The Dictator's Army

A volume in the series

CORNELL STUDIES IN SECURITY AFFAIRS

edited by Robert J. Art, Robert Jervis, and Stephen M. Walt

A list of titles in this series is available at www.cornellpress.cornell.edu.

The Dictator's Army

BATTLEFIELD EFFECTIVENESS IN AUTHORITARIAN REGIMES

CAITLIN TALMADGE

Cornell University Press

ITHACA AND LONDON

First published 2015 by Cornell University Press

First printing, Cornell Paperbacks, 2015

Printed in the United States of America

Library of Congress Cataloging-in-Publication Data

Talmadge, Caitlin, author.
    The dictator's army : battlefield effectiveness in authoritarian regimes / Caitlin Talmadge.
        pages cm — (Cornell studies in security affairs)
    Includes bibliographical references and index.
    ISBN 978-0-8014-5347-2 (cloth : alk. paper)
    ISBN 978-1-5017-0029-3 (pbk. : alk. paper)
    1. Authoritarianism. 2. Military policy—Decision making. 3. Politics and war. 4. Vietnam War, 1961–1975—Political aspects. 5. Iran-Iraq War, 1980–1988—Political aspects. I. Title. II. Series: Cornell studies in security affairs.
    JC480.T35   2015
    355'.0335—dc23   2015007580

Cornell University Press strives to use environmentally responsible suppliers and materials to the fullest extent possible in the publishing of its books. Such materials include vegetable-based, low-VOC inks and acid-free papers that are recycled, totally chlorine-free, or partly composed of nonwood fibers. For further information, visit our website at www.cornellpress.cornell.edu.

Cloth printing   10 9 8 7 6 5 4 3 2 1
Paperback printing   10 9 8 7 6 5 4 3 2 1

For my family

Contents

Maps

Acknowledgments

Writing a book is the ultimate embodiment of the paradox "You have to do it yourself, but you can't do it alone." This book is much better than it otherwise would have been thanks to the help and support of many people.

Chief among these are the mentors with whom I have had the good fortune to work at every stage of my education and career. Aaron Timmons, Alex Pritchard, Jonathan Cassie, and Mark Crotty fostered my interest in research and writing early on at the Greenhill School. At Harvard College, Steve Rosen taught me in my first courses on war and strongly encouraged me to pursue a Ph.D. (and, later, to keep pursuing it). Without him, I probably would have gone to law school.

Instead, I landed at the MIT Security Studies Program, where I had the privilege of learning from Harvey Sapolsky, Cindy Williams, Owen Cote, Ken Oye, Barry Posen, Roger Petersen, and Taylor Fravel. These latter three deserve especially emphatic thanks for the many hours they spent reading the earliest incarnation of this book and helping me improve it. I am so grateful to have benefited from the insights, patience, and generosity of each.

During my time at the George Washington University, Steve Biddle, Alex Downes, Charlie Glaser, and Jim Lebovic have continued to advise and mentor me. Each read this manuscript in its entirety—in some cases, more than once—and played a pivotal role in my ability to transform it into a book. I thank them all.

I owe tremendous thanks to my peers as well. Brendan Green read the manuscript an unreasonable number of times and offered countless suggestions that both improved the final product and steadied my personal equilibrium. Vipin Narang and Paul Staniland also each read the manuscript from start to finish several times and provided extensive comments, as well as much useful advice about revising and publishing. In addition, Keren Fraiman, Stephanie Kaplan, Elizabeth Saunders, and Austin Long each read major sections of the manuscript at various stages and offered valuable feedback. I am indebted to them all.

Many other scholars gave of their time to help my research in various ways. These include Risa Brooks, Dan Byman, David Crist, Bruce Dickson, Peter Feaver, Ben Friedman, Eugene Gholz, Mike Glosny, Madeleine Wells Goldburt, Sheena Greitens, Phil Haun, Mike Horowitz, Llewelyn Hughes, Colin Jackson, Beth Kier, Peter Krause, Jon Lindsay, Jason Lyall, Thomas Mahnken, Tara Maller, Siddharth Mohandas, Wick Murray, Dan Nexon, Suzanne Nielsen, Will Norris, Dororthy Smith Ohl, Daryl Press, Andrew Radin, Josh Rovner, Todd Sechser, Jeremy Shapiro, Joshua Shifrinson, Jessica Weeks, Alex Weisiger, Judith Yaphe, and Keren Yarhi-Milo. I owe particularly deep thanks to Richard Betts, Michael Eisenstadt, and Merle Pribbenow, who attended my book workshop and offered feedback on the manuscript in its entirety.

I also thank the members of the MIT Work in Progress Group; the Junior Faculty Working Group at GW; and the participants in the many conference panels at which I presented my work. I apologize in advance to any colleagues I have forgotten to thank, and the usual disclaimers apply.

I owe additional thanks to the people who helped me acquire the various documents cited in this book. For the Vietnam War documents, these include the historians at the Center of Military History, especially Andrew Birtle and Dale Andradé, as well as the staff of the Pike Archive at Texas Tech. For assistance with Iran-Iraq War documents from the Conflict Records Research Center, I thank Hal Brands, Jessica Huckabee, Will McCants, Wick Murray, Elizabeth Nathan, David Palkki, Joseph Simons, and most especially Kevin Woods. Malcolm Byrne of the National Security Archive at GW was instrumental in helping me understand how to identify, access, and interpret different sorts of written records. I also thank Philip Schwartzberg for the book's many maps.

For financial support, I thank the Smith Richardson Foundation, the Brookings Institution, the Olin Institute for Strategic Studies at Harvard, the MIT Seminar XXI program, the MIT Department of Political Science, the MIT Center for International Studies, the MIT Security Studies Program, the Bryce Fund of the American Political Science Association, the Georgetown Center for Peace and Security Studies, and the George Washington University, including the Political Science Department, the Elliott School for International Affairs, and the Institute for Security and Conflict Studies. I also thank my instructors and colleagues at the 2007 Institute for Qualitative and Multi-Method Research, the 2008 Summer

Institute on Conducting Archival Research at GW, and the 2008 Interuniversity Consortium for Political and Social Research, especially Tim McDaniel.

Portions of chapters 1, 4, and 5 were previously published as "The Puzzle of Personalist Performance: Iraqi Battlefield Effectiveness in the Iran-Iraq War," *Security Studies* 22, no. 2 (2013), 180–221, used by permission.

I thank my editor at Cornell University Press, Roger Haydon, along with series editor Stephen Walt, production editor Susan Specter, and my manuscript's anonymous referee. All made important suggestions on how to improve the manuscript during the last year of work.

Ultimately, my greatest debt is to those who never read a word of this book: my family and friends. I wouldn't be anywhere without my parents, John and Dana Talmadge. Their sacrifices for my education are the bedrock of any success I've attained or ever will attain. I am grateful and humbled when I think about all that I owe them and so appreciative of their love and support. I also thank my two grandmas, Violet Mancill and the late Marjorie Talmadge, who each inspired me in different ways to make the most of my academic opportunities.

I received important moral support while writing this book from my close friends Caroline Adler, Andrew Bradt, Keia Cole, Mara Karlin, Alex Lennon, Heather Grizzle, and Holly Thompson; my sister and brother, Chelsea and Jeffrey Talmadge; and my in-laws, Charlie and Susan Crawford, and Alan, Susan, and Elise Lehotsky. I thank them all.

I also thank my son Jack. The mere idea of him, not to mention the reality, encouraged me to get this book done sooner rather than later. His wonderful nanny, Yara Rojas, also was vital to my ability to complete the final revisions, and I thank her too.

Finally, I thank my husband, Steve Lehotsky. Throughout the years of research and writing, he supplied unflagging confidence and bottomless reservoirs of good humor. He made many accommodations, large and small, so that I could get my work done. But most of all, he gave me a perpetual reason to be that rarest of creatures: the happy scholar. For this he has my most profound gratitude and love.

[xi]

Abbreviations

APC   armored personnel carrier
ARVN   Army of the Republic of Vietnam
CRRC   Conflict Records Research Center
DMZ   Demilitarized Zone
DRV   Democratic Republic of Vietnam
IN   infantry
IRGC   Islamic Revolutionary Guards Corps
IRP   Islamic Republican Party
KIA   killed in action
LAW   light antitank weapon
MAAG   Military Assistance Advisory Group
MACV   Military Assistance Command, Vietnam
MEK   Mujahidin e-Khalq
MR   military region
NCO   noncommissioned officer
NLF   National Liberation Front
NVA   North Vietnamese Army
PAVN   People's Army of Vietnam
PID   Political-Ideological Directorate
PLAF   People's Liberation Armed Forces
RCC   Revolutionary Command Council
RF/PF   Regional Forces/Popular Forces
RVN   Republic of Vietnam
RVNAF   Republic of Vietnam Armed Forces
TF   task force
TOW   tube-launched, optically tracked, wire-guided
VNA   Vietnamese National Army
WIA   wounded in action

The Dictator's Army

Introduction

THE PUZZLE OF BATTLEFIELD EFFECTIVENESS

If the basic activities that produce success on the modern battlefield are well known, why don't all states perform them?[1] Why do some states successfully convert their national assets into operational- and tactical-level fighting power in war, whereas others fail even when they have the economic, demographic, and technological endowments needed to succeed?

This book proposes and tests an answer to these questions, one that focuses on the organizational practices that militaries adopt. These practices, related to promotion patterns, training regimens, command arrangements, and information management in the military, serve as the critical link between state resources and battlefield power. Where states get these practices right, battlefield effectiveness is usually the result, even if states lack many of the other inputs traditionally associated with the generation of military power. But where states get these practices wrong, national traits often associated with battlefield advantage are virtually useless.

The distribution of these military organizational practices is not random. Practices reflect the dominant, proximate threat to the ruling regime in a given state. Traditionally, international relations scholarship has highlighted the importance of external threats in shaping security decisions, but the type and magnitude of internal threats matter too, often decisively. The sort of military built to fight against other states in conventional wars is not necessarily well suited to the internal tasks of most concern to many governments: state-building, quashing mass protests, or fighting domestic insurgencies. Most important, such a military is an active liability for regimes vulnerable to military coups.

[1]

As a result, regimes facing significant coup threats are unlikely to adopt military organizational practices optimized for conventional combat, even when doing so might help them prevail in conflicts against other states (or even to combat other types of internal threats, such as conventional civil wars or insurgencies). We can most accurately assess where coup risk is likely to be high by examining two indicators: the strength of a given regime's political institutions, and key features of the state's civil-military history. Where political institutions are weak and civil-military relations deeply conflictual, coup fears are likely to dominate regimes' threat calculations at the expense of battlefield effectiveness. Where coup threats are muted, however, states have little need for the organizational practices designed to guard against military overthrow. As a result, they are free to generate maximum combat power from their material resources.

The adoption of practices optimized for conventional war is not then guaranteed, of course. Such practices require costly investments that states cocooned in benign external threat environments would have little reason to make. But the absence of coup threats does make such practices possible. Where well-institutionalized regimes with relatively peaceful civil-military relations face significant external threats or have foreign policy goals that require territorial revision, they are much more likely to adopt the organizational practices that enable conventional military success.

Understanding these connections between differing threat configurations and military organizational behavior helps resolve a number of puzzles plaguing the study of military effectiveness. Above all, it can explain why military performance seems to vary much more than existing theories predict. Most of the variables that other studies emphasize—such as national culture, the level of economic development, societal cohesion, and the presence or absence of democracy—are relatively static over long periods of time in individual states.

Such factors no doubt condition overall military performance and are relevant to explaining some cross-national variation in military effectiveness, such as the Israeli military's consistent outperformance of its Arab neighbors in the series of conflicts between 1948 and 1973. But these factors are not as well suited to explaining within-country variation in effectiveness. Such variation can occur over time, as seen, for example, in the Chinese army's excellent performances against the United States in 1950 and India in 1962, followed by a rather poor showing versus Vietnam in 1979. It also can occur across different units of the same military, as seen in the 1991 Gulf War when some Iraqi units stood and fought the coalition while others surrendered on first contact. The framework presented here shows that all three types of variation—cross-national, over-time, and cross-unit—stem from a common underlying cause operating through a common causal mechanism: the threat environment and its effect on the structure and behavior of military organizations.

For reasons elaborated in chapter 1, I use this framework to examine the battlefield effectiveness of authoritarian militaries. Compared to their democratic brethren, such militaries have been understudied. Yet the wide variation in authoritarian regimes' threat environments, organizational practices, and battlefield effectiveness suggests an area ripe for exploration. The cases studied here show that, contrary to common assumption, not all authoritarian regimes face coup threats, so not all engage in the sort of "coup-proofing" behavior that damages external battlefield effectiveness.

Indeed, past studies of coup-proofing have shed important light on the Arab regimes that gave rise to the term, but the framework presented here grounds the phenomenon in a broader argument about the requirements for generating tactical and operational fighting power.[2] It helps identify *ex ante* the states most likely to engage in coup prevention measures, by developing systematic indicators of the threat environments facing different regimes. It shows that these differing threat environments consistently result in military organizations that adopt different practices with respect to promotions, training, command, and information management—the core activities relevant to success or failure on the modern battlefield. Parsing out this variation within the broad category of "nondemocracies" enables us to explain why authoritarianism sometimes produces military juggernauts à la North Vietnam or the Soviet Union during the Cold War, while it at other times results in militaries that collapse on the battlefield even when they have the resources needed to continue fighting, as happened with South Vietnam in 1975 and with Saddam Hussein's Iraq in 2003.

Understanding these differences among authoritarian regimes is of immense practical import as well. If one believes that democracies generally do not go to war against other democracies, then we can expect that virtually all future conflicts will involve at least one nondemocratic participant.[3] Many wars may consist exclusively of such states, or their proxies: China, Iran, Russia, or North Korea, to name just a few. Simply knowing that such states are nondemocratic will offer little help in predicting their likely battlefield effectiveness. This book's framework enables us to identify the key aspects of such states' threat environments and organizational behavior that will shape their militaries' performance in war.

The framework also provides a tool for better gauging the likely battlefield effectiveness of nondemocratic allies or coalition members—an increasingly urgent proposition as the United States conducts more of its foreign policy by "building partner capacity" among nondemocratic or weakly democratic states rather than by putting U.S. boots on the ground.[4] Why do some recipients of U.S. military advising and weapons seem to bring healthy returns on the investment (Taiwan, South Korea), while others display continuing deficits even after years of training and support (Saudi Arabia, Afghanistan)? These differences remain baffling from the perspective of studies focused on external threats alone, but they are little mystery when viewed from the framework of this book. Before delving into that framework further, however, we must be specific about what battlefield effectiveness is and is not.

WHAT IS BATTLEFIELD EFFECTIVENESS?

Military effectiveness is generally defined as the power that states generate from their resources in war, distinct from war outcomes alone. Military activity at the political-strategic level is primarily about the selection of overall goals for which wars and campaigns are fought, whereas operational-tactical military activity takes those goals as givens and seeks to achieve them through the execution of actual campaigns and the application of combat techniques in battle.[5]

This book uses the term *battlefield effectiveness* to refer to a state's success at this latter level of military activity, and specifically to how well it can perform two of the key tasks of modern battle: training units to perform *basic tactics* and endowing those units with the ability to conduct what I call *complex operations*. Although I elaborate on these tasks below, the key point to note is that this definition of battlefield effectiveness posits an essentially universal, unchanging baseline that all militaries must meet in order have tactical- and operational-level fighting power in mid-to-high intensity conventional war, that is, war in which regular units fight for territory.

To be sure, the performance of these key tasks will rate as more or less impressive depending on the constraints a military faces given its resources, its environment, and its adversary—all issues discussed in the pages that follow. But effective militaries have to do certain things, whether those things are hard or easy in a particular context. Militaries that do not show the capacity to do these things cannot be said to be effective, even if their opponents are slow in making them pay the costs. Militaries that do these tasks are effective, even if they are not always victorious.

This definition has two implications. First, it means that battlefield effectiveness is a property intrinsic to a particular military or military units. Even though it is always observed in the context of interaction with external factors, enemy-generated and otherwise, effectiveness is still about the tasks that an individual organization can or cannot perform. In other words, though war is dyadic (an interaction between two states), the qualities of interest here are in fact monadic (characteristic of a single state).

Second, effectiveness is not about war outcomes. Other things being equal, we would expect that militaries displaying the highest battlefield effectiveness would also score the most victories. But other things are rarely equal. As Martin van Creveld has put it, "Victory is by no means the sole criterion of military excellence. A small army may be overwhelmed by a larger one. Confronted with impossible political and economic odds, a qualitatively superior force may go down to defeat through no fault of its own. Not the outcome alone, but intrinsic qualities as well must figure in an attempt to measure military (or any other) excellence."[6] In their classic study of the great powers' military effectiveness from 1914 to 1945, Allan Millett and Williamson Murray agree: "Victory is an outcome of battle; it is not what a military organization does in battle. Victory is not a characteristic of an organization but rather a result of organizational activity. Judgments of effectiveness should thus retain some sense of proportional cost and organizational process."[7]

Indeed, in some wars, the losing side may even be considered the more militarily effective: many characterize German performance in the world wars this way, for example, and identify a similar disjuncture in some of the tactically brilliant, strategically counterproductive Israeli operations since 1982. War outcomes depend on the political goals for which wars are fought, meaning that the same military actions can lead to victory or defeat in different contexts. Assessing military effectiveness does not mean ignoring this context—the fact that a state faces a particularly powerful opponent, for example, or that it has benefited from favorable weather or advanced technology—but it is not synonymous with these things, either. It requires measuring the performance of key military tasks, independent of externally imposed constraints or opportunities.

What are the key tasks? Stephen Biddle has usefully focused attention on what he calls "force employment" as a key component of effectiveness at the tactical and operational levels. Force employment refers to the tactics and doctrine by which forces are actually used in combat, and Biddle has shown that different methods of force employment systematically alter the combat power states produce from any given level of soldiers and weapons.[8] He argues that militaries perform best when they utilize the "modern system" of force employment, which minimizes soldiers' exposure to the increasing lethality of modern war. The system consists of a tightly interrelated complex of cover, concealment, dispersion, suppression, small-unit independent maneuver, and combined arms at the tactical level, as well as depth, reserves, and differential

[5]

concentration at the operational level. Though not without its critics, this definition undoubtedly captures key elements of fighting effectiveness in mid-to-high intensity conventional ground conflict.[9]

Drawing on Biddle's work, my definition of battlefield effectiveness focuses on two key tasks that any military employing the modern system would have to be able to perform. Together they comprise an escalating and additive series of standards by which to judge battlefield effectiveness, but it is important to spell out what is involved in each.

Basic tactics refers to whether military units demonstrate proficiency in simple skills such as weapons handling and the use of terrain for cover and concealment. These are the sort of minimal capabilities required to conduct static defenses, ambushes, orderly retreats, or planned attritional offensives—operations that depend on a basic degree of training and unit cohesion but do not necessarily require significant initiative or improvisation during battle, or extensive coordination with other combat arms or larger units. We simply want to know, do military units demonstrate basic proficiency as they resist or attack the adversary?

Complex operations refers to whether cohesive, tactically proficient units can engage in operations that require both significant low-level initiative and high-level coordination among different parts of the military. The specific content of complex operations will vary depending on the era under consideration, the medium of warfare, the type of war, and the military's tactical orientation, but within a particular context it is possible to point to some types of operations as more complex than others, and therefore a greater test of battlefield effectiveness.

For example, within the realm of modern, conventional, interstate land warfare, combined arms action is a hallmark of complex operations. Armies that demonstrate the ability to combine different types of forces, such as infantry and armor, armor and artillery, or ground forces and air forces, would be conducting complex operations. On the defensive, these operations could take the form of a mobile defense in depth, a fighting withdrawal, or the execution of counteroffensives. On the offensive, these operations could include combined arms attacks and maneuver, for example, breakthrough and exploitation, or envelopments.

What all such actions have in common is the requirement that armies integrate the activities of multiple parts of their fighting organization. Furthermore, even though this integration occurs in support of an overall high-level plan, it depends on considerable initiative and responsiveness on the part of commanders and soldiers. Units of any size, from the platoon to the corps, can conduct complex operations, although the coordination challenges grow considerably as armies attempt to integrate the activities of larger groups of soldiers, making multidivision complex operations a particularly demanding test of military performance, for

[6]

example. With these standards in mind, we can compare how well different militaries perform complex operations, how well a single military performs them across time, or how well different units within the same military perform them.

Using this basic rubric, we can distinguish theoretically among three possibilities: *excellent* battlefield effectiveness in militaries or military units that can conduct both basic tactics and complex operations; *adequate* battlefield effectiveness in militaries or military units that can do the former but not the latter; and *poor* battlefield effectiveness in militaries or military units that can do neither. It is important to note the limits of this conception of effectiveness, of course. If we think about battlefield effectiveness more broadly, as a spectrum of all tasks militaries must perform in war, then clearly other tasks also precede, coincide with, and come after the ones emphasized here. For example, the requirement to perform basic tactics presupposes the existence of cohesive units to perform them, which in turn assumes that a military has some stock of manpower that can be formed into units. Similarly, logistics undergird all aspects of military performance; it would be silly to speak of tactics if soldiers did not have adequate supplies of ammunition and food, and sometimes they do not.

In addition, there is the question of doctrine—that is, whether the operations performed are appropriate to the actual challenges posed by the adversary. For example, one could argue that the U.S. Army was at least somewhat "effective" in the Vietnam War from 1965 to 1968: U.S. soldiers were usually proficient in basic military skills such as weapons handling, and many units also routinely performed combined arms and maneuver operations requiring a great deal of low-level initiative and high-level coordination. The problem was that the content of these operations did little to undermine an adversary that mostly avoided conventional fights, especially prior to 1968.[10]

Nevertheless, there is a clear distinction between the sorts of problems the U.S. Army experienced in Vietnam and those of, say, the Argentine Army in the Falklands War. Argentina's poorly trained, short-term conscripts easily crumbled under the pressure of British engagement, repeatedly demonstrated a lack of basic military skills, and never came close to operational sophistication (the air force being the one exception).[11] One Argentine later described himself as "a civilian in the middle of war, dressed like a soldier."[12] Whatever one can say about the U.S. Army's problems in Vietnam, few would describe it as a force of civilians dressed like soldiers, especially not the officer and noncommissioned officer (NCO) corps. The Army had clear deficits, but they stemmed primarily from a poor fit between its doctrine and the nature of the enemy, not from units that had no idea how to perform that doctrine.

[7]

Some studies of effectiveness in fact focus on this type of mismatch, which usually afflicts only highly professional armies that find themselves having to prepare for and/or fight two kinds of wars at once.[13] For example, the U.S. Army had to prepare for high-intensity conventional war in Europe at the same time it was engaged in Vietnam; one could provide a similar explanation for the problems the Soviets faced in Afghanistan, or the challenges the Israeli Defense Forces face today. The conundrum merits attention, but it is essentially a question of which kinds of complex operations a tactically proficient military should perform. Indeed, recent U.S. experience in Iraq has suggested that, when properly motivated, this sort of military can at least partially transition from emphasizing one kind of complex operations (conventional high-intensity war) to another (population-centric counterinsurgency), precisely because there is an underlying tactical competence that a new doctrine can redirect.[14] It is not obvious, however, that the policies required to produce this sort of doctrinal shift in a highly professional military are the same ones that can rehabilitate a military suffering basic deficits in tactical skills.

All of this is to say that other factors no doubt influence battlefield effectiveness: manpower, logistics, and doctrine, not to mention the weather, terrain, and luck. Nevertheless, no military can be effective in modern warfare without tactical proficiency and the ability to conduct complex operations. These are the sine qua non of battlefield effectiveness. With them, militaries can generate fighting power; without them, fielded forces are more or less worthless. This book is about which states fall into which category.

AN OVERVIEW OF THE BOOK

Chapter 1 lays out the argument connecting threats, military organizational practices, and battlefield performance. In defining military organizational practices related to promotions, training, command, and information management, the chapter contrasts what I call *coup protection practices* with *conventional war practices*, explaining the causes and consequences of each. It also identifies where this framework is similar to and different from existing work and delves briefly into methodological issues of interest to more academically inclined readers. These include my approach to measuring key variables and weighing alternative explanations, why I employ qualitative case studies, and why I focus on the cases I do: a comparison of North and South Vietnam from 1954 to 1975, and of Iraq and Iran from 1980 to 1988.

Subsequent chapters use English-language and translated primary source documents to probe the argument when applied to these four instances of authoritarian regimes at war. The tremendous variation in these states' battlefield performances suggests just how much is concealed in the term nondemocracy. Furthermore, this variation is not random but rather was the product of differing threat environments. In each of the four cases, different threats led to different military organizational practices, both within and across the armies examined, which in turn resulted in differing abilities to generate tactical and operational fighting power on the battlefield. Though puzzling from the perspective of existing explanations of effectiveness, the pattern is generally what we would expect if the book's argument is correct.

More specifically, chapter 2 compares the threat environments and military organizational practices of North and South Vietnam, drawing on a variety of documentary sources, including U.S. military and civilian archives, translated North Vietnamese histories and records, captured documents, contemporary news accounts, biographies, memoirs, and secondary material. Deeply concerned about the possibility of both coups and state failure, and deliberately insulated from external conventional military threats due to U.S. aid, South Vietnamese leaders imposed coup protection practices in most of their army units. In a notable exception, however, one army division—which not coincidentally was the one stationed farthest from Saigon and closest to North Vietnam—was allowed to adopt conventional war practices. Meanwhile, North Vietnamese leaders, facing virtually no risk of coups and possessing national goals that actively required revision of the country's borders and conquest of foreign territory, adopted conventional war practices.

Drawing again on the documentary record, chapter 3 explores the dramatic consequences of these divergent practices by examining five of the Vietnam War's major battles and campaigns. Each is representative of a major phase of fighting and allows evaluation of North and South Vietnamese battlefield performance in relative isolation from the actions of third parties, notably the United States. The battles also allow comparison of different divisions within the South Vietnamese military, which provides an additional well-controlled opportunity to test my argument.

The evidence shows that the two states consistently fought differently on the battlefield. Despite the fact that North and South Vietnam were both nondemocratic and had almost identical levels of economic development, the same size populations, and common cultural underpinnings, North Vietnam's organizational practices maximized combat power, while South Vietnam's squandered it. The one major exception was the South Vietnamese 1st Division, which for various reasons had less potential to threaten the regime with a coup. It adopted organizational practices geared much more closely to conventional war and generated combat power nearly indistinguishable from that of comparable North Vietnamese units. Although not enough to overcome the deficits in the rest of the South Vietnamese army, the 1st Division's performance provides fine-grained evidence of the posited connections among threats, practices, and effectiveness, showing that the book's framework helps us understand both broad patterns at the state level as well as division-level exceptions to those patterns.

Chapters 4 and 5 conduct a similar comparison of Iran and Iraq during their war, again drawing on documentary sources, including recently released and translated records and audio tapes captured from the regime of Saddam Hussein in Iraq, a variety of declassified U.S. records, and secondary material. Chapter 4 examines the threat environments facing Iran and Iraq and the military organizational practices that resulted. Chapter 5 presents the battlefield evidence, examining a representative group of the war's major battles in which third party involvement was minimal.

In brief, the evidence shows that Saddam Hussein had a quite rational fear of coups and entered the Iran-Iraq War with exactly the practices needed to maintain himself in power against this threat. However, as the war went on, the effects of these practices increasingly became apparent, especially by 1986 when a particularly devastating series of battlefield setbacks not only threatened defeat in the war but also risked a coup by senior officers. Saddam at that point ordered his Republican Guard and select regular army units to adopt what essentially amounted to conventional war practices. Although confined only to a few divisions, this shift produced surprisingly rapid improvements in Iraqi battlefield effectiveness, resulting in the series of Iraqi counteroffensives in 1987–1988 that ended the war. Notably, these victories occurred despite the fact that Iran remained larger, wealthier, and more populous, and the Iraqi military infused with Arab culture and pathological civil-military relations—both traits that existing theories of effectiveness would expect to stymie combat effectiveness.

This Iraqi triumph was possible only because it faced in Iran an adversary that gave it the luxury of time to adapt. Iran's leaders arguably faced the most complicated threat environment of the four states I examine. The revolutionary regime simultaneously faced threats of coup, secession, civil war, and external conventional war, each of which also threatened some variety of counterrevolution. Iranian leaders prioritized coup protection even though they needed a functioning military to deal with all the threats they faced besides coups. In particular, Khomeini imposed harsh coup protection on the legacy military inherited from the Shah, which had the greatest motive and capability to unseat the new regime. Interestingly, however, the revolutionary regime was not able to erase overnight the vestiges of somewhat better military organizational practices that had evolved under the Shah. These intramilitary differences were evident in the early stages of the Iran-Iraq War, as the Shah's legacy units were clearly more tactically proficient and capable of complex operations than the newer units established by the revolutionary regime.

Unfortunately for Iran, its leaders did not successfully integrate the prerevolutionary and revolutionary armed forces, and in fact mistakenly credited the revolutionary forces rather than the legacy units with early battlefield successes. As a result, Iran's leaders only deepened their imposition of coup protection practices as the war went on, decimating whatever legacy lingered from the Shah's era. They instead relied on soldiers who were ideologically motivated to be cohesive but who lacked any ability to convert that cohesion into tactical proficiency or complex operations. Once the Iraqis finally adopted conventional war practices in their Republican Guard and select regular army units, Iranian forces became highly vulnerable to Iraqi combined arms assaults in the final battles.

Put simply, both Iran and Iraq performed poorly when their militaries were uniformly subject to coup protection practices: in the Iranian case, after about 1982, and in the Iraqi case, prior to about 1986. By contrast, in the period before these practices exerted their full effects on the regular military in Iran and in the period after these practices were lifted on the Republican Guard and select army units in Iraq, military performance by those forces was noticeably better compared both to the opponent's military and to other units drawn from the same military. The contrast was subtle in the Iranian case and dramatic in the Iraqi case, but in both instances directly attributable to differing military organizational practices that stemmed clearly from threat environments in which coups rather than other states were the major concern.

These distinctions—similar to those seen in the Vietnam comparisons—suggest again the importance of threats and military organizational practices in explaining variations in battlefield effectiveness both across and within states. They show that a common set of processes underlie military performance even in states with very different types of institutions: U.S.-backed personalist and military dictatorships (South Vietnam), a communist one-party state (North Vietnam), a personalist Ba'th dictatorship (Iraq), and a revolutionary theocracy (Iran). The next chapter examines political institutions in more depth, leveraging them along with civil-military relations as an important source of information about the threat environment facing a given regime. The resulting framework enables us to predict and explain variation in battlefield effectiveness.

[1]

A Framework for Explaining Battlefield Effectiveness

Battlefield effectiveness requires militaries to be capable of conducting basic tactics and complex operations. States can perform these tasks when their militaries adopt the right set of organizational practices with respect to four key areas of military activity: promotion patterns, training regimens, command arrangements, and information management. But these practices do not arise randomly. They evolve in response to both the domestic and international threat environments.

This chapter explains how, building a framework that the rest of the book then uses to examine puzzling variation within and across four authoritarian states at war. Although I focus empirically on authoritarian regimes, the book's overall framework is a broad one relevant to understanding the military effectiveness of any state, including democracies, and potentially even nonstate actors. The conclusion explores some of these possibilities and their implications for further research.

The chapter first defines military organizational practices and their connection to the generation of military power. It then outlines the practices best suited to conventional war and how they maximize combat power. The chapter contrasts these policies with an alternative set of military organizational practices that guard against coups but hobble conventional military performance. It then explains how we can determine *ex ante* which dangers states are likely to prioritize and therefore which practices they will adopt. Two indicators are particularly useful in assessing the threat environment facing a given regime: the strength of the regime's institutions, and the state's civil-military history. After setting up this general framework, the chapter discusses when and how regimes' choice of military organizational practices is likely to shift. Finally, the chapter elaborates on how this framework for thinking about the causes of battlefield effectiveness is similar to and different from other approaches, and describes the research strategy that the rest of the book employs to explore the argument empirically.

MILITARY ORGANIZATIONAL PRACTICES

Militaries engage in a wide range of activities: transportation, construction, maintenance, budgeting, veterans' care, and parades, to name just a few. My framework focuses on the four areas of military behavior that are most logically central to combat capability: promotion patterns, training regimens, command arrangements, and information management.

Promotion patterns generate the military's human capital, which influences virtually everything else it does. *Training regimens* determine the ends to which that human capital is directed and provide important prewar opportunities to develop military skills. *Command arrangements* structure the speed and authority with which decisions are made during conflict, with important implications for the military's initiative and coordination. *Information management* also plays a critical role in coordination, as well as in the diffusion of wartime lessons learned and related adaptations.

Although they do not constitute an exhaustive list of all military activities, these four areas of organizational behavior tell us a great deal about the likely tactical and operational fighting power a given army is likely to generate. Military organizational practices are the critical missing bridge between specific battlefield events and the broad variables that we often intuitively believe must matter for military effectiveness, such as wealth, political institutions, civil-military relations, and national culture. These traits surely matter, but we have to look at military organizational practices to see how.

Conventional War Practices: Best for Battlefield Effectiveness

States that generate high levels of battlefield effectiveness exhibit a common set of military organizational practices. *Promotion patterns* in the most effective militaries follow a simple principle: merit. The ticket to being a senior officer in these militaries is competence, demonstrated by wartime performance or by performance in training. From the perspective of an officer's career, high quality past performance is indeed a guarantee of future success. By the same token, incompetence and cowardice are quick routes to early retirement. Officers who perform poorly in war or training exercises are actively removed from command. Furthermore, an officer's own political views, ethnic or sectarian background, or other

[13]

ascriptive characteristics are largely irrelevant. This sort of promotion system enables the military to develop a much higher base of human capital over time, which in turn makes the military better at just about everything it attempts to do, including the teaching of basic tactical skills and planning of complex operations.

Training regimens in the best militaries also have particular characteristics: they emphasize rigorous, realistic, and frequent exercises, giving unit members a chance to practice key skills prior to combat. The best training regimens focus on both small- and large-unit activities, developing basic tactics in the former and practicing the aggregation of those tactics into complex operations through the latter. Exercising across different parts of the military—in particular, across different combat arms—is especially useful in this regard, making training a foundation of effectiveness.

Command arrangements in the most conventionally effective militaries are relatively decentralized and clear. While not devolving all command authority, they do give significant decision-making power to those in the field, enabling military units to engage in the improvisation and initiative required to perform complex operations. Commanders can act quickly in response to battlefield events, rather than wait for headquarters' approval of operational and tactical actions. In addition, a commander's authority over his particular unit(s) is absolute. There are never two commanders giving different orders to the same soldiers. The chain of command is clear and responsibility unambiguous, meaning soldiers can implement decisions rapidly once they have been made. This sort of clarity and rapidity are especially crucial for managing the precise timing and multiunit coordination involved in complex operations, but they are also important even for basic small-unit tactics.

Finally, *information management* policies play a critical role in the coordination required for complex operations. The most conventionally effective militaries foster extensive internal communication, both horizontally and vertically. Without institutionalized procedures to encourage this sort of information flow, it is nearly impossible to integrate action across different units or combat arms or to improvise and react quickly to reported changes in the adversary's behavior. Information sharing is the key mechanism through which battlefield learning and adaptation occur and diffuse. The result is sharper tactical skills.

In sum, proficiency in basic tactics and the execution of complex operations are most likely in militaries in which officers are hired and fired based on merit; training is rigorous, realistic, and frequent, and occurs across units of varying sizes and specializations; battlefield command is decentralized but unified; and vertical and horizontal information sharing is the norm. These practices enable militaries to extract maximum fighting power from their resources—North Vietnam, the United States, and Israel all have exhibited practices close to this ideal type.[1]

Such practices are costly, however. They require human, financial, and organizational resources that states could invest in other public goods besides the generation of military power. It would be surprising for a state to adopt ideal-typical conventional war practices in the absence either of significant external threats, such as a conventionally powerful adversary, or of foreign policy goals that required territorial revision, such as plans to invade a neighbor. In other words, states' motives in adopting conventional war practices could be offensive or defensive, but they should not be present at all in a state that does not face a serious prospect of major conventional conflict. The investments involved are too great.

A national military will still exist under such circumstances, but its activities likely will have little to do with the management of violence. Instead, they may focus on tasks such as state-building, local governance, or the running of commercial enterprises. After all, despite Charles Tilly's famous dictum that "war made the state and the state made war," many states do not live in neighborhoods characterized by a high likelihood of conventional conflict.[2] As such, the choice not to adopt conventional war practices, and even to use the military for nonconflict-related tasks, may be optimal.

Coup Protection Practices: Worst for Battlefield Effectiveness

Beyond their opportunity costs, conventional war practices can be dangerous in some situations. The same practices that generate battlefield effectiveness also improve the military's ability to launch or support a coup, defined here as the seizure of the levers of state power by a small group of armed insiders.[3] Multiple studies have emphasized the prominence of such concerns among Arab regimes and have pointed to the adoption of "coup-proofing" measures as a response.[4]

These studies are useful for understanding particular cases but have not necessarily grounded their observations about coup-proofing in a broader deductive argument about the requirements for generating tactical and operational fighting power. The framework presented here situates coup-proofing in this larger context, and explains how different threat environments systematically produce different types of military organizations, both effective and ineffective. It allows us to see that the most damaging coup prevention measures are those that deliberately interfere with the core activities relevant to military organizational strength: merit-based promotions, rigorous training, decentralized and unified command structures, and horizontal and vertical information sharing.[5] It also enables us to generate *ex ante* expectations about when the phenomenon of coup-proofing will and will not travel beyond the handful of Arab autocracies that first gave rise to the term.

What do those four key areas of military activity look like in a regime that prioritizes coup prevention? What are the ideal-typical coup prevention practices? *Promotion patterns* are likely to be entirely a function of political loyalty, with deliberate selection against proven combat prowess. It is not just that an officer's ascriptive traits or political views are relevant in selection, promotion, and demotion, but that the demonstration of competence actually harms an officer's career. Officers who easily win battles can also plot conspiracies. They are likely to command the loyalty of fellow officers and the troops, making it quite plausible that their defection from the regime would find support. Weeding out these individuals reduces the risk of military overthrow, but it also lowers human capital in the military, making officers less able to impart tactical proficiency or plan complex operations.

Rigorous, realistic *training regimens* are also dangerous from the perspective of coup prevention. Training provides opportunities for improving military skills that could be used against the regime. It also creates an easy pretext for positioning weapons and units in places that could enable the military to seize power. Restrictions on military training, outlawing live fire exercises, limiting the size and number of units that can practice at any one time, especially near the capital—all of these measures inhibit coup plotting but also hinder the development of basic military skills, not to mention the mastery of complex operations.

Preventing coups also necessitates the adoption of distinct *command arrangements*. Authority devolved to field commanders may improve performance in conventional battles, but it also opens the possibility that officers could command units to turn on the government before political leaders even realize what is happening. As a result, efforts at coup prevention usually involve the centralization of command arrangements. Command authority is heavily concentrated at the top, with virtually no authority devolved to the field, even regarding tactical matters. Political leaders may work to establish direct, personal control of important units outside the normal chain of command. They also may choose to rotate officers frequently among command posts in order to reduce officers'

[16]

chances of forming strong bonds with their units. Though excessively centralized and convoluted, these practices should make coup plotting quite challenging. But they also make it impossible for officers to engage in the sort of initiative and improvisation necessary for complex operations. Even basic, small-unit tactical activities become difficult when all decisions have to go through headquarters and the chain of command is confused.

Finally, regimes seeking to reduce coup risk are likely to adopt particular *information management* policies. Specifically, we should expect the restriction of horizontal communication within the military and distortion of vertical communication. Political leaders should be concerned about officers gathering to share information; the same conversations that convey battlefield reports could plot coups. In fact, such states would be wise to invest in an internally directed surveillance apparatus to detect and punish any potential plots. In this environment, the cross-unit coordination and rapid decision making required for complex operations should be nearly impossible. In addition, a "shoot the messenger" climate is likely to develop in which officers are reluctant to report information that they believe those higher up in the chain of command do not want to hear. These information management policies should then compound the effects of the practices already described regarding personnel, training, and command: military units are likely to be incapable of tactical proficiency, unable to conduct complex operations, and poorly situated to self-correct deficiencies even in the face of battle-

Table 1.1. Comparing military organizational practices

	Conventional war practices	Coup prevention practices
Promotions	Selection on merit	Selection against merit
Training	Rigorous, realistic, frequent, large- and small-unit	Heavily restricted
Command	Decentralized, unified, clear	Centralized, convoluted
Information	Active horizontal and vertical communication	Restrictions on horizontal and vertical communication; internally directed intelligence apparatus
Expected effectiveness	Excellent: tactical proficiency, complex operations	Poor: no tactical proficiency, no complex operations
Examples	Israel, United States, North Vietnam	Soviet Union, 1937–1941; Argentina, 1976–1983; Iraq, 1980–1986

[17]

field feedback. Examples of militaries adopting this constellation of organizational practices include the Soviet Union from 1937 to 1941, Argentina
during military rule from 1976 to 1983, and Iraq under much of Saddam
Hussein's rule.[6] Table 1.1 compares these military organizational practices with those designed for conventional war.

The Choice of Military Organizational Practices

States adopt military organizational practices that guard against the
dominant, proximate threat to the ruling regime. This distinction between state and regime is important. We often think about the prospect
of external military conquest as a threat to the state, which it usually is,
but regimes—the particular constellation of people and institutions that
actually govern the state—decide how to respond to this threat. They do
so in the context of other dangers to their rule, including internal ones.
For reasons discussed below, weakly institutionalized regimes in states
with a history of civil-military conflict are particularly likely to prioritize
protection against coups even when other threats loom.

It is relatively easy to predict the choice of military organizational
practices for a regime facing *only* conventional dangers, or *only* the risk
of coups. But for many regimes, the threat environment is more complicated. They may face conventional and coup threats simultaneously.
And they may face internal threats besides coups, against which some of
the conventional war practices would be useful. For example, a regime
facing a conventional civil war, robust insurgency, armed rebellion, or
even mass social protests might very well want military units staffed
with competent, well-trained officers ensconced in a decentralized command structure and capable of easily communicating with one another.
The pressure to invest in such practices might not be as strong as in an
external conventional war, but the adoption of coup protection practices
clearly would entail real costs in terms of exposure to other potential
dangers, both internal and external.

Ultimately, few regimes face only coup threats or only the prospect of
conventional conflict. Threat environments tend to be multifaceted. For
example, many internal threats might have common underpinnings tied
to state weakness or political illegitimacy; internal and external armed
conflict of any type might make a regime more vulnerable to a coup; coups
or insurgencies might make a state vulnerable to external conventional
attack; state failure might increase the likelihood of rebellion; and so on.

In such situations regimes have to grapple with inherent trade-offs involved in the design of coercive institutions.[7] If threats are concentrated
toward the conventional end of the spectrum (for example, conventional
interstate wars, conventional civil wars), then the trade-offs may be less

[18]

stark and more manageable despite multiple dangers. But for regimes that face serious risks of both conventional conflict and coups—two threats that call for highly divergent practices regarding the exact same set of military activities—the trade-off will be acute. Adopting coup protection practices will secure the regime against the military at home but hobble the state's ability to defeat a conventional foe. Adopting conventional war practices will maximize the state's chances of victory against the external foe but significantly raise the chances of the regime being overthrown at home.[8]

What will states do when faced with this set of choices? The contingencies of personality and circumstance should caution us against sweeping categorical predictions. Empirically, states do not always behave in accordance with the dictates of rationality, and it is not clear that there is always a single optimal path to state security. Yet states do face strong incentives to get threat assessment right, and by considering the likely reasoning of ruling regimes we can make decent guesses about how they will respond to particular threat configurations. Certainly, these guesses will not be perfect, but they generate more accurate predictions than the assumption that military organizational practices are distributed randomly.

Logical deduction and the historical record both suggest that regimes will almost always prioritize protection against coups over protection against other dangers, even if other dangers are significant. The rationale is simple: compared to rural insurgencies, poor governance, street protests, or fighting at a distant border, military coups typically present a far more immediate threat to regime stability and certainly to a given leader's power and personal safety. If a coup occurs, the leader will not be around to deal with any of the other problems, and the regime may not survive either.

Coups are, in a sense, the ultimate offense-dominant domestic weapon: they occur quickly and afford tremendous and potentially total rewards to first movers.[9] As such, the best defense is prevention, which is exactly what the military organizational practices geared toward coup protection provide. By contrast, other threats, even internal ones, are usually relatively more defense-dominant and do not require the same level of constant vigilance. For example, state failure or weakness is a serious problem, but one that erodes a regime's hold on power slowly; regimes usually have many years to respond to it before its effects become catastrophic. Social protests typically take time to become revolutions, with plenty of opportunities for negotiation, concession, and repression along the way. Insurgencies, too, are grinding affairs, and often see much of their action far from the capital. Similarly, and not withstanding some high-profile exceptions, conventional wars rarely begin with bolt-from-the-blue, large-scale, highly mobile attacks that rapidly capture large swaths of territory near the capital. Even full-scale hot wars often provide some margin of time in which states can adapt and respond before the threat becomes existential.

In peacetime, then, there is little reason to expect regimes to be as sensitive to other threats as they are to coups. Regimes often can recover from miscalculations about the dangers these other threats pose. But ruling regimes that underestimate coup threats rarely get the chance for a do-over. Coup fears therefore exert an outsize influence on the shape of military organizational practices, even in situations where regimes have legitimate and persistent concerns about other threats too.

Two related indicators help us predict *ex ante* where coup fears are likely to be highest: the strength of the regime's institutions and its civil-military history. Existing research on military effectiveness has emphasized a stark distinction between democracies and nondemocracies, which is how much international relations scholarship has come to understand the meaning of the term "regime type." On average, according to this research, democracies are said to be more effective on the battlefield due to their superior ability to choose winnable wars and the liberal political values that infuse their soldiers with fighting power.[10] But as Samuel Huntington noted more than forty years ago, the most important distinction among regimes is not necessarily their type but their strength. Both democracies and dictatorships can be well and poorly institutionalized.[11] In his telling, well-institutionalized regimes, whether democratic or autocratic, are characterized by "effective bureaucracies, well-organized political parties, a high degree of popular participation in public affairs, . . . extensive activity by the government in the economy, and reasonably effective procedures for regulating succession and controlling political conflict." Notably, such regimes also tend to have what Huntington called "working systems of civilian control over the military"—that is, they face a low or nonexistent risk of military intervention in politics.

Both Huntington's early work and a more recent wave of scholarship on authoritarianism, discussed below, suggest that weakly institutionalized regimes—particularly personalist or military dictatorships—should be the most likely to face severe coup risks. As a result, they should be the most likely to adopt the coup prevention practices that damage conventional military effectiveness. By contrast, robustly institutionalized regimes, whether democratic or authoritarian, should be the least likely to face such risks and the least likely to adopt coup prevention practices. As already mentioned, the adoption of conventional war practices is not then guaranteed, but it is at least possible. The absence of coup fears removes the major constraints regimes face in adopting practices that enable effectiveness in conventional warfare.

Notably, this means that some authoritarian regimes, particularly single-party states, are institutionalized in ways that should endow them with the same general invulnerability to coups that stable democracies enjoy and therefore the same latitude to adopt conventional war practices. The much-noted military successes of communist states, such as China's performances in Korea in 1950 and against India in 1962, seem to comport with this notion. Many autocracies certainly do embody the unstable, coup-ridden nightmare, but not all. Likewise, coups are rare in democracies, but they do happen, especially in nascent, weakly institutionalized democracies with underdeveloped economies. Turkey has experienced three (1960, 1971, 1980), Pakistan two (1977, 1999), and Bangladesh four (1975, 1981, 1982, 2007), and Thailand saw coups in 2006 and 2014.

All threats have to be perceived by the relevant actors in order to have causal power. Such perceptions are always notoriously slippery and subject to bias; they are not a perfectly rational, consistent reflection of the objective environment. Indeed, even scholars relying on the hindsight of history often disagree about how a given regime "should" have evaluated a given set of internal and external dangers. For example, historians have been unable to uncover much evidence that Stalin's worries about coups were valid, while one might marvel that Mussolini was not shot by his officers sooner.[12]

Nevertheless, the strength of political institutions in a given state offers an important initial clue as to the threat environment facing the regime, one distinct and separable from military organizational practices. Personalist regimes and military dictatorships strongly suggest a domestic political context in which coups are possible. Personalist regimes are characterized by a single individual's domination of both the military and the state apparatus. As Geddes notes, "The leader may be an officer and have created a party to support himself, but neither the military nor the party exercises independent decision-making power insulated from the whims of the ruler."[13] Personalism, then, is fragile. Deliberately devoid of institutions separate from the leader, personalist systems require only that a rival arrest or assassinate a single person (and perhaps his immediate circle) to assume the reigns of power.[14] As such, personalist leaders who want to stay in power should strongly prioritize coup prevention in their choice of military organizational practices, even when conventional external dangers loom.

Similarly, military dictatorships by their very nature raise the specter of military threats to political rule. The leadership circle in such regimes is typically larger than in personalist systems, consisting of a group of officers that decides who will rule and helps make policy. Yet the experience of having come to power through a coup should induce a similar set

[21]

of fears among leaders. Military dictatorships set a dangerous precedent the moment they come into being, which should make these regimes especially concerned about warding off future plots. For these reasons, we should expect such regimes to gravitate toward coup prevention practices much as personalist systems do.

A state's broader civil-military history offers a second important clue regarding the threat environment facing a ruling regime. Where past civil-military relations have been deeply conflictual, one can expect the regime in power to remain fearful of coups and to prioritize coup prevention in the development of military organizational practices. Evaluating the degree of such conflict is always context dependent, but we should seek to examine the indicators that regimes themselves would use in trying to assess threats.[15]

Any regime is likely to fear coups if they have happened in the past—a prediction supported by both intuition and statistical evidence.[16] In particular, in any state that has experienced a coup or attempted coup in living memory, the regime is likely to push for coup prevention practices. Even where actual coups or coup attempts have not occurred in the past, other conditions can indicate serious civil-military conflict: rulers or regimes divided from their officer corps by major societal cleavages (for example, the leader is from one ethnic or religious group, but most officers are from another); that inherit a legacy officer corps of questionable loyalty from a former regime or colonial master; that detect signs of military insubordination, especially over major policy questions, which imply a threat of coup or purposely demonstrate the capacity to mount one, even if one is not attempted; and that detect civilian support for praetorianism. In all of these situations, leaders are likely to develop concerns about internal overthrow by their officer corps, even if other threats are also very serious.

Conversely, where such indicators are absent, there would be little reason to adopt coup prevention measures. They should be missing in states with relatively harmonious civil-military relations and well-institutionalized regimes. One-party systems, which are defined by a single party's domination of access to political office and control over office (though other parties may be legal and even participate in elections), seem particularly likely to avoid these problems, despite the lack of democracy.[17] As Huntington noted, "States with one [highly institutionalized] political party are markedly more stable than states which lack such a party. States with no parties or many weak parties are the least stable."[18] More recent research confirms this intuition. One-party states are better able to co-opt regime opposition and credibly share power, muting the possibility that elite splits result in violent overthrow.[19] They can afford to direct more of their coercive power outward

[22]

rather than inward. For all of these reasons, such regimes should be much less likely to adopt coup protection practices.

In addition, where other threats are present, such as an impending conflict with another state, or if the regime has foreign policy objectives that affirmatively require territorial revision, we should expect regimes to gravitate toward military organizational practices suited to conventional war. In fact, leaders often make these concerns explicit when they deliver speeches, meet with foreign counterparts, or consult with their advisers, and in cases where states face enduring rivals, we should expect such threats to be especially prominent. As a result, it is frequently possible to observe directly the key indicators of a regime motivated to adopt conventional war practices.

Ultimately, we know that regimes do make mistakes in assessing the threat environment and in translating what that threat environment should mean for the structure of military organizations. History's long list of overthrown leaders and defeated armies certainly induces humility about any assumption of rationality. Nevertheless, the assumption of rationality on the part of ruling regimes is just that—not an asserted truth, but a useful baseline. The contention is not that regimes always will adopt the practices that they should, but that by assuming they do we gain more analytical traction than we would from simply throwing up our hands and attributing the adoption of different military organizational practices purely to the contingencies of personality and circumstance. In fact, adoption should and often does follow a reliable logic that a full appreciation of the threat environment illuminates, and which in turn enables us to make surprisingly good predictions about the fighting power a given state will generate from its resources.

ADAPTATION AND CHANGE IN MILITARY ORGANIZATIONAL PRACTICES

Military organizational practices should be self-reinforcing over long periods of time. They require investments, financial and otherwise, that accumulate as years go by. The large literature attesting to the lasting importance of initial choices in institutional design also applies to military organizations, which are known for their emphasis on tradition and established rules.[20] One can easily imagine how early decisions about practices in each of the four areas of military activity would self-perpetuate. Senior officers tend to promote junior officers based on the same criteria by which they themselves were evaluated. Military education systems are often remarkably static, generating continuity in training regimens. Patterns of command are not simply rules on paper but familiar behaviors that young officers observe and mimic. Norms surrounding commu-

[23]

nication powerfully shape what individuals do with knowledge they acquire, transmitting information management practices from today's officers to tomorrow's. Many studies have noted that this tendency to rinse and repeat is at the core of militaries' often formidable institutional strength yet also the reason that military innovation is so difficult and rare.[21]

Changes in military organizational practices do happen, however, and the threat environment is again crucial for understanding when and how these shifts can occur, despite the drag exerted by existing habits. The threat environment will determine what we might think of as the "default" setting of military organizational practices in a given country. Regimes with weaker institutions and conflictual civil-military relations, typically personalist and military dictatorships and nascent democracies, should be likely to adopt coup prevention practices, while those with stronger institutions and more harmonious civil-military relations, usually single-party authoritarian states or well-institutionalized democracies, should be able to adopt conventional war practices. Yet the nature of political power in these different systems also points to the conditions under which they are likely to seek change in their military organizational practices.

In general, any regime employing coup prevention practices should shift to conventional war practices only when leaders are convinced that a conventional adversary poses a greater threat to regime continuation than coups do. After all, regimes can be overthrown not only by the military but via conventional defeat at the hands of insurgents, civil partisans, or another state. Where such removal seems imminent—and particularly in cases where the enemy is quite literally at the palace gates—these regimes may temporarily or partially lessen their concern with coup protection and focus on these other potential threats to their power. Indeed, if battlefield disasters prompt unrest within the military, suggesting the possibility of mutiny or leader overthrow, these regimes' incentives to embrace different practices should be doubly intense.

Regimes do face a catch in making such adjustments, however. Ambiguous signals from the environment are unlikely to provide adequate motivation for such important changes in long-standing practices that protect the regime, while truly unambiguous signals may come in the form of such devastating, regime-rocking battlefield defeats that recovery is impossible in the timeframe the adversary allows. The opponent's own effectiveness therefore constrains or enables this sort of adaptation. An opponent similarly focused on coup prevention may have so many battlefield deficits of its own that even long overdue adaptation toward conventional war practices by the other side is enough to produce a battlefield edge. But an opponent whose military has thoroughly adopted

[24]

conventional war practices will provide a much more narrow margin for correction.

Furthermore, we should expect regimes that have adopted coup protection practices to need a wide margin. Interpreting signals from the environment is likely to be particularly difficult for these regimes given some of the inherent information management pathologies their practices create. We also should expect such innovations to be fragile and subject to backsliding once the conventional threat recedes. In fact, given how ingrained past practices may be, when leaders do sense a shift in the threat environment, they may find it easier to create an entirely new organization or sub-organization and imbue it with the preferred practices than to force existing organizations to change. Either way, the shift in practices should produce a shift in battlefield effectiveness.

That said, changes should be more likely to occur promptly in personalist dictatorships rather than in military regimes or weak democracies. Despite their considerable flaws, personalist regimes really do endow a single individual with near-total decision-making authority. When that person is convinced of the need for change, no institutions or individuals stand in the way. Military organizational adjustment should be relatively swift, other things being equal. In fact, we see this logic at work in historical instances of wartime adaptation by personalist dictators, such as Stalin during the period leading up to and during World War II.[22] Prior to the war, Stalin's concern about internal dangers, especially coups, led him to engage in significant coup prevention practices with respect to his military. Interestingly, these seemed to fall more heavily on units in the west rather than those who went on to fight in the eastern battles, which may partly explain why the Soviet military performed relatively well against a great power at Khalkhin Gol and so poorly against a small neighbor in the Winter War within the same short period of time. Yet as the war went on and Nazi Germany clearly became the greatest threat to both Stalin's rule and the Soviet Union's existence, Stalin pushed for adoption of more conventional war practices, which, combined with Allied aid, resulted in significant improvement in Soviet military effectiveness by 1943–1944.[23]

This turn of events suggests again the general connections among threats, military organizational practices, and effectiveness, as well as the specific nature of change in personalist regimes. By contrast, military dictators typically share power with fellow officers, and carefully managing relationships within and among these factions is an important part of both staying in power and executing policy decisions. Weak democracies often face similar problems of diffuse power and the need for consensus. Change in these cases requires widespread recognition of a major change in the threat environment, as well as agreement about how to respond.

[25]

The resulting shift in military organizational practices is therefore likely to be slower than in personalist regimes.

In all such cases, full adoption of conventional war practices is still unlikely, because of continuing coup threats and the "stickiness" of past organizational choices. Rather, the result should be deviation from the ideal-typical practices described above, in a form that I call *mixed practices*. This could involve combining coup prevention and conventional war practices so that different practices govern different military activities (e.g., orienting training toward conventional war, but maintaining or even increasing coup prevention practices with respect to promotions). Or it could mean adopting conventional war practices in some units and coup protection practices in others (and in fact, the former might make the latter more necessary).

The result should be improved battlefield effectiveness, although the fighting power of the military overall should still be lower than what we would expect were conventional war practices uniformly adopted throughout all units from the outset. For example, a military that improves training but selects against competence in the officer corps should be more skilled than a military fully subject to coup prevention practices, but the human capital of the officer corps will still be relatively low compared to a military that promoted on merit. The military might be proficient in performing scripted basic tactics, for instance, but it likely would have difficulty performing complex operations.

Similarly, a division that adopts conventional war practices should be much better at basic tactics and division-level complex operations than a comparable division in the same army subject to coup protection practices, but effective multidivision or corps-level complex operations between these two divisions will be nearly impossible. The organizational practices in the units optimized for coup protection will act as a brake on the ability to do large-scale realistic training, coordinate movement and fires, and share information. We also should expect states to choose carefully which units will adopt conventional war practices. Units with the least inherent ability to foment coups, such as those stationed abroad or far from the capital, should be the safest and most likely candidates.

States as different as Egypt under Sadat and China after Mao have adopted mixed practices, and empirically there are many varieties.[24] But generally we should expect that as militaries or military units adopt more of the conventional war practices, their effectiveness will improve. Militaries or military units that once performed poorly should perform at least adequately, and in some cases with excellence if all of the conventional war practices are adopted.

What about changes in the other direction—from well-established conventional war practices to coup prevention? The logic is the same even though the specifics are different. States should shift in this direction only when the regime experiences a dramatic rise in the threat it faces from coups. Again, the signal from the threat environment would have to be strong, such as an attempted coup, evidence of significant coup plotting, or other instances of severe military insubordination. These events would not only threaten the ruling regime but also likely fracture the military in ways that undermine conventional military performance, which should strongly motivate the regime to change practices. We would expect these phenomena to be rare in the single-party states and well-developed democracies most likely to adopt conventional war practices. As a result, shifts from conventional war practices to coup prevention practices also should be rare, though they are theoretically possible.

THE CONTRIBUTION TO OUR UNDERSTANDING OF MILITARY EFFECTIVENESS

Existing scholarship has produced important insights about the causes of battlefield effectiveness but left significant questions unanswered. Chief among these is what explains within-state variation in effectiveness—that is, variation in battlefield performance by the same state at different points in time, or by different military units drawn from the same state. Most studies emphasize relatively static national traits as drivers of effectiveness, and while these no doubt matter, they render within-state variation puzzling. For example, how can the same state or different units in the same military differ dramatically in their battlefield effectiveness if the state's wealth, demography, and culture have not changed much or at all? By highlighting the importance of military organizational practices for effectiveness—and the ways in which the threat environment prompts and can subsequently stimulate change in those practices—my framework builds on the insights of past scholarship to resolve these puzzles. The result is a more satisfying understanding of the causal mechanisms driving all three types of observed variation in military performance: cross-national, over time, and across different military units.

Existing scholarship on military effectiveness falls into two camps. The first emphasizes "what states have," that is, material resources such as wealth or a large population, and tends to treat victory as synonymous with effectiveness. The second focuses on "what states do with what they have," that is, the force multipliers or dividers that convert resources into fighting power or hinder the process of doing so. These include external threats, civil-military relations, regime type, culture, societal traits, and international norms, and the relevant studies tend to employ a definition of effectiveness more focused on battlefield processes than war outcomes. Whereas the first set of theories would expect victory and defeat in war to be largely a function of the balance of material capabilities, the second would expect significant variation in actual battlefield performance even among states with similar national resources, depending on what states chose to do with those resources.

My argument falls into this second group, but it is part of a broader body of research casting doubt on the extent to which resources alone can explain battlefield events. For example, Stephen Biddle has shown that states' gross national product is a weak predictor of their odds of victory, leaving nearly half of war outcomes unexplained.[25] He and others also point to instances in which poor, less economically developed states seem to have more than held their own on the battlefield against wealthy, economically advanced states fielding the most advanced weaponry.[26] Examples include North Vietnam during its war with the United States, as well as China in the opening phases of the Korean War and, more recently, Serbia in its defense against NATO airpower in 1999.[27]

The other major resource that some studies emphasize—manpower—also seems problematic as a predictor of effectiveness, at least as defined here. At times small states seem to outfight much larger armies, as Israel did in several conventional wars against its Arab neighbors.[28] The great variation in Chinese military performance across its wars in Korea, on the Indian border, and with Vietnam similarly suggests that there is more to explaining variation in battlefield performance than manpower availability.[29] Indeed, China arguably performed the worst in the war in which it had the greatest overall superiority in numbers—against Vietnam. What often is said to matter are not overall numbers, but rather local ratios of field forces. Biddle has shown that such ratios also do not predict battle outcomes, however.[30]

A second branch of research has focused on a variety of factors besides wealth and demography that might matter in battle outcomes. Because my argument falls into this camp and is most closely related to the existing work on threats, civil-military relations, and regime type, I briefly discuss each of these factors, explaining the connections to my argument. Rather than showing that the factors emphasized in existing work are irrelevant, my framework actually helps us appreciate when and how their causal power operates.

The Threat Environment

Realist scholars of international relations have long posited that the international system pressures states to adopt effective forms of military organization, with Waltz in particular identifying a tendency toward isomorphism among the great powers.[31] The claim is similar in many respects to well-established arguments in historical sociology connecting state development to the creation of robust military institutions geared to fighting interstate wars. Hintze, Tilly, and Ertman all tell essentially this same story about the centuries-long coevolution of modern states and militaries in Western Europe, arguing that states more or less get the militaries they need.[32]

What is puzzling about these claims are instances in which severe external threats do not seem to result in the necessary forms of military organization. Anomalies in this regard include the fall of France in 1940 and South Vietnam in 1975. Even more strange are instances in which only some units of the same military seem willing to stand and fight, while others collapse or desert at the first opportunity. Coalition forces encountered this sort of inconsistent behavior among Iraqi military units in 1991, with some breaking and running while others stood and conducted valiant but doomed tank operations.[33] If military organizational strength is all a function of external threats, these instances of variation should not be so common.

Other scholars have suggested that the explanation lies in a broader conception of the threat environment, one that also encompasses internal dangers. For example, Steven David has argued that states engage in "omnibalancing" when they make alliance decisions, taking into account enemies both at home and abroad, but the observation could just as easily apply to decisions about how to design the state's coercive apparatus.[34] Bruce Bueno de Mesquita and colleagues have argued that leaders' behavior is driven primarily by a desire to stay in office, which suggests that internal threats should be extremely important in foreign policy decisions.[35] Similarly, in his study of authoritarian durability, Slater has demonstrated that "violent internal contention can 'make the state' as surely as international warfare."[36] This indicates again that military institutions are shaped by internal rather than purely external dynamics, although, as Slater notes, the timing and type of internal threats matter greatly.

My framework concurs that threats matter, but shows their importance specifically for battlefield effectiveness rather than for alliances, general foreign policy, or regime stability. Furthermore, the critical distinction is not whether a threat is internal or external per se, but whether it makes conventional military capabilities an asset or a liability for a given regime. Coups are the most distinctive in this regard and are different from other domestic dangers such as insurgency, civil war, mass protest, or state failure. Indeed, this emphasis on regimes' coup sensitivity points directly to the importance of another major variable identified in the existing literature: civil-military relations.

Civil-Military Relations

Analysts have long suspected that the relationship between political leaders and military officers is an important driver of performance in war, but they disagree about what form this relationship should take. Some have praised military autonomy, criticizing political intervention in military affairs as counterproductive meddling. As the ancient Chinese writer Sun Tzu noted, "He whose generals are able and not interfered with by the sovereign will be victorious."[37] In the modern era, Huntington's *The Soldier and the State* resonates with this view, arguing that military effectiveness requires "objective" civilian control, that is, politicians staying out of purely military affairs and avoiding the politicization of the officer corps.[38]

Other students of military affairs have come to different conclusions. Clausewitz, for example, believed that military action was inherently political and that political involvement in military affairs was not only inevitable but crucial to success in war. As he argued, "War is only a branch of political activity; . . . it is in no sense autonomous."[39] Similarly, Eliot Cohen and Barry Posen have both pointed to cases in which civilian intervention in the military has been the linchpin of military effectiveness, noting that militaries left to their own devices often develop battle plans that are poorly integrated with the state's political objectives and at times unsound even in purely military terms.[40]

The book's framework shares the intuition that political-military relations matter greatly for military performance. But it moves beyond the two schools of thought that have focused for so long on whether to encourage or minimize political intervention in the military. Instead, it urges us to pay attention to the causes and nature of such intervention when it does occur—what political leaders actually do when they involve themselves in military affairs, why, and with what implications for battlefield performance. In short, simply knowing whether political intervention in military affairs is high or low is not enough to predict how a given military will perform. Even where political intervention in the military is extensive, it can take varied forms, some conducive to better military performance and others damaging to it. The book's framework enables us to distinguish among these different kinds of political intervention

[30]

and to estimate states' likely military effectiveness with more precision than otherwise would be possible.

For example, my argument suggests that even militaries subject to similarly high levels of political meddling could diverge sharply in their effectiveness depending on the nature of said meddling. To take two extremes, Adolf Hitler and Saddam Hussein both presided over highly politicized armies in which they exerted personal control over key activities such as promotions—but Hitler, leader of one of the twentieth century's most tactically and operationally effective fighting forces, and Saddam, leader of one of the least effective, wielded personal control toward very different ends. They both hired and fired officers, for example, but Saddam cared mostly about whether his commanders were Ba'thist, whereas Hitler promoted and demoted based largely on merit and combat performance, especially after the early years of his rule and before the assassination attempt against him in 1944.[41] Certainly, Hitler did not punish competence in the officer corps the way Saddam did, even though both prized political loyalty.[42] In short, political intervention was rampant in both cases, but Hitler intervened in ways generally consistent with conventional war practices, whereas Saddam usually enforced coup protection practices.[43] My framework helps explain why these two varieties of what Huntington called "subjective" civilian control produced such different battlefield results.

Furthermore, I show that just as political intervention is not an unalloyed evil, military autonomy is not an unalloyed good. To be sure, some very autonomous militaries do become professional and relatively effective fighting forces, such as the Pakistani military under periods of military dictatorship.[44] But other highly autonomous militaries do not, such as the Argentine military under the junta (surely a case where civilian meddling was not the problem). A focus on actual military organizational practices explains these apparent inconsistencies by drawing our attention to what militaries choose to do—and why—when they enjoy high levels of autonomy (i.e., when a military leader is more or less running the state).

This distinction helps explain why the German military went from extreme autonomy in World War I to extreme civilian control in World War II, but is generally acknowledged to have fought well at the tactical and operational levels under both circumstances. It also explains why armies subject to intrusive communist control in China and the Soviet Union varied significantly in their battlefield effectiveness across wars, and even in different campaigns in the same war, despite having consistently low autonomy. As these examples suggest, the relationship between military autonomy and effectiveness is not as straightforward as often assumed, and politicization of the military may not always be a bad thing. To the extent that politicization encourages adoption of conventional war practices, it may even enhance effectiveness.

This insight is consistent with the more recent wave of civil-military scholarship focused specifically on how coup fears shape leaders' choices about military organization and the resulting impact on effectiveness.[45] My argument shares the intuitions of this coup-proofing literature, though it refines, expands, and deductively grounds them in a broader claim about how different threat environments should systematically produce different types of military organizations. In so doing, it enables us to understand coup-proofing as a phenomenon that should travel well beyond the small handful of Arab autocracies that first gave rise to the term.

The fact that the term is used in the context of nondemocracies points directly to the relevance of a third body of existing literature, that on regime type. Indeed, it is strikingly difficult to think of autocracies that have adopted Huntington's preferred model of objective control, even if the forms of subjective control among autocracies are more varied than he supposed.

Regime Type

Some international relations scholarship has argued that democracies are more militarily effective than nondemocracies, in part because democracies are said to infuse their soldiers with liberal values that bolster fighting prowess.[46] This book joins more recent work that has moved beyond the democracy/nondemocracy distinction in trying to explain states' conflict behavior.[47] Institutions can be strong or weak in both democracies and autocracies, and as Barbara Geddes has noted, "Different kinds of authoritarianism differ from each other as much as they differ from democracy."[48]

My approach suggests that these differences matter because they (along with a state's civil-military history) provide a useful indicator of the threat environment facing a given regime, which in turn shapes choices about military organizational practices. In so doing, the argument points to a reason that democracies may generally develop organizational practices better suited to conventional war, while also providing a logically compelling explanation of the autocratic exceptions that remain puzzling from the perspective of existing theories. Democratic rulers should be far less likely, on average, to face severe internal threats, especially the coups that present an impediment to the development of conventional war practices.[49] But there are, of course, outliers. Republican Spain adopted coup prevention practices during the Spanish Civil

[32]

War, for example—an understandable response to the coup that launched the conflict.[50] Nehru's India adopted some coup prevention practices prior to the devastating war against China in 1962 that prompted major changes in Indian civil-military relations.[51] Coups do happen in weak and nascent democracies, while well-institutionalized authoritarian regimes, particularly single-party states, seem to be well insulated from them, enabling the adoption of conventional war practices if the state's external threat environment and foreign policy goals provide a reason to do so.

In addition, by emphasizing the centrality of threats and treating political institutions as an indicator of those threats, the book's framework provides a more satisfying explanation of why effectiveness can sometimes vary even when regime type does not. For example, the improvement in India's fighting effectiveness after 1962 or in Egypt's between 1967 and 1973 makes little sense in terms of shifting political values: India remained a democracy and Egypt a dictatorship. But the variation makes sense from the perspective of changes in the threat environment. In both cases, the poor early performance resulted from a regime facing more internal than external threats, and particularly concerned with coups. In both cases, the war indicated that the nature of the dominant, proximate threat had changed. It stimulated changes in military organizational practices and resulted in subsequent improvement in battlefield effectiveness—despite no major changes in political institutions. Clearly, then, political institutions are relevant to military effectiveness, but the framework here explains why, how, and under what threat conditions change is possible, even within the same country.

TESTING THE ARGUMENT

Tracking the Variables of Interest

Exploring my framework empirically requires a consistent, substantively satisfying way of measuring the variables of interest. In particular, I seek to track variation in two indicators of battlefield effectiveness: tactical proficiency and the ability to perform complex operations. Some studies measure effectiveness simply by examining war outcomes. As discussed earlier, however, there are good reasons to conceptualize tactical-operational performance as distinct from ultimate strategic-political victory, even if the two are related. Outcome-based measures also limit our ability to observe variation within a given military, because the unit of analysis is a given military in a given war, which may mask important differences across or even within divisions.

Other studies take the battle as their unit of observation and measure effectiveness by looking at the loss-exchange ratio of the two sides in a given encounter—attacker casualties divided by defender casualties.[52] This measure, too, has its uses, but it does present a problem of observational equivalence: both effective and ineffective armies can have high casualties. For example, low casualties may result from the ability to conduct sophisticated operations that shield soldiers from their enemies' firepower, which many observers pinpoint as the cause of the extremely low American casualties in the Gulf War.[53] But low casualties also can result from armies surrendering, retreating, or simply collapsing in the face of enemy contact, which occurred in the South Korean army after the invasion by the North in 1950.[54] Likewise, high casualties can result from incompetent armies repeatedly attempting the same ill-advised tactics, which many observers blame for the extraordinarily high number of battle deaths suffered by the belligerents on the Western Front in World War I. But high casualties also can result from very skilled units motivated to fight to the death, as the Wehrmacht proved in the winter of 1944–1945.[55] These examples do not mean the measure is meaningless, merely that we often need additional contextual information in order to know what it is telling us about a given military's tactical proficiency and ability to conduct complex operations.

For these reasons, I rely on a series of qualitative indicator questions that attempt to provide this context and to probe for the performance of specific tasks. Regarding the conduct of basic tactics, I ask the following:

- Do units demonstrate the ability to handle their weapons properly? Is marksmanship good?
- Are units familiar with their equipment and weapons? Are these well maintained?
- Are soldiers able to use terrain for cover and concealment?
- Can the unit execute an ambush? A static defense? An orderly retreat? A planned attritional offensive?

Regarding the execution of complex operations, I ask,

- Can the unit conduct combined arms operations? Participate in interservice operations? Division size or larger operations?
- Among defensive operations, is the unit able to conduct a defense in depth? Fighting withdrawals? Counterattacks?
- Among offensive operations, is it able to maneuver? To conduct small-unit special forces operations?
- Does the unit demonstrate a capacity for both low-level initiative and high-level coordination?

[34]

These questions can be asked of any military unit participating in a battle or campaign—ranging from a multidivision corps formation to an individual division to a brigade or even smaller units. Not only does this approach target the actual tasks of interest rather than a proxy for them, but it also enables me to detect and probe within-military variation, producing an opportunity for more rigorous testing of my claims. If my argument about military organizational practices is right, then the adoption of different organizational practices in different units should produce intra-military variations in effectiveness, which provides another opportunity to falsify or confirm my claims.

I take a similar approach to coding the independent variable, the threat environment. My coding questions aim to generate a picture of the major dangers facing a given state, and in particular to determine whether coup fears are present or absent in the period prior to and coincident with a given war. The first seven questions pertain to precisely this topic, and the more "yes" responses a given state receives, the more strongly the argument would predict the adoption of coup protection practices. The last three questions probe for other threats the state might face, which could result in the adoption of mixed or conventional war practices. The questions are crafted to detect objective features of the environment that should be observable *ex ante* and distinct from military organizational practices:

- Is the country a military dictatorship or personalist regime?
- Has the country experienced a coup or coup attempt within the leader's living memory?
- Did the current leader come to power in a coup?
- Is the leader divided from much of the officer corps and/or the military writ large by a major social cleavage?
- Has the leader inherited his officer corps from a regime of questionable loyalty (e.g., from a colonial master or a regime recently overthrown)?
- Has the military deliberately signaled a recent threat to mount a coup (e.g., explicitly making public statements to this effect or engaging in military maneuvers designed to show the ability to seize power)?
- Do elites in the country express support for military intervention in politics or military government?
- Is the state currently experiencing armed popular threats such as civil war, insurgency, or secessionist movements? Has it recently experienced such threats?

- Does the state face an enduring external rival? Has that rival made recent hostile statements or taken provocative actions indicating that war may be imminent?
- Do the leader's foreign policy goals require forcible expansion of the state's borders and/or the conquest of foreign territory?

To code the intervening variable, military organizational practices, I examine promotion patterns, training regimens, command arrangements, and information management in a given military, both over time and across different units, based on the framework developed earlier. In my analysis I ask,

- What are the primary criteria for promotion in the senior officer corps, junior officer corps, NCO corps, and among enlisted personnel?
- What is the relative weight given to political loyalty versus demonstrated military competence in the promotion process?
- How important are sectarian background and/or ideological credentials for advancement?
- Is a strong performance in training or on the battlefield good or bad for an officer's prospects? What happens to commanders who preside over battlefield disasters?
- Are there mass firings that amount to purges, and if so, how often do they occur?
- Which skills are emphasized in training?
- What size units engage in training exercises? Is it all small-unit, or are there efforts to practice coordination of large-unit activities?
- Is training rigorous and intensive, or largely perfunctory? Does specialized training occur?
- Is training realistic? How closely does it mirror the battlefield environment? Are there live fire exercises?
- Does the content of training remain static, or does it evolve in response to new information from the battlefield?
- Are training commands run by experienced and competent officers?
- Are there clear, institutionalized procedures for conveying orders during battle?
- To what extent does command authority reside with those not present on the battlefield (e.g., how many layers of approval are required before commanders can execute a tactical decision)?
- Do command arrangements generally prioritize central oversight of battlefield developments, or do they devolve authority to officers in the field?
- Are there "dual command" arrangements, for example, commissars alongside regular officers who are given a veto over battlefield decisions?

- Are officers ever fired or shuffled among commands, and if so why?
- Are units fighting on the same battlefield regularly able to communicate horizontally?
- Are senior officers and political leaders regularly updated on battlefield events as they happen?
- How often do military and political leaders interact, and what is the format and substance of their communication?
- Are commanders encouraged to deliver candid assessments of battlefield performance to political leaders?
- Is there an internally directed intelligence gathering organization that reports on the military to political leaders?

Based on our answers we can gauge whether a state's military organizational practices reflect ideal-typical conventional war practices, which should result in excellent battlefield effectiveness; whether they veer toward ideal-typical coup prevention practices, which should result in poor battlefield effectiveness; or whether they reflect mixed practices, which should result in adequate battlefield effectiveness.

The Use and Selection of Case Studies

The data demanded by this coding scheme, as well as the heterogeneous units of observation involved, make case studies the most viable means of probing my argument empirically. A "case" for my purposes is a given state in a war, although all such cases contain multiple "observations," that is, instances of military units fighting a given battle or campaign. My research strategy focuses on cases that enable both cross-case and within-case tests of my argument.

Because I want to maximize external validity, I begin by seeking out cases that display what Slater and Ziblatt call "typological representativeness"—cases that represent the full range of possible variation of the dependent variable. Rather than embodying the often-maligned approach of "selecting on the dependent variable," strategically choosing a sample of cases whose outcomes are known to mirror variation in the larger population of interest actually helps sidestep the problem of selection bias in small-N work.[56] For my purposes, this means choosing cases from all instances of interstate war since 1917 that, as a group, populate the values of the dependent variable: excellent battlefield performance (tactical proficiency and complex operations), adequate battlefield performance (tactical proficiency without complex operations), and poor battlefield performance (neither).[57] Although this approach does not allow us to say how frequently these different values will arise in the broader population, it does avoid artificially truncating the range of possible values of the dependent variable in ways that distort inference.

I also choose cases with careful attention to how they help control for theoretically generated rival hypotheses. To do this I employ what political scientists call a "folk Bayesian" approach to identify the cases that are most puzzling based on existing explanations of effectiveness.[58] In other words, rather than artificially assume a position of no prior knowledge about either a state's effectiveness in a given war or what might account for it, I explicitly use prior knowledge about both to identify cases where variation points to the need for new explanations. Specifically, I look for states whose battlefield performance seems at odds with what we would expect based on the state's wealth, population, regime type, external threats, military politicization, and national culture. For example, a case involving a rich, populous, wealthy democracy outfighting an economically underdeveloped military dictatorship would be much less useful from this perspective than a case that appeared to show the opposite.

I also seek out pairs of such states fighting in the same war. First, paired comparisons allow examination of two states in a given war rather than just one, yielding a much higher analytical return on the sunk costs involved in a detailed case study. I can extract useful data from both sides in every battle or campaign. Second, paired comparisons facilitate additional cross-national tests of my argument, rather than within-case analysis only. Wars in which battlefield effectiveness varied between two opponents, even when the two states were evenly matched along most dimensions said to matter for effectiveness, would be highly puzzling based on our theoretical priors. These are exactly the cases that one's intuitive inner statistician (or "folk Bayesian") would seek to explore in the hopes of developing and testing new arguments.[59]

Using this approach, I identified two pairs of cases whose values of the dependent variable were especially puzzling: North and South Vietnam from 1963 to 1975, and Iran and Iraq from 1980 to 1988. In addition to being long wars that afford many opportunities for observing variation, these conflicts both involved nondemocratic states whose fighting effectiveness varied cross-nationally and subnationally. For example, though South Vietnam often lived up to its reputation for military ineffectiveness, some units within the South Vietnamese military actually fought very well and proved quite capable of both tactical proficiency and complex operations. By contrast, North Vietnamese units were generally excellent, though their conventional effectiveness became notably better by 1975. All this variation within and across the two militaries occurred despite both being authoritarian, roughly even in terms of wealth and population size, and having common (though far from identical) cultural underpinnings. The national stakes were high for both

[38]

sides in the conflict as well, suggesting that realist pressures to perform well should have been strong. Also, both militaries were highly politicized, albeit in different ways. In short, the pair provides impressive range on the dependent variable while still controlling for many possible independent variables. Each state also affords some additional subnational variation, allowing further tightly controlled opportunities to test my argument.

The Iran and Iraq cases offer similar methodological advantages. Like the Vietnam War, the Iran-Iraq conflict was a long land war fought between two authoritarian neighbors, both of whom displayed subnational variation in their battlefield effectiveness. The Iraqis fought disastrously overall, especially in the war's early years, but Iraqi Republican Guard and select army units did demonstrate excellent tactical proficiency and complex operations in the series of counteroffensives that finally ended the conflict. Iran's revolutionary forces also generally proved inept, although some of the legacy military units from the time of the Shah demonstrated basic tactical proficiency early in the conflict.

In short, the two countries displayed representative variation on the dependent variable—despite the fact that neither experienced much variation in wealth, population, regime type, national culture, or degree of military politicization over the course of the war. Both states also faced high national stakes in the conflict. As a pair, Iran and Iraq were not evenly matched along every dimension, but the lopsided areas actually reinforce why the war is baffling from the perspective of existing theories. Iraq had a smaller economy, a smaller population, and an Arab culture—all factors that existing theories predict should hinder performance—yet it ultimately proved far more innovative and tactically proficient than its Persian adversary.[60]

That said, the existence of such variation does not prove that the book's framework is useful in accounting for it. Such assessments require process tracing. Process tracing is distinct from what political scientists call "congruence tests," which simply try to detect a correlation between a given independent and dependent variable. Process tracing examines the steps linking two variables to see if they accord with a hypothesized set of causal processes.[61] Here, we want to know whether a given threat environment resulted in variation in battlefield effectiveness due to the adoption of different military organizational practices. Because the four cases I have chosen are relatively data-rich and covered in detailed, accessible, English-language or translated sources, this type of analysis is possible.

In general, the more we see the detailed connections posited by the book's argument at work across multiple battles and units in a given military, especially where other variables are held constant, the more confident we can be that the framework is accurate and useful. We should be especially confident where we see it explaining variation over time or across different units in the same military, given that so many other possible alternative variables remain unchanged. Where we see it explain the full range of possible outcomes on the dependent variable, we also can have confidence that the causal relationships identified in the sample at hand likely mirror those found in the broader population of cases.

Furthermore, process tracing, in combination with the folk Bayesian approach to case selection, can bolster not only within-case but also cross-case analysis. Controlled comparisons sometimes come in for criticism because researchers cannot truly hold all confounding variables constant.[62] It is true that the pairs of states I examine in this study do not offer the precision of natural experiments. They cannot perform what Slater and Ziblatt call "inferential miracles," and they do not tell us how often the variables controlled for in the comparisons are actually controlled for in the broader population.[63] But my explicit use of existing theory to identify puzzling cases on the front end should leave us reassured that at least the most plausible candidate explanations have been ruled out in each comparison. Just as important, process tracing allows me to identify and address possible case-specific alternative explanations, an extra guard against the possibility that some other important omitted variable explains observed cross-national differences. I examine several of these in the course of each paired comparison, providing an additional means of assessing how well my argument travels within and across different cases.

[2]

Threats and Military Organizational Practices in North and South Vietnam

The contrasting battlefield performances of North and South Vietnam present an enduring puzzle in the history of warfare. Why did two states with so many underlying similarities generate armies displaying such tremendous variation in battlefield effectiveness? North Vietnam is renowned for its ferocious fighting capabilities, while South Vietnam is just as famous as a symbol of incompetence, disparaged for its seeming inability to build even a mediocre military despite massive U.S. aid.

While the reality of both sides' performances was more complicated than these pervasive images suggest, the stereotypes do capture a basic puzzle. Why was North Vietnam consistently able to generate tactically proficient armed forces capable of conducting complex operations, while South Vietnam proved unable to do so? As we will see, existing theories of military effectiveness do not provide a satisfying answer.

These explanations have particular difficulty accounting for variation within the South Vietnamese military. While South Vietnam's overall performance was clearly inferior to the North's, its armed forces were not uniformly terrible, as often assumed. South Vietnam did not develop the ability to consistently conduct the most difficult complex operations, particularly large-scale offensive operations. But some of its units proved to be tactically proficient and more operationally sophisticated than usually recognized. These units stood in contrast to other parts of the military that were indeed unable to meet even basic standards of tactical proficiency. Any explanation of the difference in performance between North and South Vietnam therefore has to account not just for the general variation between the two states but also for the variation within the South Vietnamese military—variation that proved crucial in determining the course, costs, and ultimate outcome of the war.

[41]

This chapter and the next argue that the answer lies in the very different threats facing the regimes in Hanoi and Saigon, and the military organizational practices that these environments engendered. South Vietnamese leaders believed, correctly, that they faced a multitude of internal, irregular threats, including insurgency, state weakness, and especially coups. The South Vietnamese military generally adopted coup prevention practices as a result. The alliance with the United States only reinforced this tendency, as it promised to shield South Vietnam from exactly the sort of external threat most likely to result in the adoption of conventional war practices. Furthermore, the factionalism of Saigon's military governments hindered South Vietnam's responsiveness to the external threat environment even as U.S. involvement dwindled. That said, there were some South Vietnamese exceptions to this rule, particularly in situations where the conventional threat from the North was stronger, U.S. protection weaker, and the risks of coups lower. Under these conditions South Vietnamese units adopted better organizational practices, resulting in better military performance.

In contrast to the personalist and military rule that characterized South Vietnam, North Vietnam's well-institutionalized single-party regime faced far less danger with respect to irregular, internal threats—notably, no risk of coups—and possessed foreign policy goals that affirmatively required revision of the state's borders and the conquest of foreign territory. As a result, the North Vietnamese military generally adopted conventional war practices and enjoyed consistently excellent battlefield effectiveness. This is not to argue that North Vietnam's military had no shortcomings or to deny its extensive politicization, but it faced a fundamentally different threat environment that resulted in different military organizational practices and better battlefield performance.

This chapter proceeds in three main parts. The first section provides background and sharpens the puzzle of North and South Vietnamese battlefield effectiveness. The second section delves into South Vietnam, discussing how the threat environment it faced generally led to the adoption of coup prevention practices and the implications for battlefield performance. The third section then repeats this procedure with respect to North Vietnam.

The chapter draws on a variety of documentary sources, including U.S. military and intelligence reports, translated North and South Vietnamese records, official histories, memoirs, captured documents, contemporary third party studies and news reports, more recent histories, and many others, often in an attempt to "triangulate" a given topic from a variety of perspectives. The use of any documents, much less those that have been translated, naturally raises issues of bias. I mitigate this problem by being transparent about the sources of information I use, explicitly noting the instances in which I detect differing accounts of the same issue or event, and carefully contextualizing the information I use. This conservative approach enables the reader to judge the validity of my claims, and, most important, to assess whether my use of documents in any way systematically slants the evidence in favor of my argument. Chapter 3 continues this approach, using documents to examine a representative series of battles between North and South Vietnam from 1963 to 1975.[1]

BACKGROUND: THE PUZZLE OF BATTLEFIELD EFFECTIVENESS IN NORTH AND SOUTH VIETNAM

The Origins of the Conflict from the French Arrival to 1954

In 1954 two states emerged from the remnants of French Indochina.[2] The French had first established themselves in Saigon nearly a hundred years earlier and soon controlled all of Cochin China, Vietnam's southernmost region, and thereafter the middle and northern regions of Tonkin and Annam as well (see map 2.1).[3]

The experience of French imperial rule had profound consequences for Vietnam's political development. Perhaps the most important was the political awakening it stirred among the Vietnamese elite. By the 1920s a large crop of Vietnamese had been educated in France and served in the French army during World War I. But they found that positions of authority in their own country remained closed to them, open only to better paid, often less educated Frenchmen. The resulting resentment among urban Vietnamese surfaced in a variety of forms during the interwar years, although only the nascent Vietnamese communists possessed the tight organizational discipline needed to evade French repression. As historian Anthony James Joes has noted, "It is another one of the rich ironies of the whole Vietnamese revolution that the French would search desperately in the 1950s for an effective nationalist alternative to the communists, an alternative that, by their persecution from the 1920s to the 1940s, they had all but eliminated."[4]

The Japanese occupation of Vietnam from 1940 to 1945 provided the opening for which the communists and other revolutionaries had waited. In 1941, they established the League for the Independence of Vietnam, or Viet Minh, an organization that temporarily put aside the goal of class struggle and focused exclusively on the nationalist objective of evicting the Japanese and establishing an independent Vietnamese state. Because the Japanese army controlled the cities, this revolutionary organization focused on the countryside, promising land redistribution as a way to recruit peasants.

[43]

Map 2.1. French Indochina. Adapted from George C. Herring, *America's Longest War: The United States and Vietnam, 1950–1975* (New York: McGraw Hill, 2002), 7.

For most of their occupation, the Japanese were content to rule through the French, but in March 1945 they imprisoned French officials, interned French forces, and offered the Annamese emperor Bao Dai independence. He accepted, declaring the independence of Annam and Tonkin, while the Japanese continued to rule Cochin China. Japanese surrender to the Allies soon created a power vacuum, however. Viet Minh troops moved into Hanoi, forced Bao Dai to abdicate, and declared the independence of Vietnam under the leadership of Ho Chi Minh.

The success of this August Revolution was short-lived, as the French soon reasserted their authority, especially in the south.[5] Knowing that the Viet Minh were not yet in a position to defeat the French, Ho again compromised, signing an agreement with the French representative Jean Sainteny in March 1946. The Ho-Sainteny agreement did not grant Vietnam full independence, but it recognized the legitimacy of Ho's rule over Tonkin and Annam in a government now called the Democratic Republic of Vietnam (DRV).[6]

By December the agreement had fallen apart, however, and the Viet Minh began an all-out war to evict the French.[7] The 1949 victory of Mao's forces across the border brought the Viet Minh an infusion of better weapons and equipment, but this new friend also brought a new enemy. Worried about the spread of communism via Chinese assistance, the United States established the Military Assistance Advisory Group (MAAG) as a means of channeling an ever-growing stream of military aid to the Franco-Vietnamese forces.[8]

The French belatedly recognized that they would never again rule Vietnam, but they shared with the United States the goal of a noncommunist successor regime. After protracted negotiations, the French came to support a government led by Bao Dai, who broke with the Viet Minh and was recognized by the French as ruler of an independent state of Vietnam, including Cochin China, in June 1948. The French military effort then focused on defending this government. By mid-1949, 41,500 Vietnamese troops had joined the French in the campaign, coalescing into the Vietnamese National Army (VNA), which would become the nucleus of the future Army of the Republic of Vietnam (ARVN).[9]

Unfortunately, the next several years produced little more than bloody stalemate.[10] Finally, in the spring of 1954, the war culminated in the famous battle for Dien Bien Phu, an isolated French base in a remote corner of Tonkin near the Laotian border. The French defenders, outnumbered and outgunned, capitulated to the Viet Minh in May.

The Geneva Conference ensued, partitioning Vietnam into two states. Territory north of the 17th parallel—essentially the region of Tonkin—was to be ruled by Ho Chi Minh, while land south of that parallel—essentially the regions of Annam and Cochin China—was to be ruled by Bao Dai, who would soon appoint Ngo Dinh Diem as his prime minister.[11] For one year there was to be free migration across the demilitarized zone so that people could settle under the government of their choice. Despite Hanoi's violent obstruction of this migration, close to a million northerners resettled in the south, among them many Christians and intellectuals.[12]

Meanwhile, the Diem regime rapidly dispensed with Bao Dai via a rigged referendum and then adamantly opposed holding the elections called for, albeit vaguely, in the Geneva agreements.[13] It argued that the French had had no right to commit the state of Vietnam to such elections, or to partition Vietnam in the first place. It also knew that because the population of the DRV was slightly larger, and because Ho's sympathizers could rig the vote in their own territory, any plebiscite would result in a communist takeover of all of Vietnam.[14] The stage was set for further military confrontation.

An Overview of the War between North and South Vietnam

Historical debate continues about the origins of the insurgency in South Vietnam, and leaders in Hanoi were themselves divided in the period after Geneva regarding whether to prioritize building socialism at home or carrying the revolution to the South.[15] What is known is that an insurgency was well underway by the late 1950s, aimed primarily at local administration and the middle class of South Vietnam. State officials, teachers, medical personnel, and social workers were all targets of intimidation, kidnapping, and assassination in a campaign that had killed 20 percent of all village chiefs by 1958. The insurgency had Hanoi's blessing but also gained fuel from indigenous grievances with the Diem government. In fact, those in the South often sought revolution at a faster pace than leaders in Hanoi thought wise.[16]

Sensing momentum, Hanoi did start to infiltrate more heavily armed units to South Vietnam in 1959. They formed the National Liberation Front (NLF) in 1960 as a way to unify efforts to overthrow the Diem government and to appeal directly to Southern nationalism.[17] This move continued Ho's long-running willingness to follow the Leninist principle of the united front: temporarily allying with potential noncommunist adversaries in order to achieve intermediate objectives, with the full recognition that today's comrades would become tomorrow's targets.[18] The NLF, reporting to a Central Office for South Vietnam, also helped Hanoi conceal its direction of the war in the South—something it denied at the time but proclaimed once the war was over.[19]

The NLF's studious avoidance of communism as a stated goal did little to assuage U.S. concerns about the fate of South Vietnam.[20] President Kennedy more than tripled the size of the MAAG in his first seven months in office, to 1,905 personnel. He also introduced additional personnel to support struggling South Vietnamese forces directly and moved to establish a command structure that could encompass combat troops in addition to advisers and support personnel. The result was the Military Assistance Command, Vietnam (MACV), formed in February 1962.[21] Beyond ramping up military operations, MACV assisted Saigon in attempting to secure the villages, most notably through the Strategic Hamlet Program.[22] MACV also sent numerous South Vietnamese officers to the United States for training and established dozens of training centers in South Vietnam.[23]

The year 1963 proved fateful for the Republic of Vietnam. It started with the army's disastrous performance at Ap Bac and ended with President Diem dead at the hands of his own officers. Thus began two years of intense instability in which the clique of officers that had initiated the coup, known as the Young Turks, proceeded through no fewer than seven additional changes of government, including five coups.[24] By 1965 the situation had stabilized somewhat, with an original Young Turk, General Nguyen Van Thieu, now serving as president, and Air Vice Marshall Nguyen Cao Ky serving as premier.[25] They presided over a new military governing body made up of several dozen generals known as the Committee for the Direction of the State, or the Directory.[26]

Nevertheless, the political instability of this period convinced U.S. policymakers that merely advising Vietnamese forces would not be enough to ensure the survival of a noncommunist regime.[27] The United States already had inserted more than 23,000 military advisers into South Vietnam by 1964. By the end of the next year, the U.S. commitment escalated to 184,000 soldiers, including four combat divisions that initiated a new series of offensives to find and destroy the elusive North Vietnamese guerrillas. The United States also massively increased its effort to train and equip the Republic of Vietnam Armed Forces (RVNAF), growing them to an authorized strength of over 600,000 men by 1967.[28]

For its part, Hanoi believed by 1968 that it had reached the crucial point at which it could shift from a Maoist revolutionary strategy focused purely on the countryside to a Leninist approach that would seek to cause an uprising against the Thieu-Ky regime in the cities. The result was the Tet Offensive, a series of coordinated attacks throughout South Vietnam. But although tactically impressive, Tet only hardened South Vietnamese antipathy for the North. It also enabled the United States to so badly maul its suddenly exposed guerrilla opponents that they never regained their previous influence in the South.

It would be four years before the North attempted another major offensive, although the interlude was hardly peaceful. The two sides fought numerous battles during this period, reflecting the increasing willingness of the People's Army of Vietnam (PAVN) to confront the United States and the ARVN in direct battles for control of territory. During this time South Vietnam and the United States also mounted several operations to disrupt the PAVN's foreign supply routes, collectively known as the Ho Chi Minh Trail. These operations included a somewhat successful incursion into Cambodia in 1970 and a disastrous invasion of Laos in 1971.

Neither of these ventures stopped the North from launching the 1972 Easter Offensive, a coordinated series of assaults across multiple provinces in South Vietnam. Here again, Hanoi failed to provoke its much-sought urban uprising and suffered extensive losses. But South Vietnamese combat performance proved uneven at best and remained heavily reliant on U.S. leadership and support. More important, the North knew that this leadership and support would not last forever. Having already heavily shifted much responsibility directly to the South Vietnamese through the policy of Vietnamization begun in 1970, the Nixon administration soon signed the 1973 Paris Peace Accords, officially ending the U.S. combat role in the war.

After the withdrawal of U.S. combat forces, the South Vietnamese were left to defend themselves, albeit with a large stockpile of U.S. military equipment.[29] In the early 1970s alone, for example, Saigon had received an additional $753 million in new airplanes, helicopters, tanks, artillery pieces, and other military equipment.[30] This aid rapidly dried up after 1973, however, largely due to U.S. domestic politics.[31] In January 1975, the North launched a final series of offensives, and by May 1 PAVN tanks were roaming the streets of Saigon.

The Puzzle for Theories of Battlefield Effectiveness

Why did North and South Vietnam demonstrate such varying levels of battlefield effectiveness? Having been "separated at birth" in 1954 and sharing so many important traits, the two states should have generated roughly comparable armies, at least according to existing theories focused on wealth, demography, autocracy, culture and society, military politicization, and external threats. For example, both states exhibited low levels of economic development, with their populations consisting primarily of rural peasants. Of the two, the South actually had a larger educated urban elite. North and South Vietnam also were almost exactly the same size with roughly equal populations.[32]

Similarly, both states were autocratic. The two regimes were not identical, of course, and the legacies of colonial rule and revolution played out differently in the North and South, a point discussed in more depth at the end of chapter 3. North Vietnam was a Marxist-Leninist state with a robust, well-institutionalized party system, while South Vietnam was a personalist regime under Diem and later a military dictatorship under Thieu and Ky. Nevertheless, neither country could have been said to derive any aspect of its military performance from the purported democratic advantages in strategic assessment or political culture. If anything, the supposed disadvantages of autocracy should have weighed more heavily on North Vietnam.

Cross-national cultural and social differences also do not seem to be a plausible explanation for variation. Clearly, the two states differed, and for most of their history the two regions were not unified. As Joes has observed, "North Vietnamese see themselves as dynamic and southerners as rather lazy and slow-witted. Southerners view northerners as aggressive, money-hungry, harder-working, and more enduring. They perceive themselves as more pacific than the militant inhabitants of the Red River Delta, possessing in their enjoyment of the bounties and beauties of nature the true secret of happiness."[33]

Still, North and South Vietnam were more alike than different on the cultural and social dimensions said to matter for military performance—and certainly much more alike than typical opponents in war. They shared a common religious legacy from long-standing Buddhist, Confucian, and Taoist influences. For centuries they also had shared a common social hierarchy, and later both were subject to French colonial rule, albeit in different forms.[34] Both were largely ethnically homogenous, although South Vietnam exhibited significant religious divisions between Buddhists and Catholics, as well as political tensions between native-born Southerners and refugees from the North.[35]

Ideology—not only communism, but also nationalism—did constitute an important social difference between the two states, and this will be discussed more at the end of chapter 3. But it is important to note that although North Vietnam marshaled a clear ideological advantage, it is unclear how this alone should have translated into better battlefield capabilities. It might explain why those who fought for Hanoi were better motivated and therefore had better unit cohesion, but it is harder to explain how this factor could have produced such big cross-national differences in tactical proficiency and the ability to conduct complex operations. In addition, the absence of nationalism or communism cannot explain the variation seen across different units of the South Vietnamese military, again suggesting that something besides ideology was at work.

Similarly, the degree of civilian control over the military is not a convincing explanation of either the cross-national or within-country variation in battlefield effectiveness in these cases. In both states political leaders interfered in military activities and politicized the armed forces in ways that smack of Huntington's notion of subjective control. Despite this similarity, however, the two states' battlefield effectiveness diverged sharply.

Finally, both states faced threatening external environments that should have induced strong pressures for effective military organization. If anything, this pressure should have weighed more heavily on the South than the North. Yet Saigon's decision making shows that external threats are not the only ones that matter for military organizational development. The severity and nature of the internal threats facing Saigon—and in particular, the prioritization of coup protection—led to the adoption of military practices poorly suited to confronting the threat from the North. Dependence on the Americans seems only to have reinforced these choices. Conversely, North Vietnam's threat environment encouraged the adoption of conventional war practices—despite the regime's low level of economic development, small population, autocratic character, cultural affinity with its opponent, and civilian intrusion in the military.

Threats and Military Organizational Practices in South Vietnam

From 1954 to 1975, the regimes governing South Vietnam faced multiple irregular, internal threats, especially coups—an unsurprising reality given the regime's personalist and later military character. Meanwhile, the external, potentially conventional threat posed by the North was muted during much of this time. After all, the means by which Hanoi was willing to pursue its goals were deliberately opaque, and the United States promised to shield South Vietnam from the worst-case scenarios. As we will see, however, in several limited instances South Vietnamese leaders' concern about conventional threats intensified and coup worries receded, resulting in military organizational shifts toward conventional war practices among some units. But in general, South Vietnamese regimes had little reason to adopt such measures.

The country's adherence to coup prevention practices occurred despite the fact that on paper, at least, the ARVN grew rapidly into a robust fighting organization. By 1960, the ARVN consisted of seven infantry divisions organized under three major corps headquarters, one for each of the northern (I), central (II), and southern (III) regions of the country; in 1961, a fourth corps area was added in the far south (see map 2.2).[36] Each division had roughly 10,000 men and was tasked with defense of its particular geographic area. Separate armor, airborne, marine, and aviation components of the ARVN were envisioned as more mobile forces that could engage in combat throughout the country, reacting to major

[50]

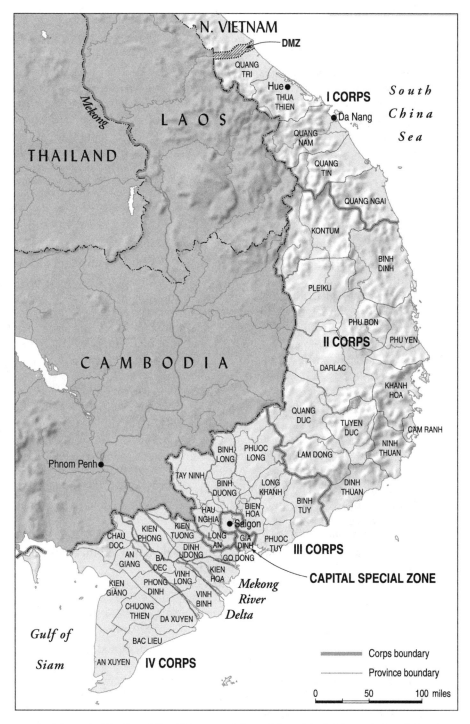

Map 2.2. The Republic of Vietnam. Adapted from Mark Moyar, *Triumph Forsaken: The Vietnam War, 1954–1965* (New York: Cambridge University Press, 2006).

conflagrations or conducting offensive operations. Separate Territorial Forces, consisting of small Civil Guard units at the province level (later known as Regional Forces, or RF) and the Self-Defense Corps at the village level (later known as Popular Forces, or PF), had responsibility for local security.[37] South Vietnam also acquired a small navy and air force. Despite growing from a 150,000-man force in the early 1960s to over a million men by the early 1970s, however, the RVNAF generated far less fighting power than most theories of military effectiveness would predict—a deficit directly attributable to the regime's threat environment and the resulting military organizational practices.[38]

The Threat Environment Facing South Vietnamese Regimes

Whatever Diem's shortcomings, he was in a terribly difficult position upon assuming the leadership of the newly formed South Vietnam. He confronted a war-ravaged postcolonial state with essentially no functioning national institutions, and his regime quickly took on a highly personalist character. Distrusting those around him, Diem sought to concentrate virtually all power in his own hands or those of close associates, particularly his wife and brother, and his solution to opposition was violent repression rather than a broadening of political representation or participation.[39]

This fragile system of one-man rule reflected the significant and immediate armed threats Diem faced upon coming to power. Chief among these dangers were coups. In September 1954, for example, Diem found himself facing a challenge from General Nguyen Van Hinh, the VNA's Chief of the General Staff.[40] Hinh "declared openly that he needed only to pick up the telephone to unleash a coup d'état."[41] These words were not an idle threat. The French Expeditionary Corps was still in Saigon.[42] Hinh had been a major in the French Air Force, was a French citizen, had a French wife, and had been picked by the French to lead the VNA. Fortunately for Diem, U.S. pressure forced Hinh into exile in France. But the incident appears to have taught Diem an early lesson on the importance of loyalty among his military commanders, especially when so many were former officers in the very colonial army that Diem had so staunchly opposed.[43]

Unfortunately for Diem, the threat from Hinh was not an outlier. Diem narrowly evaded an assassination attempt in 1957. On November 11, 1960, three Airborne and one Marine battalion attempted a coup against him. Diem was saved only when three loyal divisions converged on the capital in his defense.[44] On February 22, 1962, two of his pilots bombed the presidential palace, again attempting to kill Diem. The November 1963 coup eventually succeeded where these efforts had failed, but

[52]

the ensuing years brought their own succession of military governments. Even after the situation stabilized in 1965, Thieu and Ky were no less afraid of military overthrow, especially given that they themselves had participated in coup plotting. Indeed, South Vietnam's period of military dictatorship bore many of the same organizational hallmarks as the earlier era of personalist rule.

Despite these intense and enduring concerns about coup threats, however, South Vietnamese leaders were in no position to forego the creation and maintenance of a coercive apparatus: the state's monopoly on the use of force faced multiple internal, irregular challenges besides coups, which leaders needed some sort of military organization to manage. Chief among these threats was a mafia-like armed gang, the Binh Xuyen, that the French had cultivated in an effort to defeat the Viet Minh. Its private army did not disappear with the Tricolor. In 1954, France still had 2,000 regular troops near Saigon, organized into five main battalions, plus another 1,500 crack assault troops, and 10,000 other followers.[45] When Diem refused to renew the licenses for Binh Xuyen's casinos and brothels, they united with the forces of two religious sects, the Cao Dai and Hoa Hao, in seeking his overthrow.[46] Diem spent much of the first half of 1955 bribing the religious sects away from this alliance and then sending government forces to root out the hard core of Binh Xuyen fighters.[47]

During the mid-1950s Diem also ordered massive anticommunist sweeps, which crushed the Communist Party's presence in the South even as they created new grievances against his regime.[48] In addition, Diem dispatched military officers to assist in local and provincial government. In fact, despite his nominally civilian regime, "only 5 province chiefs were civilians; the remaining ones were all military."[49] As late as 1970, the situation had not changed: "the RVNAF [was] frequently the government's sole representative and development agent in the rural areas."[50]

These facts suggest that although South Vietnamese leaders had good reason to fear the military, they also needed the military's assistance to run the country and defend it against domestic threats. In this context, the adoption of coup prevention practices is unsurprising. Indeed, because that the United States was firmly backstopping South Vietnam's external borders through at least the late 1960s and also assisting in the internal fight against insurgents, there would have been little impetus for South Vietnam to do much else. In some instances, however, the threat environment stimulated variation in this general pattern. Here I review the most widespread ARVN practices with respect to promotions, training, command, and information before discussing some exceptions and their implications for battlefield performance.

Promotion Patterns

Consistent with his desire to prevent coups, Diem often intentionally selected against competence in the senior officer corps. Lt. Gen. Samuel T. Williams, the head of the MAAG, noted as early as 1957, "Officers who are performing their duties efficiently are relieved and transferred to other duties."[51] This trend only accelerated after perceived U.S. endorsement of the 1963 coup against Diem, leading future South Vietnamese leaders to distrust officers who had close ties to Americans, even though these were often among the most competent. As Col. Wilbur Wilson, the senior adviser to III Corps, observed in 1964: "The generals got to be generals by virtue of their ability in political intrigue, not as a result of their ability as military men," resulting in a case of "the blind leading the blind."[52] Retired general James Lawton Collins, who served in a number of assignments in South Vietnam in the 1950s and 1960s, also concluded that "the greatest obstacle in improving and training the armed forces was the lack of qualified leadership at all levels," due to the promotion system. "U.S. advisers continually cited poor leadership as the foremost reason for unit ineffectiveness."[53]

A popular line in South Vietnam in the late 1950s contended that to be an officer in the ARVN required "the three D's": D not only for *Diem*, as in the officer had to be loyal to Diem and not considered a threat to the regime, but also D for *Dao*, the Vietnamese word for religion, meaning the officer had to share Diem's Catholic faith; D for *Dang*, the Vietnamese word for party, meaning the officer had to belong to Diem's political party, the Can Lao; and D for *Du*, a designation for Central Vietnam, meaning that the officer had to have the same regional origins as Diem's family.[54] Performing well in battle was at best a secondary consideration, and often more hindrance than help.

These trends continued under the Thieu regime. As Allan Goodman, a civilian researcher who spent substantial time in South Vietnam, wrote in 1970, "The portrait of the RVNAF officer of a decade ago remains essentially unchanged. . . . Political loyalty, not battlefield performance, has long dominated the promotion system in the officer corps, with the result that there is often an inverse relationship between rank and military skill."[55] After the war, South Vietnamese officials connected the incompetent leaders that Thieu elevated to the broader problems in the army: "The majority of the high-ranking commanders were servants to the Thieu regime," they noted. The result was "a number of lazy, corrupted, and unqualified generals" who succeeded only in "destroying the fighting morale of the young ARVN officers."[56] One observer remarked that it was not simply that Thieu cared about political loyalty, but that he truly attempted to weed out those who might be competent enough to threaten him: "Thieu did not want good men in leading military positions because he was afraid that once they were in such positions they would mount a coup against him."[57]

An internal Pentagon report noted as late as October 1969 that "RVNAF commanders in the field appear to be least favored in terms of promotion."[58] Indeed, before 1966, the RVNAF did not have even the appearance of an objective promotion or officer evaluation system. That year Thieu acceded to MACV's pressure to develop one, and four kinds of promotions were established: annual, normal, battlefield, and special. Nevertheless, despite the formal creation of this promotion pathway for those who demonstrated skill on the battlefield, less than 2 percent of all officers promoted in 1968 owed their rank to combat performance.[59] A Pentagon report that year stated, "The Vietnamese simply will not promote on the basis of battlefield performance."[60] Another report in January 1969 noted, "Service in battle is clearly not the path to success in the ARVN."[61] One in 1970 observed, "While the Vietnamese have a better promotion system on paper, it has changed little in the way it operates."[62] As a result, most promotions for field grade officers and above still depended either on time in grade, or fell into the "special" category, meaning they occurred without regard to rank, length of service, or experience.[63]

Just as important, neither Diem nor Thieu made a point of removing commanders who revealed themselves to be incompetent. To be sure, U.S. advisers faced incentives to inflate the effectiveness ratings of the units with which they worked—after all, if the RVNAF commanders were ineffective, it reflected almost as poorly on the adviser as it did on the commander—so at times it could be difficult to know who deserved to retain command. Yet that makes it all the more startling that even in instances where everyone agreed South Vietnamese commanders were inept, they retained command. In 1967, for example, U.S. advisers rated the commanders of the 5th, 18th, and 25th divisions "flatly incompetent"—and the Directory generals agreed. Yet the division commanders were not replaced because they were vital political supporters of the Thieu regime.[64]

As one account notes, "The actual basis for Vietnamese intransigence lay in the political role of the officer corps and the desire of the senior generals to control its composition. Rapid promotions would destroy the existing network of local ties and personal loyalties that not only provided the current leaders with their political power but also formed the economic and social underpinnings of the Saigon regime." Even in the few instances in which incompetent commanders were inadvertently removed for other reasons, their replacements proved equally inadequate.[65]

Promotion patterns in South Vietnam eventually did shift somewhat in the early 1970s as two facts became clear: the conventional threat from North Vietnam had grown dire, and U.S. ground forces would not provide indefinite protection. Under the pressure of mounting South Vietnamese losses in the Easter Offensive of 1972, for example, Thieu removed two of his worst corps commanders during the height of the fighting and the following year continued to "sweep out many incompetent commanders, replacing them with younger, combat-hardened, U.S.-trained leaders."[66]

Despite these incremental changes, however, "Thieu remained fearful of a coup" well into the 1970s. Although "by 1973 he had successfully clipped the military's wings when it came to overt involvement in political affairs," he continued to focus heavily on internal concerns in making military organizational decisions. No doubt he pursued these mixed practices in part because he had received secret assurances from President Nixon that the United States would "react vigorously" in the event of communist violation of the ceasefire and would maintain significant military and economic aid to its ally. Confident until well into 1975 that U.S. firepower and logistics would always backstop the country's territorial integrity, South Vietnam did not feel the pressure to embrace conventional practices fully until it was too late.[67]

Training Regimens

South Vietnam's leaders generally adopted coup prevention practices with regard to training. Very little rigorous, realistic, large- or small-unit training of any type occurred during the entire war. The country did not lack the infrastructure or resources needed to conduct such training, though. Training was a top priority for the MAAG and later for MACV, and the United States grew the number of Vietnamese training centers from one in 1956 to thirty-three by 1970. It also established an additional twenty-five military schools and sent South Vietnamese officers to undergo military training in the United States. Unit training was a major focus of U.S. advisers working with their Vietnamese counterparts at all levels of command.[68]

Nevertheless, as one senior U.S. officer later reflected, "Headway in this area was generally extremely slow."[69] As late as 1970, U.S. advisers lamented that the South Vietnamese officers paid "only lip service to practical training," which had a ripple effect down the chain, producing apathy among the troops.[70] After the war a number of generals stated flatly that "leadership of service schools in South Vietnam was a sort of elegant exile for unwanted commanders, often of limited competence."[71]

Even Westmoreland observed that the academy was "a dumping ground for inept officers."[72]

Training was perfunctory at best. In 1966, for example, "MACV proposed a six-week refresher training program for all South Vietnamese infantry battalions. . . . Only a few battalions actually received the training, and the instruction for those that did was marginal. Unit commanders at all levels showed little interest in the program. . . . Commanders simply were not interested in training and found excuses to avoid it."[73] During the first half of 1969, 66 percent of maneuver battalions conducted no training whatsoever; 15 percent conducted ten days or less; and only 4 percent conducted a month or more of training.[74]

Those commanders who did participate in training often viewed the time as a leisurely break.[75] More than a decade into the war, "no 'proficiency in training' evaluations had been enforced, which meant that in most cases a new recruit 'graduated' from basic combat training based solely on the fact that he had been 'present for duty' during this five week period."[76] ARVN soldiers rarely received practical instruction on most topics and almost never had the opportunity to engage in realistic simulations of combined arms operations.[77]

At the root of these general training problems lay the military's continued involvement in governance.[78] Officers usually felt more pressure to use forces for security or administrative duties in their districts, provinces, or regions than to train them for combat. Gen. Cao Van Vien, Diem's chief of staff and later the chairman of the Joint General Staff under Thieu, noted that there was more to being a senior officer than commanding large units: "A province chief had to be an able administrator also. He had to supervise a large bureaucracy, prepare and execute a provincial budget, regulate trade and commerce, and protect national resources under his custody. . . . He had to plan for and meet the objectives set forth for security and development, and this required his involvement in countless programs and projects whose implementation needed his constant supervision and guidance. No matter how devoted he was, he simply could not perform all of his duties effectively."[79]

After the war, other generals similarly reported that the main directives they received concerned governance rather than use of the large training infrastructure established by the MAAG and later MACV.[80] Even Westmoreland was hesitant to push harder for progress in this area. As a 1967 MACV study admitted, "The military was the only body in South Vietnam with the experience and administrative skills to run the country."[81]

One might suppose that at least elite units would have received better, more rigorous training. After all, MAAG had urged the formation of specialized airborne, armor, and marine units exactly for this reason—to provide highly skilled mobile strike forces that could complement the more static corps formations responsible for each of the military regions of South Vietnam.[82] Unfortunately, the elite units' specialization became the prevention of coups: both Diem and Thieu used them as counterweights to the regular army.

Surprisingly, however, the units still received little actual military training. For example, Diem formed new armored units after the coup attempt in 1962, stationing them with the 7th and 21st divisions outside Saigon. But although these units had the newest armored personnel carriers (APCs) and appeared frequently in presidential parades, they rarely trained using the APCs with infantry.[83] The creation of Ranger units initially followed a similar pattern. Against U.S. advice, Diem simply took the fourth company out of each infantry battalion and redesignated it a Ranger battalion. Beyond the title, Rangers received no special training until 1961.[84] The Airborne had the same problems.[85] "Elite" status often indicated that a unit was volunteer only, or had better pay and access to medical care, but it rarely meant that the unit's training differed.

Command Arrangements

Diem and his successors centralized and fractured the system for giving and receiving orders. Diem initiated this approach by establishing a personal chain of command directly from the presidential palace to corps and division commanders.[86] Frequently he used this radio net to send orders "from a van in the garden of the presidential palace . . . directly to combat regiments, bypassing the Department of National Defense, the General Staff, and the field commands."[87] In this way, he ensured that large units would not be able to coordinate action against the regime and also that he could curb any operations he believed would lead to excessive casualties, which he saw as the underlying cause of the coup attempt against him in 1960.[88] The resulting climate of officer passivity persisted long after Diem was gone.[89] As Collins noted years later, one of the major problems in the ARVN was that few officers who had come up in the Diem system were willing to do anything "in the absence of detailed orders."[90]

As South Vietnamese leaders centralized command in some ways, however, they intentionally fractured it in others. For example, Diem and later Thieu maintained separate chains of command for elite forces, notably the Airborne, Marines, and Rangers. Thus they could ensure that even if one of these factions turned against the regime, the others could be contacted to counteract it. Diem also maintained a separate chain of command to the Civil Guard through the Ministry of the Interior, bypassing the Joint

General Staff in the Ministry of Defense. Because of these arrangements, it would have been very difficult for any single commander to usurp command of all of the military forces in South Vietnam at any given time.[91] Yet the arrangements also made it hard for these forces to communicate with one another or to coordinate action effectively in battle.

In addition, Diem and Thieu frequently shuffled command assignments within the officer corps. This approach prevented the development of independent bases of loyalty in the armed forces—bases that might be used to launch coups—but it also "prevented commanders from gaining the full support of their troops."[92] Junior officers could expect to have a new supervisor "every one or two months," limiting accountability with respect to any long-term tasks.[93]

Diem and then Thieu also created overlapping chains of command to constrain military commanders. As one U.S. Army study of the system noted, the command structure seemed designed to inhibit operations, containing "conflicting, duplicating chains of command and communication and . . . various major agencies . . . installed in widely separated areas so as to hamper coordination, rapid staff action, and decision-making."[94] Commanders often received orders from multiple military and/or civilian authorities. For example, under Diem, many units were only nominally commanded by the military, with the real orders coming from a Can Lao Party member who had been installed by Diem's brother, Ngo Dinh Can. Even when Diem and the Can Lao were gone, the average battalion commander could expect to receive orders in battle from both the commander of his regiment or division, as well as from the commander of the military region in which he was operating.[95] When these orders conflicted, it was safest to do nothing.

Information Management

South Vietnam's political leaders also adopted coup prevention practices with respect to information management, focused again mostly on the need to combat internal, irregular threats rather than the threat posed by the North. First, South Vietnam's leaders maintained a large intelligence apparatus designed primarily to monitor communications in their own officer corps. In the early years, there were at least six major and several minor intelligence collection groups in South Vietnam.[96] In addition, as mentioned, Diem's brother Ngo Dinh Can led a secret political party of Diem supporters known as the Can Lao. Can managed to place numerous party members in the Defense Ministry, where they provided Diem with frequent information about officer sentiment and activities. Can also helped handpick party members for division and corps commands, from which they continued to feed Diem information.

[59]

Furthermore, "cells or committees of the Can Lao existed at all echelons of the army, frequently without the knowledge of the unit commanders. The staffs of senior commanders were so riddled with Can Lao operatives and informers that some generals . . . hesitated to plan any real operations with their staffs." Unfortunately, this type of intelligence apparatus had a tendency to produce only the sort of information that spies believed Diem wanted to hear. Even as the opposition grew in strength during 1959–1960, for example, Diem continued to believe that the regime was enjoying battlefield success.[97]

Although the Can Lao disbanded after Diem's fall, the Thieu regime continued to keep close tabs on officers, with similar consequences.[98] Premier Ky ran both the Central Intelligence Office, South Vietnam's equivalent of the CIA, as well as the more mysterious Military Security Service. Both of these organizations purported to gather intelligence on the enemy, but in reality they focused on potential dissent among military officers and local officials.[99]

The Thieu regime took further measures to prevent communication among military commanders as well.[100] For example, Thieu actively discouraged officers from meeting. As one general explained after the war, "He was all the time afraid of a government by the generals. . . . He had in mind that if all these people got together to talk about the military situation, they would also discuss the political situation and make a coup."[101] As a result his commanders often had little idea what their counterparts in the next province or region were doing—or any access to their intelligence.

Variation in Threats and Practices: The ARVN 1st Division

Notwithstanding South Vietnam's general adherence to coup prevention practices, the framework from chapter 1 emphasized that when the threat environment varies, organizational practices should as well. Indeed, where the greatest threat is an external, conventional adversary, especially one with whom a state has an enduring rivalry, we should expect to see the adoption of conventional war practices. In South Vietnam this logic was often irrelevant because coup fears remained so highly salient and because subpar ARVN battlefield performance tended to stimulate U.S. involvement rather than improvements in South Vietnam's own military.[102]

Nevertheless, the logic did operate in a few instances, providing a glimpse of the organizational practices South Vietnam was capable of adopting when threats varied and further highlighting the link between threats and practices. The clearest example was the ARVN 1st Division, particularly its rapid reaction force, known as the Hac Bao, or "Black

Panther" Company. The 1st Division was tasked with operations in the territory closest to the border with North Vietnam, including the important cities of Hue and Da Nang. Notably, this area of operations also was the farthest of any ARVN division's from Saigon, making military units stationed there of little potential use in either plotting or preventing coups. This factor alone suggests that South Vietnamese leaders would have had little reason to impose coup prevention practices on units there.

What did concern them, however, were a series of Buddhist and student protests known as the Struggle Movement that swept the area from 1964 to 1966. Instead of putting down the protestors, a succession of 1st Division and I Corps commanders had sided with them against the central government. At last Ky was able to subdue the threat in late 1966 by sending in three Airborne battalions under the command of Col. Ngo Quang Truong. In the meantime, however, what had been a relatively peaceful region became the site of increasing attacks starting in 1964–1965 due to the influx of some 50,000 enemy fighters, including regular combat forces from the North. Indeed, Wiest reports that during this period, it was the "most heavily infiltrated and deadly area of operations in South Vietnam."[103]

Although it is impossible to know exactly how the Thieu government viewed the situation in the mid-1960s, two inferences are reasonable, and both lead to the expectation that different military organizational practices should have been adopted in the 1st Division. First, the environment presented little reason to adopt coup prevention practices, as coup danger was minimal here, and the other major internal threat had just been stamped out decisively. Second, the external, conventional threat in the area was growing, making it a potential source of danger to the South Vietnamese regime. Although the documentary record does not enable us to know for sure that this is what Thieu decided, his subsequent actions are consistent with this set of beliefs.

Specifically, Thieu adopted something much closer to conventional war practices with respect to 1st Division promotions and training. He gave Truong, the Airborne commander, a star and put him in command of the 1st. Although certainly Truong's loyalty against the Struggle Movement was important, he was most well known for being a highly competent tactical leader, uninterested in politics.[104] He had a proven record as a skilled officer and selected his battalion commanders based on their records.[105] As Wiest notes, "Unlike some other ARVN divisions, there were no political hacks or cronies among the combat leaders of the 1st ARVN Division." In addition, Truong pursued conventional war practices with respect to training, engaging in regular and realistic exercises.[106] For these reasons U.S. secretary of defense Clark Clifford argued in 1968 that the 1st was "comparable in quality to any U.S. Army division."[107] Indeed, I Corps was one of the first areas from which U.S. forces withdrew starting in 1969.[108] Clearly, the ARVN 1st Division had adopted military organizational practices quite different from those prevailing in most of the South Vietnamese military at the time.

Implications for Battlefield Performance

The prominence of internal threats, particularly coups, led South Vietnam regimes under personalist and military rule to optimize their promotions, training, command, and information management practices for coup prevention. But external threats drove South Vietnamese leaders to adopt different practices with respect to promotions and training in the ARVN 1st Division, resulting in a distinctive suborganization compared to the rest of the military at the time. If the argument presented in chapter 1 is correct, then most ARVN units should have performed poorly, demonstrating virtually no effectiveness: no ability to conduct complex operations and little to no tactical proficiency. By contrast, the ARVN 1st Division, including the Hac Bao Company, should have displayed at least adequate effectiveness. Because of the adoption of different military organizational practices, it should have demonstrated at least basic tactical proficiency and probably some ability to conduct complex operations compared to other South Vietnamese units.

By contrast, other ARVN units that demonstrated tactical proficiency would cast doubt on my argument, because they would show that units could still be effective even in the face of coup prevention practices. Instances in which the ARVN 1st Division failed to execute basic tactics also would undermine the argument, because they would suggest that different military organizational practices did not produce even basic improvements in battlefield effectiveness. In general, a lack of variation across units in the ARVN—or, for reasons discussed in the next section, a lack of cross-national variation between the ARVN and the PAVN—also would lend support to explanations of effectiveness focused on static national traits.

THREATS AND MILITARY ORGANIZATIONAL PRACTICES IN NORTH VIETNAM

North Vietnam evinced virtually none of the predictors of coup prevention practices present in its southern counterpart. The country was ruled by a well-institutionalized single-party regime that faced virtually no coup threats. Instead, Hanoi held foreign policy goals that the regime knew would require expansion of the state's borders by force and the probable conquest of additional territory, possibly through the use of conventional combat, all of which created strong incentives to adopt conventionally oriented military organizational practices and should have resulted in excellent battlefield effectiveness.

That said, the PAVN was a fledgling organization in the mid-1950s. Having been part of the Viet Minh's big tent, leaders in Hanoi had to consolidate and purify the fighting organization they had inherited and overcome what one observer has called the "organizational anarchy" of the nationalist movement.[109] The backbone of the PAVN consisted of six divisions that had simply been redesignated after the fight against the French, and the regime was well aware of the challenges involved in transforming "what was still a rather loosely led 'people's army' into a centralized, hierarchically organized, conventional armed force."[110]

The PAVN quickly came to comprise three different types of troops: mobile Main Force units; regional or local force units organized within particular geographical areas, akin to a national guard or standing reserve; and militia/self-defense forces. In general, it was the Main Force units that fought in South Vietnam.[111] By 1960, their strength was roughly 160,000 soldiers. This number grew to 204,000 in 1966, to 278,000 in 1967, and considerably higher by the end of the war, by which time many of the divisions had been organized into corps-level formations.[112]

It should be noted that these forces were in addition to the NLF's own units called the People's Liberation Armed Forces (PLAF), which remained tightly linked to Hanoi despite appearances otherwise.[113] Indeed, although most of the early PLAF recruits were from the South, they were usually led by Northern infiltrators.[114] Northerners were so influential in the PLAF that their dominance at times led to complaints from Southerners in the NLF.[115] For these reasons, I include PLAF units in my analysis of North Vietnamese effectiveness during the war.[116]

The Threat Environment Facing the North Vietnamese Regime

As a single-party state that could draw on long-gestating political and military institutional development dating back to the 1930s and 1940s, North Vietnam displayed virtually none of the indicators of potential coup concerns.[117] Enthusiasm for the regime in Hanoi was far from universal, but the regime had worked from its earliest days to tamp down any inkling of popular resistance or elite counterrevolution.[118] After a botched land reform campaign prompted a rural rebellion in the mid-1950s, the regime came to rely on the Ministry of Public Security as the nucleus of a carefully constructed police state. Spearheaded by the Cong An (Security Police) and Bao Ve (Military Security), this apparatus kept a close eye on both the masses and elites, including military officers,

[63]

but was primarily aimed at preventing popular uprisings, limiting foreign influence, and silencing voices of moderation within the Party leadership—not staunching coups.[119]

Indeed, the country had no history of coups or coup attempts; instead, both the political and military leadership displayed remarkable stability throughout the war.[120] As Turley explains, "Party leaders had little need to worry about the loyalty of the military leadership, as this leadership was drawn from the top ranks of the party."[121] He describes the North Vietnamese emphasis on military subordination to civilian authority as part of an "unshakeable consensus." Although Party leaders and military officers at times debated the best way to implement Party control, the principle itself was not questioned, making coups virtually a nonissue.[122] Unceasingly, North Vietnamese writings and statements reflect the belief that the military worked best when the Party maintained absolute, direct, and complete control over the armed forces.[123] As one senior PAVN general explained in 1959, "The Army must absolutely obey and accept the tight control of the Central Committee headed by Comrade Ho Chi Minh, and correctly carry out all policies of the Party."[124] General Vo Nguyen Giap echoed these sentiments in a very typical 1961 proclamation, noting, "The most fundamental principle in the building of our army is to put it under the Party's leadership, *to ceaselessly strengthen the Party's leadership* of the army. The Party is the founder, organizer, and education of the army."[125]

In short, not only were there no signs of coup fears, but there seems to have been an affirmative consensus in favor of political control over the military that freed the North Vietnamese regime from pressure to adopt coup prevention practices. The regime's ability to lay claim to the nationalist mantle and its active enforcement of communist ideology no doubt further tamped down internal dissent, allowing the formation of a military organization geared primarily toward external goals. U.S. intelligence assessments reached essentially the same conclusion in evaluating the DRV in 1959: "no significant internal threat to the regime is likely."[126] Such reports contrast sharply with assessments of South Vietnam in the same period.[127] Because leaders in Hanoi actively envisioned continued conflict with the South, the regime generally pushed for the adoption of conventional war practices—despite the fact that the military remained a deliberately and thoroughly politicized institution.

Promotion Patterns

Considerable evidence suggests that military merit took precedence over communist bona fides in the selection of leaders within the PAVN and the PLAF. Without a doubt, being a Party member guaranteed "at least some career success for a soldier," while expulsion from the Party was "the certain road to career oblivion."[128] But although Hanoi sought to root out the united front remnants in its ranks during the late 1950s, it also had to grow its military. As a directive at the time noted, "We must be extremely aggressive in promoting cadre from the worker and peasant classes while appropriately promoting cadre from other classes who have been tested and have demonstrated a progressive attitude and loyalty to the revolution."[129] In other words, political loyalty and class credentials mattered, but so did the imperative of growing the ranks, even if it meant including individuals with questionable backgrounds.

Furthermore, internal debates about the qualifications for officership repeatedly stressed the need for proven military expertise in addition to political loyalty. For example, General Song Hao, one of the most senior in the PAVN, wrote that "our Party has attached importance not only to leading our Army in building itself politically, ideologically, and organizationally, but also in leading the formulation and development of our military art."[130] He noted that the best officers were always "men with revolutionary consciousness" as well as "scientific and technical capacity."[131] A similar view apparently filtered all the way down to a captured North Vietnamese platoon leader, who noted that a good officer had to have both "talent and virtue": the talent to fight the war competently, in addition to the virtues of a correct temperament.[132]

Known as the "red vs. expert" debate, internal North Vietnamese discussions about the appropriate qualifications for officers continued well into the 1960s, but Douglas Pike concludes that the debate was essentially "settled in favor of the expert."[133] Although political commissars remained attached to virtually all units, these officials were subordinate to military commanders when it came to combat decision making.[134] Particularly as the war escalated, PAVN prisoners and defectors "indicated either that the military commander was unquestionably supreme or that an uneasy division of labor and authority had been worked out between the two in which the Political Commissar carefully kept out of combat decision making."[135]

Training Regimens

The PAVN and the PLAF largely adopted conventional war practices with regard to training. To be sure, DRV leaders heavily emphasized the importance of instilling communist ideology.[136] In 1961, for example, General Giap noted, "The People's Army must necessarily see to the strengthening of the leadership of Party and political work.... The Party has . . . given a prominent place to the activities of its organizations as well as to the political work in the army. Officers, warrant officers and armymen, all of them have followed political courses." Nevertheless, Giap and others were well aware that ideological training alone was of little use: "It is necessary to carry out regular training systematically and according to plan," he wrote. "To meet the requirements of modern war, the army must be trained to master modern techniques, tactical use of arms, coordinated tactics and modern military service."[137]

North Vietnam's official historical account states that "training was the central requirement for the completion of the work of building an army in peacetime." It discusses in considerable detail the manner in which "training activities systematically began to turn the army into a regular force" in the period after independence. For example,

> Soldiers studied weapons theory and were trained in shooting techniques, the use of bayonets, grenade throwing, and breaching and overcoming obstacles. In addition to basic weapons training, practice fire and night firing lessons were incorporated into the training program. . . . With regard to tactics, all units were trained from the squad up to the battalion level in offensive and defensive combat in regular terrain, and steps were taken to study and begin training in combat methods for use in mountain jungle terrain, in swampy rice fields, in river crossings, and night combat operations.[138]

Furthermore, military training almost always trumped political training when soldiers' time was limited.[139] According to Turley, the senior officer corps recognized by the late 1950s "that more attention to professional and technical training, instead of political activities, was necessary. . . . Time spent on training in military subjects increased and time spent on political subjects declined."[140] During this period, Hanoi established both small- and large-unit training programs covering a wide array of skills.[141] According to another account, by the early 1960s the average soldier received three months of initial training in infantry tactics, including infantry assault, basic air defense, using the bayonet and grenades, marksmanship, and movement, with only about two weeks of that time devoted to political subjects.[142]

Melvin Gurtov, a civilian researcher who conducted extensive interviews with former members of Main Force battalions during the 1960s, drew a similar conclusion about the importance of combat skills in the training process. Gurtov's interview subjects reported that "for the most part, military training took precedence even though political doctrine might, under less pressing circumstances, have seemed indispensable."[143] While cautious about drawing overbroad conclusions from his limited sample, Gurtov wrote, "What does seem fairly certain is that political training for most of the units in question was subordinated to military training. . . . Indoctrination yielded to establishing battlefield proficiency among new recruits. The priority given to war skills was reflected in the ignorance of interviewees, including cadres, about political matters."[144]

North Vietnam's training system was also highly rigorous, heavily emphasizing the demonstration of actual proficiency rather than rote learning or pro forma drills. Captured documents for a training program "reveal a well-organized and ambitious schedule" focused on "close-order drill, firing positions, bayonet drill, and grenade throwing," as well as "use and maintenance of weapons, . . . fortifications and camouflage; movement procedures; individual, cell, and squad tactics; sanitation; protective measures against toxic chemicals; military discipline; guard and patrol duty; liaison; reconnaissance; and POW [prisoner of war] escort," and "marksmanship and weapon familiarization, techniques of armored vehicle destruction, ambush tactics, surprise attack, anti-heliborne or paratroop tactics." The PAVN also developed longer-term and more specialized curricula for operators of crew-served weapons, signals operators, communications specialists, sappers, and so on.[145]

Once in the field, soldiers could expect further training. Lanning and Cragg write that "rehearsals for [an] operation began on sand tables and progressed to practices on stake-and-string replicas of the target. Depending upon the difficulty of the objective, this phase lasted from three days to well over a month."[146] One soldier reported, "Before any operation a few among us would be sent out to make a study and survey of the battlefield, and then a plan of operation would be drawn up and presented to all the men in the unit. Each would then be given a chance to contribute ideas and suggestions. Each squad, each man, would be told what action to take if the enemy was to take such-and-such a position."[147]

During the late 1950s and early 1960s, training advanced to cover more complex operations. For example, troops progressed from learning positional to mobile defenses, coordinated with combined arms counterattacks. Troops also began to learn envelopment and flanking maneuvers and to fight on different types of terrain both offensively and defensively. The North Vietnamese ensured realism by conducting regular exercises at all levels of command, across different combat arms, and on the offense and defense. As is noted in North Vietnam's official history, "The phrase 'sweat on the exercise field to lessen bloodshed on the battlefield' became a slogan in our army."[148] It is hard to imagine a starker contrast to the South.

Command Arrangements

North Vietnamese command arrangements hewed closely to conventional war practices, emphasizing the authority of officers on the battlefield. To be sure, Party control of the military's command structure was an "immutable principle," and even small units had some type of political officer.[149] But these officers usually lacked actual command authority, which was entrusted to officers selected for their military competence.

Pike reports that this system resulted in significant friction within units and that during the early 1960s, "the struggle for power between these two figures seesawed back and forth." However, as the Vietnam War escalated, the balance of power "tilted toward the military commander," and political officers were careful from then on not to interfere with combat decision making.[150] Captured documents attest to this arrangement, with one officer reporting that "in the military and administrative fields, [the political commissar] is subordinate to the military commander" at his same level of command.[151] In short, despite the formal existence of a dual-command system, in reality the military commander selected based on military qualifications made key combat decisions in the PAVN and the PLAF.

The arrangement was not perfect, and tensions persisted.[152] Pike even notes that there were "occasional bouts of open confrontation" within the dual-command system, "including a few reliable reports of battlefield disputes in which the military commander shot his Political Commissar."[153] Despite these clashes, though, the system afforded considerable latitude to most battlefield commanders in the PAVN and the PLAF. They had to report their activities to political officers and be accountable for them, but political officers did not enjoy a veto over these decisions.[154]

In fact, although political officers existed in almost all units, their role was not solely to maintain political loyalty but also to perform the duties provided in Western armies by the chaplain, the troop information and education officer, or the special services officer. Pike notes that "in PAVN and PLAF units in the South [the political officer's] duties were many and varied but chiefly involved political indoctrination, personal problem solving, and generally attending to his unit's morale."[155]

Information Management

North Vietnam seems to have adopted conventional war practices with regard to information management. First, units generally were free to communicate horizontally with one another. According to North Vietnam's official history, the Party emphasized to its tactical commanders the need to "exercise independence in battle, take the initiative in cooperating with and supporting friendly units, [and] maintain close coordination."[156]

Second, within individual units, North Vietnamese political leaders also required extensive use of what were called "self-criticism sessions": meetings in which personnel discussed recent performance and areas in need of improvement. Such sessions ensured that soldiers and officers shared feedback from battlefield experiences. They also reassured soldiers that problems were being aired and addressed, strengthening the commitment to fight while nevertheless reinforcing the politically convenient implication that military leaders were, in fact, fallible.[157] Repeatedly, North Vietnamese documents reflect a military in which political leaders encouraged candid discussion of weaknesses and ideas for improvement; there was no prize for hiding problems or punishment for delivering unfavorable information.[158]

Beyond the self-criticism sessions, there is also evidence of active debate in the North Vietnamese officer corps about military strategy and tactics. During the mid-to-late 1960s, for example, Giap thought efforts to fight the United States directly were wasteful and that Hanoi should return to a slow and protracted guerrilla war, even if it took fifteen to twenty years to win. Some officers published articles agreeing with Giap, while the commander in the South, General Nguyen Chi Thanh, continued to defend a much more aggressive strategy.[159] This was exactly the sort of debate that did not regularly occur within the South Vietnamese officer corps.[160]

Also consistent with conventional war practices in information management, the North Vietnamese regime regularly gathered and disseminated lessons from battlefield events. Information flowed in the other direction as well. From the beginning, high-level officer training in the PAVN involved reading directly from Politburo resolutions on the army.[161] Leaders of the effort in the South also annually "attended a Politburo meeting in Hanoi to consult with Party leaders and receive directions for future strategy" there.[162] Again, though not especially detailed, these facts are at least consistent with conventional war practices for information management, posing a stark contrast to the constriction of information seen in South Vietnam.

Implications for Battlefield Performance

The North Vietnamese regime faced a very different threat environment than did its Southern counterpart, leading to a very different approach to military organization. One should not infer that practices in every area were perfect, or that they did not evolve as the war went on, but the general tilt toward conventional war practices rather than those designed to prevent coups is striking. Having adopted such practices,

[69]

PAVN and PLAF units should have performed very well on the battle-field, consistently displaying tactical proficiency and the ability to conduct complex operations, despite the many underlying traits that these units shared with their South Vietnamese counterparts. Conversely, if PAVN and PLAF units demonstrated poor tactical proficiency and/or an inability to conduct complex operations, those deficits would cast significant doubt on the utility of the book's framework. In addition, a lack of cross-national variation between the performance of PAVN and PLAF units and that of South Vietnamese units would cast doubt on the argument and strengthen support for the alternative explanations focused on more static national traits.

This chapter has contrasted the threat environments and resulting military organizational practices in North and South Vietnam during the 1950s, 1960s, and 1970s. The general argument is that despite the fact that the two states shared many common characteristics said to matter for military performance, their threat environments were very different—especially when one takes into account the fear of coups perpetually wracking Saigon, the lack of such concerns in Hanoi, and the ambitious foreign policy goals that the latter embraced. These differences should have produced substantial cross-national variation in the military performance of the two sides, as well as additional subnational variation in the performance of the South Vietnamese 1st Division.

The next chapter explores whether these predictions hold up, but even the evidence presented thus far should induce significant skepticism about the variables emphasized in existing theories of military effectiveness. The contrast between North and South Vietnam suggests that civil-military relations can vary substantially across and within autocratic regimes. Even in environments of low military autonomy, politicization of the military can take very different forms, with different results for core military activities. Furthermore, the evidence of cross-unit variation in organizational practices within the South Vietnamese military suggests that these differences are not simply random or endogenous to static national traits, but rather are the product of states' efforts to manage complex and multifaceted threat environments.

None of this proves that traditional variables are irrelevant in explaining military performance. Nor does it prove that differences in military organizational practices matter for battlefield effectiveness. But it should make us curious about the material covered in the next chapter: a series of battles between North and South Vietnam from 1963 to 1975. These battles make it possible to probe further the utility of the book's framework and to compare it to existing ways of thinking about the sources of military effectiveness.

[70]

[3]

Battlefield Effectiveness in North and South Vietnam

In chapter 2 I contrasted the threat environments facing Hanoi and Saigon and the starkly divergent military organizational practices these environments engendered. The North Vietnamese regime faced few internal threats and virtually no risk of coups, enabling it to adopt conventional war practices that were consistent with its external foreign policy goals. But regimes in South Vietnam consistently faced significant coup risks and were shielded from external threats by the U.S. presence, leading to the widespread adoption of coup prevention practices, except in the 1st Division. The framework presented in chapter 1 predicts that the ARVN should have demonstrated poor battlefield effectiveness as a result: virtually no tactical proficiency and no ability to conduct complex operations, again with the exception of the 1st Division. Meanwhile, North Vietnam's PLAF and PAVN forces should have demonstrated excellent battlefield effectiveness—good tactical proficiency and a consistent ability to conduct complex operations.

This chapter explores the battlefield evidence from the war in Vietnam from 1963 to 1975 in order to see whether the variation predicted by the book's framework actually emerges in the empirical evidence, and if so why. Specifically, the chapter examines the battle of Ap Bac in 1963; the battle for the Citadel at Hue during the Tet Offensive of 1968; the South Vietnamese invasion of Laos in 1971, known as Lam Son 719; the campaigns for Hue and Quang Tri during the Easter Offensive of 1972; and the final battles of 1975.

This is far from an exhaustive list of conflict during the war, but the chapter focuses on these events for two reasons. First, these were all battles or campaigns in which the United States did not participate or in which its role was circumscribed. So, for example, the chapter does not focus on many ARVN operations from 1965 to 1968, because U.S. combat forces heavily dominated ARVN conventional activities during this period.[1] This does not necessarily mean that the ARVN's performance during this time was inconsistent with what we would expect based on the book's framework, only that the extensive U.S. combat role during the period makes it difficult to isolate the factors of interest. Instead the chapter focuses on battles in which U.S. firepower, resources, or advisory leadership were minimal, making assessments of North and South Vietnamese effectiveness more reliable.[2]

Second, this series of battles (listed in table 3.1) captures both offensive and defensive operations for both the North and the South and for different units within the South Vietnamese military, providing multiple opportunities to probe the book's argument. The chapter also captures battles across the major phases of the war: the Diem era, the period of escalated U.S. involvement, and the period after that involvement. Again, this approach enables us to extract the maximum amount of information from a relatively small number of fights. The chosen battles also were substantively important in each phase of the war, helping to ensure that the information gathered is representative of the conflict as a whole.

After providing some general background, the chapter examines each of these battles or campaigns in turn. Each section first presents the context, the forces involved on the two sides, and the key events. Then it assesses each side's ability to perform basic tactics and conduct complex operations. Notably, each battle or campaign offers multiple opportunities to observe battlefield effectiveness, because each battle involved units from both the PLAF/PAVN and the ARVN, and in some instances from different units within the ARVN.

In general, the evidence is consistent with what we would expect if battlefield effectiveness is a function of military organizational practices and if those practices arise in response to the threat environment. The battles show that North Vietnam generally performed much better than South Vietnam, with the exception of the ARVN 1st Division, which demonstrated excellent military performance virtually indistinguishable from that of PAVN and PLAF units. By itself, this observed variation should cast doubt on theories of military effectiveness that focus largely on broad, static traits that were more or less the same in North and South Vietnam. More important, however, detailed evidence from the battles affirmatively demonstrates the importance of military organizational practices in explaining this variation. Differences in overall national battlefield effectiveness and even the effectiveness of particular units within the two militaries were closely tied to the choice of military organizational practices. This connection points to the utility of the book's

Table 3.1. Vietnam War battles and campaigns examined

	On the offense	On the defense
ARVN general forces	Ap Bac, 1963	Hue, 1968
	Hue, 1968	Invasion of Laos, 1971
	Invasion of Laos, 1971	Easter Offensive, 1972
	Easter Offensive, 1972	Final battles, 1975
ARVN 1st Division	Hue, 1968	Hue, 1968
	Invasion of Laos, 1971	Invasion of Laos, 1971
	Easter Offensive, 1972	Easter Offensive, 1972
		Final battles, 1975
PAVN and/or PLAF	Hue, 1968	Ap Bac, 1963
	Invasion of Laos, 1971	Hue, 1968
	Easter Offensive, 1972	Invasion of Laos, 1971
	Final battles, 1975	Easter Offensive, 1972

framework in explaining when and how states will translate their material resources into fighting power.

Background: The Vietnam War, 1962–1975

The events discussed in this chapter occurred against the backdrop of a long and multifaceted war. Through 1965, combat was primarily a Vietnamese affair, with the U.S. role significant but still advisory. The PLAF led much of the fighting against Saigon, although the PAVN role was growing. As the 1960s went on, the war became increasingly conventional in the sense that the two sides generated regular, uniformed units of company- or battalion-size or larger to fight for and hold territory. This is not to say that the PLAF was not also conducting an insurgency, only that its combat repertoire included much more than hit-and-run attacks; it clearly sought to gain physical control of real estate in South Vietnam.

The years from 1965 to 1969 saw the introduction of U.S. combat troops and a dramatic escalation in violence against the North Vietnamese. The PAVN came to play a more prominent role in most large battles, with many of the PLAF wiped out entirely during the series of 1968 attacks known as the Tet Offensive. After the adoption of the Nixon Doctrine in June 1969, the U.S. ground presence in Vietnam began to contract, and primary combat responsibilities shifted back to the South Vietnamese. The war took on a strongly conventional character, with clashes between the ARVN and PAVN at the brigade or even division level not unusual. Thieu's government focused on breaking up North Vietnamese supply lines in Cambodia and Laos.

After considerable internal debate, Hanoi launched the series of attacks known as the Easter Offensive in 1972.[3] The offensive occurred along similar lines as the attacks in 1968, and, like the Tet Offensive, the Easter Offensive was premised on the notion that a quick succession of North Vietnamese military victories would give way to popular uprisings that would finish the job of overthrowing the Thieu regime. In fact, the Easter Offensive nearly succeeded militarily, but heavy U.S. airpower assisted the South Vietnamese in driving it back.

In 1973, the United States signed the Paris Peace Accords and soon transitioned to only a bare-bones infrastructure for continued support to South Vietnam. Thereafter the war became almost entirely a Vietnamese affair, with the North launching a final series of offensives in 1975. Bereft of U.S. help and beset by recurring political-military pathologies, the South Vietnamese crumpled, and Hanoi achieved the victory that it had sought for more than thirty years.

THE BATTLE OF AP BAC, 1963

The battle known as Ap Bac presents an initial opportunity to observe the ARVN and PLAF in a fight for control over territory, prior to extensive U.S. combat involvement. In this battle, the PLAF was essentially trying to draw the ARVN into an ambush, while the ARVN was attempting to conduct a three-pronged armor-infantry assault on the PLAF's prepared defensive position. As such, the battle enables close evaluation of both sides' tactical proficiency. The battle also saw South Vietnam attempt to conduct complex operations on the attack, trying to integrate several different battalion-sized units in a combined arms action, and it saw the PLAF attempt to engage in some minimal complex operations on the defense, trying to integrate three companies' use of light arms.

The ARVN units were drawn from parts of the South Vietnamese military subject to coup prevention practices. These included the 7th Division; an APC company, a Ranger company, and an Airborne battalion, all "elite" units whose true purpose was protection of President Diem against coups; and Civil Guard task forces, commanded by officers whose primary task was provincial government. The ARVN 1st Division, which would later develop practices more oriented toward conventional war, had no involvement in this battle.

Despite a 4:1 advantage in manpower and massively greater firepower, the ARVN forces at Ap Bac displayed serious problems with both basic tactics and complex operations. By contrast, the PLAF demonstrated remarkable tactical proficiency and a solid ability to conduct some

Table 3.2. The battle of Ap Bac, 1963

	North Vietnam	South Vietnam
Battle summary		
Tactical orientation	Defensive	Offensive
Plan	Ambush ARVN forces	Three-pronged armor-infantry assault on PLAF
Weapons	12 automatic rifles, 5 machine guns, 2–3 rifle grenades, 60-mm mortar	13 M-113 APCs, helicopters, artillery
Manpower	~350	~1200
Losses	~100 KIA [a]	~63 KIA, 109 WIA [b]
Effectiveness summary		
Tactical proficiency?	Yes	No
Complex operations?	Yes, minimally	No
As expected?	Yes	Yes

[a] Killed in action
[b] Wounded in action

minimal complex operations on the defense. Table 3.2 provides a brief summary of the battle.[4]

The Forces on Each Side

The battle began before dawn on January 2, 1963, in Dinh Tuong province, about sixty-five miles southwest of Saigon. ARVN intelligence had indicated that an enemy radio station was located near the hamlet of Tan Thoi, about a mile northwest of the hamlet of Bac (see map 3.1). Reports further suggested that a reinforced PLAF company of about 120 men, plus perhaps another 30 or so locals, guarded the radio.[5] Both hamlets were surrounded by knee-deep rice paddies bordered by a series of connecting streams and canals, covered with tree lines on both banks.[6]

The ARVN envisioned trapping the PLAF company from three directions. First, the 7th Division would land an infantry battalion of approximately 330 men to the north of the village by helicopter, who would then press southward. At the same time that this battalion (known as the 2nd Battalion, 11th Infantry Regiment, or the 2/11 IN) brought pressure from the north, a battalion of Civil Guard units divided into two task forces (A and B) were to attack from the south, preventing escape.[7] From the

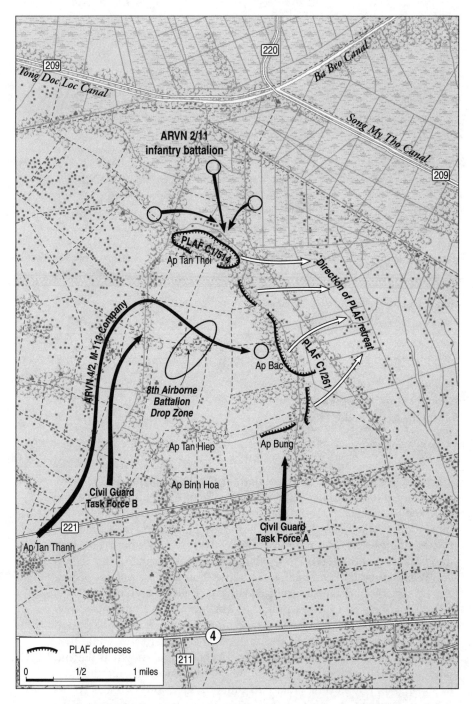

Map 3.1. The battle of Ap Bac, 1963. Adapted from David M. Toczek, *The Battle of Ap Bac: They Did Everything but Learn from It* (Westport, CT: Greenwood Press, 2001), 77; and General Donn A. Starry, *Armoured Combat in Vietnam* (Dorset, UK: Blandford Press, 1981), 26.

southwest, just along the PLAF's flank, a company of M-113 APCs with mounted infantry also were to attack. According to the ARVN plan, these amphibious vehicles, drawn from the 2nd Armored Cavalry Regiment (2nd ACR), would pivot and close with the enemy once the PLAF began to break under pressure from the infantry and Civil Guard units.[8]

Artillery as well as fighter-bombers would be on call to provide additional ARVN firepower.[9] Two reserve infantry companies also could be lifted by helicopter to the battlefield if needed.[10] In addition, the 352nd Ranger Company would be stationed northeast of the 2/11, providing a blocking force to prevent PLAF escape.[11]

Four South Vietnamese commanders were at the center of these plans. First, Colonel Bui Dinh Dam commanded the 7th Division, in whose area of operations the battle occurred and from which the infantry units were drawn. It was Dam who devised the battle plan with U.S. advisers and who was supposed to oversee its execution. Nevertheless, Dam's background was in administration, not combat, and this was his first time in command.[12]

Dam answered to the second major ARVN figure of the battle, General Huynh Van Cao, the recently promoted commander of the newly created IV Corps, whom Dam had replaced.[13] The third figure was Major Lam Quang Tho, who commanded both the M-113 company from the 2nd ACR and the Civil Guard task forces. Tho, however, was also the chief of Dinh Tuong province, meaning that his chain of command ran through the Department of the Interior, rather than through the ARVN and the Department of Defense—even though both the 2nd ACR and the Civil Guard were Department of Defense assets.[14] In other words, although Dam's plan depended on Tho's units, Tho did not answer to Dam or Cao.

Under Tho was Captain Ba, who commanded the M-113 company, usually known as the 4/2 because it was the 4th mechanized rifle troop of the 2nd Armored Cavalry. Ba had been noted as aggressive and capable.[15]

Opposing forces in the area went well beyond the single company reported by ARVN intelligence. The communists actually had Main Force companies plus additional units equivalent to a third company, totaling about 320 men, plus about 30 locals.[16] The PLAF included the 1st Company of the 514th Regional Battalion, known as the C1/514, which recently had executed a successful nearby ambush of the ARVN.[17] It now guarded the area just east of Tan Thoi. Also present was the 1st Company of the 261st Regional Battalion, known as the C1/261, guarding the area just east of Bac.[18]

The PLAF forces were lightly armed with twelve automatic rifles and four .30-caliber machine guns. They also had "two or three locally produced rifle grenades, one 60 mm mortar with three rounds, . . . and at least one heavy machine gun."[19] More important, the PLAF had carefully prepared the terrain to maximize the use of these weapons. It had established Bac and Tan Thoi as mutually supporting positions, digging carefully camouflaged foxholes behind the canal lines that jutted out at odd angles into the rice paddies. The PLAF also positioned its machine guns so as to create interlocking fields of fire along the various dikes. Indeed, these positions were so well hidden in the surrounding vegetation that even the famed American adviser Lt. Col. John Paul Vann was unable to spot any evidence of them when circling overhead at a few hundred feet during the battle. The PLAF's positions also were slightly elevated, providing an excellent downward view of the paddies through which the ARVN would have to approach.[20]

The Battle

Before dawn, the ARVN units moved into place, with the Civil Guard task forces coming into position in the south and the 4/2 moving its APCs into place toward the southwest. Dam also directed the airlifting of the 2/11 IN to the north of Tan Thoi. But fog enveloped the area, preventing the insertion of the second and third companies of the battalion. As a result, the Rangers moved southwest to reinforce the components of the 2/11 IN that had made it to the landing site, although after moving this short distance, the Rangers ceased to go farther.[21]

The noise from these initial movements was enough to alert the PLAF units, and they quickly moved into their prepared positions as the Civil Guard and 4/2 commenced the attack.[22] Knowing the range of its weapons, the PLAF let the Civil Guard get within thirty yards before opening fire.[23] Then the PLAF suddenly let loose, wounding the Civil Guard's commanding officer and killing the executive officer almost immediately.[24] The ARVN task forces quickly became disorganized and paralyzed, unable even to move to safety.[25]

As the adviser to the Task Force A reported, "I attempted to get the TF [task force] Commander to maneuver through the tree line to the right, using it for cover and concealment. He informed me that the Sector Chief had ordered him to occupy a blocking position at this location. If the TF had moved, it would have forced the VC [Viet Cong] into the same position that we were in earlier. The TF Commander either could not, or would not get permission to make the move." Instead, as the adviser related in his after-action report, "some [ARVN] soldiers cowered behind the paddie [*sic*] dyke and would not return fire, others held weapons above the dyke and fired without aiming." Artillery was no help. Although it was "timely," it was wildly insufficient and inaccurate, with the forward observer failing to adjust the volume or aim.[26]

Task Force B also refused to budge, with its adviser later reporting that it added "nothing to the friendly cause."[27] Some of its soldiers "were observed by US Advisory personnel to abandon many of their weapons while cowering in the bottom of a ditch. The District Chief took no corrective action even though he was present at the time of this occurrence."[28] According to the adviser, however, not all of the paralysis was the direct fault of the commanders on the scene. "The Commander of Task Force B requested permission to attack the main objective on at least three occasions during the afternoon but was denied permission on each occasion by the Sector Commander," that is, by Major Tho, who apparently feared losing the provincial forces on which he relied for governance.[29] Like Task Force A, Task Force B also had serious problems calling in artillery, as Task Force B had departed its base without its forward observer personnel, "who were considered 'unnecessary.'"[30]

Meanwhile, the fog had lifted, and the other two companies of the 2/11 IN were able to land to the north. Aware of the disaster with the Civil Guard, however, Dam now wanted to bring in a reserve infantry company by helicopter. Vann, who served as Dam's division adviser, circled overhead in his observation plane to find an insertion spot. Still unable to detect the well-concealed PLAF positions in the treeline, Vann recommended inserting the reserve forces only 1,000 feet away, just to the west of Ap Bac.[31]

The resulting attempt at insertion turned the battle from bad to worse for the ARVN. Until that point, despite the problems that the Civil Guard had encountered, the PLAF was still pinned in from three directions, with two of the ARVN prongs not having suffered much enemy contact at all. But bringing in the infantry reserve meant relying on helicopters—inviting targets for the PLAF.

Of the ten H-21s bringing in these troops or escorting them, one was downed almost immediately. The H-21 that went to rescue the first one was then shot down too. Another went down in an attempt to rescue the first two. Meanwhile, a fourth H-21 was forced to crash land about a mile away.[32] The PLAF also immediately pinned down the soldiers who tried to disembark.[33]

Realizing that the reserve was now more in need of help than the Civil Guard it had come to assist, Vann turned to Ba's mechanized company. Ba had a good reputation, and Vann knew that if the 4/2 could just cross the canal, its firepower and mobility could be brought to bear against the PLAF hidden away in the treeline. But Ba had suddenly become timid, resisting Vann's suggestions to cross the canal. Repeatedly, Ba refused. Only after Vann ordered the American adviser to shoot Ba—an order the adviser did not intend to follow but that Ba could hear loud and clear on the radio—did Ba relent and attempt to find a place for the M-113s to cross the canal.[34] Even then he continued to deliberately delay the crossing, though.[35]

Meanwhile, the C1/514 turned its attention to the 2/11 IN, which was now trying to press down on Ap Tan Thoi as originally planned from the north. Again, however, ARVN units walked right into well-prepared defensive positions. "Waiting until the lead company of the 2/11 IN had closed to within 20 meters of its positions," Toczek writes, "C1/514 opened fire, catching the 2nd Company almost completely by surprise." The situation quickly became stalemated, however, as the C1/514 sent another platoon to help pin down the 2/11 IN.[36] Neither the 2/11 IN nor the PLAF company was able to move.

PLAF leaders were now worried. According to Toczek, "It appeared that the 7th Division was slowly massing a coordinated assault. The 2/11 IN, although not making much progress against C1/514, was pressing firmly enough to keep the northern PLAF company fixed in place. South of Ap Bac, the two Civil Guard task forces stood a short distance away from completely enveloping C1/261. Worse, the mechanized company was crossing its last obstacle and would soon close with the insurgents who were dug into the sides of the dikes." Now would have been a good time to retreat, and, in fact, the commander of C1/261 hoped he would be told to withdraw.[37]

Meanwhile, the ARVN continued to fire artillery, although it was falling wide of the defenders' positions. Task Force A could have used this moment to attack, as the PLAF worried it would, but decided not to. Indeed, the Civil Guard soldiers decided it was time for lunch and built cooking fires. "Not taking fire, [they] casually sat or stood around," according to Toczek.[38]

Elsewhere the 4/2's situation quickly turned ugly. When Ba's APCs finally did cross the canal and move toward the PLAF, their advance was so poorly coordinated that the PLAF was able to pick off the vehicles one by one; the gunners were especially vulnerable.[39] The APCs also did not coordinate their movement with the dismounted infantry, who were quickly mowed down because the vehicle gunners were not suppressing enemy fire from the tree lines. Having waited until the APCs came in very close range, the PLAF now unleashed its carefully prepared firepower to devastating effect.

The ensuing chaos caused some of the M-113 drivers to back up, abandoning or even injuring their own wounded comrades in the process.[40] One adviser later reported that the gunner near him became so panicked that he "ducked down and was blindly firing his machine gun, mostly in the air. . . . The M-113 next to me started to back up, leaving one of their men who had just been hit." Other M-113s sought to hide behind the downed helicopters rather than attack.[41] Even the sole

M-113 with a flamethrower (instead of the normal .50-caliber machine gun) did not have much effect because "the crew had not mixed enough of the jelling agent with the gasoline to keep the jet of flame burning properly."[42] The ball of flame that should have burned the guerrillas out of their positions wound up having "the force and effect of a Zippo lighter."[43]

Despite all these problems, Ba's APC made it through and was attempting to attack. Ba was still leading from the front. But then, in an inexplicable accident, Ba suffered a concussion inside his APC and was knocked unconscious. The entire attack ground to a halt for twenty minutes as Ba struggled to regain consciousness.[44] Eventually he did, but the unit's momentum had evaporated. Ba remained "too stunned to even realize that he ought to force the four or five carriers hanging back at the canal to come forward and bolster his attack. He could not think beyond making the frontal assault that he had been taught most often to do."[45]

Ba continued to advance. But just as his APC and one or two others were about to close with the PLAF by ascending the dikes leading to the foxholes, a PLAF squad leader climbed out of his foxhole and threw a grenade right onto the M-113. Emboldened, other PLAF fighters quickly copied him. After that it was all over for the 4/2. Still stunned from his head injury, "Ba allowed the driver of his carrier to back up, and the one or two vehicles persevering with him followed. The assault had failed."[46]

At this point Vann realized major intervention was required. He suggested that Dam call in a mobile reserve unit, the 8th Airborne Battalion, for a drop east of Ap Bac, to close the cordon on the PLAF as the three prongs of the initial attack had failed to do. Vann hoped this ARVN force could at least pin the PLAF in place overnight.[47] Dam replied that the drop would be made, but only to the west of Ap Bac rather than the east.[48] The drop finally happened just before dusk but missed its target by more than half a mile. Many of the Airborne actually "landed in front of the Viet Cong positions on the west and northwest sides of Tan Thoi, instead of safely behind the Civil Guards and M-113s at Bac as Cao had planned." As a result, "they were unable to do more than launch piecemeal attacks in small units before darkness put an end to the fighting. The PLAF made short work of the newcomers and inflicted substantial casualties. Nineteen of the paratroopers were killed and thirty-three wounded, including the two American advisors."[49]

After night fell, the PLAF slipped away to the east without detection by the ARVN.[50] The next morning the ARVN entered the village, but as one adviser summed it up, "No VC were found, no weapons were found."[51] The battle had ended.

[81]

Assessing the Battlefield Effectiveness of South Vietnam

ARVN units at Ap Bac demonstrated minimal effectiveness at best. First, ARVN tactical proficiency was poor, reflecting the lack of training. At multiple points units proved unable to conduct basic activities central to their assigned functions. The APCs failed to mass for their attack, for example, allowing themselves to be picked off vehicle by vehicle. The 4/2 also proved unable to aim its .50 caliber mounts accurately or to operate its prized flamethrower, perhaps because most of its training had come in the form of presidential parades.[52] The Airborne troops proved unable to conduct a timely and accurate jump and were unable to defend themselves quickly upon landing. Throughout the battle, ARVN artillery fires also were repeatedly inaccurate and insufficient in volume to suppress the relatively light PLAF fires.

The battle also revealed the ARVN to be utterly incapable of aggregating basic tactical actions into larger complex operations. For example, units repeatedly failed to perform even relatively self-contained combined arms activities. The M-113 drivers exhibited a deadly inability to coordinate their movement and fire with dismounted infantry, even though such coordination is the entire reason to have APCs. The Civil Guard units had not bothered to bring along their artillery forward observers, resulting in a lack of effective suppressive fire when they were trying to advance on the well-defended PLAF positions. And despite everyone recognizing that the artillery was falling wide of the PLAF positions, the problem was not corrected.

More important, the ARVN repeatedly failed to integrate low-level initiative with high-level coordination. At several points in the battle, commanders could have pushed their attack forward in keeping with the overall known goals of the operation, pressing in on the defenders from all three sides with overwhelming numbers and superior firepower. But this sort of adaptation did not happen. For example, the Rangers and the 2/11 IN could have moved more aggressively south to press down on Tan Thoi, before the C1/514 had a chance to reinforce and react. But the Rangers stopped moving at the first opportunity, and the 2/11 IN moved slowly, giving the C1/514 time to turn to neutralize it. The Civil Guard task forces in the south also essentially stopped moving after their first losses. Ba's company, too, was extremely slow to cross the canals and never regrouped after its initial assault failed. Then the Airborne waited until very late in the day to make its jump, giving the PLAF an opportunity to escape under the cover of darkness. In short, ARVN commanders almost always chose inaction over action.

Much of their hesitation clearly stemmed from the ARVN's military organizational practices, notably the centralization and fracturing of

[82]

command. Even where commanders knew what to do and wanted to do it, they lacked authority to follow through, because that authority was either concentrated at higher echelons or divided among multiple lower-level commanders. For example, on three separate occasions, Col. Dam ordered Major Tho's Civil Guard units to advance. Dam outranked Tho, but because Tho was not in Dam's chain of command, the order was not followed.[53] Why were there two chains of command, one might ask? Because, as discussed in chapter 2, President Diem wanted to divide his military forces and weaken the chances of a coup. Similarly, why was Tho so unmoved by Dam's pleas to advance? Because Tho needed his Civil Guard units to survive the battle with few casualties and return to their duties helping in the governance of Dinh Tuong province.[54]

Tho also "owned" Ba's APC units—another arrangement imposed by Diem to ensure that no division commander could acquire valuable armored units that might attempt a coup. The problem, of course, was that when Dam (and Vann) then told Ba to move, he had to wait for approval from Tho. It was for this reason that Ba was "intolerably slow" and apparently showed "a lack of aggressiveness and willingness to fight," even though Ba had previously been characterized by U.S. advisers as just the opposite sort of officer.[55]

Similarly, the poor employment of the Airborne stemmed from the highly centralized nature of command. Dam wanted the drop made sooner and to the east, but he was overruled by his corps commander, General Cao, who had specifically been told by Diem not to incur too many casualties because such losses might precipitate a coup.[56] Diem also no doubt wanted to preserve his Airborne force, a mobile unit that he believed could protect him in the future if other parts of the army turned against him or if domestic dissidents engaged in an uprising.[57]

In short, the battle of Ap Bac revealed an ARVN unable to perform basic tactics or conduct complex operations. According to at least one U.S. adviser on the ground, the battle was no fluke: "Time after time I have seen the same Vietnamese officers and troops make the same mistakes in virtually the same rice paddy," he noted. "The only difference was that usually they get away with it without getting hurt because the Communists simply slip away. This time the Communists fought, and our people were torn up."[58]

As this comment implies, the ARVN's deficits were not simply the result of idiosyncratic factors. The morning's fog, the scant protection that the M-113s provided their gunners, Vann's poor choice of a landing zone for the helicopters, Ba's concussion—all conspired to make the ARVN's ambitious battle plan more difficult to execute.[59] But the ARVN's effectiveness problems ran deeper than bad luck. They stemmed from a deeply ingrained and detrimental set of military organizational practices.

As one of the advisers noted immediately after the battle, "There is still too much political interference in the Vietnamese army and . . . promotion too often depends on political loyalty rather than military ability."[60] The result was "a complete lack of discipline in battle that permit[ted] commanders at all levels, and even . . . soldiers, to refuse to obey any orders they personally [found] distasteful."[61] Indeed, no officer above the rank of battalion commander had even appeared on the battlefield to lead his forces.[62]

Assessing the Battlefield Effectiveness of North Vietnam

PLAF performance contrasted sharply with the ARVN's. First, the PLAF's tactical proficiency was excellent, with soldiers demonstrating strong basic skills. For example, all observers of the battle agreed that the PLAF made superb use of the terrain to conceal its positions.[63] "Their well sited, camouflaged, and deep fighting positions permitted them to withstand the direct fire of the M113s, as [well as] much of the artillery, and almost all of the air effort," according to one report.[64] In addition, the PLAF's own after-action report noted, "Accurate firepower was also one of our important strengths."[65] The Americans agreed: "The marksmanship of the VC riflemen was excellent. Most of the ARVN 50 caliber gunners died of head wounds within the opening minutes of the fight."[66]

The PLAF also displayed superb fire discipline, reflecting precise knowledge of their weapons' ranges. Repeatedly, the PLAF refrained from firing at the ARVN attackers until they were close enough to be trapped and hit. The PLAF after-action assessment also emphasized that it had developed detailed tactics for confronting APCs, helicopters, and airborne troops. It knew the vulnerabilities of each and fired accordingly.[67]

Second, the PLAF successfully demonstrated the ability to conduct relatively complex operations. Although it was only lightly armed, it successfully established interlocking fields of fire with its machine guns, maximizing the benefit of its defensive positions. PLAF commanders also reacted quickly to the different prongs of the ARVN attacks, fighting them off in turn and frequently shifting forces from one part of the line to another to cope with the substantially larger enemy force.[68] The PLAF considered this a key accomplishment, noting that its fighters had maintained "a combined command of 3 different types of Troops in a counter mopping up operation."[69]

The strategic implications of the battle are debatable, of course. The communists claimed it as a "great victory."[70] An internal MACV report took the opposite view, claiming that "the 2 January operation in the south is an example of what must be accomplished. . . . The 2 January operation in the south achieved a desirable confrontation of forces in which the Viet Cong came off second best."[71] Casualty data from the battle does little to resolve these interpretations, with the PLAF estimated to have lost 100 men killed in action, and the ARVN 63, with an additional 109 wounded.[72] Whatever the broader strategic interpretation of the day's events, the PLAF clearly demonstrated superior battlefield effectiveness—a direct reflection of its military organizational practices.

THE BATTLE FOR THE CITADEL IN HUE DURING
THE TET OFFENSIVE OF 1968

Occurring five years later, the 1968 battle for the Citadel in Hue offers an opportunity to examine a large-scale, extended engagement involving the ARVN forces identified as being subject to conventional war practices: the 1st Division and particularly its Hac Bao Company. Evidence from the battle demonstrates that ARVN units subject to military organizational practices more similar to those implemented in North Vietnam had much better battlefield effectiveness. Both the PLAF/PAVN and the ARVN units at Hue demonstrated strong tactical proficiency and the ability to conduct both offensive and defensive complex operations—but the ARVN's fighting prowess was particularly notable given that it was outnumbered and trying to retake territory for most of the battle. As such, the fight for the Citadel provides especially convincing evidence that military organizational practices matter for effectiveness.

The battle took place during the North Vietnamese Tet Offensive. This offensive involved coordinated, near-simultaneous attacks during late January and early February 1968 by both PAVN regulars and Main Force PLAF units in 36 of South Vietnam's 44 provincial capitals, 5 of its 6 major cities, 64 of its 242 district capitals, and more than 50 hamlets (see map 3.2).[73] The North Vietnamese had spent months planning these attacks, stealthily infiltrating men and supplies in order to take advantage of the truce typically observed by both sides in honor of the year's biggest holiday. The offensive represented North Vietnam's first true attempt to take the fight to the cities, with the expectation that the people of the South would rise up and join them in the overthrowing the U.S.-backed Thieu regime.[74]

In that respect the offensive was a colossal miscalculation, and the venture destroyed the PLAF, which was never again able to field Main Force units. In many places, it was South Vietnamese citizens themselves who helped expel the communists, curbing the offensive in a matter of hours or days. ARVN commanders also distinguished themselves in repelling

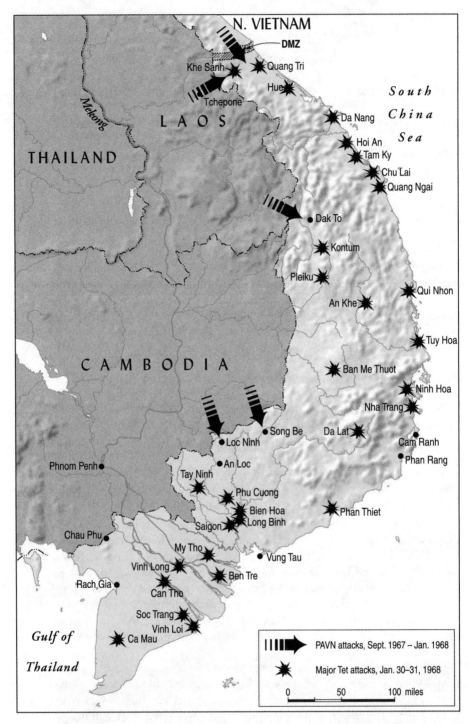

Map 3.2. The Tet Offensive, 1968. Adapted from James H. Willbanks, *The Tet Offensive: A Concise History* (New York: Columbia University Press, 2007).

attacks on Da Nang, Ban Me Thuot, and Dalat, although in many areas of the country, particularly the Delta, the Americans came to the rescue.[75] In most of the country, the offensive ended almost as quickly as it began, by the first week of February.

Intense, sustained fighting occurred at three locations, however: Khe Sahn, Saigon, and Hue. Khe Sahn was a U.S. base in the far northwest corner of South Vietnam, and therefore its defense was almost entirely a U.S. affair. In Saigon the ARVN forces played a much larger role, but the U.S. commander there had sensed an attack was coming and pulled his combat forces back from the border to defend the city. As a result, fifty-three U.S. maneuver battalions, along with a hefty dose of American airpower, were available to help defend the capital.[76]

It was in Hue, the ancient capital of Vietnam, that the ARVN faced the most sustained, intense test of its battlefield effectiveness against PAVN forces during Tet, mainly because of the minimal U.S. involvement there. There were fewer than 200 U.S. soldiers stationed in Hue, and the nearest U.S. combat base, Phu Bai, was five miles to the southeast. In addition, the North Vietnamese had correctly predicted that the country's northeast monsoon would impede aerial resupply and close air support operations in Hue, further limiting the United States' ability to aid the ARVN. Once the fight began, the U.S. forces that were there chose to divide the battlefield with their ARVN counterparts, creating a sector for which the ARVN forces were independently responsible.[77]

For all of these reasons, the battle for Hue, summarized in table 3.3, offers the best opportunity during the years of extensive U.S. combat involvement to examine ARVN and PAVN battlefield effectiveness. In particular, the fighting at Hue affords an excellent, well-controlled opportunity to evaluate both sides' tactical proficiency and performance of complex operations, both offensively and defensively.

The Forces on Each Side

The Perfume River slices the city of Hue into two parts: an ancient northern half protected by an imperial fortress known as the Citadel, and a southern residential half known as the New City. The Citadel is a square whose corners face north, south, east, and west, covering three square miles in area, with outer walls thirty feet high and forty feet thick (see map 3.3). Its southeast wall borders the river, while the other three walls are bordered by a deep moat. At the time of the battle, the inside of the Citadel housed a great many shops and homes, while its outer walls held numerous bunkers and tunnels built by the Japanese during World War II.[78] Inside the Citadel, key landmarks included Tay Loc Airfield in

Table 3.3. The battle for the Citadel in Hue, 1968

	North Vietnam	South Vietnam
Battle summary		
Tactical orientation	Offensive, then defensive	Defensive, then offensive
Plan	Take and hold the Citadel	Defend and then recapture the Citadel
Weapons	Mortars, machine guns	Light antitank weapons, machine guns, M-16 rifles
Manpower	8,000 initially, then ~16,000[a]	A few hundred initially, then rising to 12,500[b]
Losses	1,042 KIA, several times that number WIA	384 KIA, 1,800 WIA
Effectiveness summary		
Tactical proficiency?	Yes	Yes, in 1st Division
Complex operations?	Yes	Yes, in 1st Division
As expected?	Yes	Yes

[a] This is a rough estimate inferred from Willbanks, *Tet Offensive*, 45.
[b] This is a rough estimate based on the presence of the 1st Division and the insertion of three Airborne battalions. Typical ARVN divisions had about 10,000 men, and an average battalion had about 833 soldiers, so ARVN forces probably totaled no more than 12,500. This estimate is generous because it assumes that all of the 1st Division made it back inside the Citadel intact and does not reflect that fact that the Airborne forces arrived at the battle late and left early.

the western corner and the old Imperial Palace on the southeastern wall, above which flew the Republic of Vietnam flag.

The 1st Division was headquartered in the Citadel's northern corner and commanded by General Ngo Quang Truong, a highly respected officer.[79] As mentioned in chapter 2, Truong had been picked for command on the basis of merit and applied this same principle in the selection of his officers. Most of his units were outside Hue during Tet, guarding routes of advance. Only the Hac Bao was stationed inside the Citadel, commanded by First Lt. Tran Ngoc Hue, a protégé of Truong's recognized as a rising star in the ARVN. Hue, too, had earned his position based on merit rather than political connections and, as such, was a rare exception to the normal rules governing military promotion in South Vietnam.[80]

For their part, the North Vietnamese initially committed an estimated 8,000 troops to the battle at Hue, out of roughly 80,000 involved in the offensive overall. The forces at Hue included two PAVN regiments and six PLAF Main Force battalions. As the battle progressed, however, "the

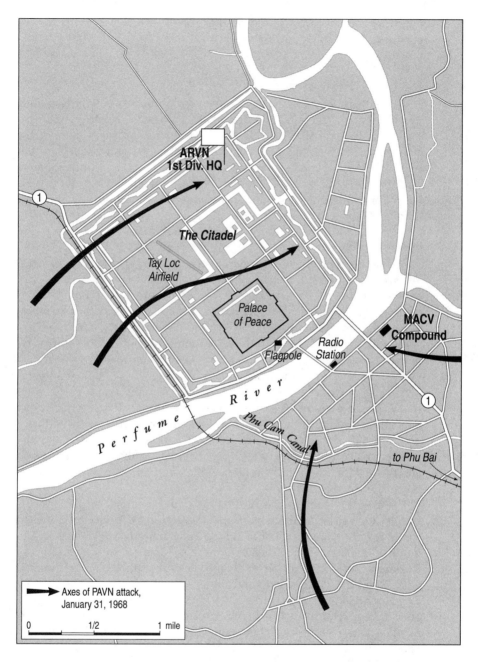

Map 3.3. The Citadel at Hue, 1968. Adapted from James H. Willbanks, *The Tet Offensive: A Concise History* (New York: Columbia University Press, 2007).

total Communist force in and around the city would grow to twenty battalions."[81]

The Battle for Hue

The battle for Hue swung like a giant pendulum between the two sides vying to control the city. The first phase involved a North Vietnamese attack that overran all but the tiny 1st Division headquarters in the northern corner of the Citadel, but then the battle's second phase saw the ARVN, led by the 1st Division and its Hac Bao Company, launch counterattacks from this outpost, gradually regaining the lost ground. The ARVN units were helped in the final days by the U.S. Marines, although for most of the battle the U.S. and ARVN forces operated separately, with the latter handling areas to the north of the river and the former to the south.[82]

On the first morning of what would become the Tet Offensive, General Truong grew suspicious upon hearing reports of enemy attacks elsewhere in the country. After reviewing recent intelligence reports from I Corps, Truong issued alert orders to confine all troops to their barracks. Although some had already gone on holiday leave, many stayed in place and began defensive preparations. Truong also sent out his thirty-six-man reconnaissance team to protect the western approaches to the city.[83]

The six platoons of the Hac Bao, numbering about 200 men and stationed in the western corner of the Citadel near Tay Loc Airfield, were sent to guard various avenues of advance. Lieutenant Hue sent three of his platoons south of the river to act as security at the provincial headquarters, a power station, and a prison. Two more were split up and dispatched to guard the gates entering the Citadel, leaving only one platoon and the headquarters staff, about fifty men in total, to thwart any attack inside the Citadel itself.[84]

The events of January 31, 1968 would prove Truong's suspicions correct. In the wee hours of the morning, PAVN and PLAF troops launched a massive attack on the Citadel. It followed a pattern similar to that seen in other cities targeted in the Tet Offensive.[85] The North Vietnamese 6th Regiment, consisting of the 800th and 802nd battalions, and reinforced with local PLAF troops, gathered along the western edge of the Citadel. Cued by a rocket barrage on the city from the mountains to the west, they attacked in the middle of the night, overrunning the ARVN forces guarding the western entrances. They soon "fanned out to begin a coordinated attack from west to east."[86] Meanwhile, separate PAVN units also overran the MACV compound south of the river and took control of the residential areas in Hue outside the Citadel, where they began rounding up those they deemed counterrevolutionaries.

[90]

According to George Smith, a U.S. adviser in Hue during the offensive, Lt. Hue led the first organized resistance to the attack inside the Citadel. His Hac Bao soldiers fired back with light antitank weapons (LAWs), machine guns, and M-16s. Fortunately, Hue had held several special training sessions for his unit on the use of the new LAWs. Also coming to the initial defense of the Citadel was a platoon from the ARVN 1st Ordnance Company that happened to be in the area near the airfield. Smith reports, "The unexpected heavy volley stopped the NVA [North Vietnamese Army, another name for the PAVN] attack cold and further disoriented the NVA troops. The enemy then tried a flanking movement to the right to skirt the fire coming from the ordnance compound and ran straight into the Hac Bao platoon. Hue's troops . . . inflicted heavy casualties. The action forced the 800th Battalion to veer to the south and held up the 802nd, which was trying to push its way toward the ARVN 1st Division HQ along the northwestern wall."[87]

With the PAVN attack temporarily delayed, Truong ordered the Hac Bao and ordnance units to withdraw into the division headquarters in the northern corner of the Citadel. This key decision both saved the valuable Hac Bao from being destroyed piecemeal and also maintained a crucial foothold in the Citadel from which to launch ARVN's eventual counteroffensive. Meanwhile, PAVN forces continued to move west, taking control of the lightly defended Imperial Palace, also inside the Citadel.[88]

Because he had managed to save his headquarters, General Truong was able to radio for reinforcement. He ordered the four battalions of his 3rd Regiment, as well as 1st Division's 4th Battalion, 2nd Regiment, and the 3rd Troop, 7th Armored Cavalry, to return to the Citadel from their various locations outside Hue. He also requested that Saigon airlift three Airborne battalions, the 2nd, 7th, and 9th, into Hue.

Unfortunately, none of these units could arrive immediately, leaving only the Hac Bao, the tiny Reconnaissance Company, and the 1st Infantry support personnel caught up in the fighting to defend the headquarters. Truong's men had no heavy weapons, just a few jeep-mounted light machine guns and a few LAWs. They also had no artillery or air support, due to the inclement weather and the priority afforded U.S. forces struggling to defend the MACV compound.[89]

As the day wore on, the communists attacked the ARVN headquarters three more times, but each time Truong's men repelled them. According to Smith, "Each attack became weaker as the enemy had to divert some of its resources to deal with ARVN reinforcements coming down Route 1 from the north. There would be one more attack on the 1st Division compound the night of 31 January, but it proved to be the last one. The enemy pulled back from the division CP [command post] and strengthened its

[91]

defenses at the airfield. Other enemy troops set up a headquarters in the Imperial Palace compound, while others moved to the southeast to put pressure on Truong's garrison from the south."[90]

By February 2, according to Smith, some of Truong's requested reinforcements, including the Airborne battalions, had made their way to the Citadel by boat and helicopter.[91] According to a South Vietnamese account of the battle, "With these additional forces, the 1st Division finally retook the Tay Loc airfield inside the old citadel after two days of heavy fighting during which the enemy lost in excess of 200 killed."[92] Shortly thereafter, other elements of the 1st Division "fought their way to the An Hoa Gate, liberating most of the northwestern wall of the Citadel and resulting in an astounding additional 693 enemy KIA. ARVN forces now controlled the more open areas of the northern sector of the Citadel and were poised to launch attacks throughout the remainder of the city."[93]

Despite this progress, Truong could see that the North Vietnamese were continuing to receive fresh supplies and troops, while his own forces were suffering attrition with no relief in sight. Unfortunately, U.S. and ARVN forces had not closed off the western resupply and infiltration routes to Hue. As a result, "enemy forces were well dug in, and, from all appearances, willing to fight it out to the end." Worst of all, the ARVN still lacked heavy weapons, a particular disadvantage when trying to retake well-defended positions nestled in the thick walls of the Citadel.[94]

This is not to say that the ARVN did not keep trying. According to Smith, "The rest of General Truong's 3rd Regiment, the 2nd, 3rd, and 4th Battalions, arrived on 7 February.... Each unit had been trying to assault the Citadel from the south after breaking free of enemy pressure at the outset of the battle. The 2nd and 3rd Battalions, which had been bypassed by the enemy invasion a week earlier, had slowly moved eastward along the northern shore of the Perfume River to the base of the Citadel, which they were unable to enter." Even the Airborne performed well.[95]

But as Airborne casualties rose, Thieu soon wanted the units to return to Saigon. When Truong protested, he was told that three battalions of Vietnamese Marines would replace the departing Airborne. Not reassured by this promise, Truong finally asked the Americans for help. In response, the United States sent in three Marine companies supported by armored vehicles.[96]

The U.S. Marines soon got a sense of what Truong's men had been up against. The Citadel's walls were sturdy and its streets narrow, making tanks necessary yet cumbersome. "The NVA forces had had a couple of weeks to prepare their defensive positions in the Citadel," Smith explains. "Firing positions were cleverly concealed not only in buildings and on rooftops but in spider holes at street level." Despite heavy pounding by naval guns and U.S. airpower, including high-explosive bombs, napalm, and tear gas, the North Vietnamese kept firing, demonstrating "fortitude and resilience."[97]

After several delays, the South Vietnamese Marines also finally arrived at the Citadel. The Hac Bao, which had just helped the 3rd Regiment break out of an encirclement toward the southern corner of the Citadel, quickly moved to guide the Vietnamese Marines into position and then helped them push the North's force back along the northwestern wall.[98] Meanwhile, the unit that the Hac Bao had just helped break free of the encirclement, the 2nd Battalion, 3rd Regiment (2/3), turned to the task of guarding the U.S. Marines' right flank as the armored companies moved through the city.[99]

The U.S. Marines did not have an easy go of it. Although the ARVN Airborne had fought well, its withdrawal by Saigon had been premature, ceding several key defensive positions to the PAVN and PLAF, which now used them to fire on the advancing Marines.[100] In fact, it was this error that lay at the root of many later Marine accounts disparaging ARVN performance in Hue.[101] Fighting was hand-to-hand at times, and U.S. Marine casualties were high.[102] Nevertheless, the U.S. Marines did have the benefit of better weapons, particularly recoilless rifles. In addition, the weather had cleared, enabling the use of supporting airpower.[103] Truong's men had enjoyed neither of these advantages.

Indeed, the ARVN 2/3 on the Marines' flank continued to face a tough fight. According to Wiest, "The NVA set up mutually supporting defensive positions in buildings that flanked the winding roads, with snipers firing from upper floors and numerous defenders in lower windows or doorways creating a deadly crossfire that converted the streets into kill zones. Lacking heavy-weapons support, 2/3 attempted to deal with such defenses by having elements of the battalion lay down covering fire while others dashed forward." Eventually, the Hac Bao went back in to help both the Marines and the 2/3 "in the final push toward the southeastern wall of the Citadel."[104]

Meanwhile, elements of the U.S. 1st Cavalry helped seal the western routes of entry that had been providing fresh troops and supplies to the North Vietnamese throughout the battle. By February 22, the PAVN and PLAF began to withdraw, ceding the Citadel piece by piece to the Marines and the 2/3.[105] Finally, "on the night of February 23–24, an ARVN battalion launched a surprise attack westward along the wall in the southeastern section of the Citadel. A savage battle ensued, but the South Vietnamese pressed the attack. The PAVN, suffering from a lack of ammunition and supplies, fell back. Allied forces overran some of the last positions; VC and PAVN troops abandoned the others as they withdrew westward to sanctuaries in Laos."[106] Members of the 2/3 soon took down the NLF flag and raised the South Vietnamese banner over the Citadel, while the Hac Bao retook the Imperial Palace.

The battle officially ended on March 2.[107] In twenty-six days of fighting, the ARVN had suffered 384 killed and 1,800 wounded, while Allied forces claimed to have killed over 5,000 North Vietnamese soldiers.[108] Later a captured North Vietnamese document revealed that losses in Hue had been significantly lower, about 1,042 killed and several times that number wounded. Among the dead were a regimental commander, eight battalion and twenty-four company commanders, and seventy-two platoon leaders.[109]

Assessing the Battlefield Effectiveness of South Vietnam

I argued in chapter 2 that because patterns of training and promotion were different for the ARVN 1st Division, particularly the Hac Bao company, its performance should have been markedly better than that of other ARVN units. In fact, the fighting at Hue bears out this expectation, showing that where military organizational practices varied within the ARVN, so did battlefield effectiveness. Compared to the earlier battle examined, ARVN soldiers at Hue performed far more skillfully, even showing the ability to perform some complex operations. In fact, they demonstrated effectiveness comparable to that of North Vietnamese forces.

First, the ARVN units in the Citadel repeatedly demonstrated strong tactical proficiency. Although severely handicapped by a lack of heavy weapons, the ARVN proved skillful in the use of the weapons it did have, notably the LAWs, as well as machine guns and rifles. The fact that these units could continue to repulse multiple attacks on their headquarters on the first night of the offensive and then even manage to retake areas like the airfield later in February further testifies to their tactical abilities. This performance contrasts sharply with the performance of other units in the ARVN that seemed to display basic problems following orders and using their weapons. Where ARVN units were trained regularly and realistically, their skills clearly improved.

Second, the ARVN in the Citadel consistently demonstrated the ability to engage in large-scale coordinated operations that conformed to an overall plan yet required substantial initiative on the part of individual soldiers and lower-level commanders. The mere fact that Truong began the battle with hardly any of his troops actually in the Citadel, yet was able to draw them all in to fight in a coordinated fashion at multiple different locations, testifies to the fact that the 1st Division was capable of more than basic tactical proficiency.

Similarly, the Hac Bao not only managed to stay intact and perform adequately in individual engagements despite its platoons' dispersal at the start of the battle, but it also repeatedly moved to different areas across the battlefield in response to the needs of the various battalions in the 1st Division and the actions of the enemy. On the initial night of the battle it proved able to conduct a fighting withdrawal from the airfield to the headquarters.

This behavior suggests that at least some parts of the ARVN were capable of complex operations that aggregated tactical skills into larger-scale, more difficult activities. Along these same lines, the 2/3 displayed a particularly strong ability to conduct complex operations as it cleared the city while operating on the U.S. Marines' right flank. It carefully coordinated its movements with firepower. It also engaged in the surprise attack that finally ended the battle.

To be sure, the battle for the Citadel at Hue was won not only by the ARVN, but also by the U.S. Marines. Indeed, some histories of the battle have referred derisively to the ARVN as mere "spectators" in the fight for the Citadel, which they claim was won solely by the Marines.[110] On this subject, a few facts about the Marines' role are worth bearing in mind.

First, the U.S. Marines did not enter the battle until late February, after significant evidence of the ARVN's independent battlefield effectiveness in the Citadel was evident. This takes nothing away from the U.S. Marines' fighting prowess but merely suggests that whatever their role in concluding the battle, the ARVN's capabilities can still clearly be evaluated in the period of battle prior to U.S. Marine involvement. Second, although there is no doubt regarding the U.S. Marines' crucial contribution to the battle's outcome, they enjoyed several advantages that the ARVN largely did not possess: organic heavy weapons, air and artillery support, aerial resupply, and clear weather.[111]

In addition, and perhaps by sheer bad luck, the ARVN was responsible for the toughest sectors of North Vietnamese resistance even after the U.S. Marines' entry. As Smith reflected, "Having witnessed fighting on both sides of the Perfume River, I believe that the enemy resistance was strongest in the Citadel, particularly in the west and southwest sectors where ARVN troops were deployed. That area of operations was the closest point to the enemy's command and resupply headquarters. The ARVN units, lacking the marines' heavy weapons capability, particularly tanks and 106mm recoilless rifles, faced fresh troops almost daily for three weeks."[112] The ARVN's performance is all the more remarkable against this backdrop. Indeed, the U.S. Marines' fight would have been even more difficult had Truong not maintained the initial foothold in his headquarters, recaptured Tay Loc Airfield, and then attached the 2/3 to the Marines' right flank as a guide through the city.[113]

Furthermore, many U.S. Marine accounts of the battle mistakenly conflate ARVN performance outside the Citadel in the southern half of Hue—the area of operations where most U.S. Marines were engaged—with that of the 1st Division inside the Citadel. ARVN units south of the Perfume River did perform poorly, even looting abandoned neighborhoods after the U.S. Marines had cleared them.[114] This behavior is consistent with what we would expect given the coup prevention practices prevalent in most of the army. But these units were not from the 1st Division or Hac Bao, and their behavior should not detract from the credit due to the ARVN inside the Citadel.[115] It was Saigon's premature withdrawal of the Airborne that forced the U.S. Marines to enter the battle from such a disadvantaged position in the first place—another unsurprising development given that the ARVN overall was still subject to highly centralized command arrangements motivated by Thieu's concern about threats besides conventional combat.

Assessing the Battlefield Effectiveness of North Vietnam

Communist forces performed in a manner consistent with what we would expect based on the adoption of conventional war practices. First, the North Vietnamese demonstrated excellent tactical proficiency, as all accounts of the battle reflect. Although they lacked anything heavier than mortars and machine guns inside the city, the PAVN and PLAF troops knew how to use their weapons and were described as "skillful" and as having clearly "rehearsed their attacks beforehand."[116] They also knew how to use urban terrain for cover and concealment while trying to take or defend territory, another area in which they had received special training.[117]

Second, the North Vietnamese showed their ability to aggregate tactical actions into complex operations. They repeatedly combined arms and coordinated the activities of multiple units to produce maximum effect, both offensively and defensively. In the attack's initial phase, for example, the infantry of the 6th Regiment coordinated its movement with the rocket barrage from the mountains to the west. Then the battalions of the 6th, the 800th, and 802nd overran Hue from west to east in a synchronized attack. The PAVN official history proudly notes, "Because our plan was detailed and the organization and command of our approach march was properly handled (in spite of the fact that we had a large number of forces and had to divide the approach march into many columns, cross many rivers and streams, and bypass many enemy outposts), all units reached their positions securely and on time."[118] As the battle progressed, the PAVN also successfully established blocking positions to attempt to interdict Truong's reinforcements converging on the city.

[96]

In addition, once they had taken over most of the Citadel, communist forces proved themselves able to conduct impressive defensive operations that again combined arms and coordinated activities across different types of units. Both the ARVN and U.S. histories note that the North Vietnamese skillfully established complex defensive positions with interlocking fields of fire.[119] Had these positions not been established, the United States' heavy firepower would not have been needed.

All of this is not to say that the communist performance was flawless. In broader military terms the Tet Offensive was a disaster, as it enabled the destruction of most PLAF Main Force units and galvanized further South Vietnamese resistance. Even at the tactical-operational level, the North Vietnamese clearly did not achieve their objectives in Hue. For example, they did not overrun Truong's headquarters.[120] Nevertheless, the sheer length of the battle testifies to North Vietnamese effectiveness—as well as to that of the ARVN units responsible for defense of the Citadel. Where military organizational practices were similar, battles between North and South Vietnam were a very close-run affair.

THE INVASION OF LAOS, 1971

The invasion of Laos offers an opportunity to gauge the battlefield effectiveness of both North and South Vietnam after more than five years of direct U.S. combat involvement in the war, including intensified attempts at training the South Vietnamese. Three years after the Tet Offensive, the conventional threat to the South had become undeniable, which should have produced strong pressures for improved ARVN performance if theories that focus on external threats are correct. Indeed, as the United States' after-action report noted of the invasion of Laos, "Operation Lam Son 719 was a real test of the effectiveness of the RVNAF and the Vietnamization program"—mainly because U.S. combat forces and advisers were not authorized to cross the border into Laos.[121]

Furthermore, the campaign in Laos involved attempts by both North and South Vietnam to engage in full-scale conventional warfare, offering a clear opportunity to examine the two sides' tactical proficiency and abilities to conduct complex operations (see table 3.4). Both sides conducted offensive and defensive operations involving multiple divisions—including, on the South Vietnamese side, the 1st Division. As such, the invasion of Laos provides an ideal opportunity to trace the impact of differing military organizational practices both across and within the two armies. The evidence again confirms the importance of these practices and suggests their close connection to the differing threat environments facing the two regimes. During the battle, ARVN units

Table 3.4. The invasion of Laos, 1971

	North Vietnam	South Vietnam
Battle summary		
Tactical orientation	Defensive, then offensive	Offensive, then defensive
Plan	Ambush ARVN forces, overrun firebases, drive ARVN out of Laos	Raid PAVN stronghold in Laos by establishing a chain of firebases, then withdraw
Weapons	Tanks, artillery, rifles, machine guns, mortars, rocket launchers	APCs, tanks, other vehicles, light antitank weapons, artillery, U.S. helicopters
Manpower	At least 30,000	17,000
Losses	~20,000	7,000+ KIA
Effectiveness summary		
Tactical proficiency?	Yes	No, except 1st Division
Complex operations?	Yes	No, except 1st Division
As expected?	Yes	Yes

generally proved themselves incapable of tactical proficiency or complex operations, in large part because of the factionalism of Saigon's military government, but the ARVN 1st Division was again an exception to this pattern. Its effectiveness was much more similar to that of the PAVN, which consistently demonstrated tactical proficiency and the ability to conduct complex operations.

The Forces on Each Side

The South Vietnamese invasion of Laos, known as Lam Son 719, began in early February 1971. It aimed to attack crucial nodes of the Ho Chi Minh Trail, particularly two major supply areas known as Base Areas 604 and 611. These were located near a deserted village known as Tchepone, about forty miles inside Laos. The sole route of approach to Tchepone was an old French-built highway called Route 9, bordered to the south by the Xepon River, which flowed under triple canopy vegetation all the way to the village (see map 3.4).[122] To the south of Route 9, just adjacent to the Laotian border, was the Co Roc highland, a 2.5-mile mountain range that provided excellent observation of both Route 9 to the west and Khe Sanh to the east. Farther west into Laos, south of Route 9 and the river, was a high escarpment that overlooked both. To the north of Route 9 was hilly terrain with heavy vegetation.[123]

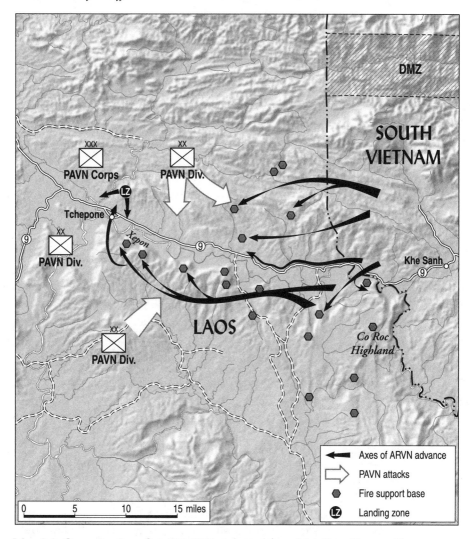

Map 3.4. Operation Lam Son 719, 1971. Adapted from Maj. Gen. Nguyen Duy Hinh, *Lam Son 719*, Indochina Monograph (Washington, DC: U.S. Army Center of Military History, 1977), 26; and James Willbanks, *Abandoning Vietnam: How America Left and South Vietnam Lost Its War* (Lawrence: University Press of Kansas, 2008), 104.

To conduct Lam Son 719, the ARVN marshaled the 1st Division, as well as elements of the 1st Armor Brigade, 3 Ranger battalions from I Corps, the Airborne division, and two Marine brigades—about 17,000 troops in total.[124] The 1st Division was commanded by Brigadier General Phu, a man with extensive combat experience who was described as

[99]

"competent and hard-working." Unfortunately, the other ARVN commanders in the operation did not have similarly sterling reputations. The I Corps commander, in charge of the overall operation, was Lt. Gen. Hoang Xuan Lam, a man with little combat experience of his own who had earned the nickname "Bloody Hands" because of his fatally inadequate attention to operations.[125] His primary interests were military administration and his daily game of tennis.[126]

Lt. Gen. Du Quoc Dong, equal in rank to Lam, commanded both the Airborne and Armor forces involved in the battle. A close political ally of Thieu, he too had little command experience and had already shown himself to lack initiative during an incursion into Cambodia the previous year. The Marine commander, Lt. Gen. Le Nguyen Khang, was not much better. An ally of Ky, he remained in Saigon throughout the operation and delegated most command decisions to Col. Bui The Lan, who was considered more competent.[127]

The ARVN plan envisioned the Armor units moving directly down Route 9 while the other forces established a series of firebases along the sides of the narrow path to protect the advance. Specifically, the 1st Division was to secure the Co Roc and the escarpment south of Route 9, while the 1st Airborne battalion and 1st Ranger battalion were to be dropped into the hilly terrain north of Route 9. The northern flanking forces were then to converge on Tchepone and Base Area 604, while the southern flanking forces were to move in and clear out Base Area 611. Meanwhile, the Vietnamese Marines were to serve as reserve forces in the Khe Sanh area.[128] In many ways, the operation was intended to be a replay of the previous year's successful, largely unopposed incursion into Cambodia.[129]

Precisely because that operation had wrecked supply routes through Cambodia, however, the North Vietnamese now recognized the importance of defending their bases in Laos. According to the PAVN's official account, in late 1970 North Vietnam formed the 70th Corps-Sized Group, consisting of the 304th, 308th, and 320th divisions, plus a number of specialty branch regiments and battalions, to counter any potential South Vietnamese moves into Laos. By early 1971 North Vietnamese forces in the area had "grown to 60,000 troops, consisting of five divisions (308th, 304th, 320th, 324th, and 2nd), two separate infantry regiments (27th and 278th), eight artillery regiments, three engineer regiments, three tank battalions, six anti-aircraft regiments, and eight sapper battalions, plus rear service and transportation units."[130] South Vietnamese estimates put enemy combat strength at more like 30,000, but either way, it is clear that North Vietnam had a large concentration of forces in the area.[131]

Sent to the front as the representative of the Central Military Party Committee and the High Command was Colonel General Van Tien Dung,

[100]

and in command was Major General Le Trong Tun, deputy commander of the Joint General Staff. The PAVN adds in its official history that "many senior cadre from the general departments and specialty branches were sent to reinforce the front's staff agencies. This was a strong command structure with sufficient ability and authority to command all forces participating in the campaign and to coordinate operations."[132]

The Battle

The initial phases of the invasion went well for South Vietnam. The ARVN Armor column advanced approximately twelve miles along Route 9 and linked up with the Airborne. Five firebases were established along the way, with Airborne and Ranger units guarding the northern flank of the westward advance and the 1st Division guarding the southern flank. By the end of the first week, however, the forward advance of the Armor and Airborne had slowed, in part because of the need to repair the road, so "a decision was made to step up the operation by having the 1st Infantry Division quickly occupy the higher mountain tops south of the Xepon River and establish fire support bases there to support the Airborne Division's push toward Tchepone."[133]

Although the 1st Division succeeded in this task, pushing south and successfully engaging the enemy at several points, ARVN Armor progress remained very slow, in part because Route 9 needed to be repaired along the way. According to one account, "on 11 February, the attack ground to a halt. . . . The ARVN force just stopped attacking." Lacking orders urging them forward, "the South Vietnamese forces in Laos sat where they were."[134] Meanwhile, the initial sluggishness of the Armor advance had given the PAVN time to reinforce its presence in the area, activating what was soon revealed to be a dense network of defenses. The PAVN began to lay siege to stalled ARVN units isolated along Route 9, massing infantry, armor, and artillery to attack them piecemeal.[135]

Soon the PAVN overran the Rangers' firebase, leaving the remaining two firebases guarded by the Airborne even more exposed. The first of these was then overrun in a combined armor-infantry attack that the Airborne failed to repel, despite having significant quantities of light antitank weapons. U.S. airpower was of little use in defending these bases, because the PAVN intentionally hugged the South Vietnamese positions.[136]

Seeing the Airborne's losses, Thieu again became anxious that the division would be destroyed, so he suggested that it be removed from battle and replaced with the Marines.[137] Lam had the sense to see the infeasibility of this suggestion: "such a relief under the combat conditions on that battlefield would be very hazardous."[138] Flying to Saigon to

[101]

meet with Thieu, Lam instead proposed that the Airborne simply drop back to protect Route 9 from the north, while allowing the 1st Infantry alone to continue west. It would now be the 1st Division that would make a heliborne assault on Tchepone, with the 1st Marine brigade following behind it and the 3rd Marine brigade remaining in reserve.[139]

Thieu accepted this plan and then adjusted the overall objective of the operation as well: the goal was now simply to reach Tchepone, rather than to destroy the base areas. Reaching the town "had become more of a political and psychological symbol than an objective of practical military value. There was nothing of military importance in the ruined town; enemy supplies and war materiel were all stored in caches in the forests and mountains."[140] But the ARVN now had to press on in service of this new directive.

The Airborne soon lost its remaining firebase under continuing heavy infantry-armor attacks from the PAVN.[141] But the 1st ARVN successfully executed heliborne assaults to the west, establishing three bases in the face of intense resistance.[142] Then the 1st Division "fought aggressively, repeatedly engaged the enemy, and defeated him everywhere," getting to Tchepone in just three days.[143] The next day the 1st Division's rapid reaction force, the Hac Bao, also successfully landed near Tchepone and extracted the crew of a U.S. aircraft that had gone down as it supported the final attack.[144] According to a South Vietnamese general whose memoirs are otherwise quite critical of ARVN performance in the operation, "The Black Panthers scored a major combat exploit by rescuing all the Americans and subsequently made contact with the enemy, sustaining light casualties but killing more than 60 Northern troops. During this violent action, they also seized 30 NVA automatic rifles, destroyed an anti-aircraft gun position, and found another 40 NVA soldiers killed by airstrikes."[145]

Inside Tchepone, the 1st Division found modest amounts of rice, weapons, and enemy dead, but the North Vietnamese had already moved most of their supplies farther west. Nevertheless, with some ability to claim victory, President Thieu made the decision to end the operation right away, on March 15. The extremely difficult task of returning to South Vietnam along Route 9 now fell to the 1st Division. Instead of the road having been secured by Armor and Airborne units as originally planned, the PAVN could now pounce on it from all directions: the 308th Division from the north; elements of the 320th and 304th Divisions from the east; the 2nd Division directly in the path of the ARVN 1st; and the 324th Division near the Co Roc, where the Marines had tried to enter the battle as reinforcements. A South Vietnamese general likened the PAVN to a hunter about to kill his prey by "locking its head and gripping its tail."[146]

The 1st Division suffered extensive casualties as it fought its way back to positions from which it could be airlifted to South Vietnam.[147] As the rear guard element, the 4th battalion of the 1st infantry regiment suffered particularly high losses in a day-long battle that left only thirty-two survivors. Nevertheless, the battalion did not break. It "had accomplished well its rear guard mission and in the process, had sacrificed nearly every man," while inflicting much larger casualties on the North Vietnamese units. By contrast, the Armor and Airborne units did return, but their "withdrawal along Route No. 9 surely did not proceed as planned in an orderly and controlled manner."[148] The Marines also chose to make a hasty withdrawal rather than waiting for orders from General Lam.[149]

Total ARVN casualties were 9,065. The PAVN's were estimated to be above 20,000, although this total includes numerous men killed by U.S. air strikes and artillery.[150] Both sides claimed victory.

Assessing the Battlefield Effectiveness of South Vietnam

Lam Son 719 was a nearly unmitigated disaster for the ARVN, which other than the 1st Division demonstrated virtually no battlefield effectiveness. Certainly, the North Vietnamese had known an attack was coming, and their defenses were prepared along the ARVN's inevitable axes of advance. The terrain and bad weather further slowed the ARVN's advance. Nevertheless, with the exception of the 1st Division, most ARVN forces showed serious deficits in tactical proficiency and the ability to conduct complex operations—deficits that were clearly linked to South Vietnam's military organizational practices.

First, most ARVN forces continued to display severe problems with basic tactical proficiency. For example, although the Airborne troops faced difficult odds in defending their firebases, they were armed with light antitank weapons that could have significantly impeded the PAVN's armor-infantry attacks (and, in turn, protected the 1st Division's eventual withdrawal down Route 9). But the Airborne troops repeatedly fired the weapons inside the minimum range needed to arm the projectile, rendering the weapons virtually useless. The Airborne troops apparently believed, or at least later reported, that the weapons were defective, though retesting revealed that the weapons were in working order.[151] The problem was not with the hardware but with the ARVN's lack of basic tactical skills.[152] As a South Vietnamese history put it, "The Airborne Division did not perform as brilliantly as its reputation would indicate during Lam Son 719." Instead, "when a FSB was threatened with being overrun, the only course of action our unit commanders took was to destroy the artillery, abandon the base, and extricate their troops by

[103]

helilift."[153] A U.S. general shared this impression, bluntly noting that "the effectiveness of the ABN DIV [Airborne Division] is below required standards."[154]

Similar problems plagued the Armor units, which the same U.S. general characterized as "dissappointing [sic]."[155] Hihn notes, "Gunners proved to be confused and hasty, firing from too far away and often too soon, thereby frequently causing deflections." In addition, armored vehicles were used primarily for transportation, not for maneuver or even firepower. As one ARVN general later lamented, "We had 300 armored vehicles but they could barely control 12 miles of road."[156] In fact, the Armor units ultimately abandoned two-thirds of their vehicles on Route 9, even though many were still in working order.[157] These included twenty-one tanks, twenty-six armored personnel carriers, thirteen bulldozers, two graders, and fifty-one other vehicles that had to be destroyed by U.S. airpower and artillery the next day to prevent them from falling into enemy hands.[158]

Meanwhile, none of these basic tactical problems were reported with regard to the 1st Division.[159] It was instead described as "topping the honor roll," "well led," "the number one ARVN combat unit," and producing "splendid results" and a "fine performance."[160] Where the 1st Division demonstrated "discretion and initiative" and was able to maneuver after first contact with the enemy, other ARVN units tended toward passivity. According to Hinh, the 1st Division's performance was "commendable" in situations in which other units "tended to stop and wait for support, rather than conduct probes and maneuver to attack or close in on the enemy."[161]

Beyond basic tactics, Lam Son 719 was a damning indictment of the ARVN's ability to conduct complex operations. Repeatedly, ARVN forces displayed an inability to combine arms. For example, more than eight years after Ap Bac, the ARVN still failed to coordinate movement with artillery or air support.[162] Indeed, this shortcoming as described in the Laos operation was virtually identical to that noted by U.S. advisers during the early 1960s.[163]

More important, the fracturing of the ARVN command structure profoundly hindered the application of low-level initiative in support of a higher-level plan, the real key to complex operations. For example, even if the Armor, Airborne, and Ranger units had been more cohesive or tactically proficient, it is not clear that these improvements would have translated into much greater fighting effectiveness, because the politically powerful commanders of these units refused to participate in the joint campaign plan devised by Lam.[164] According to a South Vietnamese officer's account, Lam was virtually ignored by the two commanders of the Airborne and Marine divisions, lieutenant generals themselves who were more accustomed, as commanders of national strategic reserve forces, to answering directly to Saigon rather than responding to a corps commander. They contested Lam's orders and directives at every opportunity. Although Lam appealed to President Thieu for support, Thieu refused to reprimand Lam's subordinate commanders, even when their actions bordered on insubordination during the heat of the battle.[165]

For example, it was Dong who ordered the Armored units to stop moving forward early in the operation and Khang who ordered his Marines to withdraw early.[166]

Why did Thieu refuse to rebuke, or better yet fire, Dong and Khang? Not because he lacked information about how his command arrangements were affecting the course of the battle.[167] Rather, Thieu did not intervene because he believed Dong's Airborne was the best safeguard against a coup, and because Khang's Marines secured the power of Thieu's rival, Ky, whom he did not wish to provoke.[168] Thieu needed Dong's loyalty and Khang's continued neutrality. As one general put it, "the most important problem . . . was insubordination on the part of general reserve unit commanders who like many other generals considered themselves," correctly, "the pillars of the regime."[169] This is consistent with what the book's framework would expect given the nature of the South Vietnamese regime at the time.

Just as this sort of fracturing presented one set of problems, however, the centralization of ARVN command posed another. Thieu allowed a paralyzing division of authority to persist among his generals, but he used the authority he did retain to control the movement of units from Saigon, rather than devolving this power to Lam. Thieu's intervention in the course of the battle explains why the initial advance slowed, why the Airborne was replaced by the Marines midway through the operation, and why the goals of the campaign were scaled back in a manner that made withdrawal far more difficult.[170] Ultimately, the same elite forces tasked with conducting the invasion played vital roles in securing Thieu in power domestically, so he intervened to preserve them.

Only the 1st Division, stationed far from Saigon and largely irrelevant to maintaining Thieu in power, had anything resembling a unified, decentralized command structure. The division was directly controlled by Phu, who did not have to share authority with other generals or take tactical and operational orders from Saigon. Only the 1st Division, which was not responsible for backing any of the Republic's political leaders, actually followed Lam's orders and demonstrated some ability to conduct complex operations.[171] The result of these differing practices was clear. The deputy senior adviser to I Corps commented in his after-action report that despite the many ARVN shortcomings on display during Lam Son 719, "The 1st Division demonstrated the ability to conduct a large scale airmobile operation against a well trained, locally superior force. Many problems arose during the operation but most were solved on the spot."[172]

None of this suggests that Lam himself was a particularly worthy general. Even during this campaign, in which more than 7,000 ARVN soldiers would eventually lose their lives, Lam took breaks every day to play tennis.[173] Thieu had promoted him primarily based on political loyalty, and as the battle wore on Thieu eventually realized his error. On February 23, he tried to replace Lam with General Do Cao Tri, the III Corps commander who had proven himself competent during the incursion into Cambodia the previous year. Unfortunately, Tri was killed in a helicopter crash on his way to take command, leaving Lam in charge.[174] It is little wonder, then, that the larger ARVN force did not prove able to conduct complex offensive or defensive operations.

Assessing the Battlefield Effectiveness of North Vietnam

Although Lam Son 719 inflicted heavy losses on the North Vietnamese and probably delayed the Easter Offensive of 1972, the battles in Laos reflected well on the PAVN's actual battlefield effectiveness. The campaign is full of examples of the PAVN's clearly demonstrated tactical proficiency. For instance, PAVN units consistently made excellent use of the terrain surrounding Route 9 to conceal their positions, as well as to establish observation points for accurate fire.[175] According to the U.S. after-action report, PAVN forces "registered mortar, artillery, and rocket fires on most potential landing or pick up zones in the area. . . . Consequently, nearly every landing and pick up zone came under indirect fire attack soon after any allied airmobile operation began."[176] The PAVN also used the terrain to create "mutually supporting, well dug-in, crescent-shape, covered trench segments," called horseshoe blocks, which greatly slowed the ARVN advance.[177]

In addition, the PAVN demonstrated great proficiency in air defense. The U.S. after-action report from Laos notes, "The NVA skillfully deployed throughout the Lam Son 719 operational area an extensive, sophisticated, well-integrated, highly mobile air defense system. Large numbers of anti-aircraft weapons of several calibers were strategically positioned, well-camouflaged, and effectively dug-in."[178] It seems clear that PAVN soldiers possessed basic tactical skills and applied them more consistently than did the ARVN.

Most important, the PAVN demonstrated the ability to aggregate basic tactical skills into complex operations at both the small- and large-unit levels. The PAVN's own account of the battle emphasizes this strength, pointing to "the power of combined arms operations and innovative combat tactics" and recounting the PAVN's "outstanding combat record."[179] Both U.S. and South Vietnamese sources confirm these claims. For example, a U.S. report noted that even in very small units of ten to twelve members, the PAVN soldiers were capable of effectively combining arms such as small weapons, machine guns, mortars, and rocket launchers, to devastating effect and with excellent consistency.[180] According to an ARVN officer, "The enemy effectively coordinated all his capabilities, to include antiaircraft, artillery, mortars, and massive infantry formations."[181] Indeed, infantry and antiaircraft gunners coordinated their movements especially closely so as to "hug" ARVN positions and prevent the application of U.S. air support.[182]

Again, this coordination speaks to an operational sophistication missing in most of the ARVN. U.S. commanders also noted this integration in their reports during the campaign: "The enemy has demonstrated a knowledge of RVNAF tactics and techniques and an ability to coordinate the employment of AA [anti-aircraft], arty [artillery], infantry, and armor in his attempt to counter the RVNAF drive."[183] The PAVN also proved able to coordinate the movement of a multidivision force, another task that the ARVN's convoluted command structure rendered impossible. In short, there is a consensus that the PAVN demonstrated high levels of battlefield effectiveness in the campaign.

The Easter Offensive, 1972

Given the dwindling U.S. presence, one might envision the large-scale fighting involved in the PAVN's 1972 Easter Offensive as the perfect opportunity to gauge North and South Vietnamese effectiveness.[184] In reality, the battles do not offer as clean a test as one would like, because U.S. advisers and firepower were still decisive in most engagements.[185] Nevertheless, the U.S. role in the northernmost part of the country (Military Region 1, or MR-1) was initially more limited, providing a chance to examine the PAVN and ARVN—including the 1st Division—conducting both offensive and defensive operations in relative isolation. The battles there for Quang Tri and Hue show a notable contrast in the effectiveness of North and South Vietnamese forces, and between the ARVN 1st Division and other ARVN units, which is consistent with my argument.

Furthermore, the months-long series of battles provoked some changes even in the military organizational practices of these other ARVN units

[107]

Table 3.5. The Easter Offensive, 1972

	North Vietnam	South Vietnam
Battle summary		
Tactical orientation	Offensive, then defensive	Defensive, then offensive
Plan	Three-prong, multidivision attack to take and hold territory throughout South Vietnam	Defend and then re-take areas captured by PAVN forces
Weapons	T-54 tanks, 130-mm guns, 160-mm mortars, rockets, antitank missiles, antiaircraft guns and missiles	M-41 tanks, TOW missiles,[a] artillery; plus U.S. airpower, artillery, and naval gunfire
Manpower	14 divisions, 26 independent regiments, supporting armor and artillery units	13 divisions, 2 independent regiments, supporting armor and artillery units, plus Territorial Forces
Losses[b]	~85,000–100,000 casualties	~30,000 KIA, 78,000 WIA, 14,000 MIA[c]
Effectiveness summary		
Tactical proficiency?	Yes	No, except 1st Division
Complex operations?	Yes	No, except 1st Division
As expected?	Yes	Yes

[a] Tube-launched, optically-tracked, wire-guided missiles.
[b] Andradé, *America's Last Vietnam Battle*, 487, 492.
[c] Missing in action.

as the external, conventional threat to their country became increasingly severe. The Easter Offensive (see table 3.5) truly raised the prospect of national destruction for South Vietnam, and for the first time the country's leaders pushed units other than the 1st Division to move away from coup prevention practices and toward conventional war practices. In combination with massive U.S. firepower, these changes were enough to turn the tide against the North Vietnamese and save the country, at least temporarily. They suggest again the connection between threats and military organizational practices.

The Forces on Each Side

The Easter Offensive involved a massive PAVN conventional assault along three avenues of advance into northern, central, and southern South Vietnam. In the north, the primary region of focus here, three North Vietnamese infantry divisions attacked into Quang Tri province across the demilitarized zone (DMZ) and from sanctuaries in Laos on March 30, 1972. Total PAVN forces in this area of operations included three infantry divisions, two antiaircraft divisions, nine field artillery regiments, two tank and armored regiments, two engineer regiments, and sixteen battalions of sapper, signal, and transportation troops.[186]

Facing the PAVN in Military Region 1 was the ARVN I Corps, commanded by General Hoang Xuan Lam—still in charge despite his disastrous performance in Lam Son 719 the previous year.[187] Directly defending the DMZ was the ARVN 3rd Division, under the command of General Vu Van Giai, considered to be a very good officer.[188] In addition to this newly established division, formed to replace the departing U.S. Marines, I Corps included the 1st Division, still under the command of Major General Pham Van Phu, as well as the 2nd Division, the 51st Infantry Regiment, the 1st Ranger Group, and the 1st Armor Brigade.[189]

The Initial Battles in the North: The Fall of Quang Tri Province

North Vietnam's opening salvo caught the ARVN off-guard as the 3rd Division rotated its troops among their firebases on March 30. Unleashing well-planned and highly accurate 130-mm artillery fire, the PAVN launched well-coordinated armor-infantry attacks from the north across the DMZ, as well as from the west through Khe Sahn.[190] According to a South Vietnamese account, "Enemy forces conducting these initial attacks included elements of the NVA 304th and 308th Divisions, three separate infantry regiments of the B-5 Front, two armor regiments, five artillery regiments, and at least one sapper battalion."[191]

Over the next several days, the PAVN quickly overran the 3rd Division's network of small outposts intended to prevent the capture of the province. As North Vietnam's official account of the campaign relates, "After the artillery's destructive barrages, combined-arms forces launched assaults in the main sectors. . . . We also launched coordinated operations to encircle enemy forces, make deep penetrations to the east, cut supply routes, and isolate the campaign area from the south. During the first two days of combat our troops overran one entire group of strong points . . . [and] shattered the enemy's strong outer defensive perimeter."[192] Indeed, panic engulfed ARVN units as they observed refugees fleeing the areas of PAVN attack, and fire support coordination to these outlying areas was poor.[193]

The ARVN was soon forced to contract to a much tighter defensive perimeter around the obvious target of the attack: the provincial capital, Quang Tri City (see map 3.5). As an ARVN account of the battle notes,

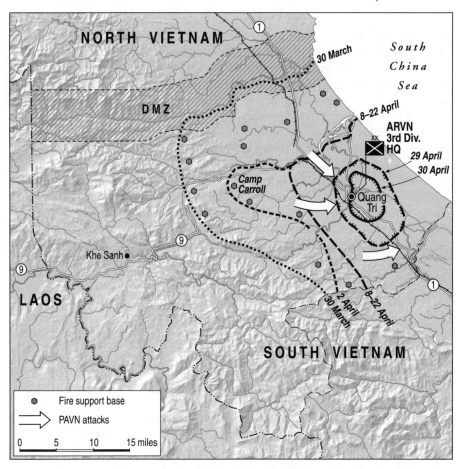

Map 3.5. ARVN defensive lines in Military Region 1, 1972. Adapted from Lt. Gen. Ngo Quang Truong, *The Easter Offensive of 1972* (Washington, DC: U.S. Army Center of Military History, 1980), 42.

"Both ARVN regular and territorial forces seemed to hold extremely well along this new line. To their credit, they had stopped the NVA invasion— for the time being. They had performed their task well, not through reliance on U.S. air support but with their own combat support."[194]

The last claim is somewhat true, in the sense that bad weather did prevent close air support to most units during this initial phase.[195] Lack of air support was also somewhat the ARVN's own fault, however, as its disorderly retreat made avoiding friendly fire difficult. Furthermore, the

[110]

ARVN still benefited from immense U.S. naval gunfire and B-52 strikes. As one history notes, "Before April 1972, U.S. air activities in MR-1 were at a low level. Any 24-hour period with more than 10 tactical air sorties was considered a busy day." This tempo changed dramatically after March 30, with U.S. air sorties rising to 300 or more per day, every day. It was common to see more than 30 B-52 missions in a single 24-hour period.[196] Notably, ARVN troops were not subject to reciprocal attack; the PAVN did not have air forces over South Vietnam.

In any event, General Lam was not especially concerned. Without having visited the front to inspect the 3rd Division's line, Lam ordered a counterattack to the west on April 14, although he was careful to check his horoscope first so that he could choose the correct hour. Despite clear weather that enabled a significant surge in U.S. air support, the ARVN units defending the line refused to attack as ordered.[197] "The troops still clung to their trenches and made no significant effort to move forward," according to a South Vietnamese account of the battle. "By the end of the first week of the operation, no unit had advanced more than 500 meters from the line of departure." Part of the problem was morale, according to this same source: "It seemed that the subordinate commanders knew that their units lacked the strength to break through the NVA formations facing them, that the enemy's artillery would surely catch them in the open and destroy them, and that the coordinated fire and logistical support they would need to carry the attack was beyond the capability of the 3rd Division or I Corps to provide."[198]

These doubts stemmed directly from broader problems with General Giai's command of the 3rd Division, which bore a strong resemblance to the ARVN difficulties seen the previous year during Lam Son 719. Although Giai was technically responsible for all of the forces holding the line against the PAVN, he actually had authority over only his own division, not over the Marines, Armor units, or Rangers in the area. This might have been just as well given that, as a division commander, he lacked the headquarters needed to truly control such a large group of forces.[199]

The problem was that the Marines and Rangers also were not controlled by I Corps. Instead, the Rangers remained under their separate command out of Da Nang, while the Marines continued to be led from their headquarters in Hue. As one ARVN officer later speculated, "Perhaps General Lam did not feel certain he could handle the Marine Division commander who, during Lam Son 719, had failed to comply with his orders but still came out unscathed."[200] After all, the Marine commander, General Khang, was a close political ally of President Thieu's rival Ky, and reprimanding or threatening him risked upsetting the delicate political balance that underlay the regime's stability.[201] The result—again—was a chain of command that was not much like a chain at all, but instead like a series of scattered links, each perhaps solid on its own but not connected together to forge anything stronger.

Lam did directly control the Armor units in I Corps, although this centralization posed its own set of problems, as he gave orders to these units without telling Giai.[202] Indeed, "Lam let Giai take responsibility for the battle, but he did not grant him any real authority. From Da Nang, Lam personally interceded at all levels, sometimes going so far as to personally issue orders by radio to individual brigade commanders without notifying the division operations center. Both Giai and his division advisers often learned of new orders only as they were being carried out."[203]

Predictably, Giai now found "that the orders he gave to his attached units had no effect until the subordinate commander had checked and received guidance from his parent headquarters. This was especially true if the orders required a difficult operation," such as an attempted counteroffensive.[204] In light of these delays, it is not difficult to understand why the 3rd Division was less than enthused about participating in a difficult attempt to retake territory. Even though Giai was competent, he lacked the authority to lead all the forces required to make the operation successful.

With the ARVN having failed to launch this initial counteroffensive, a week later the commander of the 1st Armor Brigade decided of his own accord to pull some of his units south in order to clear elements to his rear. Again, Giai was out of the loop, this time with dire consequences. As soon as other ARVN forces saw the Armor Brigade's tanks moving south, they were "gripped with panic, broke ranks, and streamed along." Before Giai even realized what had happened, many of his troops had abandoned their positions, and the line of defense collapsed—not because of PAVN attacks but because of an internal ARVN command problem. Once Giai recognized the issue, he managed to reestablish the defenses, but this time in an even tighter circle around Quang Tri City.[205]

As April wore on, Giai's lines continued to move closer and closer to Quang Tri. Unit discipline began to collapse as the 3rd Division became increasingly isolated.[206] Then on April 27, the North Vietnamese launched a new assault. The 308th, 304th, and 324th divisions, along with artillery and tank support units, overran the remaining defenders outside the city in a series of well-coordinated attacks.[207]

By April 30, Giai realized the city would fall and began planning for withdrawal. But at the last minute, on the morning of May 1, General Lam called Giai to tell him not to withdraw after all: "All units were to remain where they were and hold their positions 'at all costs.'" Lam added that "no withdrawal of any unit would be permitted unless he personally gave the authorization" after receiving it from President

Thieu, who was apparently now directing events from Saigon.[208] Lam was afraid to share with Thieu and the Joint General Staff the true scale of the threat, downplaying PAVN advances and overstating ARVN capabilities.[209]

In a disturbing echo of what had happened in Laos, and a preview of what would happen in 1975, this sudden change in orders from an uninformed Thieu was a disaster, resulting in neither a robust defense of the city nor a clean withdrawal. "And so within the space of four hours," as an ARVN general later put it, "the ARVN dispositions for defense crumbled completely."[210] Or as the North Vietnamese history later recounted, "Surrounded and isolated, the enemy troops . . . broke and ran. Our troops clung to and pursued them. Accurate fire from our long-range artillery positions created added terror among the enemy troops. Abandoning their vehicles and artillery pieces, enemy troops fled on foot."[211] The ARVN abandoned the city, with General Giai attempting unsuccessfully in the final moments to catch up with his own fleeing troops in a commandeered armored vehicle. Thieu had him arrested in Da Nang on May 5.[212]

The Second Set of Battles in the North: The Defense of Hue and the Retaking of Quang Tri Province

All of Quang Tri was now in the North's hands, the first time in the war that the DRV had gained control of an entire province. This conquest opened the door to Hue, the imperial capital only about forty miles away that the PAVN had tried so hard to capture in 1968. The 304th and 308th divisions had already been attacking it since March, with the 1st Division again holding them off in a series of battles in the foothills to the west of the city.[213]

The 1st Division also had conducted a major counterattack into the A Shau Valley on March 5, successfully airlifting forces into six landing zones and coordinating movement with ARVN artillery and U.S. airpower to drive back the North Vietnamese. The 3rd Regiment of the 1st Division temporarily retook territory at the mouth of the valley, holding it long enough to kill more than 200 PAVN soldiers who stood and fought for it viciously. Massively outnumbered, the ARVN regiment eventually had to withdraw on March 16, but the operation had clearly upset the PAVN's offensive timetable for Hue.[214]

The PAVN gradually moved closer to the city throughout March, until Hue seemed on the verge of being attacked.[215] This reality, combined with the loss of Quang Tri province and the panic engulfing civilians in the area, finally forced Thieu to reconsider his military's organizational practices, at least with respect to promotions. First, Thieu removed

[113]

General Le Nguyen Khang from command of the Marine Division, replacing him with Colonel Bui The Lan, the more competent field commander from the Laos operation in 1971. Second, he removed General Lam from command of I Corps, replacing him with the highly able General Truong, the former commander of the 1st Division and now the commander of IV Corps.[216] In short, Thieu fired the two officers responsible for the disasters in 1971 and 1972 and put competent, proven combat leaders in their stead.

In his memoir, Truong recounted that the command shake-up took effect immediately, enabling him to establish a new forward headquarters for I Corps at Hue. He quickly assembled a new staff of officers "who had solid military backgrounds, both in the field and in staff work, a rare assemblage of talents." As he explained, "I had wanted to make sure that they knew how to use sensibly and coordinate effectively all corps combat components and supporting units in a conventional warfare environment." These moves buoyed I Corps, bringing about "a restoration of confidence among combat units. They all felt reassured that from now on they would be directed, supported, and cared for in a correct manner."[217]

Unfortunately, the only functioning units left in the area were the 1st Division and the Marines. Nevertheless, Truong began to organize a defense in depth of Hue—the type that should have been established in the first place by the 3rd Division around Quang Tri City—and the Americans initiated a massive barrage of naval gunfire, artillery, and aerial bombing against PAVN forces to the west.

During May and June, both the 1st Division and the Marines launched limited but effective counterattacks from their forward positions. In the face of the Marine attack, the North Vietnamese units were surprised, "resisted weakly and incurred extremely heavy losses." The 1st Division also retook two of the westernmost firebases that had been lost earlier, conducting another round of carefully coordinated airborne operations to seize them. Meanwhile, the Marines fought off PAVN armor-infantry attacks to the northeast, and Colonel Lan was promoted to general.[218]

Again, however, it bears noting that U.S. firepower continued to play a crucial role. In the month of May alone, for example, the United States flew more than 6,000 sorties in I Corps. South Vietnam's air force played only a very limited role. U.S. naval gunfire was also massive, with as many as thirty-eight destroyers and three cruisers committed to the effort during the month of June. On a light day, these ships might fire 1,000 rounds of support, while on heavy days the expenditure rose to as many as 7,000 rounds. To be sure, General Truong deserved great credit for improving the fire support coordination procedures, including the emplacement of forward observer teams to call in naval gunfire, which enabled the effective use of these U.S. assets.[219] Nevertheless, the fact remains that the ARVN was highly dependent on these sources of nonorganic firepower for its very survival, a fact that the PAVN history notes.[220]

Throughout May and June, Truong also oversaw an aggressive refitting and retraining effort in I Corps consistent with conventional war practices. As he explained, "A two-week quick recovery training program was conducted at each unit by ARVN and U.S. mobile training teams, usually at battalion level with all officers and NCOs attending. This program included both the theory and practice of marksmanship, the handling of individual and crew-served weapons, reconnaissance and tactics." Instructors also emphasized the proper use of the new TOW (tube-launched, optically tracked, wire-guided) antitank missile. Artillery units underwent counterbattery fire training, another crucial deficit that had been evident at least since Lam Son 719. The 3rd Division also was reconstituted, undergoing a complete retraining program. Many of the soldiers who had abandoned it returned when it was placed under the leadership of Brigadier General Nguyen Duy Hinh.[221]

Having made these preparations, Truong launched Operation Lam Son 72 to retake Quang Tri province on June 28. In this two-pronged counteroffensive, the Marines and the Airborne (who had been called in from Saigon) were to attack north, while the 1st Division would continue to pin down enemy forces southwest of Hue so that they could not join the offensive. Unfortunately, yet again the Airborne and Marine spearheads moved "slower than expected," and enemy resistance became heavy.[222] The PAVN defenders proved "ferocious," repeatedly interdicting the counteroffensives with infantry and armor attacks.[223] As General Truong later recalled, it became clear that the North planned to hold Quang Tri City "to the last man. . . . The enemy continued reinforcing; he was determined to go all out for the defense of this city. The ARVN drive was completely stalled."[224]

As had happened during Lam Son 719, the slowness of the ARVN offensive (or in this case, counteroffensive) had given the PAVN time to reinforce. By September, the North Vietnamese had flooded the area with their forces, which now included six infantry divisions: the 304th, 308th, 324B, 325th, 320B, and 312th. For its part, South Vietnam had only three divisions in northern I Corps and no additional reserves available.

As South Vietnamese officers readily admit, these forces soon became heavily reliant on U.S. firepower to break up the building concentrations of PAVN forces. Only after two months of heavy B-52 strikes and U.S. artillery bombardments did the South Vietnamese Marines finally retake Quang Tri City on September 15. The Airborne also retook two of the firebases remaining in enemy hands, while the 1st Division continued to defend Hue and eventually retook several of the firebases to the west of Hue, again with heavy U.S. air support.[225]

By October, MR-1 was stabilized. Although the ARVN certainly deserves credit for this eventual outcome, and in particular for changes in promotion, command, and training processes, it is also clear that these efforts would have been moot without U.S. support. ARVN forces would not have lived to make these changes, nor been able to reap the benefits of them, absent their superpower patron. As the PAVN history notes, "Eighty percent of our casualties were caused by U.S. air attacks and U.S. naval gunfire support."[226]

Assessing the Battlefield Effectiveness of South Vietnam

The Easter Offensive is often hailed as an ARVN triumph because the North Vietnamese ultimately failed to take Quang Tri and the other major areas of South Vietnam that they attacked. But a close look at the evidence suggests that this "victory" occurred largely despite ARVN combat performance rather than because of it, and because the PAVN was severely overmatched by U.S. firepower. Most of the ARVN units displayed serious deficits in tactical proficiency and the ability to conduct complex operations. Furthermore, these problems were directly attributable to their embrace of coup prevention practices. As one authoritative history notes, "The South Vietnamese army exhibited many of the same problems in 1972 as it had ten years earlier. . . . Clearly progress was being hampered by something other than manpower and materiel. Indeed, at the beginning of the offensive the South Vietnamese army was among the best equipped in the world."[227]

Most ARVN forces continued to exhibit significant problems with basic tactical proficiency. It is notable that when Truong took over I Corps, he did not simply reorganize the command structure and fix broken equipment; he initiated marksmanship training and basic instruction in handling individual and crew-served weapons. With three PAVN divisions breathing down his neck and the imperial capital of Vietnam at stake, it is hard to believe that Truong would have invested time and effort in these endeavors if ARVN troops had exhibited basic tactical proficiency during the opening stages of the battle.

Beyond basic tactics, the Easter Offensive presented a damning indictment of the ARVN's ability to conduct complex operations. Repeatedly, the ARVN displayed an inability to combine arms, whether on the offense or the defense. The extensive need for U.S. airpower was both a symptom and a cause of this problem. As one commander noted, "Since U.S. air support was so effective and always available, ARVN tactical commanders tended to disregard their own supporting weapons which were seldom used properly. Eventually the tendency to rely on B-52s or tactical air in the place of organic fires and maneuver became so commonplace that it inhibited initiative and often caused delays in conducting attacks."[228]

More important, the fractured, overly centralized ARVN command structure profoundly hindered the application of low-level initiative in support of a higher-level plan, the real key to complex operations. The few good officers who did exist repeatedly found that they had responsibility without authority. Command over their forces had to be shared with less competent colleagues, or units received disastrous direction from Saigon. Ultimately, even when groups of ARVN soldiers had been retrained, they often showed an inability to aggregate their skills into larger operations. For example, Truong had difficulty getting his troops to actually go on the offensive in retaking Quang Tri. Again, only the 1st Division proved able to conduct consistently well-coordinated offensive and defensive operations—an unsurprising feat given that it was the only major unit subject to long-standing conventional war practices. Overall, evidence from the Easter Offensive reinforces the connection from threats to practices to effectiveness.

Assessing the Battlefield Effectiveness of North Vietnam

Although the Easter Offensive inflicted heavy losses on the North Vietnamese and was a strategic failure, most of the fighting reflected well on the PAVN's actual battlefield effectiveness. First, the Easter Offensive is full of examples of the PAVN's clearly demonstrated tactical proficiency. Reports from all sources describe PAVN artillery barrages as highly accurate, its marksmanship as excellent, its antiaircraft fire as effective, its tank movement as generally adequate, and its antitank fires as especially impressive. Such evaluations reflect units that had engaged in rigorous and realistic training processes, producing skilled soldiers capable of using their weapons.

Second, the PAVN demonstrated the ability to aggregate basic tactical skills into complex operations at both the small- and large-unit levels. The PAVN generally was able to conduct combined arms operations. For example, it repeatedly proved successful in integrating artillery fires with infantry movement. Although the PAVN did not demonstrate total mastery of armored warfare, displaying some problems integrating the use of tanks with dismounted infantry, it is unclear how much these problems were a function of actual deficiencies in the PAVN and how much the result of the disorientation and disruption caused by U.S. firepower. To be sure, the North Vietnamese were critical of their own performance afterward and vowed to do better, but the contrast with the ARVN is nevertheless stark.[229]

In addition, the PAVN proved able to coordinate the movement of a multidivision force, another task that the ARVN had never executed successfully. North Vietnam's sheer ability to get fourteen divisions into the field and have them implement three separate corps-level attacks along multiple avenues of advance, all while taking a massive pounding from the air, reflects a unified, decentralized command structure. Moreover, in numerous instances these formations proved able to react appropriately to opportunities and setbacks on the battlefield, demonstrating an important integration of low-level initiative with a higher overall plan. For example, PAVN troops quickly exploited the gaps that they found in ARVN defensive lines around Quang Tri City. The PAVN performance was not perfect, but it certainly revealed a superior ability to conduct complex operations.

THE FINAL BATTLES, 1975

Despite their devastating losses in 1972 and the restrictions imposed by the Paris Peace Accords, the North Vietnamese retained an estimated 170,000 regular troops and 30,000 other soldiers inside South Vietnam after the 1973 U.S. withdrawal.[230] With the United States finally out of the picture, North Vietnam renewed its drive to conquer the South, culminating in the final series of battles in 1975.

The overall contours of this drive mimicked those of 1972 and even 1968, with many of the same units locking horns over the same real estate. What is remarkable about these battles is how rapidly Saigon fell and how little actual fighting occurred. Instead of devolving into a stalemate or showcasing another dynamic series of attacks and counterattacks, the battles of 1975 highlighted improvements in performance by the North Vietnamese and exposed just how heavily dependent on the United States most of the ARVN truly had been. Stripped of U.S. firepower and command structures, the ARVN's poisonous political-military relations exerted their full force, even in units that had previously been exempt, such as the 1st Division. The ARVN did not so much lose the final battles as self-destruct (see table 3.6).

Although some accounts of the final battles emphasize the North's numerical superiority or the South's shortages of ammunition and equipment, these factors do not tell the whole story.[231] Military organizational practices in the two states continued to exert a powerful and direct influence on fighting power. Although they were not the only factors that mattered, it is impossible to explain what happened in 1975 without

[118]

Table 3.6. The final offensives, 1975

	North Vietnam	South Vietnam
Battle summary		
Tactical orientation	Offensive	Defensive
Plan	Initial probe into MR-3, followed by major attacks in MR-1 and MR-2, culminating in attack on Saigon	Defend attacked areas; then execute strategic withdrawal from MR-1 and MR-2; defend Saigon
Weapons	Armor, artillery, air defense	Armor, artillery
Manpower	200,000, formed into 13 combat divisions, plus numerous independent regiments	300,000, formed into 14 combat divisions and 2 independent regiments
Losses[a]	~16,135 KIA	~13,847 casualties
Effectiveness summary		
Tactical proficiency?	Yes	No
Complex operations?	Yes	No
As expected?	Yes	Yes

[a] Figures calculated based on Michael Clodfelter, *Warfare and Armed Conflicts: A Statistical Reference to Casualty and Other Figures, 1500–2000* (Jefferson, NC: McFarland, 2001), 743.

them. Indeed, it is important to remember that the fall of Saigon was not preordained and came as a surprise to those on the ground. As late as 1974 the United States' own assessment indicated that the ARVN was "strong and resilient," and Hanoi was only slightly more optimistic, predicting that it could not conquer the South until 1976 at the earliest.[232]

The Forces on Each Side

The North Vietnamese retained roughly 200,000 soldiers in the South after 1973, up against about 300,000 ARVN combat soldiers (out of a total ARVN force of about 1.1 million). Despite their numbers, ARVN troops were spread thin, offering a variety of targets against which the North Vietnamese could mass forces and strike.[233] Furthermore, the PAVN had built more combat divisions out of its manpower. The ARVN had thirteen divisions, plus several independent regiments and numerous specialty units, while the PAVN fielded sixteen total divisions plus a large array of independent and specialty forces.[234]

The final battles came in three phases. First, the North Vietnamese probed a lightly defended province in MR-3, known as Phuoc Long, in

January 1975. Then they initiated full-scale attacks on MR-1 and MR-2 during March. Finally, they returned their focus to MR-3, converging on Saigon by the end of April.

On both sides, the forces and commanders were familiar, with many characters reprising earlier roles. General Truong still commanded the ARVN I Corps, where the Marines and Airborne were now stationed in addition to the 1st, 2nd, and 3rd divisions, one armored brigade, and four Ranger groups.[235] Despite this impressive show of force, the ARVN was outnumbered in MR-1. According to Veith, "While Truong controlled the most powerful command within the South Vietnamese military, he had few reserves, his units were under-strength, the terrain placed him at a tremendous disadvantage, and his firepower was drastically reduced."[236] By contrast, the PAVN had seven division equivalents in MR-1 by early March 1975, as well as several additional PAVN reserve divisions just north of the DMZ.[237] PAVN forces inside MR-1 included the 308th, 312th, and 320B divisions, as well as the 304th, the 325th, and the 324th.

More important, the North Vietnamese had vastly improved their road networks in MR-1 (and throughout South Vietnam), creating new lines of transportation referred to in the ARVN as "Ho Chi Minh east." These routes essentially gave the PAVN internal lines within South Vietnam, greatly shortening the distances the North Vietnamese had to traverse in order to get within striking distance of key cities and substantially increasing the speed of resupply efforts.[238]

Meanwhile, the ARVN II Corps had acquired new leadership—General Phu, the former commander of the 1st Division. Despite his strong reputation as a combat commander, however, Phu admitted that he felt unready for this new position, as he had little experience as a "headquarters man." Moreover, his predecessor, General Nguyen Van Toan, had not left II Corps in good shape. Toan "had turned the command into a petty fiefdom, parceling out provincial posts and other assignments on the basis of various personal gratuities. . . . Phu had been left with the vestiges of Toan's style of command—an inept staff with almost no feeling for the troops."[239]

Phu's troops included the 22nd and 23rd divisions, which both had new leaders since 1972, as well as several Ranger groups. Arrayed against these ARVN forces in MR-3 were five PAVN divisions: the NT3, F10, 320th, 968th, and 316th, plus fifteen independent regiments specializing in armor, artillery, antiaircraft fire, and engineering, for a total of more than 75,000 soldiers.[240]

PAVN forces again were led by General Van Tien Dung, who as a colonel general had led forces in Laos during Lam Son 719.[241] Dung shared Giap's belief that professional merit was more important than Party status in determining promotions.[242] Following the Politburo's direction to

[120]

assess the lessons of the Easter Offensive, Dung had overseen a massive review and retraining effort within the PAVN, with significant emphasis on improving tactical skills from the individual soldier up to large-unit formations.[243] He also had sought out Soviet instruction in combined arms tactics.[244]

Under Dung's leadership, the North Vietnamese had held a variety of realistic exercises emphasizing the use of combined arms at multiple levels of warfare. "In 1974," according to the PAVN history, "units held many staff and command-level exercises at the corps and division level to practice our different combat tactics." These included special exercises by the PAVN 1st Corps "involving an offensive campaign operation aimed at liberating a large city and attacking enemy forces mounting counterattacks on the outskirts of the city. Command and staff cadre at three levels, corps, division, and regiment, participated in the exercise."[245] Clearly, North Vietnam was prepared for conventional battle.

The Battles in II Corps

A January 1975 probe of Phuoc Long province in MR-3 convinced Hanoi that the United States would not intervene to defend South Vietnam. On March 10, the real offensive began as the PAVN launched a multidivision attack on Ban Me Thuot, the provincial capital of Darlac, in the very heart of the Central Highlands. II Corps forces were responsible for this area but were widely dispersed, with only one regiment of the 23rd Division defending the capital.[246] Dung had built up a substantial local superiority in numbers.[247] Following a powerful artillery barrage, two divisions of PAVN infantry and armor directly attacked the city from three directions, overrunning almost all of its defensive positions by the end of the day and bypassing the remaining pockets of resistance in order to attack the heart of the city.

The South Vietnamese air force also did the PAVN a favor by accidentally bombing the 23rd Division's command post, severing the defenders' communications and flattening any hope of organized resistance. One Ranger group made it to Ban Me Thuot to try to rescue the 23rd, but no sooner had it arrived than the division commander diverted it to secure a landing zone for the evacuation of his wife and children.[248] By the time the Rangers had completed this task, the battle was over, and Ban Me Thuot was in North Vietnamese hands.

Observing this disaster, President Thieu ordered General Phu to retake the city by airlifting another regiment of the 23rd into nearby Phuoc An. But this process took much longer than either Thieu or Phu expected. "Even more disastrous," according to the recollections of ARVN generals after the war, was that the troops lifted into the area " 'were not ready to fight' and began to desert in order to take care of their families" as soon as they arrived. Instead of trying to retake Ban Me Thuot, soldiers from the 23rd took off their uniforms and abandoned their weapons, hoping to blend in with the civilian population and escape.

Phu, who previously had enjoyed an excellent reputation as commander of the 1st Division, expressed grave reservations about the operation to those around him, complaining that he had done it only because of Thieu's order and that he remained "pessimistic about the chances of reoccupying the province capital." By March 14, Thieu must have agreed, because his approach to the fighting soon changed radically: instead of trying to save Ban Me Thuot, he told Phu that the remaining forces in II Corps were to abandon the two large provinces to the north, Pleiku and Kontum, and move to the coast, from which they would supposedly later be in a position to retake Ban Me Thuot. Not only were the forces to make this withdrawal immediately, but they were to execute it in secret, leaving behind the soldiers' own dependents, as well as the RF/PF troops. Moreover, II Corps was to accomplish the withdrawal using an old back road, Route 7B, that was heavily mined and had been in disrepair for some time.[249]

Thieu's orders were so bizarre, and so obviously infeasible, that even years after the war many ARVN officers and high-ranking officials had difficulty explaining them. South Vietnam's speaker of the House of Representatives went so far as to suggest that the decision to abandon the highlands might have been purely instrumental, aimed at "creating a state of emergency in the country which would consequently muzzle the mounting opposition" to Thieu's rule and possibly provoking U.S. intervention.[250] Certainly, this policy stood in stark contrast to Thieu's "four no's": no negotiations with the North Vietnamese, no North Vietnamese political activities south of the DMZ, no coalition government with the North Vietnamese, and no surrender of territory.

So entrenched was the four-no's policy that Phu's officers at first did not believe the orders, and many expressed their preference to stay in Kontum and Pleiku and fight. Perhaps sharing their shock, or fearing that he would be captured as he had been after Dien Bien Phu, Phu appears to have all but abdicated his command. He gathered his staff and departed for the coast, leaving behind a colonel to execute the withdrawal of 165,000 men, with "no staff, no planning, and no guidance from the [Joint General Staff] in Saigon, who themselves were at first unaware of Thieu's redeployment order." When the troops heard the order and realized their dependents were to be left behind and that their leaders had abandoned them, they lost all discipline. Local forces began to riot, and the colonel who had been left in charge had to use his pistol just to keep order at the airfield in Pleiku.[251]

Despite attempts to rapidly repair Route 7B during the next several days, the withdrawal quickly bottlenecked, alerting the population to its impending abandonment and causing hordes of refugees to join the withdrawing column (see map 3.6). The PAVN quickly began to attack the road. Years later, military officials present at the scene recalled the disaster: "Jammed with civilians and military alike, the road from Pleiku rapidly became a nightmare. Unit integrity completely disintegrated as did all semblance of control."

To make matters worse, an ARVN armored unit trying to clear an alternate route was hit by South Vietnam's own pilots, crushing any remaining morale in the withdrawing column. In some cases, soldiers actually began killing their officers and readily surrendering to the PAVN. "The despair was so great that at one point two or three guerrillas arriving at the scene could make prisoners of a hundred Rangers," according to witnesses.

Ultimately, "only about 20,000 of the 60,000 troops that had started out from Pleiku and Kontum finally got down to Tuy Hoa [on the coast], and these were no longer fit for combat. . . . Of the some 400,000 civilians who had attempted to flee . . . , only an estimated 100,000 got through," and they were still trickling in by April 1. RVN officials later called this withdrawal "the greatest disaster in the history of ARVN" and lamented that it "must rank as one of the worst planned and the worst executed withdrawal operations in the annals of military history."[252] The PAVN had certainly outfought the ARVN at Ban Me Thuot, but with his extreme centralization of command, President Thieu's interventions managed to turn the defeat of a single regiment into what would soon become the collapse of an entire corps.

The quick pace of events surprised even Hanoi, where the Politburo soon issued new orders to proceed with taking all of South Vietnam in 1975.[253] With the 23rd Division demolished, the PAVN was able to attack the 22nd, situated in the northernmost part of II Corps. Soon the 22nd was trapped from the north and south, and was driven almost into the sea by mid-March.[254]

Meanwhile, the other provinces of II Corps quickly collapsed despite strong resistance from the RF/PF forces. There was a complete breakdown in command and control of units in these areas, with several observers later defining the basic problem as a case of "no one was in charge." Phu himself never recovered from Thieu's initial orders to withdraw from the Central Highlands. After his initial abandonment of his corps, Phu later walked out of his headquarters and flew to Saigon. The other senior commanders in central Vietnam soon followed him. North Vietnam controlled almost all of the highlands and the coastal areas of II Corps by early April.[255]

[123]

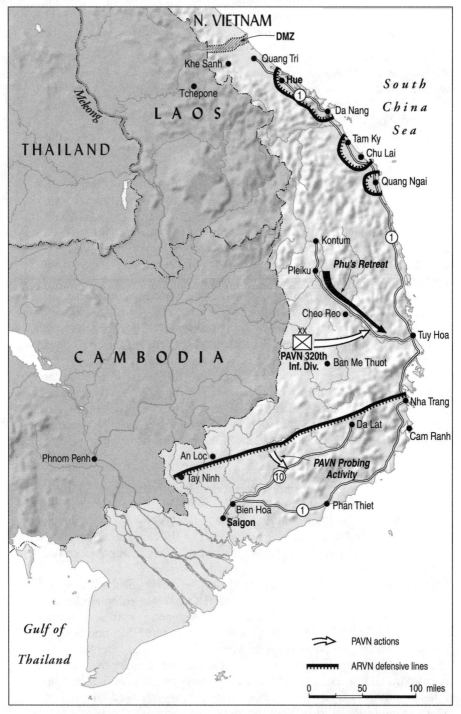

Map 3.6. The withdrawal from the highlands, 1975. Adapted from Frank Snepp, *Decent Interval* (New York: Random House, 1978), 205.

The Battles in I Corps

Simultaneously with their attacks in II Corps, the North Vietnamese launched an enormous offensive in MR-1 during early March, led by the 324th Division. Under General Truong's command, the ARVN did a decent job fighting off initial attacks near Hue and farther south in Quang Tin province, holding up in the face of the PAVN onslaught. New defenses-in-depth created by the 1st Division had "worked perfectly," imposing significant losses on the 324th.[256] But on March 10, Thieu apparently grew nervous about the possibility of a coup in Saigon and ordered the Airborne to return immediately from southern I Corps to protect him, similar to what had occurred during the operation in Laos in 1971.[257]

Apparently General Truong had become a little too effective for his own good. Ever since his success in retaking a province during the response to the Easter Offensive in 1972, Truong had enjoyed growing national stature, and now Thieu was suspicious that he faced a rival for national power.[258] As it later turned out, Thieu's fears were not entirely unfounded: according to one source, "Ky, by his own admission, had begun to approach other senior officers about removing Thieu after the loss of Ban Me Thuot," and it is possible that Truong was among them.[259] Regardless, Thieu did not want five divisions within Truong's orbit, despite the four-plus PAVN divisions threatening MR-1.

Truong, shocked by the military implications of Thieu's recall of the Airborne, coped as best he could with the sudden change. He moved two of the three Marine brigades in Quang Tri down to Quang Nam to defend the area formerly secured by the Airborne. But all of these rapid and unusual troop movements alarmed the population, causing them to initiate a massive refugee flow south, similar to what had just occurred in II Corps. Indeed, as news of the defeat at Ban Me Thuot and the abandonment of Kontum and Pleiku spread throughout the population of I Corps, the panic worsened. Many near the DMZ believed a secret deal had been struck to partition Vietnam anew and cede the northern regions to Hanoi.[260]

By March 13, these fears proved half-founded as Thieu informed Truong that "he had to give up most of I Corps," keeping only Da Nang and the immediately surrounding areas. Thieu described the new strategy as "light at the top, heavy at the bottom." In other words, the ARVN would give up much of I and II Corps, withdrawing to fight from the coasts and the areas surrounding Saigon.[261] Soon, however, even this strategy proved futile, as 2 million refugees flooded into Da Nang, a coastal city of only 300,000 people, and clogged the major roads in I Corps.

On March 19, Truong tried to convince Thieu to reconsider his decision to withdraw all the way to Da Nang, explaining that such a withdrawal was infeasible due to the refugee situation and that it was better "to stay in Hue and fight" because he had established "good defensive positions around Hue." Thieu eventually agreed with Truong's suggestion and re-assured him that the Marine Division would remain in I Corps as well, a critical point on which Truong sought reassurance for planning pur-poses. According to witnesses, "after hearing this new decision, General Truong reported he 'felt good,'" that he could still sustain the defense of his region for some time. Immediately after the meeting, however, the prime minister privately informed Truong that "there were indeed plans under way to bring back the Marines." Truong was "crushed" and filled with despair.[262]

Matters only worsened the next day when Truong returned to Da Nang, and the Joint General Staff relayed a new and confusing set of ad-ditional instructions. In what remains a matter of historical controversy, Truong interpreted these new instructions as telling him to abandon Hue.[263] According to Joint General Staff officers interviewed after the war, the message was intended only to warn Truong that Saigon had a limited ability to support forces in I Corps and that he had permission to withdraw from Hue to Da Nang when he felt it necessary. To Truong, however, the ambiguous message came across as meaning Saigon would not support the defense of Hue in the first place and that he must go ahead and withdraw to Da Nang. As several high-ranking RVN officials noted after the war, "This misunderstanding was but one manifestation of the serious problems in communication and coordination that existed between the I Corps and Saigon staffs. . . . When the Americans had been in Vietnam, I Corps could rely on U.S. channels. However, with the de-parture of U.S. forces, coordination was no longer 'appropriate' to deal with the situation."[264]

Even this debacle became somewhat moot by the next day, however. Two PAVN divisions, the 324th and 325th, cut the road between Hue and Da Nang, "despite intensive close air support and a determined counter-attack by a Marine battalion rushed to the area." The PAVN also put pres-sure on ARVN forces north of Hue, threatening a total envelopment of the city. In the face of these developments, "the cohesion of the South Vietnamese forces began to give way. The I Corps Chief of Staff stated that 'everything was out of control' and that the commanders 'reported back that they could not control their troops, that the troops deserted, that they did not have enough supplies and that they could not control the situation. They reported that they had to abandon Hue.'"[265]

Similarly, the PAVN history notes that "under the pressure of our at-tacks, enemy troops in Hue collapsed into disorder."[266] The Navy and Marines that were supposed to provide evacuation for ARVN forces by sea failed to arrive at the right locations on time. Though they had "fought valiantly," many 1st Division soldiers were now drowned in rising tides in the areas where they were supposed to await evacuation, while others were killed by PAVN forces because the Marines had not secured the rendezvous points as planned. All vestiges of discipline evaporated.[267] Ultimately, "less than half of the troops scheduled for evacuation . . . arrived in Da Nang, and those that did make their way there were completely disorganized. . . . The 1st Infantry remnants [then] dispersed in an effort to find their dependents and were no longer of fighting value." Amazingly, despite the Joint General Staff's message of the previous day, "Hue's abandonment apparently came as a surprise to President Thieu."[268]

Meanwhile, the battle was not over in the southern part of I Corps. There the PAVN overcame the 2nd Division's defenses and cut all routes to Da Nang, splitting the Corps area in half. The 2nd Division was totally surrounded and had to be evacuated by sea. Only about 2,000 of the division's troops ever made it to Saigon.[269]

With the ARVN 1st and 2nd Divisions utterly dismantled, the PAVN could now turn to the remaining 3rd Division, two Marine brigades, and various RF/PF units in and around Da Nang. Not only were these forces outnumbered, but the city behind them was raging out of control with refugees, looting, lack of sufficient food and water, and nowhere near enough police. General Truong was unwilling to turn back the hordes of people seeking safety and desperately sought aid from Saigon, but "except for a few transport flights, no help was forthcoming."[270]

Desertions by both officers and enlisted men increased rapidly as it became a situation of every man for himself and his family.[271] The North Vietnamese history of the battle claims that all of the Marine units in Da Nang simply abandoned their defensive positions.[272] Not mentioned in this history is that the PAVN also began shelling Da Nang, including areas teeming with civilians. Observing the carnage, Truong asked Thieu for permission to withdraw, but Thieu again equivocated and refused to make a decision. After PAVN artillery cut communications with Saigon, "General Truong made the decision on his own to withdraw."[273]

In one of the many ironies of 1975, the Marines, whose recall to Saigon had prompted much of Truong's despair, were virtually destroyed as a fighting force in the withdrawal. Less than half the division made it out by sea. Similarly, out of the 12,000-man 3rd Division, only about 5,000 men made it to the evacuation point, and of them only a thousand could board the single ship that arrived. In an odd contrast to the many previous years of high casualties, South Vietnamese combat losses in I Corps in March are estimated to have been only 1,000–2,000 soldiers—regrettable, certainly, but relatively light given the stakes involved. As the ARVN chief of staff observed after the war, "I have to say there was no big battle.

Only small engagements so the losses were not much. Maybe a thousand, maybe two thousand. But not much because no big battles."[274]

The Battles in and around Saigon

With the rapid collapse of I and II Corps in March, the PAVN was able to turn its full force against the remaining ARVN forces in and around Saigon. So much of the ARVN had self-destructed that the North Vietnamese advantage in numbers was by now overwhelming.[275] ARVN defenders held in a few areas, most notably in the 18th Division's heroic eleven-day defense of the town of Xuan Loc northeast of Saigon.[276]

Overall, though, PAVN forces quickly were able to converge on the capital, which had the equivalent of four to five divisions defending it: the full-strength 5th and 25th divisions, elements of the 18th, remnants of the 22nd, and a hodgepodge of Airborne, Rangers, Marines, RF/PF, as well as other stragglers. Poorly organized, these forces were demoralized, ill-disciplined, and "no longer wanted to fight." They stood in stark contrast to the PAVN divisions, most of which had yet to see hard fighting and "were up to strength, fresh, and obviously buoyed by their enormous successes in the north." The collapse in the north had happened almost too fast for the PAVN to exploit it fully.[277]

By the end of April, after overcoming some final ARVN resistance in Ninh Thuan and Long Khanh provinces, the PAVN assembled thirteen divisions on the outskirts of Saigon, plus four more in reserve. On April 21, Thieu resigned in favor of the vice president, Tran Van Huong. A week later, on April 28, General Duong Van Minh, known as "Big Minh," replaced Huong, as Minh was said to be the only leader acceptable to the North. Minh attempted to negotiate a ceasefire, to which North Vietnam responded by strafing the presidential palace with captured South Vietnamese aircraft. With its overwhelming numbers, perhaps as great as 4:1, the PAVN overran Saigon quickly in a mechanized attack from five directions, targeting key government sites and facing almost no organized ARVN resistance. On April 30, Minh unconditionally surrendered. The war was over.[278]

Assessing the Battlefield Effectiveness of South Vietnam

In 1975, the ARVN essentially self-destructed. In both MR-1 and MR-2—the two key arenas in which the ARVN had at least a chance to resist the North Vietnamese—ARVN soldiers repeatedly chose to stop fighting, take off their uniforms, drop their weapons, and blend in with the fleeing civilian population. Although even the best armies sometimes need to withdraw from engagements in which they are outnumbered,

[128]

the ARVN's retreats were so disorderly that most of the forces were never reconstituted as combat units.

In both regions the mass exodus began after Thieu overruled his field commanders and gave them unrealistic and unclear orders to execute. This extreme centralization of command obviated the influence of the good commanders who did exist in the ARVN and the preparations that they had made to fight, particularly in I Corps. For example, Thieu's order to withdraw the Airborne and Marines from MR-1 due to coup fears crippled the ability of even General Truong, a very good corps commander, to keep his units intact and to fight from prepared defensive positions.[279]

Likewise, Thieu's absurd order to withdraw immediately from the Central Highlands essentially caused another corps commander, General Phu, to give up. Phu had demonstrated himself to be capable in the past as a division commander. Although some South Vietnamese officials interviewed after the war condemned Phu's behavior in 1975, most officials believed the real blame lay with Thieu. In their view, "the withdrawal operations should never have been left in Phu's hands in the first place." It was not reasonable to think "that II Corps could withdraw forces already under enemy pressure and preserve their morale and combat effectiveness, much less retake Ban Me Thuot."[280]

Thieu's negative impact was further compounded by the subsequent lack of clear procedures for communicating orders from the president to the Joint General Staff to field commanders, and for sending information about the battlefield back up the chain.[281] Especially in MR-1, the corps commander remained confused about when and where the president planned to withdraw various forces, particularly with regard to Hue and Da Nang. South Vietnam's practices with respect to command arrangements and information management, which the Americans had been able to paper over in previous battles, crippled whatever fighting power the ARVN had now that it was on its own.

Although one can speculate about what would have happened in 1975 absent these practices—whether and for how long the ARVN might have been able to hold out against the PAVN, and what sort of costs the ARVN might have imposed on the PAVN in the process—such conjectures remain just that. The overall nature of the country's military organizational practices obviated the impact of the few units that had been geared toward conventional war, leading to a force that was fundamentally unable to resist the PAVN advance.[282]

Assessing the Battlefield Effectiveness of North Vietnam

The final offensives illuminated an even greater contrast in North and South Vietnamese capabilities than had appeared earlier in the war, when the United States had been able to compensate for what turned out to be critical flaws in the ARVN's battlefield capabilities and to keep heavy pressure on the PAVN. In 1975, the PAVN actually improved its tactical proficiency and ability to conduct complex operations compared to earlier battles.

First, tactical proficiency in the PAVN remained excellent. The results of Dung's intensive training program were evident, with virtually all ARVN officials agreeing after the war that the enemy "had greatly improved his proficiency in using his equipment, especially armor."[283] Another example of the well-honed PAVN tactics came in the area of air defense, where North Vietnamese soldiers displayed extraordinary fire discipline, reflecting careful and specialized training. The PAVN history of the campaign reports: "Our anti-aircraft artillery troops waited until enemy aircraft dove down to a low level before opening fire," which made such efforts particularly effective.[284]

Most important, the PAVN proved itself able to perform difficult combined arms operations. The PAVN had mastered the art of using tanks for maneuver, repeatedly demonstrating the ability to bypass obstacles on the outskirts of major South Vietnamese cities and move directly to key targets inside, all the while closely coordinating armor movement with infantry. As the PAVN history notes, "Our infantry stuck close to and supported our tanks while they overran enemy pockets of resistance." The PAVN also repeatedly demonstrated the ability to coordinate artillery with infantry and armor.[285]

Moreover, the PAVN demonstrated the ability to combine low-level initiative with a higher-level coordinated plan. Although the Politburo had set the overall goals of the campaign for 1975–1976, the PAVN repeatedly showed the ability to react intelligently to events in the field, such as the quick ARVN collapse in MR-1 and MR-2. Although the PAVN leaders had planned to fight large battles for some of the cities in these regions, they adjusted when ARVN units began withdrawing; the PAVN soldiers instead pursued the retreating ARVN columns and disrupted their ability to evacuate by sea. As the PAVN's own history put it, there was "unanimity of thought from the top to the bottom regarding the opportunity we faced and the tactics to be employed" but significant room for commanders to execute their plans within the framework of the overall attack. The PAVN history emphasizes that in 1975 its soldiers truly demonstrated "their ability to conduct combined-arms combat within the context of large-scale campaigns"—the goal that had been set after 1972.[286] In short, not only did North Vietnam fight better, but its superior performance seems directly attributable to the military organizational practices that it had adopted.

What else might account for the variation in battlefield effectiveness between North and South Vietnam? Several alternative explanations seem possible besides those extrapolated from the theoretical literature on military effectiveness. Some point to possible additional reasons for poor ARVN performance, such as the role of doctrine inherited from the United States. Others focus on ideological differences between the two states, especially the roles of nationalism and communism, and on North and South Vietnam's differing post-colonial legacies. Here I address each of these alternatives.

The Role of ARVN Doctrine

Some scholars suggest that the fundamental problem with South Vietnamese military effectiveness was the doctrine the United States imparted, which emphasized large-unit conventional fighting on the model of Korea, rather than small-unit counterinsurgency.[287] Putting aside the considerable resources the United States devoted to building counterinsurgency capabilities among South Vietnam's RF/PF troops, this argument mistakenly presumes that the state of South Vietnam's conventional capabilities was somehow irrelevant to the course and outcome of the war. The narrative also tends to imply that South Vietnam was reasonably effective at conventional warfare and lost the war simply because North Vietnam refused to engage in stand-up battles and instead won the hearts and minds of the South Vietnamese people.

As my analysis of battles has shown, however, the war actually took on a remarkably conventional character after 1968, precisely because the North Vietnamese were unable to win over the South's population through political means. There is no doubt that the United States failed to fully understand the nature of its adversary in Vietnam and that this shortcoming hobbled its efforts to strengthen the ARVN. But if the problem for South Vietnam were simply that it had borrowed an initially inappropriate conventional doctrine from the United States, that doctrine should have served it well, especially after 1968. Ultimately, the problem for South Vietnam was not a mismatch between its doctrine and the nature of the war, but rather that it was unable to implement its doctrine competently in the first place. South Vietnam's military organizational practices produced deficits in tactical proficiency and the ability to conduct complex operations that would have been disastrous no matter what the army's doctrine.

[131]

The Role of Communist Ideology

Other studies emphasize the role of communist ideology in motivating PAVN and PLAF soldiers and also in winning over the population of South Vietnam.[288] According to this argument, the primary driver of North Vietnam's effectiveness was the regime's ideological apparatus, which instilled incredible loyalty and inspired immense sacrifice. Certainly, the North Vietnamese themselves must have believed that their ideology had power, because they invested considerable time in disseminating it to both civilians and soldiers.

Nevertheless, as chapter 2 demonstrated, the PLAF and PAVN devoted considerably less time to political indoctrination of soldiers than often assumed, and, when push came to shove, ideology and party credentials almost always took a backseat to rigorous military training consistent with conventional war practices. Furthermore, although communist ideology might help explain soldier motivation and, in turn, some aspects of unit cohesion, an army cannot propagandize its way to competence in basic tactics and complex operations (a point the next two chapters also illustrate in the discussion of revolutionary Iran). The development of these skills requires good officers, thorough training, appropriate command structures, and solid information management—all of which Hanoi repeatedly prioritized.

Even Pike, one of the foremost scholars of Vietnam and not one to dismiss the overall importance of communism in the war, notes the tautology and illogic of explanations that over-emphasize these variables in explaining the fighting prowess of North Vietnam. He is worth quoting at length on this point:

> Americans and others often assumed that the NLF army members were fanatics. Because they performed well in combat, it was argued, they were highly motivated, which meant dedication to an ideological cause. Thus the search was for the essence of this belief. It proved elusive, largely because it did not exist. The best of the military units—the Main Force units—were highly effective because they were composed of professionals. These were not young green Vietnamese farmers, only recently introduced to the rifle, but experienced guerillas who had been fighting most of their adult lives. What impelled them was not ideology so much as professional competence, much like the United States Marine or the French Foreign Legionnaire. The men in the best of these units were very good; their discipline was superb; they knew how to use camouflage well, a requirement for survival; they were well skilled in small-unit tactics, especially the ambush in its many variations; they trained hard, rehearsed, and practiced attacks until letter perfect, and then they fought hard.[289]

[132]

In addition, the evidence showed that when ARVN units adopted the same military organizational practices as their PAVN and PLAF counterparts, the South Vietnamese fought much better, despite their lacking communist indoctrination. Although this does not prove that ideology was irrelevant to North Vietnamese fighting power, it suggests that generating military power mostly hinges on adoption of the right set of military organizational practices, which in turn depends on the threat environment. To be sure, leaders may be able to use ideology to manage or to prevent some types of internal threats, in which case we should not be surprised that the more ideologically potent of the two states performed better on the battlefield. But the book's framework points toward an understanding of the causal mechanisms through which ideology must operate in order to influence effectiveness. Where ideology is not accompanied by conventional war practices, it should have little positive effect.

Finally, the notion that the government of South Vietnam fell because its people were ultimately won over by communism is simply wrong. First, although the South Vietnamese may not have felt a deep affinity for their own government, many were deeply anticommunist, as the repeated refugee flows in the face of the major North Vietnamese advances demonstrated. Despite the desertions that plagued the South Vietnamese military, for example, virtually none of them resulted in actual defections to the North, and surveys repeatedly demonstrated that public support for communism was low.[290] Although some aspects of the communist program, such as social justice and the demotion of landed elites, clearly appealed to the peasantry, the fact remains that Hanoi had to rely on highly coercive tactics to get many peasants to support the insurgency.[291] Meanwhile, Hanoi never was able to spark urban uprisings against the South Vietnamese government—not in 1968, 1972, or even 1975. Although one cannot dismiss the role of communism, it is worth noting that North Vietnam had to win the war militarily through a conventional assault precisely because it was unable to use the power of ideology alone to achieve its goals.[292]

The Role of Nationalism

Nationalism is another factor often mentioned in explanations of the variation in fighting power between North and South Vietnam.[293] According to this perspective on the war, the North fought better because only Hanoi was able to claim the nationalist mantle of independence, while the South was a puppet regime tainted by its association with the United States.

Nationalism was an undeniable advantage for North Vietnam, one that Ho and his followers carefully cultivated throughout their decades of revolutionary struggle. The key question is, How did nationalism affect events on the battlefield? It probably helped guarantee North Vietnam a steady supply of manpower, but a shortage of manpower was not the primary driver of South Vietnam's effectiveness problems during the war, nor is plentiful manpower a guarantee of effectiveness (as the next two chapters also demonstrate in their examination of revolutionary Iran). More important, perhaps, nationalism may have helped North Vietnamese society deliver more motivated soldiers to the PLAF and PAVN, potentially bolstering unit cohesion. By changing the way that soldiers conceived their interests, nationalism also could have made these soldiers more willing to conduct dangerous tactics or more able to perform difficult operations away from direct supervision by their officers.[294]

No doubt PAVN soldiers exhibited an unusually strong sense of their normative obligations to perform military service. But South Vietnam also was able to generate motivated soldiers capable of fighting skillfully when the military organizational practices in those units hewed closer to the requirements of conventional war. Even in many cases where units disintegrated, as in 1975, this problem seemed more attributable to the highly pathological ARVN command structure and the officers who ran it than to the political views of the average soldier. This does not mean that nationalism did not provide a boost to the North Vietnamese side, but it does suggest that nationalism is not necessarily required for battlefield effectiveness.

As with communism, however, nationalism may have conferred its biggest advantage on Hanoi indirectly, by helping secure the North Vietnamese regime internally and making coup prevention practices unnecessary. Likewise, perhaps if South Vietnamese regimes had ruled a more nationalistic population, they would have been more likely to treat all of the ARVN the way they treated the 1st Division. The book's framework suggests that nationalism alone is neither necessary nor sufficient for good military performance, and it points to the mechanisms that we should expect nationalism to have to activate in order to influence effectiveness—a lesson that the battlefield experience of revolutionary Iran drives home as well.

The Role of Organizational Legacies

Beyond specific arguments about communism or nationalism, one also could posit that the entire course of the war was determined long before armed struggle began, because of organizational legacies dating to the pre-war period. In other words, the very processes by which North and South Vietnam came into being arguably exerted powerful effects on their subsequent abilities to build and sustain effective military organizations.

After all, the French had killed or imprisoned most credible, noncommunist nationalists who struggled for revolution, especially in Cochin China, the nucleus of the future South Vietnam. Here French (and then Japanese) control had been tightest and virulent anticolonial sentiment weakest.[295] These patterns of foreign rule left Vietnamese with two choices by the 1950s. On one side were the communists, strongest in the north, the only revolutionary group that had evaded French repression and gained experience and credibility in the process. On the other were the privileged Vietnamese elite leading the Saigon regime, most of whom had either actively collaborated with the French or Japanese, or sat on the sidelines in the struggle for independence, and many of whom had little appreciation for issues of concern to the country's mostly rural population.[296] One certainly can imagine why many Vietnamese would have preferred the former over the latter, especially given that Hanoi deliberately avoided emphasizing its communist ambitions, stressing themes of independence and unification instead. In this sense, the regime in Saigon was born with some significant disadvantages.

Similarly, the revolutionary struggle had endowed Hanoi with a vast and sophisticated political network in both South and North Vietnam, providing ready-made infrastructure for its later armed struggle.[297] The regime in Saigon could draw on no such base. The units that went on to form the PAVN also had gained significant combat experience fighting the French.[298]

Nevertheless, it can be misleading to tell a "just so" story with the benefit of hindsight. North Vietnam was not born with a ready-made fighting organization. Recently uncovered historical evidence emphasizes just how turbulent the late 1950s were for Hanoi, because of the ways in which it had conducted the revolutionary struggle against the French. Its united front strategy had created such a broad movement that Hanoi spent the late 1950s rectifying the "organizational anarchy" that had resulted (in fact, this was part of the motivation for maintaining the commissar system). The leadership in Hanoi also was wracked with internal divisions about how to build socialism in Vietnam and whether to prioritize reforms at home or the struggle for unification.[299] Though internal threats—especially coup risk—were far less pressing in North Vietnam, and the regime there was better institutionalized, the PAVN was not a completely ready-made "organizational weapon" destined to defeat a doomed South Vietnam, as sometimes depicted.[300] For years Ho Chi Minh actually worried about the prospect that Diem, "whose nationalist credentials were almost as sterling as his own," would become the leader of a unified Vietnam, rather than Ho.[301]

To make matters worse, Diem was highly effective in destroying Hanoi's infrastructure in the South in the mid-1950s, arresting and executing many with only the loosest connection to communism.[302] Although these sweeps ultimately created more problems than they solved for Saigon, they also illustrate that North Vietnam's supposed organizational advantages from the war against the French did not go unchallenged on Southern territory. Indeed, Party leaders fretted that their organization had been nearly destroyed in the South during this period.[303]

In short, it is difficult to look at the scene in the late 1950s and believe that victory was inevitable for the North, especially in light of the infusion of U.S. aid flowing to Saigon at the time—although, counterintuitively, that very aid may have shielded South Vietnam from the external threats that would have been most likely to prompt widespread adoption of conventional war practices. Combined with South Vietnam's extensive internal threats, the escalating U.S. presence made adoption of coup prevention practices a rather logical choice for South Vietnam, though it was far from inevitable in 1954.

In general, the battlefield evidence from the Vietnam War is consistent with what we would expect if effectiveness is a function of military organizational practices, and if those practices arise in response to the threat environment. The evidence is largely inconsistent with what we would expect based on existing theories of military effectiveness. First, the battles showed that there was significant cross-national variation in effectiveness between North and South Vietnam, in addition to significant variation within the ARVN itself. The PLAF and PAVN demonstrated tactical proficiency and an ability to conduct complex operations much more consistently than did the ARVN. These facts alone suggest that arguments focused on the roles of wealth, democracy, culture and society, and military politicization cannot adequately account for all the observed variation, because North and South Vietnam were very closely matched along these broad dimensions.

Second, the evidence affirmatively demonstrates the importance of military organizational practices in explaining this variation. The ARVN units subject to coup prevention practices—including most infantry divisions, the Airborne, the Rangers, the Marines, and the Armor squadrons—performed poorly, as seen in the battles at Ap Bac, during the Tet Offensive, in Laos, during the Easter Offensive, and in the final offensives. This general pattern, reflecting a prioritization of internal threats, especially coup prevention, is consistent with what we would expect given the country's history and the personalist and then military nature of South Vietnamese regimes.

When these practices varied within the ARVN, however, so did battle-field effectiveness. Evidence from the battle for the Citadel at Hue in 1968, the invasion of Laos in 1971, and the Easter Offensive in 1972 showed that the ARVN 1st Division displayed much better effectiveness. In many engagements it would have been very difficult for an outside observer to tell which forces were North Vietnamese and which were South Vietnamese based on the 1st Division's actions. This variation shows that there was nothing inherently inferior about ARVN forces. Using essentially the same human and material resources as the rest of the South Vietnamese military—and facing the same set of disadvantages as well—the 1st Division generated significantly more fighting power because it was subject to different military practices, especially with respect to promotions and training.

Furthermore, changes in leadership, aggressive retraining, and shifts in command led to at least some observable improvements in the performance of other ARVN units after the initial losses in the Easter Offensive. Although these units did not radically transform overnight and still displayed serious problems in 1975, some did fight better than before, again suggesting that where concerns about coups were lower—and conventional, external threats higher—military organizational practices shifted, and so did battlefield performance.

Meanwhile, PAVN and PLAF units consistently performed well in all the battles examined, displaying good tactical proficiency and a steadily improved ability to conduct complex operations. This is not to say that North Vietnam had no military shortcomings. Particularly when fighting against the Americans, Hanoi showed a willingness to accept high casualties, which was often counterproductive, and the North Vietnamese were often critical of their own efforts. Nevertheless, what successes the North did enjoy were clearly tied to the very different military organizational practices it adopted, which stemmed from a different threat environment. As a well-institutionalized, single-party state, the North Vietnamese regime faced few internal dangers and almost no coup risk. Furthermore, the state's leaders had foreign policy goals that affirmatively required territorial revision. These divergences again speak to just how different nondemocratic regimes can be, even when they have similar cultures, economic parity, and high levels of military politicization.

Finally, close examination of the battles detected minimal disconfirming evidence. There were no significant instances of widespread PLAF/PAVN ineffectiveness.[304] Conversely, in only a handful of instances did ARVN units other than the 1st Division demonstrate even minimal effectiveness. For example, the Marines did show some surprising cohesion in Laos in 1971, and the 18th Division demonstrated impressive ferocity and competence at Xuan Loc in 1975. Probably the strongest evidence to cast doubt on the book's argument is that the 1st Division did not fight better in 1975, though it still fought well initially and the evidence shows that its collapse was attributable largely to problems of command, a disadvantageous starting position, and the fact that its units were significantly understrength.[305]

Still, overall the evidence from the Vietnam War suggests that the book's framework has substantial explanatory power. Although imperfect, the framework better accounts for both the cross-national and within-country variation observed in the North and South Vietnamese cases than do existing theories of effectiveness. Differences in threats and military organizational practices go a long way toward explaining the fighting power each army was able to generate from its national resources.

[4]

Threats and Military Organizational Practices in Iraq and Iran

From 1980 to 1988, Iran and Iraq fought one of the largest and bloodiest land wars of the twentieth century, a war that ended with hundreds of thousands of people dead and nearly a million more wounded, with billions of dollars diverted from the economies of both sides toward war needs. Despite producing virtually no change in the territorial holdings of either belligerent, the war, by its sheer persistence and scale, fundamentally reshaped the politics of the Middle East and led to profound shifts in U.S. foreign policy.[1]

To name just a few of its consequences, the war helped solidify the Iranian revolution while deepening Iran's diplomatic isolation. It provided a firm rationale for the already growing U.S. conventional military presence in the region.[2] Perhaps most important, the war built the military of Saddam Hussein, massively indebting Iraq to Kuwait in the process. The 1990 invasion of Kuwait was in large part an effort to resolve the economic difficulties this debt created. Absent the 1990–1991 war, in turn, one can draw a whole series of fairly uncontroversial conclusions about just how different the region, U.S. foreign policy, and the U.S. position in the world might be, even today.

Crucially, it was the merciless persistence and ever-escalating scale of the Iran-Iraq War—almost eight entire years of multidivision battles along an 800-mile border, eventually involving chemical weapons, missile attacks on urban areas, and a campaign against tanker traffic in the Gulf—that produced most of these regional and international consequences. Had either Iran or Iraq been able to bring the war to a swifter conclusion, many of these effects never would have come to pass. Not only would the human and economic costs of the war have been far lower, but the entire architecture of the region and the U.S. role there also likely would have assumed very different forms.

The puzzle for observers of the war is why this did not happen. Why did the war last so long, despite some initial Iranian battlefield successes that suggested it might end quickly? Why was neither side able to end the conflict decisively on the battlefield prior to 1988, the year that a quick series of Iraqi counteroffensives finally did so? Why was neither side able to capitalize consistently on the resources and advantages it possessed in order to sustain an effective fighting apparatus? And what explains the surprising shift in the performance of key Iraqi units at the eleventh hour?

As we will see, the existing explanations of military effectiveness are unsatisfying in explaining both the generally poor performance of Iran and Iraq, compared to what one might expect given their national resources and characteristics, as well as the limited early successes of the Iranians and the late triumphs of the Iraqis. Only by understanding the nature of threats facing the two states, and the military organizational practices these threats engendered, is it possible to resolve the puzzle of the two countries' battlefield performances—and in particular to explain the within-country and over-time variation seen in particular units of both militaries.

In the Iraqi case, Saddam Hussein presided over a personalist regime, one characterized by a well-founded concern about coups, in addition to other internal, irregular threats.[3] These fears led Saddam to impose coup protection practices in his military with respect to promotion patterns, training regimens, command arrangements, and information management. Indeed, his concern about coups ran so deep that he clung to these practices despite mounting evidence of their battlefield costs. Finally, in 1986, Saddam seems to have calculated that not only would these practices likely lose the war against Iran, but they might well result in the overthrow of his regime—either through Iranian conquest or at the hands of his frustrated officer corps. As a result, Saddam ordered a shift to conventional war practices among Republican Guard and select army units, resulting in the improved Iraqi effectiveness that helped end the war.

That said, this shift was possible only because Iraq faced an adversary in the midst of revolutionary upheaval whose military also was beset by organizational pathologies. The nascent Iranian regime faced multiple threats in addition to its Arab neighbor, including civil war and secession by ethnic minorities. As much as it needed the military to combat these dangers, the regime also feared that the armed forces inherited from the Shah posed a substantial danger of counterrevolution by coup. As a result, the regime imposed coup protection practices, eventually eroding the adequate tactical and operational effectiveness the Iranian military had acquired under the mixed practices of the prerevolutionary period. The legacy of these earlier practices was evident in some of the early battles of the war, in which the preexisting military units displayed notably better tactical proficiency than the new units formed by the revolutionary regime. Unfortunately for Iran, however, the regime never successfully integrated prerevolutionary and revolutionary armed forces, and in fact mistakenly credited the revolutionary forces rather than the legacy regular units with stopping and turning back the initial Iraqi invasion.

As a result, the Iranian regime actually solidified its imposition of coup protection practices as the war went on, squelching whatever battlefield effectiveness lingered from the Shah's era. Iran's military strategy instead came to rely on revolutionary soldiers who were ideologically motivated to be cohesive but who lacked any ability to convert that cohesion into tactical proficiency or complex operations. Iran thus was very vulnerable to the improvement in Iraqi practices that finally occurred late in the war.

It is important not to overdraw these contrasts, of course, especially in the Iranian case where the variation was quite subtle. Nevertheless, the overall pattern is striking: both Iran and Iraq performed poorly when their militaries were uniformly subject to coup prevention practices—in the Iranian case, after about 1982, and in the Iraqi case, before about 1986. By contrast, in the period before these practices exerted their full effects on the regular military in Iran and in the period after these practices were lifted on the Republican Guard and select army units in Iraq, military performance by those forces was noticeably better compared both to the opponent's military and to other units drawn from the same state. These findings, which also are consistent with the evidence from the Vietnam comparisons, strongly suggest the importance of threats and military organizational practices in explaining battlefield effectiveness.

This chapter proceeds in three main parts. The first section provides background on the Iran-Iraq War, sharpening the puzzle presented by the two sides' battlefield performances. The second section relies on the series of questions presented in chapter 1 to show how the threat environment facing Iraq gave rise to a particular set of military organizational practices. The section then generates predictions about how different units of the Iraqi military should have performed over time. The third section repeats this procedure with respect to Iran. Chapter 5 then turns to the empirical evidence needed to adjudicate among these predictions, examining a series of battles between Iraq and Iran from 1980 to 1988.

Both chapters 4 and 5 draw for their evidence on recently declassified and translated documents and audio tapes from the regime of Saddam

[141]

Hussein, made available at the Conflict Records Research Center (CRRC) of National Defense University; on archival material made available through the National Security Archive and Digital National Security Archive, including transcripts of FBI interviews with Saddam Hussein and intelligence and military documents pertaining to U.S. foreign policy in the region; and on secondary literature, including published interviews with ex-officers from both countries. As in the Vietnam cases, my approach triangulates issues of interest by examining multiple sources of information, although I readily acknowledge that no source is unbiased. I carefully contextualize and note the origins of information I use and flag areas of disagreement among sources in an effort to allow the reader to evaluate my judgments. The result should leave the reader reassured that there is no systematic bias in favor of my argument and that any disconfirming evidence has been detected and reported.

BACKGROUND: THE PUZZLE OF BATTLEFIELD EFFECTIVENESS IN THE IRAN-IRAQ WAR

The Origins of the War

In one sense, the cause of the Iran-Iraq War was narrow and immediate: a border skirmish in September 1980 (see map 4.1). But it is hard to see how this dispute could have escalated into the war it became absent broader differences between the regimes in Baghdad and Tehran. Iraq was a staunchly secular dictatorship run by Sunni Arabs, while Iran was a theocracy run by Shi'i Persians.

In the narrow sense, the war arose from a territorial dispute over the waters of the Shatt al-Arab, where the Tigris and Euphrates meet and separate the two countries in the south (see map 4.2). A 1937 border treaty had given Iraq control of the Shatt up to the river bank on the Iranian side, except for a five-mile stretch in which Iraqi control extended only to the center of the channel. Starting in 1969, the year after the Ba'th came to power in Iraq, "Iran unilaterally renounced the 1937 treaty and systematically began to challenge Iraqi control of the Shatt al-Arab by not flying the Iraqi flag on its ships and by refusing Iraqi pilots."[4]

In 1975, the two countries resolved these disagreements with the Algiers Accord, negotiated on the Iraqi side by the country's second-in-command at the time, Saddam. This accord adopted the center line as the boundary along the entire river, but in return for this contraction of Iraqi territory, which essentially internationalized the Shatt, Iran agreed to end all support for the Iraqi Kurds, who had been conducting an ongoing insurrection against Baghdad.[5] The agreement held until 1979, at

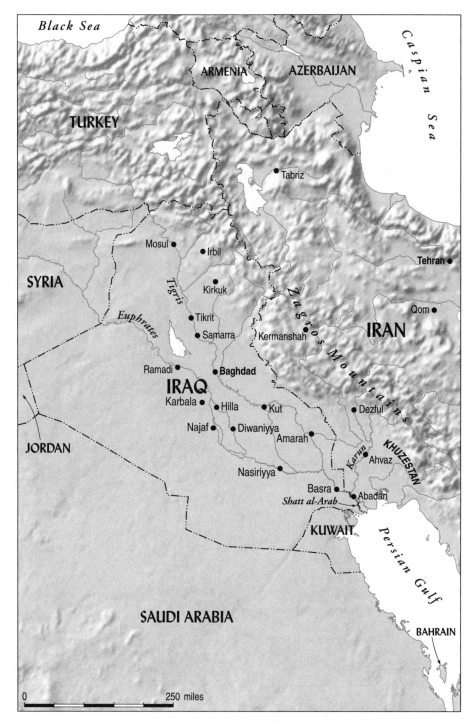

Map 4.1. Iran and Iraq

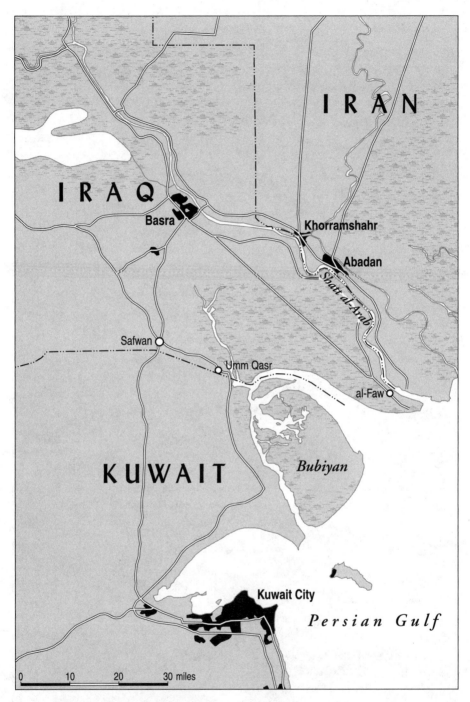

Map 4.2. The Shatt al-Arab

which time Iran still occupied small areas that were to have gone to Iraq according to the 1975 terms. Although the new regime in Tehran did not formally renounce the Algiers Accord, "neither did it offer assurances that the treaty would be observed. On the contrary, revolutionary leaders almost casually let it be known that they did not consider themselves bound by any of the Shah's agreements."[6]

Accounts vary regarding the 1980 border clashes that preceded Iraq's all-out attack on September 22.[7] Yet in a broader sense the attack was not surprising given escalating bilateral tensions during the previous two years. Both regimes were engaged in efforts to shore up their own power, but the very methods by which each chose to do so threatened the other. For his part, Saddam had just replaced General Ahmed Hassan al-Bakr as the country's top leader. Circumstantial evidence suggests that Saddam's timing stemmed in part from Bakr's pending move to join Iraq in a Ba'thist alliance with Syria, which would have made Hafez al-Asad— rather than Saddam—the clear successor to Sadat as leader of the Arab world after the Camp David Accords.[8]

Saddam's status as a pan-Arabist, secular Ba'thist, and Sunni ruling over a majority Shi'i population also gave him good reason to fear the example of the Iranian revolution. Tehran did nothing to quell this fear when it initiated a propaganda campaign calling for the removal of the "non-Muslim" Ba'thist regime in Baghdad.[9] Tehran radio during this period also proclaimed a leading Iraqi Shi'i cleric in Najaf, Ayatollah Muhammad Baqir al-Sadr, the "Khomeini of Iraq." A wave of antigovernment bombings swept the country, apparently with Iranian blessing, and the major Shi'i party, al-Da'wa, began to organize active opposition to the Ba'th regime. Antigovernment riots broke out in the Shi'i holy cities of Najaf and Karbala, resulting in the execution of seventy-nine Iraqi dissidents, some of them military officers, in March 1979.[10] Indeed, some evidence suggests that Bakr's hesitation to execute these officers was the final disagreement with Saddam that prompted Bakr's ouster.

By 1980, Iran also was providing guerilla training to Iraqi Shi'a.[11] In April a new wave of bombings swept across the country, culminating in assassination attempts against two high-ranking Iraqi officials. Baghdad responded by executing al-Sadr and his sister, a move that so outraged the Shi'i community that even twenty-six years later, guards present at Saddam Hussein's execution were heard yelling, "Long live Mohammed Baqir Sadr!"[12]

As Gary Sick has noted, "In retrospect, it is evident that the events of April 1980 represented the crucial turning point that eventually led to war."[13] Just as the very nature of the Iranian regime in this period seemed to threaten Iraq, so too did many aspects of the Iraqi regime appear threatening to leaders in Tehran. And just as Khomeini stoked Saddam's fears, Saddam stoked Khomeini's.[14] Iraq gave safe harbor—and radio stations—to numerous officials from the Shah's regime, including former prime minister Shapour Bakhtiar and the former commander of Iranian ground forces, General Gholam Ali Oveisi, allowing them to broadcast antirevolutionary messages into Iran.[15]

In fact, these exiles "filled Saddam's head with visions of a weak fundamentalist regime that would collapse if given a shove but that otherwise would subvert Iraq's oppressed Shi'ah population if not stopped immediately."[16] It was an odd logic: the Iranian regime was so strong that it had the potential to unseat Saddam's regime simply through ideological appeal, but so weak that it could be toppled by a quick military incursion that would leave Iran's major cities, including the capital, untouched. Saddam apparently believed he could undo the Iranian revolution by appealing to the Iranian Arabs who lived near the southern sector of the border, just as Iran's leaders apparently believed that they could spread their revolution easily to coreligionists in southern Iraq.[17] Against the backdrop of these fresh tensions and mutual suspicions, festering for almost two years, the border clashes of September 1980 proved to be one skirmish too many, drawing both sides into a war that would last eight years.

An Overview of the War between Iran and Iraq

Most of the war took the form of ground combat along the border, which comprised three sectors: a northern sector roughly adjacent to Iraq's Kurdish areas; a central sector where the border curves inward toward Iraq and the Zagros mountains rise up on the Iranian side, roughly parallel to Baghdad; and an oil-rich southern sector with extensive marshes and several major rivers.[18] Although fighting occurred in all three, most of the decisive ground combat occurred in the central and especially the southern sectors, as these were the areas that protected Iraq's capital and access to the Gulf. Furthermore, the southern sector was home to Iraqi Shi'a and Iranian Arabs, the two populations to which Tehran and Baghdad, respectively, believed they could appeal.

Though complex and multifaceted, the Iran-Iraq War (or the Imposed War, as it is known in Iran) consisted of three major phases.[19] The first began with the Iraqi invasion of Iran in 1980 and continued into early 1981, at which time Iran initiated a series of counteroffensives. This phase of the war was fought almost entirely on Iranian territory and lasted into the early summer of 1982.

By mid-1982, Iran had regained most of the land Iraq had conquered. A second phase then began when Iran rejected Iraq's attempts at a

[146]

ceasefire and invaded in July. For the next five years the war took place almost entirely on Iraqi territory. Though the Iranians scored some victories in this phase, notably the conquest of the al-Faw Peninsula in 1986, for the most part the fighting devolved into a war of attrition. The Iraqis defended their territory at great cost but were unable to decisively drive out the Iranians, who also suffered extremely high losses in their repeated assaults on Iraqi positions.

In an attempt to break the stalemate, the Iraqis began using chemical weapons as early as 1983, and by 1984 the war spilled into the Gulf, with each side attempting to interdict the other's access to oil and shipping. In 1985, Iraq initiated large-scale missile strikes against Iranian cities.[20] Such attacks were one of Iraq's only ways to compensate for Iran's immense strategic depth: Tehran was always more than 500 miles from the scene of the ground battles, while Baghdad was often little more than 60 miles away.[21]

Finally, in late 1987, the short but crucial third phase of the war began, in which the Iraqis conducted five counteroffensives in quick succession. During the first half of 1988, Iraq regained virtually all the territory it had lost in the previous five years, drove the Iranians back across the border, and called for a ceasefire, which Iran accepted in August. The terms of this ceasefire were essentially the same as those Iran had rejected in 1982, and they secured for Iraq virtually no gains over its position at the outset in 1980.[22]

The war had been a disaster for the participants in every sense—social, economic, political, strategic. Iran's total losses were estimated at 200,000–220,000 battlefield deaths and 350,000 to 400,000 wounded, plus approximately 16,000 civilian deaths.[23] Iraq's losses amounted to at least 105,000 killed and 400,000 wounded.[24] By some calculations, the total cost of the war reached over $1,190 billion. This figure included more than $41.94 billion worth of weapons imported by Iraq and $11.26 billion imported by Iran.[25]

Furthermore, neither side realized its major goals. The Iraqi invasion consolidated rather than upended the Iranian revolutionary regime, damaged rather than strengthened Iraqi standing in the region, and alienated rather than liberated the Arabs of Khuzestan. Similarly, the Iranian invasion in 1982 was also counterproductive: it rallied even Shi'i Iraqis to Saddam and terrified the region and the superpowers into supporting Iraq.[26]

Indeed, initial international reaction to the war reflected Henry Kissinger's rumored remark, "Too bad they can't both lose."[27] At first many countries, including the United States, declared themselves neutral, but as time went on and it appeared Iran might prevail, they tilted toward Iraq.[28] Egypt, Kuwait, and Saudi Arabia all became open supporters of their Arab neighbor, providing various forms of aid, including loans, outright grants, weapons, transit rights for the shipment of weapons, and assistance in getting Iraqi oil to market. Meanwhile, Iran still was able to buy weapons and spare parts from North Korea, China, Vietnam, Britain, and numerous European companies.[29]

U.S. policy proved more ambiguous, following the lines suggested in a government memo from the period that "our interests are best served by a military stalemate."[30] The United States provided some tactical intelligence to the Iraqis and publicly engaged in Operation Staunch to stem the flow of weapons to Iran, but the United States also secretly funneled arms to the Iranians through Israel in what became known as the Iran Contra affair.[31] Remarkably, however, despite all this external intervention in the war, little changed on the battlefield until the Iraqi counteroffensives in 1988.

The Puzzle for Theories of Battlefield Effectiveness

The Iran-Iraq War remains puzzling for scholars of military effectiveness. Why did the war last so long, with neither side able to bring it to a decisive end despite some initial Iranian successes? Why did each side seem unable to capitalize on the particular national assets it possessed—Iraq's tremendous access to international arms, for example, or Iran's greater strategic depth and larger population? And why did the situation then change so dramatically in 1988, with the Iraqis able to conduct counteroffensives so effectively that Iran suddenly accepted terms it had been rejecting for six years?

Existing theories do not provide a satisfactory answer, for several reasons. First, along many of the dimensions said to matter for the generation of military power, such as the presence of democracy or the severity of external threats, Iraq and Iran were evenly matched. Neither regime was democratic, so neither state should have benefited in its battlefield performance from the supposed advantages of democratic strategic assessment or liberal political culture.

In addition, both states should have experienced strong external pressures to improve their military performance, given the intense human and economic costs of the war. This was not some great game played in distant lands; it was a border conflict in populated areas. As chapter 5 discusses, there is some evidence that each side did do better when fighting on the defensive. But it remains unclear whether these slight improvements were due to nationalism or simply to the fact that defensive operations are often less militarily challenging than offensive ones.

What is clear is that despite many years of feedback telling both states that their military strategies were failing, neither demonstrated much improvement until the Iraqi changes in 1986–1987. In fact, the Iranians drew the wrong lessons from the initial successes they did have in turning back the Iraqi invasion. Overall, this pattern is quite puzzling for theories focused on external threats, which would expect a major land war to produce rapid incentives for military improvement, especially as losses mounted.

Along other dimensions said to matter for military power, such as wealth, demography, and culture, the two countries were not evenly matched, but their differences deepen rather than resolve the puzzle surrounding battlefield performance. For example, Iran was the wealthier of the two states, in terms of gross domestic product, its cash reserves, and the ability to export oil. Iran also had a population roughly three times that of Iraq.[32] Its demographic advantages were even more pronounced. In 1980 Iran had 8.6 million men between the ages of fifteen and forty-nine, 5.1 million of whom were militarily fit; Iraq had only 3 million men in the same age bracket, and only 1.7 million of them were militarily fit.[33]

Iran and Iraq also had different national cultures, with Iran reflecting its Persian roots and Iraq its Arab ones. Yet contrary to theories emphasizing the detrimental effects of Arab culture on military performance, the Iraqis ultimately outperformed the Iranians in the war.[34] This over-time improvement in particular Iraqi units is surprising if a large structural variable such as Arab culture was the systematic driver of performance. Also puzzling for cultural explanations is the fact that for most of the war the Iraqis and Iranians had many of the same tactical problems on the battlefield, suggesting the importance of some underlying similarity rather than cultural difference.

Furthermore, both countries had highly politicized militaries characterized by low levels of autonomy. In fact, some histories have diagnosed much of the Iranian and Iraqi problems on the battlefield as the result of "civil leaders interfer[ing] directly and constantly in all levels of military activity."[35] Had there been no early Iranian battlefield successes and no improvement in Iraqi performance in the final phase of the war, political interference in the military might indeed be a satisfactory explanation for the battlefield performance of both states. But the decline in Iranian effectiveness and the improvement in Iraqi effectiveness—despite the low level of military autonomy in both states—suggest that something besides the mere level of civilian control of the military drove the two sides' performances. Ultimately, what mattered were the threat environments these regimes faced and what those environments drove political leaders to actually do when they intervened in their military organizations. Even the quintessential personalist regime, Saddam's Iraq, was able to perform well on the battlefield when the external threat environment created strong incentives to do so.

[149]

THREATS AND MILITARY ORGANIZATIONAL PRACTICES IN IRAQ

Historically, external conventional conflicts were low on the list of threats that Iraq's military and personalist regimes had to surmount in order to remain in power. Instead, the country's litany of irregular internal dangers, most notably coups but also recurrent Kurdish and Shi'i rebellion, led its leaders to adopt virtually all of the coup protection practices identified in chapter 1. Iraqi battlefield effectiveness generally was poor as a result. Nevertheless, there were some important exceptions to this pattern—exceptions that arose because of shifts in the threat environment over time. Only when these moves toward conventional war practices occurred did the Iraqi military begin to maximize its material resources, accounting for its adequate and at times excellent performance toward the end of the Iran-Iraq War.

These resources were substantial even in the late 1970s when Saddam launched a major military expansion effort.[36] By 1979, Iraq's ground forces were second in size only to Egypt's among the Arab states. The regular army had twelve active-duty divisions, including four armored and two mechanized infantry divisions, totaling approximately 200,000 men.[37] During the course of the war with Iran, the army ballooned to an astounding 40 divisions encompassing at least 700,000 active-duty soldiers, 250,000 reservists, 4,000 tanks, 3,800 other armored vehicles, 3,500 artillery pieces, and 600 combat aircraft.[38] Lack of material capability was not the primary Iraqi problem in fighting Iran.

The Threat Environment Facing the Iraqi Regime

Throughout modern Iraqi history, the country's military posed a recurring dilemma: political leaders relied heavily on the army to protect their regimes against internal opponents, but the military itself repeatedly proved to be the greatest threat to anyone wearing the mantle of power.[39] Even prior to independence, during the British occupation after World War I, the Iraqi army had focused primarily on internal missions.[40] The instability of the early years of independence, including the formation of no fewer than twelve different cabinets during the period 1932–1939, invited praetorianism. Iraq's military launched its first coup in 1936, and by 1941, six more had occurred.[41]

Thereafter, a period of relative stability emerged under the British-influenced Hashemite monarchy, but this, too, ended with a coup in 1958. This time the plotters were the Free Officers, led by nationalist General Abd al-Karim Qasim. Although Qasim succeeded in finally curtailing the British hold on Iraq, he did little to end the systems of patronage and coercion that many Iraqis despised. Also unresolved were

[150]

the competing claims to political power made by communists, the Shi'i al-Da'wa Party, the Sunni Muslim Brotherhood, and the emerging Ba'th party.

It is not surprising that Prime Minister Qasim himself was soon a target, surviving an assassination attempt in 1959 at the hands of a twenty-two-year-old Ba'thist apparatchik named Saddam Hussein. Saddam fled the country, but in February 1963 Qasim's luck ran out. A group of twelve Ba'thists and four Arab nationalist officers shot him dead and declared themselves in charge of the country. Squabbles among this new ruling clique paved the way for another coup in November 1963, this time orchestrated by General Abd al-Salam Arif, again with help from two Ba'thist military officers who had grown disillusioned with their earlier collaborators.

For the next five years, President Arif and, after Arif's death in a helicopter accident, his brother Abdul Rahman Arif, ruled Iraq, relying on the military as a pillar of the regime. They formed the Republican Guard as an elite unit to protect the palace, and Ba'th members were purged from the officer corps. In fact, the entire party had to go underground, where its security apparatus was now built and managed on a day-to-day basis by Saddam.[42] Saddam himself eventually was imprisoned for plotting with his cousin Bakr against Arif, and he later noted that the era had a profound impact on his political trajectory.[43] "A leader is not made in a factory in Europe," he observed. "Leadership is developed gradually. This was done underground."[44]

In July 1968, Bakr and Saddam finally saw their chance to regain power, again with help from the armed forces. Collaborating with three disillusioned officers, the Ba'th plotters overthrew President Arif in a bloodless coup.[45] Within two weeks, Saddam and Bakr then moved to preclude a repeat of the mistakes of 1963. They orchestrated a second coup, dumping their military allies and declaring themselves the country's sole political authority—in Saddam's case, by personally escorting one of the ruling generals at gunpoint to a new assignment as ambassador to Morocco.[46]

This move was the first in a series of deliberate steps to wrench political power away from the armed forces and place it permanently in Ba'th hands. The most important institutional change occurred in late 1969, when Saddam and President Bakr stacked the Revolutionary Command Council (RCC) with Ba'thist civilians, turning the country's highest decision-making institution from a military-dominated body to a tool of the party overnight.[47] Under Saddam's direction, the Ba'th also purged the army of potentially disloyal officers and arrested large numbers of communists, Nasserists, dissident Ba'thists, former politicians, and Western-oriented businessmen, among others.[48] Several prominent senior

[151]

officers died of conveniently timed heart attacks or in mysterious car accidents as well.[49]

Saddam summarized his objectives during this period when he noted, "The ideal revolutionary command should effectively direct all planning and implementation. It must not allow the growth of any other rival center of power." He added that "with party methods, there is no chance for anyone who disagrees with us to jump on a couple of tanks and overthrow the government."[50] The regime later codified this view at a 1974 party congress, where a statement noted, "From the earliest days, the Party urgently had to . . . consolidate its leadership in the armed forces; to purge them of suspect elements . . . ; to establish the ideological and military criteria which would enable the armed forces to do their duty as well as possible and would immunize them against the deviations which the Qassem and Aref regimes and their military aristocrats had committed in the army's name."[51]

In 1970 Saddam oversaw the formation of the Popular Army. The nucleus of this paramilitary force already had played key roles in the 1963 coup and the initial consolidation of Ba'th power in 1968. Now Saddam sought to develop the Popular Army as a full-fledged counterweight to the regular military, growing it to 250,000 men by 1980. Its membership would reach over half a million during the war with Iran.[52] The Popular Army came in addition to the Republican Guard inherited from Arif. That force would grow from two brigades during the early years of the war to more than two dozen by the end of the conflict.[53]

Despite his later prominence, however, in the early years of Ba'th rule Saddam remained behind the scenes, with Bakr the figurehead not only because of his age and title but also because of his continuing links to the officer corps. Saddam had no military background or standing, having failed the entrance exam to the Baghdad Military Academy, which Bakr considered a good thing. As Efraim Karsh and Inari Rautsi explain, "As long as the Party was in opposition, the primacy of the military faction was indispensable since the army was the only institution which could help the Party regain power. [But] having achieved the country's top position, Bakr no longer needed a strong military faction. On the contrary, ambitious independent officers . . . posed a permanent threat to his position. . . . In these circumstances, an able and ruthless, yet loyal operator like Saddam Hussein, who was equally determined to break the military's hold on Iraqi politics, seemed the ideal number two man."[54]

As the 1970s wore on, Saddam became more prominent and took a number of steps to place the armed forces even more directly under his personal control. The Ba'th party also became an instrument for executing his individual will rather than an independently powerful institution constraining his actions.[55] With Stalin as his role model, Saddam "uncovered" a number of antiregime plots within the security apparatus, although only one of these, in 1973, has ever been confirmed as real. Then, in 1976, Saddam had Bakr grant him an honorary military rank of lieutenant general, equivalent to chief of staff of the army. From this position, he appointed numerous relatives to key positions in the officer corps, most notably naming a cousin as minister of defense, a position previously held by Bakr. The cousin then used this position to further purge the officer corps of those who might be disloyal to Saddam.[56]

By 1979, Bakr—and his sway with the officer corps—had simply become unnecessary to Saddam's hold on power.[57] Under murky circumstances, the ailing Bakr abruptly resigned in July, leading to Saddam's immediate ascendance as Iraq's president.[58] He also became chairman of the RCC, commander in chief of the armed forces, and Field Marshal.[59] Shortly thereafter Saddam announced the discovery of a Syrian plot against him, leading to a wave of show trials and purges within the party leadership.[60] These included an extraordinary meeting of the RCC and top party officials on July 18, at which Saddam "exposed" those in the audience who had participated in the supposed plot and called out plain-clothes security officers to arrest them. Saddam then gave handguns to those remaining and compelled participation in the execution of their colleagues.[61] Saddam later distributed videotapes of the entire event to the rest of the party membership.[62]

It remains unknown regarding this and other similar incidents whether Saddam's fears were genuine or instrumental. He had noted cryptically in 1978 that "the revolution chooses its enemies," suggesting that he might see some political value in manufacturing plots.[63] Conversely, Saddam probably was correct that some in the party did oppose his takeover from Bakr.[64] Furthermore, it was reasonable for Saddam to have been haunted by the very events that had brought him to the presidency. As he reportedly commented, "I know there are scores of people plotting to kill me, and this is not difficult to understand. After all, did we not seize power by plotting against our predecessors?"[65]

Saddam reflected later that well into 1980, the primary job of the military was still "countering the sabotage," that is, protecting the regime from internal threats rather than external ones.[66] Besides coups, Saddam feared armed rebellion by the Kurds or Shi'a. In addition to the crackdown against perceived Shi'i conspiracies in 1979–1980, Saddam executed an unknown number of Kurds and communists whom he worried might have aspirations to unseat him.[67]

Some observers have implied that Saddam's worries might have been paranoia. For example, a 1979 U.S. National Intelligence Estimate referred agnostically to a regime that "believes it has a host of enemies among its own people."[68] Adeed Dawisha similarly has noted that even "at the height of his popularity" in 1980, Saddam "still could not be convinced of the solidity of his people's support for him and his regime."[69] Yet one has to wonder if he could not be convinced because the reality was not very convincing. In addition to the tumultuous events of 1979–1980, Saddam faced five assassination attempts in 1981, two in 1982 (including one in which the presidential motorcade was pinned down for several hours before being rescued by the army), and another in 1987, all linked to Shi'i opponents of the regime.[70]

To sum up, at the same time that Saddam relied on the military to protect him against domestic enemies, the military itself posed a potential threat, even after Ba'th civilians had secured the levers of political power.[71] The threat of coups only intensified as Saddam concentrated more power in his hands and in those of his small inner circle. As one of his generals later reported Saddam to have said, "The Iraqi army was the only force capable of conspiring against me. The only power we fear is this army will take over the party's leadership. The army is like a pet tiger"—so Saddam "pulled out its eyes, teeth, and claws."[72] These facts all suggest that Saddam entered the war deeply preoccupied with concerns about internal, irregular dangers, and most especially coups. Even the Iranian revolution was threatening for primarily domestic reasons; Saddam's worry was not that the Iranian military would overrun the border but that Khomeini's radical ideas would undermine the basis of Saddam's rule inside Iraq.

These preconceptions notwithstanding, Saddam eventually came to believe that his chosen military organizational practices were endangering rather than protecting his regime, especially after 1986. To be sure, the disastrous battlefield results of his approach had been evident relatively early in the war, even to him, which prompted some limited initial modifications of his practices. But a series of battlefield setbacks in 1986—including the loss of the strategically vital al-Faw Peninsula and a costly attempt to take the Iranian town of Mehran—seem to have pushed Saddam to reassess his policies. In particular, Saddam likely realized that the Iranians had both the will and the potential ability to take more Iraqi territory, including territory only a short distance from Baghdad, which meant that winning the conventional war was now vital to maintaining his own hold on power.

Adding fuel to the fire, Saddam's officers, the people whose lives and professional credibility were most directly at stake in implementing his choices, all but threatened his overthrow if he did not shift his policies.[73] As a diplomatic report noted in April 1986, "Unity among the three major forces of power, the Baath party, the army and other armed forces, and the president, has been broken. The army is unwilling to assume responsibility for the failures at Al Faw, and there are many voices now openly mentioning the role of the president and his immediate entourage in this failure. Military leaders eager to fight demand that they should be given a free hand in eliminating the consequences of this failure that had destroyed their prestige."[74]

We cannot know for sure how Saddam viewed this crisis. But his actions suggest that he realized changes were necessary in order to stave off both the Iranians and his own frustrated officers. Iraq needed to launch new offensives, and it needed a bigger—but most important, better—Republican Guard in order to do so.[75] As a result, Saddam rapidly and dramatically shifted organizational practices in those units and some regular army divisions, strongly suggesting a connection between the changed threat calculus and changed policies. The fact that Saddam apparently reverted to his prior practices soon after the war ended lends further support to this linkage. With the Iranian threat gone, he again had much more to lose than gain from a capable military.

Still, the Iraqi improvements in the final years of the war testify to the impact of the shifting threat environment on military organizational practices and, in turn, on battlefield performance. They also suggest that even though personalist regimes are likely to default to coup prevention practices, such regimes can change practices with surprising rapidity once the dictator's threat calculus shifts. Because there were so few institutionalized constraints on Saddam's decision-making authority, shifts in Iraqi military organizational practices occurred quickly after he became convinced that such shifts were necessary to preserve the regime.

Promotion Patterns

As Saddam rose to power in the 1970s, he had focused almost solely on political loyalty as the key criterion for officer selection and advancement. As one general noted in an interview decades later, "Whereas the saying in the early part of the Baath rule had been 'better a good soldier than a good Baathist,' it changed to 'better a good Baathist than a good soldier.' " As this same general noted, Saddam "ordered politicians to serve at the army level and . . . emphasized the principle . . . that as long as one was a Baathist he can always be a leader, since the Baathist is a truly natural leader."[76]

In fact, the regime actively selected against military professionalism in forming its officer corps, a trend that only accelerated when Saddam became president. One authoritative study notes that "the emphasis was now on political reliability and unquestioned obedience to orders rather than on serious military professionalism. . . . Once firmly in charge, Saddam acted to promote a number of lieutenant colonels to major general, and subsequently to the command of divisions, without

[155]

requiring them to hold any of the traditional or intermediate level command positions."[77]

Audio tapes of Saddam's deliberations with his advisers confirm that he paid close personal attention even to junior officer appointments.[78] He cared somewhat about the professional qualifications of his potential commanders but also showed interest in a candidate's family background, political views, and likelihood that he would support Ba'th objectives.[79] In one exchange on this topic in 1980, a division commander reported to Saddam that a capable officer had been passed over promotion to brigade commander because "he is not a party member. I am saying it frankly. . . . There is no other reason." Although in this particular case Saddam eventually relented and allowed the promotion of the officer, the very fact that he and his officers had such an extensive conversation about whether the officer could be trusted—despite the fact that all agreed "he is a good officer"—reflects the overriding importance of political credentials early in the war with Iran.[80]

Furthermore, Saddam repeatedly purged the officer corps of those he deemed disloyal. By the eve of the war, "the high command structure had effectively become Saddam Hussein and his political supporters, none of whom had practical military experience and training. . . . Much of the high command was chosen more for loyalty than competence." The formation and rapid expansion of the Popular Army epitomized these practices, as "low-grade Popular Army 'brigades' were rapidly created with officers whose own real qualification was party membership and loyalty to the regime."[81]

According to one general, however, "Saddam began looking for more competent individuals to run things" as early as 1982, the year of the Iranian invasion.[82] Saddam purged the Popular Army of its worst commanders, in part to shift blame for Iraq's defeats.[83] He also ordered the execution of as many as 300 senior officers for poor performance.[84] Saddam then sought to identify and promote officers who had performed well and eliminated the distinction between Ba'thist and non-Ba'thist officers in making promotion decisions.[85] Still, many incompetent senior officers remained in place or even advanced during this time. For example, generals Tali al-Duri and Ma'ahir Rashid, close personal friends of Saddam later described by a peer as "two of the dumbest generals in the army," remained in command through 1987, despite having presided over multiple battlefield disasters.[86]

After 1982, Saddam reduced the use of the Popular Army and focused on enlarging and improving the leadership of the Republican Guard. According to one of his generals, "Saddam began to choose commanders from the best Iraqi armored battalions to command Republican Guard battalions, whereas previously he had chosen only his relatives. . . . He

[156]

started picking the best officers, commanding officers, and junior officers within the Iraqi army and put them in the Republican Guard, and he aimed to save this new force for the major counterattack. . . . This was in line with the recommendations of the general officers to create a special armored force that was well equipped and well trained, led by expert, high-ranking officers, with great experience."[87]

Nevertheless, this expansion and improvement in the Guard was quite limited. The same general who noted some of the early changes in 1982 commented that even four years later, "a substantial number of Republican Guard commanders were brave but professionally unprepared and often incompetent in the positions they held."[88] Some evidence suggests that Saddam felt this way as well, as tapes from 1984 reveal him brainstorming about the possibility of bringing generals out of retirement to lead companies because the junior officer corps was so inept.[89]

After 1986, the merit component of promotion standards was made much more stringent due to Saddam's selection of a new army chief of staff.[90] Though still overwhelmingly Sunni, the top command of the Guards was reconfigured, with its highest post now filled by an officer "known for his courage and achievements" on the battlefield.[91] In addition, "initiative on the battlefield was rewarded over political loyalty or blood relations to Hussein, and incompetent officers who were friends or relatives were purged."[92] Saddam then combed the rest of the army to pull out the most "outstanding and exceptional" officers for transfer to the Guard, which expanded to over two dozen brigades by 1988.[93] These officers—again, personally identified and promoted by Saddam—provided the human capital driving much of the improved Iraqi performance in the closing stages of the war.

At the same time Saddam shifted the nature of his promotion policies with respect to the Guard, he created a new force known as the Special Republican Guard to continue to protect him in Baghdad. Its soldiers came primarily from the original membership roster of the Republican Guard, which had been created to protect the regime.[94] During this time Saddam also "tightened up his control of the state apparatus" in nonmilitary domains, transferring or dismissing from government service anyone outside his immediate circle of kinsmen and trusted long-time associates.[95]

Furthermore, as soon as the war was over, Saddam ousted many of those who had led the Guard during the period 1986–1988.[96] "What is sad," explained one general, "is that we had heroes who survived the war, but they were dismissed by Saddam because he accused them of something or another."[97] In short, the officer corps with which Saddam went to war in 1980, 1991, and 2003 was not the same one that saw action during 1987–1988.[98]

Training Regimens

Prior to and during the early years of the war, Saddam adopted coup protection practices with respect to training. The Popular Army provided only nominal training to its members.[99] Soldiers usually received about two months of instruction focused on the use of small arms and low-intensity conflict, with little attention to the use of heavy weapons or combined arms.[100] As Anthony Cordesman and Abraham Wagner write, "These People's Army units were usually led by senior members of the Ba'th rather than professional officers. They were not properly organized, led, or equipped for intense combat."[101]

There is some evidence that the Republican Guards were given better training prior to the war, although even for them, there were limits.[102] Despite an infusion of modern weapons, for example, few Iraqi officers received foreign military training in how to use those weapons, because of Saddam's fear that they would bring subversive ideas back with them.[103]

Perhaps the greatest indication of how little training the Iraqi military had received prior to the war is that, once the war escalated, Saddam had numerous conversations with his generals about how to correct training deficits.[104] Only a month into the conflict, for example, one officer subtly warned Saddam, "Our soldier is raw material, we can accomplish miracles with him if he is better used and guided."[105] Saddam noted in another conversation, probably in the mid-1980s, "We have formed a large army to be trained," but "our infantry training is a bit a lagging. . . . We have been in war . . . without training and of course all of you knew before the war we were in need of training. If there was any blame to be placed, it would be for not having the training done before the war started."[106]

Saddam himself initially gave specific instructions to improve training.[107] By 1984, he also had assigned a highly competent corps commander, General Aladdin Hussein Makki Khamas, to the task. Notably, Makki was not a Ba'thist and had been educated at Sandhurst; his father had been minister of defense during the monarchy. Makki tightened the standards for Iraqi officers assuming command, developed an after-action process whereby battles could be assessed to provide direction for future training, undertook a comprehensive review of Iraqi doctrine, and published new training manuals, all of which Saddam reviewed personally.[108]

In addition, Makki launched a professional military journal modeled on the U.S. Army's *Military Review*.[109] The content of this journal, which Saddam himself read, is in some ways striking in its banal exposition of basic military principles. For example, a 1984 article noted,

[158]

Training and maintenance are essential, basic elements in all circumstances. They are needed to build a qualified human and material base superior to that of the enemy, and to maintain the momentum and impact of that base in various stages of the conflict to achieve decisive results and to effectively remedy shortages and losses stemming from the length of the war. In this regard, emphasis must be placed on not restricting training and maintenance to a certain aspect or area to the exclusion of another.[110]

Although perfectly unobjectionable, the fact that a senior officer devoted the time to write an article explaining the importance of unrestricted training—four years into the war—speaks volumes about the legacy of Saddam's prewar policies. One can draw a similar inference from another article published in the same issue, in which the author observed, "Constant drilling in peace based on the most likely scenario tends to produce good action in warfare. Training alone ensures gradual improvement in all exercises. . . . The constant execution of realistic procedures in peacetime will make matters proceed automatically and easily in war, which increases the chances of success in battle."[111] Clearly, it seems, some in the Iraqi military and political leadership were not yet convinced of these arguments.

Indeed, although Iraq attempted to improve training for particular units starting as early as the fall of 1980, these efforts remained sporadic at best well into 1984–1985.[112] In one recorded conversation with Saddam, for example, an officer carefully approached the topic of seeking foreign help with training, commenting, "We cannot say that the [foreign] officers are smarter than the Iraqi ones. . . . On the brigade level our officers can hold their own, but in other areas we can do better if some of those [foreign] officers can come here and train us. . . . We should have put more emphasis on training our troops. . . . Education in the military should take a larger scale and requires planning."[113] Saddam eventually did authorize a return to foreign military education.[114]

As late as 1986–1987, Saddam's advisers still had to work to convince him to ease restrictions on training. In one 1986 conversation, for example, the defense minister noted, "The process of building the warrior and building the human being, it is not a haphazard process, it is not just giving a weapon to a person and train him for two weeks and tell him go ahead and fight, the process of building the fighter is a very difficult one and requires time."[115] In another conversation the following year, a commander struggled to convince Saddam of the need to reconsider Iraq's training methods, or lack thereof: "if these brave troops were to be given room for training . . . , if they were to be given three to four months to be trained, our position will be much better. Sir, each battalion needs a month or a month and a half to be trained. . . . Can you see how it works, sir? . . . If you allow me, sir, everything will be explained."[116] The general gingerly concluded that more so than the size of the Iraqi army, the "quality, and the shortage of its training, [were] very important too."[117]

Finally, in late 1986 and early 1987, Saddam formed a new command for his rapidly expanding Republican Guard brigades, known as the Republican Guard Forces Command.[118] Saddam rotated brigades away from the front to train intensively on mobile operations, and he personally replaced commanders who resisted these efforts. As one general later put it, "He knew he could not win the war with these people."[119] According to one recent historical account, "There was [now] a greater willingness at the top to pay serious attention to the recommendations of the more professional officers to build up the Republican Guard's capabilities. . . . This effort to improve the Republican Guard involved more extensive training at all levels to improve tactical and battlefield proficiency of officers commanding Republican Guard units."[120]

For the first time, Saddam ensured that his forces actually practiced conducting both small-unit and large corps-level offensive and defensive operations in highly realistic, full-size mockups of Iranian defensive positions.[121] One general recounted years later, "There was an extensive training curriculum, day and night. . . . Saddam Hussein continuously followed up with us to see how our training was coming, and the readiness of our forces. . . . We had several active firing ranges and training grounds that would run 24 hours a day." In fact, many officers no longer wished to serve in the Guard because of these responsibilities.[122]

Iraq also formed Republican Guard naval infantry units during this period, and a few regular army armored and mechanized infantry divisions received additional training, too.[123] As Cordesman and Wagner report, "Iraqi armor and infantry were given special training in maneuver and combined-arms operations. . . . Iraq conducted corps-level exercises in fluid defense and counterattack tactics. . . . Iraqi artillery units were given special training in concentrating and shifting fire and in providing fire at the call of forward air controllers in the forward area rather than prepared fire."[124] Notably, these skills atrophied after the war as Saddam reimposed his prior restrictions on training.[125]

Command Arrangements

Iraq began the war with a command system that was both centralized and fragmented. It was centralized in the sense that virtually all battlefield decision-making authority lay in Saddam's personal hands or those of a small inner circle in Baghdad.[126] For example, Saddam "sent an order to all frontline units . . . stating the exact dimensions of the trenches to be dug."[127] He also ordered that soldiers could not retreat unless they were outnumbered by particular force ratios. Saddam even created a Punishment Corps that operated in rear areas to enforce this policy, and he approved commanders' executions of their own soldiers after battlefield defeats.[128] As a result, soldiers feared taking any action without specific authorization from higher headquarters or their unit's political officer.[129] Cordesman and Wagner note, "Every level of command tended to refer all decisions upwards. The entire burden of command eventually rested on Saddam Hussein and his immediate staff in Baghdad, a burden of command they lacked both the communications and the expertise to bear effectively."[130] This was in some sense what Saddam wanted, however, as he had explicitly modeled his command system on Stalin's.[131]

Saddam also intentionally fractured command lines to different parts of the military, ensuring that he personally controlled them and that no one unit could easily assume command of the others. For example, Saddam ensured that the chain of command for the Popular Army ran outside the armed forces and the Ministry of Defense, so that he could control it independently. The Republican Guard also bypassed the normal chain of command, reporting only to Saddam. In addition, Saddam frequently shuffled officers to prevent them from forming personal relationships with men under their command that could then be used to foment a coup.[132]

As the war went on, Saddam realized that these practices were detrimental to Iraqi effectiveness, particularly the ability to conduct complex operations. In one discussion with his generals, for example, he explicitly voiced his realization that "it is hard for the higher command to have a good control system when you have a large army with many brigades and it lacks coordination between its units."[133] It seems that although the centralization and fracturing of command might have been feasible when the army's main tasks were palace protection, monitoring the Shi'a, or shelling the Kurds, these practices proved paralyzing and dangerous for a multidivision army operating across three huge fronts in a conventional war. The aforementioned Iraqi military journal observed that "there is a limit to the number of individuals which one supervisor can manage effectively" and that Iraqi lines of command authority needed to be clarified to avoid conflicting orders and "duplicate leadership."[134]

In another conversation, an officer concurred with Saddam's dawning realization that a more decentralized command structure might allow better coordination across different branches of the Iraqi military. According to this officer, "In other armies they make different branches of the military interact and have the same tasks. Usually the armed forces break soldiers of different branches into working together by forcing them to do joint tasks. As they ease into it, it becomes a routine." Saddam agreed that Iraqi command arrangements needed to be restructured to "hinder any chances that the enemy would use the lack of coordination or communication for his advantage." He also listened as another officer suggested that Saddam needed to halt the destructive practice of frequently shuffling officers among different commands.[135] Still, there is little evidence that Saddam made any actual changes to these practices early in the war.[136]

Finally, in 1986–1987, Saddam did make significant changes to his command arrangements. First, he initiated a major devolution of command authority.[137] Ward writes that starting in mid-1986, "the Iraqi dictator limited his micromanagement of operations" and "allowed Iraq's increasingly competent and professional commanders more control."[138] Cordesman and Wagner also report that Iraq's field commanders were given a much stronger voice in directing battles and campaigns.[139] Saddam recalled many of the political officers, often called commissars, who had formerly been assigned to all Iraqi units above battalion strength, and those who remained found their command authority curtailed.[140]

Saddam never ended the fracturing of command, in the sense that the Guard continued to be separate from the Popular Army, which was separate from the regular army. But he did nothing to divide the Guard further and more than tripled its size. He also encouraged the formation of a functioning general staff system among Guard officers, reversing some of the intra-Guard fracturing that had existed earlier. In addition, he halted the constant rotation of officers.[141] Again, however, these policy changes did not outlast the war.[142]

Information Management

Saddam entered the war with information management practices oriented toward coup protection. Iraqi intelligence was generally more concerned with tracking political developments inside Iraq and monitoring the loyalty of the armed forces than with gathering information on Iran.[143] In fact, on the eve of the war Iraq had only three intelligence officers in the entire country tasked with Iran. Saddam had instead spent most of the 1970s constructing a vast spy network to report on the activities of military officers and the general population. One study notes that "when the war started, political commissars, who did nothing but report back to Saddam, were attached to all units. This system was still in place in 1982, an indication of Saddam's continued distrust."[144] In fact, in one conversation with his generals, Saddam responded to their disagreement about part of a report by noting, "The Intelligence Officer will settle this matter, because he was eavesdropping on you."[145]

[162]

Internal correspondence from the Iraqi General Military Intelligence Directorate similarly noted that after the war started, the government was facing difficulties gathering intelligence from its own population, because Iraq's citizens were so used to an intelligence apparatus focused on them instead of Iran. One document stressed that the government needed to work to "convince the masses that the staff intelligence directorates were established to watch the enemy and not our various sectors; we should end this sort of stereotype and convince them that intelligence is part of the armed forces and not a dominating department—with the only concern—of watching and looking for adversaries."[146]

The same writer also noted that thus far in the war, "intelligence is still not up to the required standard due to some organizational reasons."[147] Indeed, one of the first articles in the aforementioned Iraqi military journal emphasized the importance of basic tactical information, which it described as "the vital nerve in warfare." The article's author added that "long ago, it was said 'Give me information and I will give you victory.' The basis of warfare is the collection of information before and during the war. Information is indispensable to any commander regardless of his capability or status."[148] Again, the fact that an officer had to spell out these facts suggests continuing problems with information flow in the Iraqi military.

Given this climate, Saddam's officers rarely reported information that they thought he might not want to hear. As one general explained in an interview after the fall of the regime, "Saddam put great pressure on Iraqi commanders on the ground to avoid losses, which led them not to report failures. Withholding losses from reports and thus not receiving reinforcements or other support left commanders in impossible combat conditions. However, this was better than reporting their failures and suffering execution."[149]

Commanders often exaggerated their claims about battlefield events or chose not to convey important developments up the chain of command, which may explain why Saddam was so slow to recognize the effects of his policies and to attempt changes.[150] Iraqi officers also were afraid to speak to one another, fearing that they might be accused of coup plotting. As Cordesman and Wagner put it, "The command-and-control system was incapable of transmitting the true tactical situation. Senior Iraqi officers later noted that they often got more timely information from the media than they did from their own commanders at the front."[151]

That said, the problem was a two-way street: political leaders also severely limited the information that battlefield commanders received, even about events occurring directly in their areas of operation. According to Al-Marashi and Salama, "Controlling the dissemination of information served as a means of manipulating the military during the war"—and of preventing military units from collaborating in any potential internally directed actions that might threaten the regime. "Tactical field commanders rarely received timely intelligence down from the chain of command and thus never had a full picture of the nature of the Iranian forces in their theater."[152]

Starting in 1983, Saddam initiated some changes in his information management policies. First, he fired the security chief who managed the spy network in the armed forces.[153] The next year he made some attempts to gather more realistic information from his field officers, evident in their more frequent inclusion in high-level political meetings about the war.[154] Quite a bit of evidence suggests that by 1984 or 1985 Saddam was seeking a more realistic assessment of how to win the war. For example, a memo from Saddam to his commanders dated February 16, 1984, admits, "We must quietly examine our defensive measures and find out what type of activity we could add to those measures to increase their effectiveness."[155]

Still, only in 1986 or 1987 did Saddam institutionalize major changes in information management in the Republican Guard. According to Al-Marashi and Salama, Saddam finally embraced "the need for combined arms operations, even though in the past these had been discouraged due to political reasons. . . . To conduct these combined arms tactics, the officers had to convince Hussein to allow cooperation between the military services and devolve command and control authority to the commanders on the field."[156] Saddam complied, slashing "the number of bureaucratic barriers to the rapid transfer of information to field commanders" and lifting restrictions on interservice communication.[157] Unfortunately for Iraq, Saddam reversed these moves when the war ended, refocusing the Iraqi intelligence apparatus internally and resurrecting barriers to information sharing within the Iraqi military.[158]

The Implications for Iraqi Battlefield Effectiveness in the Iran-Iraq War

A personalist dictator, Saddam entered the Iran-Iraq War with military organizational practices optimized for regime protection against coups, rather than for the generation of conventional fighting power against an external opponent. Only when the resulting deficits actually posed a threat to Saddam's hold on power—by risking Iranian conquest or Saddam's overthrow by his frustrated officer corps—did Iraqi military organizational practices become more mixed, as the Republican Guard and key army divisions adopted conventional war practices distinct from those in the rest of the military.

As a result, one would expect that virtually all Iraqi units should have displayed poor effectiveness in the early years of the war against Iran. Their battlefield performance should have reflected essentially no tactical proficiency and no ability whatsoever to conduct complex operations. After 1986, however, there should have been substantial improvements in the battlefield effectiveness of Iraqi Republican Guard units and select regular army divisions. These units should have been tactically proficient and capable of at least some complex operations, especially when compared to other regular and Popular Army units.

Iraqi units that demonstrated tactical proficiency and/or the ability to conduct complex operations prior to 1986 would cast doubt on the argument from chapter 1, because they would show that the military was effective even under coup prevention practices. Similarly, Republican Guard and select regular army units that failed to demonstrate tactical proficiency and the ability to conduct at least some complex operations after 1986 would cast doubt on the utility of the framework, because they would show that major shifts in both threats and military organizational practices did not prompt corresponding changes in effectiveness.

By contrast, if the book's argument is wrong and alternative explanations focused on static national traits are right, then there should have been little variation over time or across different units of the Iraqi military. There also should have been little cross-national variation between Iraqi and Iranian units after 1986, for reasons that the next section brings into focus.

THREATS AND MILITARY ORGANIZATIONAL PRACTICES IN IRAN

Iran was a weakly institutionalized state whose leaders were deeply concerned about irregular, internal threats, particularly coups. This was as true of the revolutionary theocracy that took over in the 1980s as it had been of the Shah's monarchy. Neither regime fits neatly into ideal-typical autocratic regime type categories, but both had a strong strain of personalism (centered first on the Shah, then Khomeini), as well as other prominent indicators of coup threat. As a result, both regimes adopted military organizational practices designed largely to fend off this danger rather than to maximize performance in conventional war, and this focus persisted even as it traded off with other vital functions that each regime needed the military to perform: in the Shah's case, protection from revolution, and in Khomeini's case, protection from Iraq.

Fear of coups was particularly intense in the latter case, because the revolutionary regime was forced to go to war with a military inherited from the Shah. Revolutionary leaders strongly suspected that this legacy institution, known as the Artesh, would attempt to restore the prerevolutionary order. After all, the Shah had harbored residual worries about conventional, external threats, and—though far from embracing conventional war practices—he had allowed his military to engage in some U.S.-led training that made the Artesh seem especially dangerous to Iran's new leaders. In response, these leaders built parallel military organizations to watch over the legacy force and imposed coup prevention practices on both.

This section discusses the evolution of the Iranian military under these conditions and the implications for battlefield effectiveness. If the argument from chapter 1 is correct, Iranian performance generally should have been quite poor, but especially so as the war went on and the country's revolutionary leaders deepened their imposition of coup protection practices on the regular forces and eliminated any lingering benefits of the training that had occurred under the Shah. Meanwhile, the newly constituted Iranian revolutionary forces should not have displayed tactical proficiency or the ability to conduct complex operations.

These potential deficits notwithstanding, Iranian forces expanded rapidly over the course of the war. In 1980, the Artesh numbered 150,000 men, while revolutionary forces amounted to 75,000, in addition to some 400,000 men in the reserves. By 1986, the Artesh had more than doubled in size to 305,000, while revolutionary forces had grown to 350,000. When combined with the air force, navy, and remaining reserve forces, total Iranian strength was well over a million men.[159] As reflected in the slogan "Revolution before Victory," however, these forces were not primarily oriented toward defeating Iraq.[160]

The Threat Environment Facing the Iranian Regime

Despite the conventional threat from Iraq, leaders of the Islamic Republic essentially never budged from the belief that their greatest enemies lay within Iran, particularly in the armed forces. This belief was more than a mere by-product of the revolution, though, as the military had long been a central focus of political contestation in modern Iran, serving as both a source of power and a constant threat to it.

Iran had ended World War I as a British protectorate after invasions by both Russia and Britain. Fearing instability and Soviet influence, Britain supported a 1921 coup led by a young colonel, Reza Khan, who overthrew the last ruler of the Qajar dynasty and in 1925 established Pahlavi rule. Although Reza Shah Pahlavi wore a crown, his regime was better characterized as a military dictatorship.[161] The Shah enlarged the Iranian army, now called the Artesh, in order to assert central authority over Iran's many tribes and to undermine the clergy. At the same time, rumors of coup plotting were frequent, and the Shah was careful to promote only those military officers whom he personally knew to be loyal.[162]

During World War II, British and Soviet forces again invaded large swaths of the country, in part because of Iran's strategic location and good relations with Nazi Germany. Seeing that the Artesh could not hold up against these foreign armies, the Shah accepted Allied terms in August 1941 and abdicated in favor of his son, Muhammad Reza Shah Pahlavi, who took the throne in September.[163]

The postwar years brought turmoil to Iran. The young Shah faced growing opposition from both the communist Tudeh party and the Nationalist Front, led by Muhammad Mossadeq, who became the country's prime minister in 1951. Mossadeq's growing political popularity eventually forced the Shah to give him control of the war ministry, a position from which Mossadeq immediately began to reduce the military's size and purge it of the Shah's supporters.[164]

Army officers responded by conspiring to remove Mossadeq. Given his decision to nationalize Iranian oil—a threat to British profits, which had been one of the main rallying cries of the Nationalist Front—British intelligence soon joined the plotting, as did the Central Intelligence Agency. The result was a 1953 coup in which the army carefully orchestrated Mossadeq's ouster and restored to the Shah wide-ranging powers more akin to those his father had enjoyed. Over the next several years, the CIA also assisted the Shah in establishing an internal intelligence organization, eventually known as the SAVAK, which assisted in further consolidating the Shah's rule and ridding the Iranian armed forces of Tudeh supporters.[165]

His power thus fortified, the Shah spent the next twenty-five years building the Iranian military into the largest and best-equipped force in the Middle East. With extensive aid from the United States, the Shah developed the military as the key pillar of his authority.[166] Keenly aware that both he and his father had come to power through coups, the Shah lavished the officer corps with pay and perks.[167]

During the 1960s and 1970s, the military's role was primarily internal, focused on implementing the Shah's reform and modernization programs and ruthlessly quashing opposition.[168] Under the Shah, "senior officers were assigned to run provinces, important government ministries and large state enterprises, particularly major industrial installations." Even the last major expeditionary operation mounted by the prerevolutionary Artesh, a campaign to help the Sultan of Oman defeat an insurgency in 1973, reflected a military that had evolved to perform mostly irregular, internal tasks related to state-building or regime protection, rather than to combat external, state-based threats in conventional warfare.[169]

[167]

Nevertheless, the Shah did worry about external threats ranging from the Soviets to the Iraqi Kurds to the Egyptians. By the late 1970s, some 45,000 Americans were living in Iran to provide various kinds of training and support to help secure Iran externally.[170] But the year 1978 shattered this equilibrium as a diverse series of popular grievances with the Shah led to violent uprisings across the country. Exiled Shi'i cleric Ayatollah Ruhollah Khomeini skillfully capitalized on the citizenry's discontent with enforced secularism, economic inequality, and dependence on the Americans. He also cleverly appealed to the military not to defend the Shah's regime, sparking desertions and mutinies. For his part, the Shah proved unwilling to order the sort of harsh crackdown that might have saved his regime, though perhaps he refrained simply because the military had not been trained to put down riots or control crowds.[171] In January 1979, the Shah fled.

Khomeini arrived two weeks later, and within a matter of days what remained of the Iranian military returned to its barracks.[172] The revolutionaries had triumphed, but the diverse anti-Shah coalition displayed little consensus. Secular nationalists, liberals, leftists, communists, and various Islamists all had different ideas about the shape of the new order.[173] Between February and November 1979, Khomeini began to systematically neutralize other centers of power in postrevolutionary Iran. As Menashri has observed, "Khomeini, who had labored strenuously to keep them together as long as he needed their aggregate strength, now turned against them. To do so he applied an old Persian proverb: 'if you want to smash a bunch of sticks, don't do it in one blow. Break them one by one.'"[174]

Khomeini started by pressuring the new prime minister, Mehdi Bazargan, into accepting members of the clerically dominated Islamic Republican Party (IRP) into his administration.[175] These members then lent further support to the armed groups known as the Islamic Revolutionary Guards Corps (IRGC), or Pasdaran, springing up around the country in support of Khomeini. During 1979, the country descended into virtual civil war as the Guards fought against their former allies, especially the Tudeh and the Marxist movements such as the Fedayeen e-Khalq and Mujahidin e-Khalq (MEK).[176] According to Ward, the Fedayeen and MEK at the time "had between fifteen thousand and twenty thousand armed guerrillas, while the Tudeh Party had about seven thousand armed men and women in Tehran alone. Militant Islamic groups aided by cadres of Lebanese Shia and Palestinians had nearly twenty thousand fighters, while another twenty thousand or more armed Iranians were in the streets after the military's armories were looted."[177] The Guards also put down ethnic revolts during this period by nearly all the major non-Persian groups in Iran, including the Kurds, Arabs, Turkmen, Baluchs, and Azeris.[178]

[168]

November 1979 then brought what some have called "the second Islamic revolution" or the "clerical coup d'état."[179] Angered by news of a meeting between Bazargan and U.S. national security adviser Zbigniew Brzezinski, Iranian students—probably with direction from the Guards—stormed the U.S. embassy and took hostages in protest. Bazargan resigned, and his government fell. Khomeini supporters then quickly pushed through constitutional changes granting the ayatollah absolute power under the concept of guardianship, also known as clerical rule. He was now the commander-in-chief of the armed forces and the Guards as well.[180]

January 1980 brought the election of a moderate secular intellectual, Abol Hasan Bani Sadr, as president. Having become allies during their anti-Shah days in France, Khomeini backed Bani Sadr and delegated to him the responsibility for commanding the military, including the Guards. But the Guards soon rejected Bani Sadr's authority, and, as had been the case with Bazargan, the gulf between Bani Sadr and the radical clerics who supported Khomeini grew too great. Bani Sadr was dismissed in June 1981.[181] With this step, the Khomeini faction was no longer just a faction; it had transformed into a juggernaut in full control of the legislative, executive, and judicial branches of government.[182]

Khomeini had recognized early on that gaining a monopoly on the use of force would be essential to consolidating the Islamic regime. In particular, he had shown immediate concern in the spring of 1979 about the threat posed to the revolution by the professional military. Although the Artesh's return to the barracks had been instrumental in the Shah's demise, it was not exactly a hotbed of support for the new clerical regime.[183] Nikola Schahgaldian, who interviewed dozens of exiled Iranian officers in the 1980s, notes, "From the very beginning of the Islamic regime, the ruling clerics were intensely aware of the potential threat that the Shah's military posed to their own political survival."[184] Guard units were stationed at the exits to Artesh garrisons, ensuring that Artesh soldiers did not move without permission from Khomeini, and these fears only worsened as the regime learned of six coup plots in the first half of 1980.

Against this backdrop, Khomeini ordered the establishment of the Revolutionary Guard in May 1979. The force grew from 30,000 in 1980 to more than a quarter of a million during the war.[185] The Guard also helped oversee volunteer militias of young Iranians known as the Basij, which would eventually swell to 200,000 members at the height of the war.[186] Both of these forces helped ensure that Khomeini had at his disposal a large coercive apparatus committed to the ideals of the revolution.

It is crucial to note, however, that Khomeini formed this apparatus with the destruction of domestic enemies in mind. Antiregime violence continued in Iran, peaking in a spectacular attack on IRP headquarters in June

1981, followed by the assassination of the president and prime minister in August.[187] The regime executed thousands of opponents that summer.[188]

After this crackdown, violence against the regime lessened considerably.[189] By 1982, for example, the U.S. Department of State described the regime as "in firm control of Iran with no meaningful opposition within the country."[190] The Defense Intelligence Agency made a similar assessment, noting, "Politically, the Khomeini regime has defeated most of its immediate internal opponents and continues to consolidate control."[191] Although an additional coup plot was discovered in April 1982, and 1983–1984 brought further assaults on the Tudeh, in general the regime had stabilized.[192] It is important to realize, however, that this stabilization occurred not because the regime had suddenly built well-functioning political institutions that managed opposition, but because the regime had used the brute force of an internally directed coercive apparatus to kill or repress all dissenters. The regime remained focused on internal threats.

To the extent that Iran's leaders even considered Iraq a threat prior to the war, this fear had meaning largely within the context of Iran's own domestic battles. For example, while still in office Bani Sadr wrote the UN Secretary-General that "from the very beginning of our revolutionary victory . . . , Iraq has been . . . sending Iraqi agents and armed units . . . for the purposes of committing acts of sabotage and assisting counter-revolutionary groups. . . . Iraq has been a haven for the remnants of the previous regime and other reactionary and criminal elements involved in propagandistic and terroristic activities against the Islamic Republic of Iran."[193]

These suspicions were not paranoia. As mentioned, Saddam had given refuge to the Shah's last prime minister and last army commander, who were now broadcasting attacks on Khomeini from Iraq. Iraq also supported anti-Khomeini coup efforts. Notably, though, Iraq was a threat not because of its conventional military capabilities but because of its counterrevolutionary activities inside Iran. Hence as Iran expanded the Revolutionary Guards into a force of several hundred thousand by August 1981, it did so primarily with the goals of providing a counterweight to the regular military and protecting the regime from internal threats.[194] It was this evolving force that faced Iraq on the battlefield.

Promotion Patterns

The idea of promotion on merit was relatively unknown in Iran, even under the Shah. As Ward argues, "The original sin of the Shah's armed forces was that political considerations took first priority in managing the officer corps, even if this meant removing capable officers or promoting mediocre ones loyal to the court."[195] The Shah did not simply hire cronies—he actively fired anyone who appeared competent enough to threaten him.[196]

This was the so-called professional military that Iran's new leaders inherited in 1979. Khomeini further weakened it by initiating a massive wave of purges, comparable to Stalin's on the eve of World War II. Schahgaldian reports that "by the end of 1979 almost all of the hardline pro-Shah officers and those who had been known for their pro-American views were eliminated, regardless of rank, in one way or the other. These reportedly included all of the 14 army division commanders, the eight commanders of the independent army and army air command brigades, and all the military governors." Starting in 1980, the purges reached into the lower ranks, and "membership with any political group not in favor of the newly instituted clerical regime came to be regarded as a sufficient ground for purge."[197] According to Ward, extensive purges, even below the rank of major, continued throughout the first half of the 1980s. "The Iranian officer corps may have lost as much as 40 percent of its strength by the eve of the war with Iraq," he estimates.[198]

Although Khomeini sought to strip the Artesh of its imperial taint, in a certain sense his policies reflected continuity rather than disjuncture. The definition of political reliability shifted—from loyalty to the Shah to loyalty to the clerical regime—yet it remained a far more important criterion for advancement than demonstrated military competence. In the Islamic Republic, officers gained their commissions primarily through family ties to the clergy, who were able to manipulate promotion and selection even of senior officers. In many cases captains and lieutenants were promoted to fill senior billets recently vacated by disfavored colonels and generals.[199] The result was an officer corps supportive of the new regime but even more poorly situated than its predecessor to handle the challenges of conventional interstate war.

These coup protection practices seem to have abated slightly as the war went on. Relations between the Artesh and the Pasdaran did improve a bit, and the pace of purges slowed somewhat after 1982.[200] Many former officers were called up, in some cases from prison. There is also evidence that the regime came to value battlefield competence in making some leadership decisions after 1983.[201] But there was no sign of any systematic improvements in promotion practices. Furthermore, restoring officers from the Shah's military hardly was equivalent to embracing true conventional war practices, given the manner in which the Shah himself had chosen officers.

[171]

Training Regimens

Under the Shah, military training at least had purported to prepare the armed forces for combat, although his methods had been far from consistent with conventional war practices. Extensive and realistic training at the small- and large-unit levels was rare in the Shah's army, for example.[202] The training that did occur tended to consist of set-piece exercises organized by the United States.[203] "Not wishing to risk mistakes or raise suspicions," Ward writes, "unit commanders showed a marked lack of interest in collective training or in developing their abilities to handle larger combined forces."[204]

Clearly, training under the Shah was not ideal, but it did exist. After the revolution, even the limited military school system all but collapsed.[205] As Ward explains, "The clerics were content to allow logistical problems to fester while they focused on the military's political reliability. . . . Advanced training came to nearly a complete halt."[206] The purges also caused enormous turnover in the institutions responsible for training, such as they were, and dramatically lowered the standards of instruction. Schahgaldian reported based on his interviews with exiled military officers that "in general, the professional military has become much more lenient both in admission and graduation requirements of most training centers. . . . They lowered the professional competence of the officer corps."[207] Even Iraqi intelligence noted in 1980 that many Iranian units had "not conducted any exercises since the fall of the Shah."[208]

To the extent that the new regime did prepare soldiers for the battlefield, the lessons tended to consist of ideological indoctrination rather than realistic, live fire opportunities to develop and hone military skills. The military academy now devoted more than one-third of all courses to an ideological and political curriculum. Khomeini's new Political-Ideological Directorate (PID) assigned clerics from the joint staff down to the platoon level to provide ideological and political education, write new training materials, hold daily prayers, and enforce Islamic standards of behavior.[209]

In short, Khomeini was more concerned that soldiers accept the ideas needed to consolidate the revolution than that they develop the tactical and operational skills needed to defend against the Iraqis.[210] To be sure, he probably considered the two related: soldiers who believed in the ideals of the revolution would be more motivated to evict the "infidel" Saddam and "liberate" the Shi'a. But clearly Iran prioritized ideological indoctrination over even very basic training.

Many soldiers reportedly received only a few weeks of instruction of any type.[211] This reality appears to have been confirmed by Iraqi interrogations of Iranian prisoners of war.[212] Basij training in particular was nominal, usually consisting only of very basic small arms training and perhaps a few hours of exercises in penetrating defensive obstacles.[213] Iran did not restore the training systems that had existed under the Shah and conducted little refresher training.[214]

Furthermore, large segments of the Guard were focused on local policing and enforcement of Islamic laws and regulation, the defense of the regime against counterrevolution, the protection of government buildings, the collection of internal intelligence, the sponsoring of proregime rallies, publication of proregime literature, and so on.[215] Thus, to the extent that training occurred, its content was geared toward duties unlikely to have prepared Iranian soldiers for fighting a conventional war against an opposing land army. Even six years into the war, a senior Iranian minister emphasized this distinction: "The mission of the Guards of the Revolution is to protect the Islamic revolution, which may be from threats other than those across the frontiers."[216]

Command Arrangements

Iran adopted coup prevention practices with regard to command arrangements. Even under the Shah, Iranian command arrangements had been highly centralized and intentionally fractured, in order to maximize the Shah's personal control of the armed forces. As one study notes, "The Shah ensured loyalty to himself by applying the divide-and-rule principle among his generals, accomplished by exacerbating intense personal rivalries among his generals and placing 'personal enemies alternately in the chain of command' to preclude the possibility of a coup."[217]

In addition, the Shah "frequently shuffled commanders to ensure that they could not form power bases or enduring alliances. Under his micromanagement, no regular chain of command developed. Every general viewed himself as responsible to no one other than the Shah, and the field commanders regularly bypassed the SDC [Supreme Defense Council] and their service chiefs to contact Muhammad Reza."[218] The entire system was so dependent on the personal authority of the Shah that his direct permission was required for any general to visit Tehran.[219]

Ironically, this command structure helped doom the Shah during the revolution. According to Ward, "Muhammad Reza could not break his habit of using rivalry and resentments among his senior commanders to prevent the rise of a potential alternative to his rule. The result was a senior command structure unable to coordinate action to stop the revolution."[220] Roberts has made a similar observation, noting that because "the Shah insisted that the heads of the armed forces deal with him directly on all matters and prohibited direct contact among service chiefs," the military was unable to coordinate an effective counterrevolutionary campaign.[221] Although the Iranian revolution later purged individuals loyal to the Shah, in some sense the new regime also perpetuated the underlying command structure the Shah had developed: overlapping chains of command reporting directly to political leaders. Now these leaders were all clerics, but the resemblance was notable.

Certainly, centralized control broke down in the period immediately surrounding the revolution; many military units acted independently with little direction from Tehran.[222] Nevertheless, Khomeini reasserted his personal control over the military by inserting mullahs throughout the command structures of both the Pasdaran and the Artesh.[223] According to Ward, "Clerical supervision was arranged for all Pasdaran units down to the local level."[224] During 1980–1981, the revolutionary regime was so worried that Bani Sadr was trying to isolate the regular army from Islamic influences that the Supreme Defense Council, dominated by clerics, insisted that religious commissars be attached to all Artesh units. Even when Bani Sadr fled Iran, these commissars—with the power to override the commands of regular army military officers—remained in place.[225]

In essence, the mullahs had developed "their own separate chain of command through the various religious commissars in the forces and often exercised a command authority which overrode that of the regular commanders."[226] It became common for senior commanders "to bypass regular command chains and go directly to leading clerical figures in order to resolve internal military problems."[227] In fact, in what must have been a somewhat awkward observation given Saddam's own command structure, an Iraqi assessment noted the damaging effect of these conflicting and confusing chains of command: "the units are driven by committees consisting of three persons that are mostly clergymen. This has left a bad effect on the psychological state of the commanders and leaders."[228]

Even more striking than these moves toward centralization in Iran's command structure was Khomeini's repeated willingness to fracture command, a pattern rooted in the establishment of the Guard in May 1979.[229] The emergence of two parallel militaries, each with its own chain of command, created hostility and tension within the country's armed forces, hindering coordination.[230] Again, even an Iraqi assessment picked up on the rivalry, noting, "The relationship between the Guards and the Armed Forces is full of tension. The members of the Guards feel that they are the real power of Al-Khomeini. They behaved improperly with the members of the armed forces and degraded them. This has built grudge [*sic*] and hatred towards them. The statements of Bani Sadr and the commanders of the guards show the size of the exploitation, the chaos that has spread between their flanks, and the differences between their commanders."[231]

[174]

Iran's leaders wasted repeated opportunities to rectify the problem. A joint military command between the army and the Guard was announced as early as 1982, but real integration never happened, often because of interference from senior mullahs. Ultimately, Iran's leaders did not want to resolve the division between the regular army and the Guards. The two entities exchanged some officers, but tensions remained high. According to Cordesman and Wagner, "reports of clashes between clerics, officers of the regular forces, and officers of the Revolutionary Guards continued through 1988."[232] The two organizations maintained separate budgets, recruiting systems, and intelligence arms as well.[233]

Although the mullahs' interference and the intramilitary tensions lessened somewhat as the war went on, they never disappeared.[234] Iranian leaders continued to require centralized religious approval for most military decisions and to maintain military institutions that were deliberately and formally divided.

Information Management

As with the other areas of military activity, the Shah had not developed information management practices oriented toward conventional war. Rather than optimize his officers' ability to acquire, share, and use information in wartime, the Shah had developed an elaborate internally directed intelligence apparatus to report on his own forces. According to Ward, the Shah "used multiple organizations, including SAVAK, his own secret intelligence bureau, and military intelligence, to watch the armed forces and each other, ensuring that officers could not confidently make alliances with each other or regime opponents."[235]

The Shah also severely restricted horizontal communication among his officers.[236] "For example," according to Schahgaldian, "the three service chiefs, the commanders of the national police force and gendarmerie, and the directors of various security and intelligence organizations all reported directly to the monarch and received orders from him and were permitted to communicate with one another only through the Shah or his own personal staff."[237] While these measures lessened the likelihood of a coup, they also all but eliminated the ability of different units to communicate. In addition, they created a political-military climate characterized by distrust, suspicion, and hesitation on the part of the officer corps to take any action absent direct approval from the Shah.[238]

Khomeini continued the essence of many of these policies, establishing multiple organizations with overlapping domestic spying responsibilities. These agencies were intended "partly to keep watch over the regular military and potential opposition groups and partly to keep watch over each other."[239] In this way, Ward argues, the regime was able to generate "a large number of overlapping control mechanisms" that produced multiple independent streams of information about any potential threats in either the regular military or Iranian society writ large.[240] Military officers, NCOs, and civilian defense employees all could expect to be monitored closely by a network of clerical spies. [241] The same PID representatives who oversaw ideological indoctrination in every unit also "spied on the soldiers and served as snitches."[242] In general, the system was set up to manage information about activities inside Iran—not to gather intelligence on external adversaries such as Iraq.[243]

Khomeini also continued the Shah's strict limits on horizontal communication among officers.[244] By and large, officers simply were not allowed to discuss military matters or anything else outside politically approved channels.[245] For the new government in Tehran, the risk of counterrevolutionary plotting seemed too great. As Schahgaldian observed based on his interviews with escaped officers, "It is believed that three or more senior or middle-level officers from different branches or units cannot meet in a group and hope to remain unreported."[246]

The Implications for Iranian Battlefield Effectiveness in the Iran-Iraq War

The Iranian regime adopted coup prevention practices with respect to promotions, training, command, and information. Broadly speaking, these measures departed little from the Shah's, with the exception of practices governing training, although even here the difference was subtle. As a result, the framework presented in chapter 1 would expect Iranian revolutionary units (the Pasdaran and Basij) to have displayed poor battlefield effectiveness—no tactical proficiency and no ability to conduct complex operations. Iranian regular units (the Artesh) should have displayed comparatively adequate battlefield effectiveness early in the war, reflecting the lingering influence of training practices under the Shah. In particular, they should have displayed at least some tactical proficiency. Still, the overall fighting effectiveness of these legacy units should not have been especially high and should have declined over the course of the war as the revolutionary leaders' organizational practices exerted their full force.

Iranian revolutionary units that displayed high levels of battlefield effectiveness despite the consistent application of coup protection practices would cast significant doubt on my argument. Iranian regular units that displayed increasing rather than decreasing levels of battlefield effectiveness over the course of the war would also cast doubt on the connections posited here among threats, practices, and performance. In

[176]

addition, if there were little to no variation over time or across different units of the Iranian military, or little cross-national variation between the performance of Iranian regular units and Iraqi military units in the early years of the war, that would lend support to alternative explanations focused on static national traits.

This chapter has examined the nature of prewar and intrawar threats and military organizational practices in Iraq and Iran. The general argument is that irregular, internal threats, especially coups, dominated the calculations of leaders in both states when it came to designing their military organizations. The result in both was a strong tendency toward military organizational practices that protected against coups instead of maximizing combat power for conventional war.

Two important exceptions arose, however. First, Saddam thoroughly shifted toward conventional war practices after 1986 in the Republican Guard and in some regular army units. As a result, we would expect that the performance of the Iraqi Republican Guard and select regular army units should have begun to improve significantly toward the end of the war. They should have demonstrated good tactical proficiency and even the ability to conduct complex operations, especially compared to earlier Iraqi performance and to Iranian performance during the same period. Evidence that Iraqi effectiveness did not improve after these changes, that it improved before they happened, or that Iraqi forces did not perform better than Iranian forces after this shift, would cast doubt on my argument.

Second, the Iranian military exhibited some variation as well. The regular Iranian military units that had existed prior to the revolution had been subject to different training practices than the units formed after the revolution. Although Khomeini's policies overall proved quite similar to the Shah's, training constituted an area of subtle difference. As a result, there should have been at least somewhat better battlefield effectiveness by the regular forces compared to the revolutionary forces early in the war, and the effectiveness of the regular forces should have declined over time as coup protection practices were more fully imposed.

These predictions will be tested in the next chapter, but even the evidence presented thus far should induce skepticism about some of the variables emphasized in existing theories of military effectiveness. The evidence from the Iraqi case, for example, suggests that Arab culture and autocracy do not completely predetermine a military's trajectory. By the same token, the fact that populous, prosperous Iran, a beneficiary of significant U.S. aid, adopted military organizational practices under both the Shah and Khomeini that were very similar to those used initially in Iraq suggests that material power alone does little to guarantee any particular type of military institutional development.

That said, these anomalies do not indicate that the variables emphasized in existing theories are irrelevant for explaining military performance. Nor do these observations prove that differences in threats and
military organizational practices really matter for battlefield effectiveness. The next chapter turns to these questions, examining a series of
battles between Iran and Iraq from 1980 to 1988 in order to adjudicate the
relative causal weight of different factors in explaining actual fighting
power.

[5]

Battlefield Effectiveness in Iraq and Iran

This chapter examines the impact of threats and military organizational practices on battlefield effectiveness in the Iran-Iraq War from 1980 to 1988. Specifically, it focuses on the Iraqi invasion and initial battles in Iran from September to November 1980; the Iranian counteroffensives from January 1981 to May 1982; the battle for Basra in July 1982 and subsequent Iranian attacks inside Iraq, including the battles for the Hawizeh Marshes in 1984 and 1985; the battles for al-Faw and Mehran in 1986; Iran's Karbala offensives from December 1986 to April 1987; the second battle for al-Faw in April 1988; and the Iraqi final offensives during the spring and summer of 1988.

These battles are useful in probing the book's framework. Each battle saw minimal involvement by other actors, allowing us to isolate the fighting effectiveness of the Iraqi and Iranian forces of interest.[1] This series of battles also captures both offensive and defensive operations for Iran and Iraq involving military units whose organizational practices varied (see table 5.1). As such, the battles enable multiple opportunities to examine whether Iraqi and Iranian battlefield effectiveness was consistent with what we would expect based on the threat environments and military organizational practices outlined in chapter 4.

In general, the battlefield evidence is consistent with what we would expect: coup prevention practices were a consistent barrier to effectiveness in both countries, with two exceptions. The lingering effects of some conventional war practices under the Shah led to adequate effectiveness by Iranian regular forces early in the war, and Saddam's shifts toward such practices produced improvements in select Iraqi units late in the war. These patterns again suggest the connection between the threat

Table 5.1. Iran-Iraq War battles and campaigns examined

	On the offense	On the defense
Iraqi general forces	Invasion, 1980 Mehran, 1986 Al-Faw II, 1988 Final offensives, 1988	Counteroffensives, 1981–1982 Basra and subsequent battles, including Hawizeh Marshes, 1982–1985 Al-Faw I, 1986 Karbala offensives, 1986–1987
Iraqi Republican Guard	Invasion, 1980 Al-Faw II, 1988 Final offensives, 1988	Al-Faw I, 1986 Counteroffensives, 1981–1982 Karbala offensives, 1986–1987
Iranian regular army (Artesh)	Counteroffensives, 1981–1982 Basra and subsequent battles, including Hawizeh Marshes, 1982–1985 Al-Faw I, 1986 Karbala offensives, 1986–1987	Invasion, 1980 Mehran, 1986 Al-Faw II, 1988 Final offensives, 1988
Iranian revolutionary forces (Pasdaran/ Guard and Basij/ Militia)	Counteroffensives, 1981–1982 Basra and subsequent battles, including Hawizeh Marshes, 1982–1985 Al-Faw I, 1986 Karbala offensives, 1986–1987	Invasion, 1980 Mehran, 1986 Al-Faw II, 1988 Final offensives, 1988

environment, military organizational practices, and battlefield effectiveness. That said, other factors also mattered to the military performance of both countries, and the end of the chapter addresses those alternative explanations.

BACKGROUND: THE IRAN-IRAQ WAR, 1980–1988

The battles examined in this chapter occurred in the context of a much larger war.[2] As already mentioned, ground combat in the Iran-Iraq War comprised three major phases. The first began with the Iraqi invasion of Iranian Khuzestan in 1980, which encompassed battles for the Iranian cities of Dezful, Abadan, Mehran, and Khorramshahr

[180]

during September–November 1980. Despite the Iraqi advantage of surprise, operations generally involved surrounding and besieging outnumbered Iranian defenders. Iran began to marshal its forces for offensive action starting in early 1981 and kicked off a major counteroffensive in September. Gradually Iran regained much of the territory it had lost, conducting operations in Khuzestan into the spring of 1982, including the very large battle of Khorramshahr in April and May.

The summer of 1982 marked the beginning of the war's second major phase with the Iranian invasion of Iraq. After nearly succeeding in taking the southern city of Basra in a large battle in July, the Iranians settled into a pattern of annual offensives, as exemplified in the battles of 1983 and a series of inconclusive struggles during 1984 and 1985 for control of the strategic Hawizeh Marshes, a large swampy area of the border containing significant oil reserves. Most of the fighting during this period amounted to a grinding war of attrition, living up to Chaim Herzog's characterization of the conflict as a "delicate balance of incompetence."[3] The one exception was Iran's surprising conquest of the al-Faw Peninsula, Iraq's gateway to the Gulf, in February 1986. After this momentary victory, though, Iran continued to launch offensives during the rest of 1986 and in 1987 with few gains.

The year 1988 saw the dramatic third phase of the war, as the Iraqis returned to the offensive, launching a series of operations to drive out the Iranians. In April, the Iraqis decisively regained control of al-Faw. The Iraqis followed this success with four more quick offensives from May through July of that year, virtually collapsing the Iranian military and forcing Iran to accept a ceasefire in August 1988.

My analysis focuses on the ground battles, the arena in which the majority of fighting took place and in which the war was decided. A focus on ground warfare also allows for the most consistent comparison between the Iran-Iraq and Vietnam cases. Still, the war was far from a land-only affair, with both sides using strategic and tactical airpower. The Iranians also deployed significant naval forces in an attempt to strangle Iraq's access to the Gulf. For their part, the Iraqis used chemical weapons early and often, eventually mounting them on long-range missiles targeted at Iranian population centers. The Iranians also engaged in some missile attacks on Iraqi cities.[4]

Third parties did participate in the war. In addition to Kurdish involvement, the United States eventually deployed naval forces to keep shipping open in the Gulf. Indeed, the war probably ended more expeditiously because the United States trounced the Iranian navy in an apparently unrelated skirmish the very day after the Iraqis retook al-Faw in 1988.[5] Overall, however, the war was fought on the ground by the Iraqi and Iranian armies, so it is on these interactions that the chapter focuses.

THE IRAQI INVASION: SEPTEMBER–NOVEMBER 1980

The Iraqi invasion of Iran and the latter's initial defense of its territory offer an important opportunity to observe the battlefield effectiveness of both states in their first large-scale encounter. In addition to
providing a chance to observe both countries' tactical proficiency, the
campaign shows the Iraqi military attempting to conduct offensive
complex operations. The Iraqi campaign plan envisioned a series of
lightning strikes against key Iranian targets across the border and was
to have relied on a combined force of armor, artillery, infantry, and some
airpower.

Evidence from the battles is largely consistent with what we would
expect based on the book's framework. Despite having a significant advantage in manpower and catching the Iranians by surprise, the Iraqis'
advance was slow, clumsy, and very costly in terms of casualties and
equipment losses. The Iraqis displayed serious tactical shortcomings and
little competence in complex operations. The Iranians did not perform
much better. Only the regular forces displayed any tactical proficiency,
and neither the regular nor the revolutionary forces attempted to conduct complex operations. Close examination of battlefield events suggests that both sides were more lucky than good, owing the gains they
made more to the mistakes of the other side than to their own performance of key tasks.

The Forces on Each Side

At the war's outset, Iraq's twelve active-duty divisions were deployed
at various points along its eastern border: five in the north, near the
Kurds; two in the central front, roughly opposite Baghdad; and five in
the south opposite Khuzestan, the oil-rich, Arab-populated area of Iran
that also offered excellent access to the Gulf. The Iraqi battle plan envisioned an initial Israeli-style air attack followed by armored thrusts into
Iranian territory, with the bulk of the effort in the southern sector (see
map 5.1).

In addition to its substantial inventory of tanks and other armored vehicles, Iraq had ample artillery and antitank guided missiles.[6] Saddam's
spending spree in the 1970s had ensured that much of this arsenal was of
high quality. The Iraqis possessed T-72 main battle tanks, the best Soviet
export at the time; BMP-1 infantry fighting vehicles; and MiG-23 Flog-
gers in addition to older Su-22 Fitter fighter-bombers.[7]

Arrayed against this juggernaut were one Iranian infantry division in
the far north, an infantry division slightly farther south, an armored

[182]

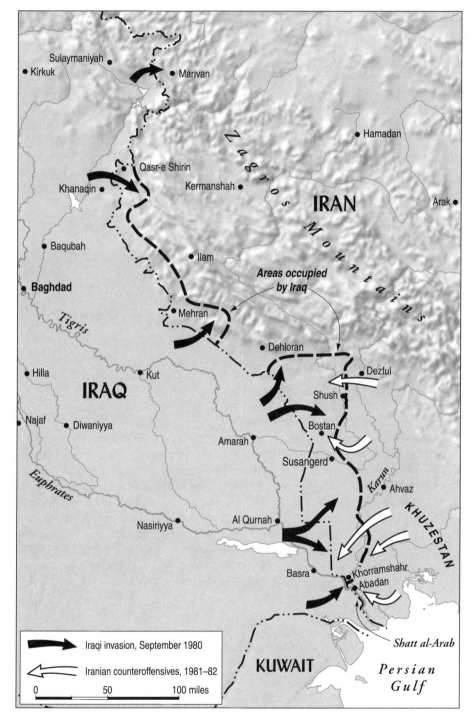

Map 5.1. The Iraqi invasion of Iran, 1980. Adapted from Steven R. Ward, *Immortal: A Military History of Iran and Its Armed Forces* (Washington, DC: Georgetown University Press, 2009), 250.

Table 5.2. The Iraqi invasion of Iran, fall 1980

	Iraq	Iran
Battle summary		
Tactical orientation	Offensive	Defensive
Plan	Air attack followed by multipronged invasion	Ambushes and roadblocks, then retreat to urban areas
Weapons	2,750 tanks, 1,400 artillery pieces, 4,000 APCs, 340 fighter-bombers	500 tanks, 300 artillery pieces, <100 aircraft[a]
Manpower	In south: three armored and two mechanized infantry divisions	In south: two understrength divisions, two under-strength brigades, border forces
Losses	10,000	15,000[b]
Effectiveness summary		
Tactical proficiency?	No	Yes, among the regular forces
Complex operations?	No	No opportunity to observe
As expected?	Yes	Somewhat

[a] Order of battle data from Pollack, *Arabs at War*, 186.
[b] Loss figures from Cordesman and Wagner, *Lessons*, 108.

division in the central sector, a brigade at Qasr-e Shirin, a brigade at Mehran, and an armored division at Ahvaz. Iran had one more armored division and an airborne division in reserve, but only two divisions and two brigades sat opposite the main lines of Iraqi attack in the south, the key sector. These Iranian forces were also significantly understrength. Most combat units stood at only 30–50 percent of their authorized manpower due to the upheavals of the revolution and the purges (see table 5.2). Available manpower consisted primarily of Pasdaran, that is, units from the Guard, not the Artesh, or regular military.[8] Iran's armor was mostly Chieftain and Patton tanks.

The Battles

The Iraqi attack on September 22, 1980, began with a series of air strikes that attempted to mimic Israeli operations in 1967. Although Iraq's strikes inflicted negligible damage—in part because the Shah had hardened and dispersed his air bases according to U.S. standards, and in part because the Iraqis planned and executed their attacks poorly—the Iraqis proceeded with their invasion.

At the northernmost points of the invasion and in the central sector, the Iraqis were able to overrun the towns of Qasr-e Shirin and Mehran within the first day. Penetrating Iranian territory to depths of nearly thirty miles in some places, the Iraqis faced only disorganized and scattered resistance. They soon spread out in a thirty-mile front along the central sector, guarding potential routes to Baghdad.

In the south the Iraqis launched their major offensive thrust. Deploying three armored and two mechanized infantry divisions, they quickly reached the outskirts of Khorramshahr and Abadan. Along the way, the Iranians had formed some initial roadblocks and ambush sites, but the Iraqis broke through with heavy artillery and antitank missiles. Recognizing their odds, the Iranians withdrew to more defensible urban terrain—a feat made easier by the fact that Iraqi forces never went after Iranian rear areas or vigorously pursued retreating Iranian forces.

The Iraqis soon found themselves facing a four-week battle in Khorramshahr, a town of 70,000 where 3,000 Artesh soldiers and thousands of Guards had burrowed into the classic advantages of an urban defense despite having little more than rifles, grenades, and Motolov cocktails.[9] Iranian efforts were then aided by the Iraqi decision to "soften up" the city with heavy artillery fire. This tactic not only roused the local population to their city's defense but later made it far more difficult for Iraqi armor to move through the area.

Indeed, Cordesman and Wagner note, "Iraq rapidly found that it could not send tanks unescorted into the city and that it had to send in infantry support." But because Iraqi forces had received no training in urban warfare, "they moved far too cautiously in maneuvering through the less-defended parts of the city and repeatedly became the victims of Iranian ambushes. Neither Iraqi armor nor infantry conducted aggressive reconnaissance, and both tended to wait until massive firepower could be brought to bear. Iraq was forced to slowly secure the perimeter of the city with the armored division it had initially committed to the attack and then rush a special forces brigade and Republican Guard brigade through a quickly improvised course in urban warfare," giving the Iranians several weeks to reinforce.[10]

Although Iraq eventually took the city with its Republican Guard brigade (which was quickly returned to Baghdad after the fight), doing so required a street-to-street grind at the price of 8,000 Iraqi casualties and 100 tanks and armored vehicles.[11] As Ward notes, "The Iraqis paid a heavy price for moving into urban terrain."[12] One Iraqi general similarly recalled that "the Iranians displayed ferocious resistance during the urban fighting, to the point where it became difficult and costly for us to occupy [Khorramshahr]. They would always attempt to retake their last bases. . . . They would hold every point to the bitter end, so they were

[185]

able to inflict heavy losses."[13] The Iranians suffered an estimated 7,000 killed or wounded, with some reports indicating that the Guards shot Artesh soldiers who attempted to flee the battle.

In addition to halting the overall Iraqi advance, the battle for Khorramshahr diverted Iraqi efforts to besiege another crucial node in the south, Abadan. An oil refining town of 300,000, the city was defended by about 10,000 Iranian fighters, including about 5,000 Pasdaran and an armored brigade with fifty tanks.[14] Even though Iraq started shelling the city on September 22, it did not attack until October 10, giving Iran ample time to bolster its defenses. The initial Iraqi entry to the city required a difficult crossing of the Karun River, demonstrating an impressive feat of combat engineering. But Iraq soon found itself fighting street by street again, unable to take the entire city.

In fact, September 1980 proved to be the high point of Iraq's territorial gains in the war. After taking Khorramshahr and making inroads at Abadan, Iraq never extended its grasp farther into Iran.[15] Pollack attributes this outcome in part to the superior skill of Iranian regular army armor crews compared to their Iraqi counterparts (and, it can be inferred, compared to the Revolutionary Guard). "In armor duels," he notes, "small numbers of Iranian tanks regularly outfought larger Iraqi units." Pollack points in particular to an instance in which an understrength Artesh tank battalion, reinforced by Revolutionary Guards, fought off an Iraqi armored division's advance on the town of Dezful. Iranian armor was better because crews actually maneuvered and their fire was more accurate.[16]

By contrast, Iraqi armored forces practically halted in place during October, moving forward only in early November. By that point, Iraq faced near parity in manpower, even though it retained a significant advantage in heavy weapons. Soon all Iraqi forward momentum ceased, as the rainy season forced a pause in the fighting.[17] Iraq still had failed to take any major cities in the south besides Khorramshahr, and, crucially, it had neglected to seal the passes of the Zagros mountains, enabling the Iranians to reinforce their positions.[18] On December 7, 1980, Saddam announced that Iraq would henceforth pursue only defensive goals.[19]

Assessing the Battlefield Effectiveness of Iraq

Iraqi forces generally displayed poor battlefield effectiveness in their initial campaign. It is true that Iraqi forces were somewhat cohesive. Pollack, for example, gives the Iraqis high marks for remaining solid during the vicious house-to-house fighting in Khorramshahr, relating that they displayed "tenacity, courage, and endurance in combat."[20] Nevertheless,

Iraq demonstrated a number of very basic tactical shortcomings in the invasion. Despite having a huge initial advantage in numbers (as much as 6:1 in some places) and a sustained edge in technology, the Iraqis displayed serious problems turning these advantages into fighting power. In addition to the inaccurate and virtually irrelevant air strikes conducted at the outset, Iraqi artillery units repeatedly made simple fusing errors that limited their weapons' impact, and artillery crews remained in static positions that left them highly vulnerable to counterbattery fire. Iraqi infantry did not conduct reconnaissance patrols, and reserve units were rarely committed in an efficient manner. Tank movements were slow and overly cautious, their fire often inaccurate. As Pollack notes, "Tank crews could not fire on the move and had very poor marksmanship even when stopped. Iraqi tank commanders did not use the mobility of their vehicles to maneuver against the enemy."[21]

The Iraqis demonstrated virtually no ability to conduct complex operations, with little to no combined arms activity during the invasion. The Iraqi air forces and ground forces worked in nearly total isolation from each other. Iraqi armor, infantry, and artillery showed little ability to coordinate attacks on the cities of Khorramshahr and Abadan. The Iraqis repeatedly missed chances to maneuver, relying on their tanks more as big guns than as tools of offensive speed and shock.[22] As Ken Pollack has observed, "Iraqi armored and mechanized formations never used their mobility to bypass Iranian positions, nor did they envelop Iranian defensive positions, nor did they use their shock power simply to overrun what were usually small numbers of ill-trained Iranian infantry with little or no antitank weaponry . . . . Iraq did not once employ airborne or helicopter-borne troops to conduct a vertical envelopment of Iranian positions to speed the passage of their mechanized forces."[23]

Ultimately, in what should have been an ideal environment for conducting complex operations, the Iraqis opted out. Their operations showed virtually no initiative and no coordination across different units, as evidenced by the almost complete halt of operations after the first week. A former Iraqi general noted years later, "Our troops were just lined up on the border and told to drive into Iran. They had an objective, but no idea how to get there or what they were doing, or how their mission fit the plan, or who would be supporting them."[24] Indeed, it turned out that the entire invasion plan had been based on an old British staff exercise organized at the Baghdad War College in 1941.[25]

Despite these shortcomings, combat engineering was one bright spot in the Iraqi invasion. An entire armored division was able to conduct a river crossing under cover of darkness during the advance on

Khorramshahr, and Iraqi units were generally well supplied, reflecting good logistics.[26] The Iraqi skills in this area suggest that other deficiencies may have been less the product of large structural factors such as culture and economic development, which arguably should have impeded capability across the board, and more the result of deliberate choices by the regime about which skills were and were not safe for the military to have. The ability to build pontoon bridges and efficiently deliver spare parts would have been considerably less threatening to Saddam's hold on power than the ability to conduct tank maneuvers or coordinate air strikes.

Assessing the Battlefield Effectiveness of Iran

The Iranians put up a stiff defense, and at times their efforts actually fared better than the framework from chapter 1 would predict. Iranians from both regular and revolutionary units had some success in forging basic urban defenses, suggesting at least some tactical proficiency. Most notably, the Iranian regular forces clearly showed tactical skills in tank battles, conducting basic maneuvers and exhibiting good marksmanship. In several instances, this proficiency was the key factor that halted the Iraqi invasion.

That the revolutionary forces displayed any tactical proficiency at all is surprising in light of the coup prevention practices under which these forces operated. Their performance may have been a function of the extreme external threat they faced. Iranian soldiers were defending their families and homes in these battles, and perhaps that pressure led to tactical improvisation among individuals even in the absence of the organizational grounding that such proficiency usually requires.

That said, the regular, or legacy, forces' relatively better proficiency makes sense in light of the training they had received under the Shah. Despite the other coup protection practices that he imposed with respect to promotions, command arrangements, and information management, one would not expect the results of the long-standing U.S. training programs to have disappeared overnight. The overall pattern—Iranian regular forces displaying greater tactical proficiency than their revolutionary brethren or Iraqi opponents—is consistent with what we would expect based on the book's framework.

It appears that the Iranians did not attempt to perform complex operations during this period. On the one hand, this behavior might be considered reasonable, given the balance of forces and the shock of invasion.[27] On the other hand, Iranian forces could have done far more to attack the Iraqis' vulnerable fixed positions.[28] The absence of such efforts is consistent with what we would expect from a military subject to coup prevention practices.

THE IRANIAN COUNTEROFFENSIVES, JANUARY 1981–MAY 1982

As 1981 dawned, Iraq held the city of Khorramshahr and threatened Qasr-e Shirin, Susangerd, Dezful, Ahvaz, and Abadan. Regaining its equilibrium, Iran launched an escalating series of counteroffensives to regain territory and prevent further incursions (see map 5.1). This campaign included battles at Ahvaz in January 1981, Qasr-e Shirin in March, Abadan in September, Bostan in November and December, Dezful in March 1982, and Khorramshahr in April and May. As a group, these battles are useful because they occurred on the same terrain and with roughly the same forces and weapons as the invasion, but with the tactical orientations of the two sides reversed.

Overall, the battles are consistent with what we would expect based on the book's framework. The Iraqis displayed routine deficits in basic tactical proficiency and repeatedly failed to conduct complex defensive operations. Their inability to maneuver, protect their flanks, conduct reconnaissance, or engage in combined arms activities repeatedly led them to cede territory at a huge human cost. At the same time, Iran's territorial gains would have been possible only against an opponent such as Iraq. Iranian human wave attacks reflected a strong will to fight, but the country's overall effectiveness was poor relative to what it could have achieved. The one exception were the Iranian regular forces, which again demonstrated some solid tactical proficiency and even a minimal ability to conduct complex operations.

The Forces on Each Side

By the end of 1980, Iran already had begun to erode Iraq's sizeable local manpower advantage. What had been a 6:1 Iraqi edge shrank to no more than 2:1 as Iranian volunteers flooded into the south.[29] In fact, Ward reports that "more Iranians volunteered to fight Iraq than could be absorbed by the Guard and army."[30]

Over the course of 1981 and 1982, Iran gained a manpower advantage, marshaling nearly 140,000 troops in the southern sector. About 60,000 of these were from four Artesh divisions, while the other 80,000 were Guard and Basij forces. Against them stood about 80,000 Iraqis, comprising three infantry divisions, two armored divisions, one mechanized division, and some independent infantry brigades (see table 5.3).[31] In general,

Table 5.3. The Iranian counteroffensives, 1981–1982

	Iraq	Iran
Battle summary		
Tactical orientation	Defensive	Offensive
Plan	Hold territory gained through static positional defense	Re-take territory through infantry attacks followed by mechanized exploitation of breakthroughs
Weapons[a]	Roughly the same as in 1980	Roughly the same as in 1980
Manpower[b]	80,000	140,000
Losses[c]	Tens of thousands KIA and WIA; tens of thousands POW	Tens of thousands KIA and WIA; a few thousand POW
Effectiveness summary		
Tactical proficiency?	No	Yes, among regular forces
Complex operations?	No	Minimal, among regular forces
As expected?	Yes	Somewhat

[a] Hiro, *Longest War*, 59.
[b] Ward, *Immortal*, 256.
[c] Significant information on losses is missing for both sides. These rough estimates are based on the sources referenced in the discussion of each battle.

the balance of weaponry remained the same, except for Iraq's acquisition of some new Mirage fighters.[32]

The Early Battles, January–September 1981

As early as January 1981, Iran launched counteroffensives near Qasr-e Shirin, Mehran, Ahvaz, and Abadan, which continued to suffer under an Iraqi siege. In several areas the Iranians managed to push the Iraqis back a bit, but the operations were driven more by the regime's need to appear to be responding to the invasion than by strategically sound military imperatives.[33]

The battle for Abadan rapidly became a disaster for the Iranian armored forces. The first brigade sent into the fight quickly bogged down in mud and became an easy target for the Iraqi defenders. According to Cordesman and Wagner, "If Iran had halted at this point, its losses would have become acceptable, but Iran did not stop its attack or attempt a different line of advance. Instead, the Iranian commander committed his second brigade against virtually the same Iraqi defenses the next day," allowing Iraq to grind down yet another brigade's worth of Iranian armor using infantry equipped with anti-tank weapons, artillery, and some armor. The process was repeated a third time the next day, finishing off nearly an entire Iranian armored division.[34] Iran was saved only by the fact that the Iraqis did not pursue their retreating opponents.[35]

Unfortunately, Iran's leaders interpreted this disaster as evidence that Iranian regular forces were worthless and unreliable. In fact, some sources suggest that the revolutionary leaders actually wanted the regular forces to suffer battlefield defeats in these initial operations so that the regular forces would lose credibility as a potential counterweight to the new regime.[36] Iran's leaders then accelerated their imposition of coup prevention practices. According to Cordesman and Wagner, "Iran ceased giving proper emphasis to acquiring and training high technology forces and trying to build upon its past cadre of military professionals. Priority clearly shifted to the Pasdaran."[37] Indeed, the only remaining secular leader, commander-in-chief Bani Sadr, was publicly blamed for Iran's losses and forced to flee the country.[38]

The Battle for Abadan, September 1981

Iran and Iraq had some smaller engagements over the spring and summer, but Iran turned most of its attention to plans for relieving Abadan. On September 2, Iran began with a feint, launching a 30,000–40,000-strong mixed force of armor, artillery, and infantry toward Basra. This deployment had its desired effect, convincing the Iraqis to keep their reserves there rather than move them toward Abadan and Khorramshahr, where the Iraqis already had about 50,000–60,000 soldiers. Meanwhile, the Iranians managed to ferry 15,000–20,000 additional soldiers to Abadan to shore up the 9,000 Artesh and 4,000–6,000 Guard members already in place. This stealthy move soon gave the Iranians a sizeable local advantage over the five Iraqi brigades guarding the eastern end of the city.

On September 26, Iranian forces attacked. According to Cordesman and Wagner, "Iraqi forces fought hard but did not receive effective reinforcement or artillery and air support, although Iraq had some 150–200 major artillery pieces within range." Iranian forces also managed to infiltrate behind Iraqi lines, leading to the isolation of some units and heavy Iraqi losses. "This seems to have driven their command into a panic, and what started as a tactical withdrawal became a rout. The Iraqi troops abandoned their armor and heavy equipment" and rapidly retreated.[39] Even a Republican Guard armored brigade sent in to counterattack "was easily beaten back with the loss of over one-third of its tanks."[40]

Within days, Iraq was forced back across the Karun River and had lost dozens of tanks and some 200 armored vehicles and artillery weapons while suffering thousands of casualties.[41] Iran suffered about 3,000 killed in action.[42] Still, lacking a numerical advantage, and with minimal armor and almost no air support, Iran had managed to end the siege of Abadan. Unfortunately for Iran, the commanders responsible for this victory were killed in a plane crash on their way back to Tehran, suddenly depriving Iran of the very leaders that had successfully melded together Pasdaran and regular forces during the battle. The crash victims included the minister of defense, chief of staff, army chief of staff, and the regional commander of the Pasdaran.[43]

The Battle for Bostan, November–December 1981

After a lull in the fighting, an Iranian force of 10,000–14,000 Guard and regular soldiers attacked the Iraqi salient near Susangerd, south of Bostan. According to Cordesman and Wagner, "The attack was confused . . . because Pasdaran attacked without waiting for either a regular army artillery barrage or support."[44] Nevertheless, the first use of the human wave attacks terrified Iraqi Popular Army units in the area, which broke and ran when they saw Pasdaran units attacking over the slain corpses of Basij who had thrown themselves on Iraqi minefields.[45]

Iran retook Bostan but at a heavy price in casualties. The Iraqis also suffered at least 1,000 dead and 500 taken prisoner. In December, the Iranians launched another attack farther north in Qasr-e Shirin, achieving tactical surprise in a week-long battle. Due to the Iraqis' failure to react quickly and to make use of artillery and airpower, Iran succeeded in retaking this area as well. The remaining Iraqi positions in the south now looked vulnerable.

The Battle for Dezful, March 1982

By February 1982, Iraq had about six divisions—three infantry, two armored, and one mechanized—defending its positions in the south. Against this force of approximately 80,000 men, Iran had assembled four divisions comprising about 60,000 soldiers, plus 200 tanks and 150 artillery pieces, in addition to 80,000 Guard and Basij troops.[46] On March 22, these forces attacked the Iraqi salient near Dezful, using human waves spearheaded by the Pasdaran to overwhelm posts manned mostly by the Popular Army.

These waves eventually achieved breakthroughs into which regular army units then rushed to attack the Iraqi flanks. Because Saddam had decreed that units were not allowed to cede any ground, the Iraqi defense was poorly coordinated and ineffective, eventually inducing panic. The corps commander ordered frontal counterattacks by two Iraqi armored divisions and an armored brigade of the Republican Guard, but these proved futile in the muddy terrain. Iranian forces then initiated a double pincer movement to trap the Iraqi forces still in the salient.[47] As these Iraqi forces were ground up over the next several days, the remaining segments of the Iraqi army fled in disarray.[48]

Though costly, the battle became a significant victory for Iran. Iraq was largely evicted from northern Khuzestan and suffered as many as 50,000 casualties. Another 20,000–25,000 Iraqis were taken prisoner, and multiple Iraqi units were destroyed outright, including a mechanized division and armored division. In addition, the Pasdaran captured so much Iraqi equipment and ammunition that they were able to form new units of their own.[49]

The Battle for Khorramshahr, April–May 1982

Iran's victories at Abadan, Bostan, and Dezful positioned it to make a final attack on the city of Khorramshahr. Iraqi forces in the area were formidable, consisting of 70,000–90,000 soldiers dug into well-established static defenses. As at Dezful, the Iraqis guarded their positions with barbed wire and minefields, but these proved no deterrent to the Iranians, who launched a three-pronged assault on the night of April 30.

In the north, in the first of the three prongs, an Iranian armored division attacked an Iraqi armored division. From the south, another Iranian infantry division and large numbers of Pasdaran crossed the Karun River and overran the Iraqi reserve and Popular Army forces stationed in the area. Then, in the offensive's third prong, another armored division and additional Pasdaran struck Iraq's eastern lines, which were being held by several infantry brigades.[50] The Iranians sent as many as 40,000 Pasdaran and Basij directly into the teeth of the Iraqi defenses, persisting until the Iraqis grew exhausted or panicked.[51] The waves targeted Popular Army units in particular, which broke most easily.[52]

Once Iraqi lines ruptured, regular Iranian forces with more firepower and mobility surged into the gaps, exploiting the breakthrough to attack the Iraqi flanks, which, again following orders from Saddam, generally remained in place instead of conducting a fighting withdrawal or counterattacks on the exposed Iranian flanks.[53] The Iraqis did try to conduct a counterattack with one of their armored divisions, but this effort was slow. According to Pollack, "By the time it got moving, the Iranians had penetrated across the front and routed most of the Iraqi frontline formations."[54] As a result, the Iranians easily parried the counterattack, leading Saddam to call in air strikes, which had little effect. Iraq tried again on

May 6 to counterattack with two armored divisions, but Iranian armor pushed them back to the border.

Realizing its units were trapped, Iraq vacated Khuzestan except for Khorramshahr itself. Then on May 22, 80,000 Iranian troops assaulted the city, retaking it in two days of intense street fighting.[55] The Iranians captured as many as 15,000 Iraqi prisoners of war, including many from Popular Army units that showed little sign of combat stress or battle fatigue. The Iranians again captured hundreds of Iraqi tanks and artillery weapons, as well as enormous supply caches. Iran essentially had destroyed two Iraqi mechanized brigades and two infantry brigades, albeit at the cost of 15,000–25,000 dead and tens of thousands wounded. Iraqi casualties were similarly high.[56]

By May 1982 Iraq had lost all territory acquired in the invasion. The situation was so bleak that a CIA assessment at the time virtually declared the war to be over, noting, "Iraq has essentially lost the war with Iran. . . . There is little the Iraqis can do. . . to reverse the military situation."[57] All told, Iraq probably suffered 50,000 or more killed and 45,000 captured. Iranian losses were estimated at 70,000 killed, perhaps an additional 50,000 wounded, and 5,000 taken prisoner.[58] Saddam reacted by shooting twelve generals and regrouping Iraq's defenses, while Iranian leaders appear to have credited the Pasdaran and Basij for the victories, reaffirming the attachment to human wave attacks.[59]

Assessing the Battlefield Effectiveness of Iraq

Iraqi battlefield effectiveness during the Iranian counteroffensives was poor, consistent with what we would expect from a military subject to coup prevention practices. At Abadan, Dezful, and Khorramshahr, the battles ended with Iraqi soldiers fleeing in disorder and leaving behind large quantities of armored vehicles, artillery, and other equipment. Thousands upon thousands of Iraqis were taken prisoner during this period of the war, often with few signs of resistance.

More important, serious tactical shortcomings were evident even where Iraqis did stand and fight. Although at times the Iraqis were proficient in establishing basic static defenses relying on machine gun and artillery fire, minefields, and barbed wire, Iraqi limitations were pronounced. Even Saddam, in a meeting with his officials around this time, observed Iraq's continuing basic tactical problems, stating, "As for the artillery, it is certain that we see some negatives. . . . There are negatives in the accuracy, coordination and usage. The concentration is inaccurate and not hitting the target. . . . In the discipline of artillery I believe it is one of those areas where we are still in need of someone to teach us."[60] The Iraqis also continued to be surprised by Iranian attacks because most

Iraqi units failed to conduct regular patrols, and even where they did, they did not pass on the information they learned.[61]

Given the continued Iraqi advantage in weaponry, one also has to question why the human wave attacks managed to be so successful—either the Iraqis broke and ran, or they simply did not operate their weapons properly. A U.S. analysis of the situation pointedly noted, "Our estimate is that equipment shortages have not been a major factor in Iraq's battlefield reverses . . . . Iraqi failures to date have been due mainly to weak leadership, morale, tactics, and intelligence weaknesses."[62]

Furthermore, Iraq demonstrated virtually no ability to conduct complex defensive operations. What was needed in response to the Iranian attacks was an elastic defense in depth rather than a static positional defense, but Iraq's decision to dig in its forces and forbid any retreats made these units prisoners in their positions and allowed Iran to destroy them piecemeal in battle after battle. Iraq repeatedly displayed an inability to conduct fighting withdrawals, maneuver, or counterattack by committing its reserves, even in situations where Iranian units were exposed and vulnerable. Part of the problem appeared to be that Iraqi officers in the field lacked the authority to redeploy forward troops or to call on reserves. Even in situations where the Iraqis reportedly fought hard, as at Abadan, the lack of combined arms integration doomed their efforts.

One has to question whether Iraq could have held such a long front forever. But the nature of the Iraqi command system and, indeed, the commanders themselves, made it impossible to consolidate to more defensible positions. Instead, the Iraqis' lack of tactical proficiency and inability to perform complex operations made their retreat enormously costly.[63]

Assessing the Battlefield Effectiveness of Iran

The years 1981 and 1982 witnessed the peak of Iranian battlefield effectiveness during the war. A combination of revolutionary fervor, nationalism, and Shi'i beliefs about martyrdom made for an enormous and highly motivated stock of infantry soldiers, as will be discussed further below. Nevertheless, it is important not to treat this cohesion as synonymous with effectiveness. The Iranians designed their offensives as they did precisely because they required so little tactical proficiency, something that the poorly trained Pasdaran and Basij units lacked. Iranian "tactics," such as they were, consisted of walking into Iraqi minefields, cutting through barbed wire, and using children as human shields against heavy weapons fire. While perhaps "effective" in a certain way, this approach did not reflect mastery of modern military skills such as weapons handling or careful use of terrain for cover and concealment. Furthermore, had these tactics been used against an adversary adept at coordinating its own movement and fire, it is doubtful that they would have delivered territorial gains.

That said, the regular Iranian forces did display some tactical proficiency and, in a few instances, the ability to conduct complex operations. Although the first battle for Abadan was a disaster, this was partly because the regular forces had been pressured to respond to the invasion before they were ready. In general, the Iranian regular army units displayed competence in the operation of their heavy weapons, notably armor. In addition, the Iranians deserve credit for conducting better reconnaissance than the Iraqis, as repeatedly demonstrated in the targeting of vulnerable Popular Army units.[64] No source explicitly identifies the regular forces as being better at this task than the revolutionary forces, but one account does single out the Pasdaran as frequently failing to do more than attack whatever Iraqi position was directly in front of them.[65] This suggests that it was probably the regular forces who were doing most of the reconnaissance and infiltration seen in the battles, again reflecting a skill differential.

Although far from consistent, the regular forces also were at times able to exploit the breakthroughs created by the human wave attacks, an action that required coordination among infantry, armor, and artillery.[66] It was probably not a coincidence that in one of the chief instances of this phenomenon, the battle for Abadan in September 1981, "Iranian preparation for the attack had been left largely to regular officers believed to be fully loyal to the regime," and revolutionary forces "were subordinated to the regular army command."[67] When regular forces were in charge, even the combat power of the revolutionary forces could be harnessed to greater effect.

It is important not to overstate these contrasts. Although one must give credit to the Iranians for their gains, it is very difficult to see how the Iranian methods could have yielded such significant results had their opponent offered even slightly more effective resistance. In other words, it is important not to mistake Iraqi errors for Iranian military prowess.[68] That said, the Iranian counteroffensives show that there were some real differences between the prerevolutionary and revolutionary forces, in part because of the nature of the Shah's earlier policies.

Unfortunately for Iran, most of its leaders drew the wrong lessons from what happened, crediting the revolutionary rather than regular forces for Iran's victories—and the few leaders who might have told them otherwise perished in the plane crash. As we will see, these events set the stage for a decline in Iranian effectiveness among even the regular forces in subsequent battles.

THE IRANIAN INVASION AT BASRA, JULY 1982, AND
SUBSEQUENT ATTACKS INTO IRAQ, 1982–1985

After regaining its territory, Iran invaded Iraq in July 1982, focusing its initial efforts on Iraq's second largest city, Basra (see map 5.2). The
battle of Basra therefore offers the first opportunity to observe the Iranians on the offensive against Iraqis defending their own soil. In Operation
Ramadan, Iran launched a major assault to take the heavily defended
city. After a protracted fight, the Iraqis managed to keep Basra. Nevertheless, the costs Iraq paid for this victory were exorbitant, and both sides
demonstrated poor battlefield effectiveness, especially in the realm of
complex operations, where the Iranian decline was clear.

The fight for Basra established a pattern that was to govern the ground
war for the next several years. The analysis that follows briefly discusses
subsequent Iranian offensives, showing that the performances of the two
sides in 1982 were typical rather than anomalous. Subsequent battles included Iranian attacks in the south during 1982 and 1983 and efforts to
take the Hawizeh Marshes in 1984 and 1985. Assumed by the Iraqis to be
impenetrable, this swampy terrain on the central front had the potential
to provide Iran with access to the major road connecting Basra and Baghdad, as well as to dozens of Iraqi oil wells.

The Forces on Each Side in the Battle for Basra

Iraq retained a decisive overall advantage in weapons.[69] Its advantage
in armor and artillery was close to 3:1, and it retained a 4:1 edge in airpower. The two sides were more evenly matched in terms of the local
balance of manpower, with both having something on the order of
70,000–90,000 men near Basra (see table 5.4).[70]

Iraq now fought on its home turf, affording the military greater famil-
iarity with the terrain and much shorter and more secure lines of communication, resupply, and reinforcement.[71] Certain that they would be
welcomed by Basra's Shi'i populace, the Iranians had broadcast news of
their impending attack.[72] Since the retreat from Iran, Iraq had devoted
considerable effort to establishing defenses in the south. Parallel to the
main north-south roads, the Iraqis had built giant berms that provided
good fighting positions for tanks, machine guns, and cannon. Opposite
this line, the Iraqis established a free-fire zone filled with mortars, mines,
and barbed wire.[73] In addition, Iraq converted a small fishery east of
Basra into an enormous artificial water barrier. Known as Fish Lake, the
water concealed concertina wire, mines, and an electrocution system.

The Iranian plan reflected some awareness of these defenses. It called
for two divisions to conduct a diversionary attack across the Iraqis'

[197]

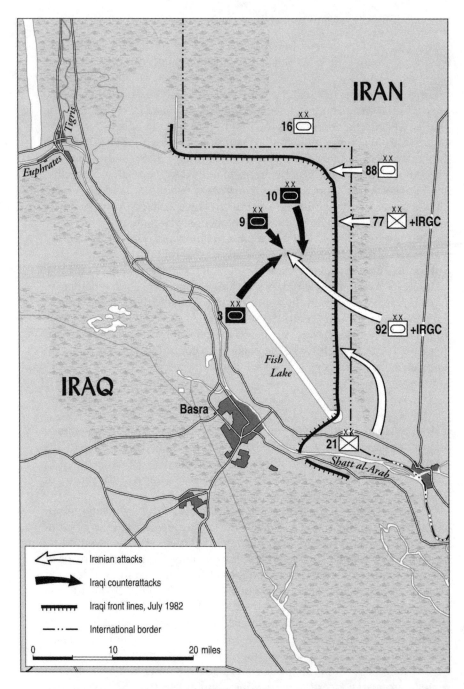

Map 5.2. The Battle of Basra, 1982. Adapted from Kenneth Pollack, *Arabs at War: Military Effectiveness, 1948–1991* (Lincoln: University of Nebraska Press, 2002), 204.

Table 5.4. The battle for Basra, July 1982

	Iraq	Iran
Battle summary		
Tactical orientation	Defensive	Offensive
Plan	Layered positional defense using heavy firepower against Iranian infantry	Cut off Basra, then engage in infantry-armor assault
Weapons[a]	>700 tanks; dug-in armor, artillery, machine guns, mines, wire, mortars, water barriers	200 tanks, 200 APCs, 300 artillery pieces
Manpower[a]	70,000–90,000 men: five reinforced divisions, plus three more armored divisions in reserve	90,000 men: Revolutionary Guard and Basij, plus six understrength army divisions
Losses[b]	>3,000 KIA, 1,400 POW	20,000–30,000 KIA and WIA
Effectiveness summary		
Tactical proficiency?	No	No
Complex operations?	No	No
As expected?	Yes	Yes

[a] Pollack, *Arabs at War*, 204.
[b] Hiro, *Longest War*, 88.

northern flank, while two mixed army-IRGC task forces would assault the Iraqis' eastern flank. Eventually the two forces were to link up and encircle the Iraqis. Meanwhile, the 21st Infantry Division, along with Revolutionary Guard forces, was to swing south of Fish Lake and flank the entire Iraqi position defending the city.[74]

The Battle for Basra

The battle for Basra began on the night of July 13–14, 1982. Iraqi firepower halted the Iranians' diversionary attack in the north and one of their two thrusts from the east. But the second thrust from the east broke through the Iraqi lines, causing the Iranians to call off the planned attack by the 21st Infantry Division to the south of Fish Lake and instead call that unit north to reinforce the breakthrough.

Rather than providing momentum for the Iranian attack, however, this decision created a giant target for the Iraqis, who attacked the Iranian penetration from three sides.[75] The Iranians were driven back almost to where their attack had begun, and their cohesion soon deteriorated.[76] But

Iraqi forces, too, suffered heavy losses as they failed to maneuver or to operate in combined arms teams.

Rather than pause, the Iranians quickly regrouped and crossed the Iraqi border again on July 21 from a position slightly south of the original avenue of attack. Again, Iranian Basij walked into the Iraqi defenses, clearing paths through the minefields for Pasdaran and army forces. This effort broke through the Iraqi defenses east of Fish Lake, but Iraqi forces again drove back the Iranian penetration with heavy fire from tanks, helicopters, and artillery. This basic scene repeated itself during the last week of July and first days of August, as another Iranian breakthrough was driven back by another Iraqi defensive onslaught.[77]

In the end, Iran suffered perhaps 20,000–30,000 casualties and lost up to a quarter of its equipment in these efforts.[78] Iraqi casualties were considerably lower, somewhere around 3,000 killed, but the main armored division involved, the 9th, was permanently destroyed.[79]

Subsequent Iranian Attacks into Iraq, 1982–1983

The battle at Basra set a pattern that both sides were to repeat during the remainder of 1982 and throughout 1983. During this time, Iran launched additional attacks in the northern sector and against Basra (late 1982), as well as another five offensives (February–November 1983).[80]

Reflecting the ascendance of the revolutionary forces, the Iranian approach continued to rely on human wave attacks. As in the initial battle for Basra, these attacks sometimes were able to penetrate the first line of Iraqi defenses but always proved difficult to direct thereafter. Iran's decreasing stocks of armor and mechanized vehicles also made it ever more difficult to exploit the breakthroughs that did occur.[81] Even several years into the war, "Iran still was willing to throw thousands of Basij into combat, almost straight from their cities and villages. It provided them with little military equipment and resupply capability and gave its volunteers few instructions other than to advance to their primary objective and obtain supplies from the newly liberated Iraqi Shi'ites."[82]

Despite launching offensives involving tens of thousands of men and suffering casualties that were often three to four times those of Iraq's, Iran's offensives in 1982 and 1983 resulted in virtually no lasting, strategically significant territorial gains.[83] Iran never proved able to launch more than one major assault at a time and tended to develop such assaults slowly, so the Iraqis always were able to shift their forces to the point of attack.[84]

For its part, Iraq continued to rely on the large fixed defenses that it had employed at Basra.[85] Again reflecting good combat engineering, the Iraqi fighting positions, bunkers, and fortifications integrated the use of mines, artillery, armor, and various manmade obstacles, including water barriers.[86] Iraq also employed chemical weapons for the first time in 1983.[87]

The entire front devolved into trench warfare reminiscent of World War I. By 1983, Iran had suffered about 180,000 killed in total, with several times that number wounded and 8,000 taken prisoner. Iraq had suffered about 65,000 killed in total, with several times that number wounded and 50,000 taken prisoner. The war was not yet at its halfway mark.[88]

The Battles for the Hawizeh Marshes, 1984–1985

Undeterred by previous losses, Iran launched an amphibious assault on the marshes farther north in 1984 (see map 5.3). Overall, Iran followed the same formula of human wave attacks backed by heavy weapons. The operation reflected the continuing limitations of this approach, yielding small territorial gains at high cost of human lives: an estimated 18,000–26,000 Iranians were killed and another 20,000–30,000 wounded.

Iraq repeated its basic defensive approach as well, relying on heavy firepower (including chemical weapons) to mow down Iranian infantry, while engaging in only very limited counterattacks. This approach kept Iraqi casualties much lower (about 6,000 killed in action and perhaps twice that number wounded) but failed to decisively stop the Iranian attacks. Indeed, Iran even gained control of the manmade Majnoon Islands at the southern edge of the marshes, which afforded easy access to the oil in the area. Iraq eventually recovered about one-quarter of the southernmost of the two Majnoon Islands but was unable to dislodge Iran from the rest or to retake the northern island, despite an enormous advantage in weaponry. In fact, although Iran did deploy some better armed Artesh units, the Basij and Pasdaran fighters involved lacked almost any artillery, anti-tank weapons, or other sources of heavy firepower.

In March 1985, Iran launched a slightly more cautious version of the same operation. The goal was to sever the Iraqi south from the rest of the country, cutting through the Hawizeh Marshes to split Basra from Baghdad. Again, it had relatively little success and brought massive casualties, even as the Iraqis proved unable to decisively evict the Iranians.[89]

Assessing the Battlefield Effectiveness of Iraq

The battles fought from 1982 to 1985 reveal a consistent pattern of poor Iraqi effectiveness. Iraqi tactical proficiency continued to be minimal at best. The Iraqis did establish basic defenses around Basra, but the fact that the Iraqis had to use tear gas and, later, chemical weapons to break

[201]

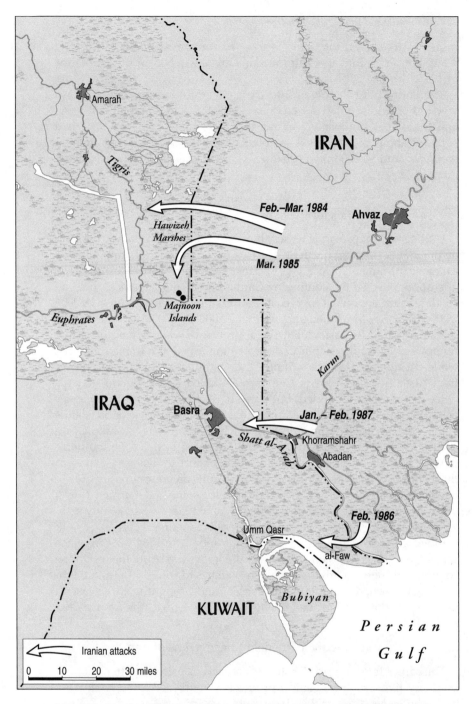

Map 5.3. Iranian offensives, 1984–1987. Adapted from Steven R. Ward, *Immortal: A Military History of Iran and Its Armed Forces* (Washington, DC: Georgetown University Press, 2009), 262.

up Iranian formations suggests continuing skill deficits. As Pollack puts it, "The Iraqis were employing all the weaponry available to a modern army to fight what was basically a light infantry force. They generally outnumbered the Iranians, except temporarily at the point of attack, where the Iranians might muster an advantage in manpower for their human-wave assaults. The Iraqis could bring to bear vastly greater firepower . . . and were considerably more mobile."[90] Yet despite these advantages, the battle for Basra permanently destroyed an Iraqi armored division and cost Iraq thousands of casualties.

Strangely however, Saddam actually considered these massive losses a sign of effectiveness, which perhaps explains why the Basra approach was used repeatedly.[91] In the marshes, for example, Iraq eventually was able to halt most Iranian advances but only through immense firepower. And Iraqis frequently found themselves surprised by Iranian attacks because they did not conduct patrols. Iraq's only real tactical success continued to be in the area of combat engineering, particularly the use of water barriers, though this alone hardly marks the Iraqis as a paragon of tactical effectiveness.

Most notably, Iraq still displayed no ability to conduct complex operations. It had multiple air and ground combat arms at its disposal in the battles for the marshes, yet it did not integrate them into combined arms operations. There are virtually no examples of the Iraqis using their ground forces to pin down Iranian units that could then be attacked from the air, even though the Iraqis had near-total air superiority during the battle.

One detailed analysis attributes this sort of coordination failure directly to Saddam's coup concerns, noting,

> A number of officers in the Air Force were not from his network of loyal clans and tribes and were not politically reliable. . . . Due to these considerations, Hussein discouraged inter-service cooperation so that the Air Force and the Army could not coordinate a coup. On the battlefield, this arrangement resulted in the ground forces failing to work effectively with the Iraqi Air Force. By the time information from ground commanders on the battlefield filtered through the various political circles to the Air Force, it would be too late for them to perform in an effective manner. An example of such failures occurred during the battle in the Marshes in 1984 when the Iranian military was able to build a massive 17-kilometer [10.5-mile] pontoon bridge without Iraqi aircraft taking any actions to disrupt this effort.[92]

Furthermore, despite the extensive nature of the Iraqi defenses, they remained simple and rigid, rather than layered and flexible. Iraq did not adopt a defense in depth, even though it had the equipment, weapons, and numbers needed to do so. Iraq rarely engaged in offensive action in general. Cordesman and Wagner have noted that even as the campaign became more and more intense, "Iraq continued to fight relatively passively. . . . It failed to give proper emphasis to increasing its infantry and assault capability."[93] Instead, the Iraqis relied on their technological edge and fixed positional defenses to simply grind down the Iranians. In the one location where this approach did not work, the Majnoon Islands, the Iraqis had to cede the territory.[94]

Assessing the Battlefield Effectiveness of Iran

The battles that took place from 1982 to 1985 shone a harsh light on Iranian tactical limitations. Iranian cohesion remained robust, with tens of thousands of soldiers willing to walk directly into Iraqi defenses. Still, even the human wave tactics were not executed proficiently, especially as compared to some of the infantry successes Iran had experienced in the earlier battles where the regular forces had been given more command authority. For example, Iran now launched its attacks in broad daylight, when the attackers were most vulnerable to Iraqi firepower. The attacks often were not timed to launch simultaneously, giving the Iraqis ample opportunity to concentrate firepower wherever they were most threatened. Iranian soldiers also "persisted in their habit of congregating indecisively once they had achieved their objective, providing ideal targets to the well-entrenched Iraqis."[95] As Ward notes, "Iran's basic strategy was roughly equivalent to trying to use a hammer to destroy an anvil. The Guard formations allowed the commanders to commit large numbers of infantry in repeated attacks, but the divisions were slow and plodding and lacked the training and mobility needed to counter Iraq's strong armored reserves."[96]

Iranian effectiveness utterly broke down in the realm of complex operations. Iranian fearlessness—that is, the willingness of its soldiers to execute the "tactic" of martyrdom—could not compensate for serious deficits in coordination. Iran's command structure was so fractured that the human wave assaults were poorly integrated with the mobility and firepower that Iran did possess. Those willing to walk into minefields tended to be from the Pasdaran and the Guard, while those who operated armor and artillery tended to be from the Artesh. Because these forces were controlled separately, "the ability to shift fires or change attacks to take advantage of opportunities was seriously circumscribed."[97] For all the terror they may have inspired, the human waves "could not maneuver quickly or effectively, particularly once forces were committed to battle. Command and control was difficult."[98]

Furthermore, the reliance on human waves wasted what armor and skilled manpower the Iranians did have. As Cordesman and Wagner note, "There often was no clear role that Iranian armor could play except to provide fire support for the infantry. Iranian armor could occasionally flank an Iraqi force but could not maneuver in depth against Iraqi opposition without infantry support, and the bulk of Iran's infantry lacked the equipment and skill needed to operate as a mechanized force. Further, Iran's tactics presented major problems in . . . exploiting a breakthrough."[99]

The reliance on human waves to breach the Iraqi lines had worked better on Iranian territory than it did once the Iraqis were defending established positions on familiar terrain. The battle of Basra epitomized this problem, but it repeatedly appeared. Iran "never brought an end to the feuding and lack of coordination between the Pasdaran and regular force, and it continued to reward loyalty and belief, rather than professionalism."[100] A CIA assessment at the end of 1982 agreed that Iran was basically incapable of offensive operations and would remain so given the threats facing the state at the time: "the Iranian Army is basically a defensive organization. . . . The Army will never be fully exonerated under the current regime: political controls have been tightened over the military."[101] The net result was a subtle but noticeable decline in Iranian fighting effectiveness compared to the initial battles of the war.

THE BATTLES FOR AL-FAW AND MEHRAN, 1986

In 1986, Iran launched another major offensive, including a successful attack on the al-Faw Peninsula (see map 5.4). Because it provided Iraq's only access to the Gulf as well as a foothold into the Shi'i-populated, oil-rich Iraqi south, al-Faw was prized real estate. Some observers point to its capture as representing a major improvement in Iranian fighting capabilities.[102] Closer inspection of the battle reveals more continuity than change, however. Iran performed somewhat better at al-Faw—perhaps because the operation was designed by an Artesh officer—but even so, the Iranians continued to have serious deficits in tactical proficiency and sustaining offensive complex operations.

Iran's victory was as much the product of Iraqi weakness as of real changes in the Iranian military. Additional fighting in the immediate aftermath of al-Faw, near the Iranian town of Mehran, illustrates just how deficient Iraqi forces continued to be due to the imposition of coup prevention practices. The experiences at Mehran and al-Faw caused leaders on both sides to reconsider their approaches to the war, however—with important consequences for subsequent battles.

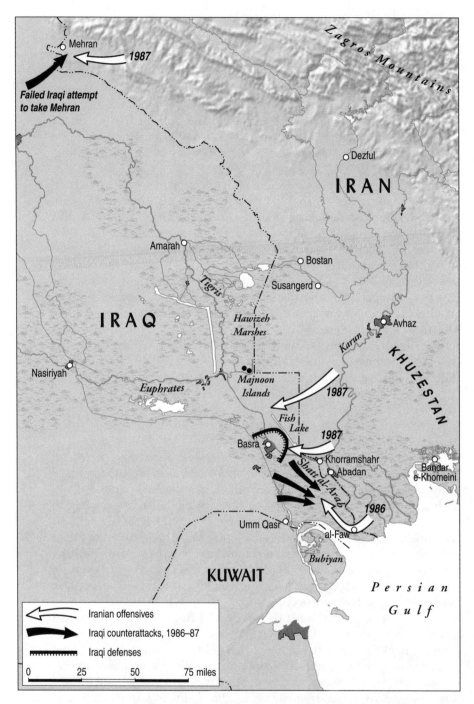

Map 5.4. Iranian offensives, 1986–1987. Adapted from Kenneth Pollack, *Arabs at War: Military Effectiveness, 1948–1991* (Lincoln: University of Nebraska Press, 2002), 222.

The Forces on Each Side

Iran had kept nearly half its regular army and two-thirds of the Guard deployed in the south, amounting to about 200,000 troops there at the start of 1986.[103] A sizable portion of this force was devoted to the attack on al-Faw—probably a corps containing several divisions.[104] Iranian troops had some new arms, such as antitank missiles, as well as chemical protective gear.[105] Iran also had stockpiled supplies and bridging equipment in the area and deployed some units specially trained for amphibious assaults and fighting in wetlands.[106]

For its part, Iraq continued to enjoy a qualitative and quantitative advantage in all types of arms.[107] On the peninsula, however, Iraq had stationed only its 26th Division, consisting of Popular Army soldiers, and within the city of al-Faw itself, Iraq had only 1,000 reservists (see table 5.5).[108]

The Battle for al-Faw

Al-Faw was not Iran's only target in February 1986. It also initiated several large but unsuccessful attacks in the Hawizeh Marshes and on Umm al-Rasas, a group of islands in the Shatt north of al-Faw. The Iraqi high command apparently believed that these efforts were feints designed to divert their attention from Basra, where the Iranians had initiated a massive artillery barrage.[109] The Iraqis were wrong, however; the real attack was coming much farther south.

On February 10, the Iranians launched an amphibious assault on al-Faw. In the midst of a rainstorm, Iran began a massive artillery barrage while also sending forward an infantry division that quickly overran the first line of Iraqi defenses. According to Ward, "The attackers were lightly armed but were trained to use captured Iraqi tanks and ammunition, which they put to immediate use in mopping up the last few positions on the Iraqi front lines before advancing against Iraqi strongpoints and rear area facilities."[110]

As this spearhead punched forward, another 20,000 Iranian troops flooded in, attacking straight through the Iraqi defensive obstacles, which included trenches, wire, and mines.[111] Most of these defenses were poorly prepared, despite the peninsula's strategic importance. Although some of the troops held out until February 14, the Popular Army units panicked within the first two days, abandoning their positions and equipment.[112]

According to one Iraqi general, "Everything was happening so quickly that even after the battle started, the leadership in Baghdad and Basra still believed there was another main attack coming."[113] The leadership's

Table 5.5. The battle for al-Faw, February 1986

	Iraq	Iran
Battle summary		
Tactical orientation	Defensive	Offensive
Plan	Defend existing positions; later, regain al-Faw	Capture al-Faw as part of larger offensive
Weapons	Armor, including T-72 tanks; chemical weapons; barriers, wire, mines	Antitank missiles; pontoon bridges and boats; surface-to-air missiles and antiaircraft artillery; later, captured heavy weaponry and equipment
Manpower	On al-Faw, 26th Popular Army Division; 1,000 reservists	On al-Faw: several divisions out of overall southern force of 200,000
Losses	8,000–10,000 casualties, including 30 percent among Republican Guard units; 20–25 aircraft	27,000–30,000 casualties
Effectiveness summary		
Tactical proficiency?	No	Yes
Complex operations?	No	No
As expected?	Yes	Somewhat

misperception also may have stemmed from the unwillingness of Iraqi commanders at al-Faw to report initial losses up the chain for fear of punishment.[114] Finally realizing the seriousness of the situation, Iraq sent reinforcements to al-Faw. But the Iraqis' initial counterattacks floundered as armor and infantry elements failed to coordinate their movements and the poor weather impeded aerial attacks. Even the Republican Guard division eventually sent into the fight proved unable to conduct an effective infantry assault against the dug-in Iranians. The Iraqi troops simply were not proficient in close fighting, especially on swampy terrain.[115]

Through the massive application of firepower, Iraq at last managed to break the Iranians' momentum on February 14. According to Ward, "Many of Iran's losses came from Iraq's heavy use of chemical weapons. Despite the greater availability of masks and protective gear, the Basijis were poorly trained in using their equipment." During this intense week, the Iraqis also burned through 200 of their tanks' main gun barrels and expended so much ammunition that Baghdad rushed to secure new stocks.[116]

[208]

The Iraqis now were able to hold their lines, but repeated attempts to counterattack failed.[117] For nearly a week, the Iraqis pounded the Iranians, who by now were fully dug in. Pollack writes, "The Iraqis threw everything they had at the Iranians. They committed the air force in full, flying as many as 200 . . . sorties per day, in addition to enormous quantities of artillery and heavy doses of chemical agents. However, after three weeks of constant attacks, the Iraqis had made little progress. Iraqi infantry—even the elite units—continued to perform poorly and had to rely heavily on the firepower of their tanks and artillery. Iraqi armor had to stick to the roads because of the soft terrain, and even where the ground was firmer, they refused to maneuver against the Iranians. . . . Iraq was unable to suppress or defeat Iranian antitank teams either with artillery fire—slow to respond and inaccurate as ever—or with infantry, who simply did not know how to cooperate with tanks."[118] Even with the use of mustard gas, Iraq's inability to maneuver cost it entire battalions in the attempt to regain territory.[119] Iran, too, suffered immense losses, with an estimated 27,000–30,000 killed or wounded.[120]

On March 9–10, the Iraqis made a last stand, attempting to conduct amphibious landings that would outflank the Iranians. But these, too, failed at great cost, and the Iraqis finally ceased their attempts at regaining territory.[121] An uneasy, exhausted stalemate settled over the peninsula, where 20,000–25,000 Iranians and some 25,000–32,000 Iraqis now sat in their positions less than a thousand feet apart.[122] Iran now occupied a substantial chunk of the peninsula, which it kept supplied through pontoon bridges across the Shatt, where five divisions stood at the ready.[123] Iraqi defensive lines rimmed the edges of the Iranian holdings and were soon connected to the large Iraqi road network in the south, which rapidly brought in more weapons and equipment.[124]

The Aftermath: Strategy Debates and the Battle for Mehran

Strategically, the 1986 offensive damaged Iraq's position. In addition to the disaster at al-Faw, Iranian forces had moved to within ten miles of Sulaimaniyah, a major Kurdish city in the north, and huge concentrations of Iranian troops were still poised to attack again across al-Faw.[125] Iraq could at best defend these areas but had no ability to threaten comparable Iranian targets.

In Iran, a serious strategy debate ensued, although its details remain murky.[126] What is clear is that Iran's leaders emerged drawing the wrong lessons. In August, Khomeini removed from command a Shah-era officer named General Ali Seyyed Shirazi, the architect of the al-Faw operation. Shirazi had been one of the voices calling for Iran's legacy forces, the Artesh, to have a greater role in the development of strategy, and his removal even more firmly secured the dominance of the revolutionary forces, particularly the Guard, which was commanded by Shirazi's rival, Mohsen Rezai.[127]

A similar debate occurred in Iraq, though with very different results. There, the events of 1986 had shaken the regime to its core. A diplomatic report from Baghdad in April noted that "the military leaders responsible for events in the south have been relieved, transferred to other posts, or even executed."[128] Just as important, the report noted that military leaders were increasingly frustrated with Saddam's military organizational practices. Indeed, a CIA analysis at the time proved prescient in predicting that "the military probably will press Saddam for policy and operational changes to improve Saddam's war making ability."[129]

Saddam doubled down in response. In May 1986, he ordered four Iraqi divisions to seize the virtually abandoned area of Mehran across the border in Iran, which was guarded by only about 5,000 troops.[130] Saddam then offered to exchange Mehran for al-Faw, an offer Tehran rejected.[131] But Saddam's real miscalculation had been in rejecting his generals' advice to seize the heights surrounding Mehran, which were vital to defending the territory. Apparently, Saddam refused to let the general on the scene take the heights because it would have required the use of elite forces needed to defend Baghdad.

Predictably, the Iranians soon seized the heights and used them to attack the Iraqi concentration of forces in Mehran. The general in the field, trying to defend his disadvantaged position, requested air support after he came under attack, but because his request had to be routed through Baghdad due to restrictions on army–air force communication, the approval came after the Iraqi ground forces already had been forced to retreat from the town. The general was recalled to Baghdad and is believed to have been executed.[132] Iran rapidly regained control of Mehran.[133]

Coming on the heels of al-Faw, this debacle only deepened the crisis within the regime.[134] Iraqi generals blamed Saddam's military organizational practices for both sets of losses, raising a serious danger of overthrow from within even as the Iranian threat loomed. This combination of circumstances seems to have led to the shift in Saddam's military organizational practices discussed in chapter 4.[135] Paradoxically, adopting conventional war practices became the best way for Saddam to keep himself in power—a shift that would have important consequences for the war's final battles. As a personalist dictator, Saddam was in a good position to execute these changes quickly once he became convinced of their necessity.

Assessing the Battlefield Effectiveness of Iraq

Iraqi tactical proficiency continued to be limited. The amount of fire-power the Iraqis required to halt what were essentially light infantry attacks again suggests that Iraqi heavy weapons were not used with much competence.[136] Ward notes that the Iraqis repeatedly "relied on firepower over skill and maneuver."[137] This seemed to be true even as Iraq threw supposedly more proficient units into battle, replacing the Popular Army units with regular army units, and then the regular army units with Republican Guard units. None of these forces were able to counterattack successfully, and many were destroyed trying. When it came to close fighting, even Republican Guard units simply were not able to perform well. Only through an escalation to chemical weapons were the Iraqis able to stabilize the situation.[138]

Furthermore, Iraqi units continued to display serious problems with complex operations. Their response to the attack on al-Faw was slow and late, largely because commanders lacked the initiative—or permission—to organize defenses at the first sign of Iranian attack. They also did not report up the chain the seriousness of the attack. Had the Iraqis reacted more quickly, the entire battle might have turned out differently. A similar story can be told about the defeat at Mehran, where the lack of independence for the field commander led to predictable losses.

Coordination remained the Achilles' heel of Iraqi operations. The Iraqis missed repeated opportunities to conduct combined arms operations that could have smashed the massed Iranian forces at al-Faw. To be sure, the terrible weather impeded Iraqi air operations, neutralizing a major advantage. But even with the combat arms that were in perfectly good working order during the battle, notably armor and infantry, the Iraqis repeatedly failed to integrate fire and movement. The same was true at Mehran, where Iraqi airpower was not impeded by weather. The Iraqi command structure was so fractured that ground forces were unable to get air support in time to save them from the disastrous position in which Saddam's choices had placed them.

Assessing the Battlefield Effectiveness of Iran

Iran did capture territory during 1986, and Iranian forces continued to display a strong will to fight, but Iranian tactical proficiency remained poor overall. It is true that initial Iranian operations at al-Faw were better prepared and coordinated due to the leadership of an officer from the Shah-era regular forces.[139] The amphibious training that some Pasdaran had received also helped. Yet Iran never progressed past its initial breakthrough on al-Faw, and the seemingly impressive river crossing succeeded mostly because it was unopposed. The Iraqis were caught by complete surprise, at night, in terrible weather; they were locally out-numbered by the Iranians at a ratio of something like 20:1; and the op-posing Iraqi soldiers were drawn from the Popular Army. As soon as these factors shifted—the Iraqis realizing the scale of the attack, the weather clearing, better trained reinforcements arriving—even minimal, unskilled Iraqi resistance managed to stop the Iranian advance. The Ira-nians also continued to be far more vulnerable to Iraqi chemical weapons than they had to be, suffering numerous casualties from gas even though soldiers had protective gear. In fact, the impact of Iraqi chemical weap-ons would have been far worse had the rain and wind not dispersed much of the gas.

Furthermore, Iran continued a long-standing pattern of being unable to use other combat arms to exploit its infantry's initial penetrations.[140] It was this deficit that ultimately limited what the Iranians could achieve on al-Faw, despite the positive initial influence of the legacy Artesh com-mander. Although they had prepared better for this attack than for oth-ers and benefited from favorable circumstances, the Iranians' fundamental approach to battle had not changed.

THE KARBALA OFFENSIVES, DECEMBER 1986–APRIL 1987

Iran's last attempt to take significant territory in Iraq occurred from De-cember 1986 to April 1987, when Iran launched the Karbala offensives, a series of attacks in the northern and southern sectors (see map 5.4). These battles, particularly the Karbala-5 battle for Basra in early 1987, offer a final opportunity to view Iran attempting to conduct complex offensive operations with leaders from the revolutionary forces firmly in control of the military. They also offer an opportunity to examine Iraqi attempts at complex defensive operations, as well as complex counterattacks.

Generally speaking, both Iran and Iraq evinced the same effectiveness problems that they had displayed earlier on this same terrain, and it would be hard to call the offensives a victory for either. Iran did not pre-vail in taking Basra, but neither did Iraq in evicting the Iranians from their new positions on the Iraqi side of the Shatt al-Arab.

Nonetheless, some improvements in Iraqi tactical effectiveness were evident in the Republican Guard units called into the fight. These changes, though subtle, suggest that some of the shifting military organi-zational practices adopted during 1986 were already beginning to in-crease the battlefield effectiveness of these units. This variation was an important harbinger of changes that were to become fully evident in 1988.

The Forces on Each Side

At the time of the Karbala offensives, the two sides each had 150,000–200,000 soldiers in the south (see table 5.6).[141] Iraqi forces consisted of army units, though they were later backed by Republican Guard. Iranian forces were primarily Guard and Basij, although about one-third of the forces were Artesh.[142] As before, Iranian forces were mostly light infantry, although they were better armed now with antitank weapons, including new TOW missiles. Iraqi forces still enjoyed superiority in armor, artillery, and airpower.

The Iraqis also made extensive use of defensive obstacles, including Fish Lake.[143] They had expanded the lake to create two additional channels to the north and south, essentially forming a giant moat guarding eastern routes of advance on Basra.[144] Iraqi defenses ringed the city itself.[145]

The Battle

The Iranians launched the first part of their offensive, Karbala-4, on the night of December 23. Fifteen thousand Iranian soldiers crossed the Shatt

Table 5.6. The Karbala offensives, December 1986–April 1987

	Iraq	Iran
Battle summary		
Tactical orientation	Defensive, then offensive	Offensive, then defensive
Plan	Defend approaches to Basra; push Iranians back from any territory gained	Cross Shatt, launch two-pronged assault around Fish Lake, converge on Basra
Weapons	Armor, artillery, air power, chemical weapons	Rockets, missiles, antitank weapons, HAWK antiaircraft system
Manpower	In the south: 200,000 soldiers, including some Republican Guard	In the south: 150,000–200,000 soldiers, mostly Pasdaran and Basij
Losses[a]	8,000–15,000 KIA	50,000 KIA, tens of thousands WIA
Effectiveness summary		
Tactical proficiency?	Better in Republican Guards	No
Complex operations?	No	No
As expected?	Yes	Yes

[a] Cordesman and Wagner, *Lessons*, 261; and Murray and Woods, *The Iran-Iraq War*, 296.

[213]

al-Arab along a twenty-five-mile front stretching roughly from Basra to Abadan. Specially trained commandos and frogmen quickly captured several weakly defended islands in the Shatt. A much larger force of up to 60,000 Pasdaran and Basij then used these islands as stepping stones to surge across to the Iraqi side.

Despite this initial success, Iranian forces made virtually no progress once they attempted to move up the road toward Basra. Iraqi minefields and barbed wire guarded huge emplacements of Iraqi heavy weapons, creating a massive killing zone. Iran's daytime light infantry attacks were no match for these defenses, especially given that the only Artesh support for the Basij and Guard spearheads was artillery fire from the western bank of the Shatt.[146]

After suffering 9,000–12,000 casualties, the Iranians quickly retreated back across the Shatt. The entire episode was a disaster, with Cordesman and Wagner noting, "The Karbala-4 offensive may have been the worst planned and executed major Iranian offensive since Bani Sadr's ill-fated offensives early in the war. It had much of the character of the hopeless mass infantry assaults that Britain, France, and Germany had launched against well-entrenched defenses in World War I."[147] The Iraqis, safe behind their defenses, had experienced far fewer losses, around 1,000–2,000.

Despite this catastrophe, Basra continued to be the bloody fulcrum on which the Iranians had decided the entire war balanced. In the early days of January 1987, they renewed their campaign with the Karbala-5 offensive. This effort did appear to benefit from better planning, including some division-level combined arms exercises in the Caspian.[148] Recognizing that the Iraqis expected an attack on Basra to originate from al-Faw—a credible threat, given the events of 1986—the Iranians instead launched a two-pronged attack north and south of Fish Lake, just to the northeast of Basra. Each prong contained about 60,000 soldiers, with the idea that they would encircle Iraqi forces and then converge on the city.[149]

Launching their assaults on January 9, the first spearheads consisted of about 50,000 troops, mostly waves of Basij followed by Revolutionary Guards. According to Cordesman and Wagner, "initial battle management was good, and the leaders of the assault included large cadres of experienced officers, NCOs, and troops." Iran made some territorial gains along the border, as the first Iraqi counterattacks proved unsuccessful. Indeed, the Iraqi advantage in armor was of little use in the marshy terrain, and Iraq proved unable to maneuver in the face of the Iranians' light antiarmor weapons. In addition, the pressure of the human waves caused some Iraqi infantry formations to disintegrate, allowing the Iranians to puncture two of the major defensive lines around Basra.[150]

On January 12, however, the Iranian advance slowed dramatically for two reasons. First, Iraq recognized the direction of the main attack and committed its Republican Guard forces. Second, the closer the Iranians got to Basra, the more formidable the Iraqi defenses became and the drier the land on which Iraqi armor could operate. Meanwhile, Iranian supply lines grew longer. By mid-January, Iranian losses had risen to 40,000, and Iraq's to at least 10,000. Nevertheless, Iran soon committed another 50,000 troops, and in the following days it managed to make a few additional gains, though these were typically measured in feet due to Iraqi use of artillery, including chemical weapons.[151]

Iraq then attempted a major counterattack, aiming to sever the southern prong of the Iranian attack by driving south from behind Fish Lake. But according to Pollack, "The operation went nowhere. Although the counterattacking force began as a combined arms team, it almost immediately separated into its different components, with the infantry veering off to the southwest, the armor veering off to the southeast, and the artillery failing to effectively support either."[152] Making matters worse, the soft ground continued to absorb much of the impact of Iraqi shells and conventional fragmentation bombs, and Cordesman and Wagner report that "a few of Iraq's secondary positions were virtually abandoned, along with large stocks of equipment and munitions."[153]

Through continued fighting, Iranian forces managed to get within just a few miles of Basra, but they then found themselves trapped in the narrow strip of land between the Shatt and Fish Lake. The offensive devolved into a siege by early March, and when Iran finally called off the offensive, Saddam quickly ordered an attempt to retake the lost territory. Iraqi armor, backed by artillery and air sorties, again attempted to drive the Iranians back from their positions surrounding Fish Lake. But the Iraqis failed to maneuver adequately, instead preferring simple frontal assaults, and although airpower was available, it was not provided in an accurate or timely manner.[154]

A stalemate resulted: Iraq could defend Basra but not counterattack, and Iran could invade Iraq but not take its prized city. Other Iranian attacks elsewhere along the front led to a few territorial gains, which, combined with the ongoing fighting at Basra, appear to have deeply concerned Saddam. On March 15, 1987, he called a five-hour meeting with his commanders, which apparently led to the decision to expand the Republican Guard, as well as to escalate the tanker war and expand the use of chemical weapons.[155]

Assessing the Battlefield Effectiveness of Iraq

Iraqi battlefield effectiveness generally continued to be poor. Iraq again required enormous firepower to mow down what were essentially light infantry forces. The use of artillery was particularly futile given the terrain.[156] Iraqi pilots also seem to have delivered their ordnance late, inaccurately, and in insufficient quantity. All of these misjudgments and inefficiencies make it difficult to rate the Iraqis as tactically proficient outside the area of combat engineering. Indeed, Pollack argues "there was little or no discernible enhancement in [Iraqi] tactical competence."[157]

Some accounts do give the Republican Guard forces slightly higher marks for tactical proficiency during the Karbala offensives. For example, Woods and colleagues argue that "the major factor in the Iraqi ability to hold off the Iranian attacks lay in the skill and capabilities of the expanded and improved Republican Guard formations."[158] Cordesman and Wagner, too, make the general observation that "Iraqi ground forces performed better than in previous years" during the battles of early 1987. In their view, "it was already clear that some aspects of Iraqi performance were improving. Iraq's new elite forces showed increasing capability to act as a strategic reserve."[159] This evidence is consistent with the predictions made in chapter 4 that as the Republican Guard military organizational practices changed, these units' battlefield effectiveness should have risen.

It is important not to exaggerate the extent of these shifts by early 1987. Iraqi forces, even the Republican Guard units, still were unable to perform complex operations.[160] Cordesman and Wagner are careful to note, for example, that Iraq "still could not efficiently counterattack Iranian forces with armor. . . . Its forces continued to fail to coordinate its ground, air, and helicopter forces efficiently. It still lacked an effective overall command structure, and it consistently committed its technology and firepower piecemeal rather than in a coherent form or in support of some coordinated form of maneuver warfare."[161] Iraqi armor and infantry repeatedly counterattacked separately and in frontal assaults that left them vulnerable to what few capabilities the Iranians possessed.

Assessing the Battlefield Effectiveness of Iran

Iranian battlefield effectiveness was relatively poor among both the regular and revolutionary forces. The human wave attacks still reflected little tactical proficiency and no ability to conduct complex operations. The Iranians did manage to cross the Shatt, but it was essentially undefended. As soon as Iranian forces arrived in Iraqi territory, they plowed straight into Iraqi defenses, in broad daylight, with little effort to time the infantry assaults for maximum effect. This resulted in minimal territorial gains for Iran at a catastrophic human price.

These tactical shortcomings finally began to have strategic effects for Iran in 1987, severely hobbling the supply of manpower before the battles of 1988. The Iranians seem to have done slightly better in the Karbala offensives in terms of their use of amphibious operations, antitank weapons, and antiaircraft missiles.[162] But overall, the Iranian forces continued to reflect their amateur leadership, highly fractured command structure, and lack of training.

These deficits were most clear when the Iranians attempted to conduct complex operations. Virtually all attempts to combine arms—for example, by relying on artillery from across the Shatt to support infantry in Karbala-4, or by linking up the two major prongs of the assault on Basra in Karbala-5—failed.[163] Iranian battlefield effectiveness among both regular and revolutionary forces was therefore generally consistent with what we would expect based on the book's framework.

THE SECOND BATTLE FOR AL-FAW, APRIL 1988

In the spring of 1988, Iraq returned to the offensive, seeking to retake the al-Faw Peninsula as the first part of a larger campaign (see map 5.5). The Iraqi effort at al-Faw offers a useful opportunity to view Iraq attempting complex offensive operations after the shift in its military organizational practices in the Republican Guard. The substantial changes in Iraqi promotion, training, command, and information management practices should have led to an observable improvement in Iraqi battlefield effectiveness by this point. The contrast should have been especially evident in comparison with Iranian performance, which should not have shifted because there was no major change in Iranian military organizational practices during this same period.

The battle was consistent with these expectations, showing greatly improved Iraqi tactical proficiency and a much better ability to conduct complex operations. It is important not to overstate the extent of these changes and also to acknowledge that in this particular battle the Iraqis also had strong numerical and material advantages. But the Iraqis already had enjoyed superiority in weapons and the local balance of manpower at numerous points in the war, without ever demonstrating the ability to perform complex operations. A close analysis of the fighting at al-Faw in 1988 makes it clear that the Iraqis were more skilled now. Given the nature of their opponent—a military fully subject to coup prevention practices, and finally cracking under the enormous human cost of its suicidal tactics—this edge was more than enough to finally deliver victory.

The Forces on Each Side

The balance of forces had shifted dramatically after the Iranian disasters of 1986. Iran's total manpower had fallen to only 600,000, while Iraq

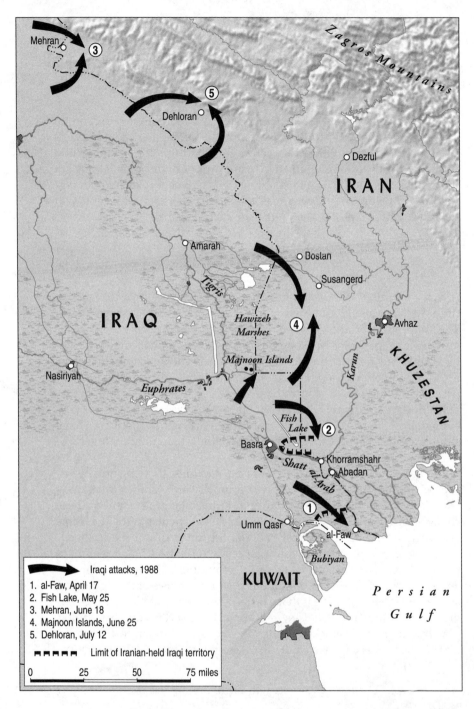

Map 5.5. Iraqi offensives, 1988. Adapted from Kenneth Pollack, *Arabs at War: Military Effectiveness, 1948–1991* (Lincoln: University of Nebraska Press, 2002), 226.

now had a million-man army.[164] Indeed, Iran was experiencing serious mobilization problems. Whatever Iranians' beliefs about the revolution, Arab invaders, or the rewards of martyrdom, the massive casualties and strategic futility of the human wave attacks had become obvious to the Iranian populace.[165]

By the spring of 1988, Iran had reduced its presence in the garrison at al-Faw from some 30,000 troops to half that or less, mostly older soldiers and volunteers rather than Artesh (see table 5.7). The light force may partly have been in preparation for a troop rotation but also reflected mobilization problems and some complacency about the Iraqi threat.[166]

By contrast, Iraq marshaled roughly 100,000 troops at al-Faw, mostly Republican Guard, as well as III and VII Corps forces. As discussed in chapter 4, the Republican Guard had not only expanded in size during the last two years but had also been subject to major changes in how its combat leaders were chosen, the rigor and frequency of its training, the nature of its command structure, and the way it managed information.

In addition, Iraq had brought large stockpiles of artillery, chemical weapons, and ammunition into the area in preparation for a combined arms amphibious assault. For its part, Iran retained significant armor and artillery at al-Faw. But as Cordesman and Wagner note, "The Iranian defensive positions were surprisingly badly developed. They lacked depth and were not particularly well sheltered or reinforced with tank

Table 5.7. The second battle for al-Faw, April 1988

	Iraq	Iran
Battle summary		
Tactical orientation	Offensive	Defensive
Plan	Combined arms amphibious assault to evict Iranians	Fixed defense from prepared positions
Weapons	Artillery, armor, chemical weapons, air support	Infantry, artillery, mines, barbed wire
Manpower	100,000 soldiers, headed by Republican Guard units	8,000–15,000, mostly Pasdaran and Basij
Losses	1,000	Heavy, but number unknown
Effectiveness summary		
Tactical proficiency?	Yes	No
Complex operations?	Yes	No
As expected?	Yes	Yes

barriers. The only major sheltered area was the central Iranian command post in the town of al-Faw. Many defensive facilities had been left unfinished, and there seems to have been little training or preparation for gas warfare."[167]

The Battle

Saddam carefully planned the attack on al-Faw in consultation with six senior officers.[168] At dawn, the Iraqis launched a massive air and artillery bombardment, subjecting the defenders to both chemical and conventional munitions.[169] A multipart ground assault then began. First, a Republican Guard naval infantry brigade launched an amphibious assault on the peninsula's southern edge, gaining a foothold on the southern coast.[170] Then at least two division equivalents of Republican Guard troops attacked the southern end of the Iranian lines. Still more Republican Guard forces moved into the city itself. At the same time, the regular army's VII Corps hammered the Iranians from the north by driving directly down the bank of the Shatt. One division broke through the Iranian lines, while another managed to link up with the Guard units that had pushed up from the south.[171]

Iraqi forces advanced through minefields, barbed wire, and water barriers, continuing to rely liberally on nonpersistent nerve gas, yet according to Cordesman and Wagner, Iraqi artillery was finally "effective" and "clearly benefited from its improved training in 1987. [It] moved more quickly, was more responsive to commanders in the forward area, and did a much better job of shifting and concentrating fires."[172] In addition, the Iraqi air force flew over 300 sorties in support of the attack, reflecting an improved ability to work with ground forces.[173]

The Iranians did receive some fire support from the eastern bank of the Shatt, but they were too surprised, outnumbered, and outfought to hold for long. Cordesman and Wagner report, "Many Iranian forces put up only a brief defense, and the local commanders showed little ability to rally their troops. Few units showed any of the willingness to die that had characterized Iranian forces in previous campaigns. The Iranian defenders began to pour back across the Shatt, but Iraqi fighters also knocked out two of the three pontoon bridges across the Shatt al-Arab from Iran to Faw. This still allowed Iranian troops to retreat but forced them to retreat in disarray and without their equipment."[174]

Although exact figures do not appear in reports of the second battle for al-Faw, all sources agree that Iranian losses were "heavy" in terms of both men and equipment.[175] Iraqi casualties, too, are unclear based on reports of the battle, but one reliable source suggests a figure of 1,000.[176] Within thirty-five hours, Iraq had restored its control of the peninsula and captured virtually all of the Iranian armor, artillery, and equipment at al-Faw.[177] It was, as a U.S. intelligence cable noted, "by far the biggest Iraqi military victory since 1981."[178]

Assessing the Battlefield Effectiveness of Iraq

Iraqi tactical proficiency at al-Faw was better than it had been two years earlier on the same terrain. Artillery and airpower were used in a more accurate and timely fashion, suggesting greater skill. Iraqi forces were able to penetrate Iranian lines quickly, suggesting that the increased infantry training had paid off. The Iraqis also demonstrated proficiency in amphibious warfare, reflected in their landings and the rapid destruction of the Iranians' pontoon bridges. Despite the fact that much of the war had already been fought on marshy terrain, these capabilities were new.

Most important, the Iraqis for the first time showed that they could execute complex operations. The assault on al-Faw integrated different combat arms so that they each supported and enhanced the power of the others. Artillery and air power responded to the needs of the ground forces, for example. The battle also reflected impressive coordination among large Iraqi ground units themselves, something the Iraqis had thus far failed to demonstrate. The Iraqi plan required synchronized movements among multiple different divisions. The fact that the Iraqis managed to position and move these forces without any detection by the Iranians showed significantly greater effectiveness than before. For example, the Republican Guard units driving up from the south did in fact link up with the VII Corps forces driving down from the north.

Part of the reason that the Iraqis could advance so quickly and execute these sorts of plans was that command decisions no longer had to be routed through Baghdad.[179] Commanders were able to take advantage of the improved training and information sharing that had occurred among their forces. Certainly, the Iranians' poor performance also accelerated the Iraqi victory at al-Faw. Some accounts, particularly those written in the period just before the 1991 Gulf War, perhaps have overstated just how much the Iraqis improved by the war's final years.[180] But the shifts that had occurred in Saddam's practices were very real—and essential to Iraq's ability to exploit Iran's long-standing deficiencies.[181]

Furthermore, even Pollack, who is highly skeptical about the military capabilities of Arab armies, notes that al-Faw was the beginning of a period that saw "a higher degree of effectiveness than the Iraqi military had ever hinted at previously." Pollack emphasizes that the Iraqi attacks, at al-Faw and elsewhere, remained heavily planned, even rigid, and argues that at a tactical level the Iraqis "did not internalize any of the concepts that lay behind these carefully scripted moves."[182] In his view, the Iraqi improvements were mostly the result of better general staff planning and limited primarily to Republican Guard units.

In short, Pollack's claim is not that there was no improvement in Iraqi performance, only that the Iraqis still did not meet the standard of combined arms maneuver warfare set by, say, the best U.S. divisions during the Cold War or the Israelis in 1967. No doubt this is true, but it also does not deny that Iraqi units subjected to different practices still performed remarkably better than they had only a short time earlier using essentially the same weapons and human capital, fighting the same opponent on the same terrain, and under the influence of the same broad structural factors such as culture, regime type, and level of economic development. These other variables are not irrelevant to a full explanation of all aspects of Iraqi military performance in 1988, but clearly the changes in military organizational practices produced important shifts in battlefield effectiveness as well.

Assessing the Battlefield Effectiveness of Iran

Iranian effectiveness was poor and reflected a military firmly under the grip of coup prevention practices. By the spring of 1988, ideological fervor could no longer compensate for the reality that a great many young Iranians simply did not want to fight and die in futile infantry attacks.[183] Moreover, in what little fighting they did in this battle the Iranians continued to demonstrate serious tactical deficits. Whatever traces of competence the Shah's practices had left behind were gone. For example, despite having been ensconced in al-Faw for two years, Iran's fixed positions were poorly prepared. The Iranians never managed to use most of the armor and artillery that they apparently had. The Iranian retreat was so disorderly that it left behind most equipment and weapons. There also had been little preparation for defense against chemical weapons, even though the Iraqis had been using such munitions since 1983.

Finally, it almost goes without saying that the Iranians were unable to conduct complex operations at al-Faw, as had been the case in most earlier battles. The Iranian command structure continued to be so fractured due to the divisions between the Artesh and the revolutionary forces that such operations remained virtually impossible.[184]

THE IRAQI FINAL OFFENSIVES, MAY–JULY 1988

Iraq's victory at al-Faw was but the first in a string of five major offensives it conducted in 1988. The other four occurred near Fish Lake outside Basra; in Mehran in the central sector; on the Majnoon Islands in the Hawizeh Marshes; and in Dehloran, also in the central sector (see map 5.5). In each of these battles, the Iraqis sought to retake territory defended by Iranian forces, providing useful opportunities to observe Iraqi attempts at complex offensive operations and Iranian attempts at complex defensive operations.

The evidence from these battles confirms the pattern seen in the second battle for al-Faw: the Iraqi armed forces demonstrated significantly improved effectiveness, while Iranian forces continued to perform poorly. The consistency of the evidence across these multiple additional offensives suggests that the Iraqi victory at al-Faw was no fluke. Instead, it reflected a sustained increase in the degree of military power that Iraq was able to generate from its national resources—an increase directly attributable to the shifts in Iraqi military organizational practices. By contrast, continuing Iranian problems reflected the country's full adoption of coup prevention practices.

The Forces on Each Side

The overall balance of forces during Iraq's final four offensives was essentially the same as it had been during the second battle for al-Faw (see table 5.8). The Iraqi attacks were led by the Republican Guard Forces Command, usually acting in conjunction with some armored, mechanized, and/or infantry elements from the regular army corps located near the sites of particular battles. Total Iraqi manpower involved in this series of battles was well over 100,000 men, giving Iraq a substantial local advantage. Although the exact number of Iranian forces in each of these confrontations is unknown, most reports refer only to division-size or smaller formations. Additionally, the Iraqis still enjoyed an overwhelming superiority in armor and artillery, including chemical weapons.

The First Battle

After retaking al-Faw, the Iraqis sought to end the threat to Basra once and for all. Iran still retained something on the order of five divisions near the city from the Karbala-5 offensive in early 1987, creating a large salient south of Fish Lake.[185] According to Cordesman and Wagner, "The Iranian defenses in the area involved a well-designed mix of trenches, sand-mound fortifications, barbed wire, tank snares, and minefields." Already in early 1988, Iraq had begun to drain Fish Lake in order to dry out the terrain surrounding these Iranian positions and enable easier use of armor. The Iranians did their best to reflood the area but failed.[186]

In May 1988, Iraq surged more than 100,000 soldiers to the area, building up a local manpower advantage of at least 3:1. Iraqi forces included

[223]

Table 5.8. Iraqi final offensives, May–July 1988

	Iraq	Iran
Battle summary		
Tactical orientation	Offensive	Defensive
Plan	Evict Iranian forces from Basra, Majnoon Islands, Hawizeh Marshes, Mehran; capture Dehloran	Defend positions, then retreat
Weapons	Armor, fixed and rotary wing aircraft, artillery with chemical and conventional munitions, pontoon bridges	Fixed defenses containing mines, barbed wire, water barriers; minimal armor and artillery
Manpower	100,000+: multiple Republican Guard units, including special naval infantry brigade; additional armored, mechanized, and infantry forces	Probably no more than 2–3 divisions at any point
Losses	Unknown but usually minimal	Significant, including POWs
Effectiveness summary		
Tactical proficiency?	Yes	No
Complex operations?	Yes	No
As expected?	Yes	Yes

the newly trained and expanded Republican Guard units, including the same special naval infantry forces that had been used the previous month at al-Faw. They enjoyed an enormous advantage in armor, as high as 15:1 or 20:1, according to Pollack.[187] Iraq also created attack routes for these forces to use in moving out of the defenses around the city, which now included additional rings of fixed fortifications interlaid with observation and artillery posts.[188] Iraq also managed to conduct some deception operations that convinced Iran the real attack was coming from farther north.[189]

On the morning of May 25, Iraq launched a massive attack reminiscent of the assault on al-Faw, bombarding the Iranians with artillery, including chemical munitions. Before Iranian forces had to time to recover or react, Iraqi armored and mechanized forces charged into the Iranian flanks, rapidly enveloping them. Iran initially attempted a counterattack, imposing high losses on the Iraqis who tried to penetrate their lines. But Iraq called in fixed wing aircraft for close air support and also used them as spotters for artillery, which provided additional support to the ground forces.

Within hours, the Iranian forces retreated in disorder, leaving much of their equipment and weapons behind. These included more than 100 tanks and 150 artillery pieces, many of them captured by Iraq without signs of combat damage. In fact, observers who later walked the battlefield found the Iranian positions littered with soldiers' personal effects, as well as a great deal of unused ammunition, grenades, bullets, gas masks, and small rockets. There was little sign of the high Iranian casualties that had characterized earlier battles; indeed, at least 350 Iranian soldiers surrendered without resisting.[190] In one fell swoop, Iran had surrendered all of its gains in the area from 1987, achieved at the cost of tens of thousands of war dead.[191]

The Second Battle

The next Iraqi attack came in mid-June against the Iranian city of Mehran. Again, Mehran had been the scene of an ugly Iraqi defeat in 1986. And again Iraqi forces followed the pattern they had established to reverse earlier losses, massing several divisions and initiating an enormous artillery barrage that included chemical munitions. Without giving the Iranian defenders time to react, Iraqi armor rapidly conducted a double envelopment, virtually destroying the two Revolutionary Guard division equivalents defending the town.[192] Iraq easily overwhelmed the Iranian defenses and advanced almost twenty miles into Iran. Neither side appears to have suffered high casualties, though the Iranians lost their equipment.[193]

The Third Battle

Only a week after retaking Mehran, Iraq launched a third attack, this time on the Iranian positions on the Majnoon Islands in the Hawizeh Marshes. The assault followed the same pattern. After a massive artillery barrage, Republican Guard forces, including the same naval infantry brigade that had fought at al-Faw and Basra, executed an amphibious assault to take the islands, supported by air power and Iraqi tanks that had been carefully pre-positioned in the marshes. After Iraqi infantry streamed onto the island in small boats and amphibious armored vehicles, combat engineers rushed in to build pontoon bridges and earthen causeways so that Iraqi armor could move in to defend the islands against any Iranian attempt to retake them.[194]

Led by two Republican Guard division equivalents, the Iraqis then initiated a double envelopment of the remaining Iranian forces in the area. According to Pollack, "The RGFC's [Republican Guard Forces Command's] Hammurabi and Madinah Armored Divisions, supported by

[225]

the Nebuchadnezzar Infantry Division, swung around to the north and linked up with mechanized formations from the III Corps that had looped around to the south thirty kilometers [about 19 miles] into Iran."[195] Enjoying an enormous superiority in weapons by this point—Iraq had perhaps 2,000 tanks and 600 artillery pieces, compared to 50–60 Iranian tanks and a handful of artillery pieces—the Iraqis obliterated the Iranian defenders. Iran suffered thousands of casualties, and many of its soldiers surrendered to the Iraqis after putting up little more than token resistance.[196] As Pollack writes, "The Iraqis mauled six to eight army and Revolutionary Guard divisions in their envelopment, seizing all of their weapons before pulling back across the border."[197]

The Fourth Battle

On July 12, Iraq launched the last attack, seeking to capture the Iranian city of Dehloran. Located in the central sector of the front, Dehloran had no particular importance except that its capture would clearly demonstrate the full implications of Iraq's new offensive power: it had the capability not only to retake its own territory but also to make gains inside Iran.

The Republican Guard Forces Command again led the attack, this time in conjunction with mechanized elements of the army's IV Corps. Again, Iraq launched an artillery bombardment, then "conducted a double envelopment, with the Republican Guard forming one prong and the IV Corps forming the other." In this attack, "the Iraqis met little resistance and drove 40 kilometers [25 miles] into Iran, encircling and routing a number of enemy formations."[198] Within hours, all Iranian defenses had crumbled.

On July 13, Iraq issued a public threat to invade all of southern Iran if Iran did not abandon its only remaining positions on Iraqi soil, all in the north. Meanwhile, rather than attempt to hold 1,500 square miles of newly conquered territory, Iraqi forces retreated back across the border with some 2,500 prisoners and large amounts of captured equipment in tow. Iran quickly complied with Iraqi demands, and Khomeini accepted a ceasefire. The war officially ended on August 8, 1988.[199]

Assessing the Battlefield Effectiveness of Iraq

Iraqi performance in the final four battles of the war demonstrates that the improvements in battlefield effectiveness at the second battle for al-Faw were not anomalous, nor were they solely the product of Iran's decline, though such a decline clearly had occurred. Iraqi tactical proficiency continued to be quite good compared to earlier in the war. It is important not to ignore the significant Iraqi advantage in weaponry in these final offensives, of course, but this was nothing new. Iraq had been better armed in terms of quality and quantity throughout the war, yet this edge, even with the use of chemical weapons, did not translate into a war winning advantage until 1987–1988. The improvement occurred because Iraqis finally knew how to use the weapons that they had. Airstrikes and artillery reached their targets; tanks were well positioned to provide fire support to advancing forces; amphibious forces actually gained control of marshy areas so that combat engineers could build the necessary bridges to transport heavier weapons and equipment. These activities reflected improvements in basic tactical skills that Iraqi forces had repeatedly failed to demonstrate earlier in the war.

Most important, Iraq continued to demonstrate a much better ability to conduct complex operations. Cordesman and Wagner, for example, repeatedly characterize Iraqi operations in this period as "effective combined arms and maneuver warfare."[200] A contemporary U.S. military assessment went so far as to claim that the final Iraqi offensives represented "the perfection of the Iraqi attempt to develop combined arms practices." This sort of praise must be taken with a large helping of salt given that it was written as the U.S. military prepared to fight a war with Iraq; surely, no U.S. analyst wanted to make the mistake of underestimating the capabilities of a soon-to-be adversary. Nevertheless, the assessment correctly noted that Iraqi forces in 1988 "were the beneficiaries of tested training techniques, experienced cadres, and especially of training time. . . . As they began operational training for the final campaign, their use of mock-ups—upon which entire divisions trained repeatedly—was highly effective."[201]

In other words, there had been real changes in how well the Iraqis were able to integrate different combat arms in operations that required both coordination and initiative—and, crucially, these changes stemmed from the very different military organizational practices that the Iraqis had adopted after 1986, particularly with respect to training. Even Pollack, a skeptic on Iraqi capability in general, writes that Iraqi forces in this period "conducted fairly deep maneuvers that led to the encirclement of sizeable Iranian forces. The offensives were preceded by highly effective deception operations and benefited from excellent intelligence regarding the disposition of Iranian forces at the start of the battle. What's more, all of the Iraqi operations moved crisply and efficiently." He continues to stress, however, that the Iraqi improvement was only "relative," "adequate," and "modest," especially given the country's overwhelming material advantages by 1988.[202] Clearly, there is some daylight between his view and the U.S. military's interpretation that by war's end the Iraqi military had become "a first-class fighting institution."[203] Still, it seems clear that Iraqi fighting effectiveness did grow substantially in 1988, consistent with what we would expect based on the book's argument.

Assessing the Battlefield Effectiveness of Iran

Iranian battlefield effectiveness in the final four battles was poor. Repeatedly, Iranian forces put up little resistance and retreated in disorder, abandoning huge quantities of perfectly good military equipment and weapons.[204] Iranian tactical proficiency and complex operations were almost irrelevant in the final battles. Only in the fighting at Fish Lake did the Iranians even try to counterattack, and their efforts quickly failed. Iranian forces generated virtually no combat power from their resources in the final year of the war—a fact that Iran's own leadership seemed to acknowledge by finally accepting a ceasefire that gave it more or less the same territory it had held in 1982.

ALTERNATIVE EXPLANATIONS

The battlefield evidence from the war was generally consistent with what we would expect if military organizational practices drive military performance, and if the practices themselves stem from the threat environment facing a given regime. Iranian and especially Iraqi units demonstrated considerable over-time and cross-unit variation in their effectiveness—variation that makes sense in light of the book's framework but that is hard to explain from the perspective of theories focused on wealth, democracy, culture, or the degree of civilian intervention in the military.

That said, some evidence from the war was surprising. Although Iranian units lacked tactical proficiency and the ability to conduct complex operations, for example, their will to fight was incredibly high until the war's final phase. Early in the war the legacy Artesh units also fought particularly well, perhaps better than can be explained simply with reference to their prewar military organizational practices under the Shah.

This section examines the role of ideology in driving Iranian military performance. It also delves into the possibility that Iraq's seemingly good performance was entirely a function of material factors rather than shifting organizational practices.

The Role of Ideology

Despite being subject to the effects of coup prevention practices—incompetent leaders, inadequate training, a convoluted command

[228]

structure, and poor information sharing—soldiers in the Iranian ground forces rarely surrendered, deserted, or retreated before 1988. More than a million Iranians were willing not just to stand and fight but to engage in battlefield tactics that in many cases all but guaranteed death. Iranian soldiers, particularly those in the Basij, were more than brave or resilient; they were suicidal.

Although this behavior did not make Iranian forces "effective" in terms of tactical proficiency or the ability to conduct complex operations, it did prolong the war and impose significant costs on the Iraqis. Moreover, this unusual behavior had ideational sources not accounted for in the book's framework: in this case, a unique cocktail of religion and revolution.[205] Of crucial significance here was the Shi'i emphasis on martyrdom as a righteous act—a theme emphasized repeatedly to Iranian soldiers in their training and indoctrination.[206] Rather than recoil from the horrendous losses incurred in the human wave attacks, Iranian leaders glorified them in a manner that seemed religiously sanctioned; sacrificing oneself was not just acceptable but a duty that brought rewards. Even though the threat environment should have pushed Iran toward conventional war practices, the country actually deepened its attachment to coup prevention as the war went on, suggesting that perhaps the country's leaders simply had a few different, deeply flawed conception of how to fight and win wars.

The Iranian regime also was able to link the war with Iraq to the cause of safeguarding and expanding the revolution, which provided further motivation for Iranian soldiers to stand and fight.[207] All these ideas combined to form what Sepehr Zabih has called "the new Islamic Shia nationalism." Notably, Iranian troops had not fought with this sort of fervor prior to the revolution. For example, in the Iranian deployment to Oman during the 1970s, British observers characterized Iranian performance as relatively lackluster.[208] Put another way, Iranian cohesion during the Iran-Iraq War stemmed from something besides simply being Iranian or Shi'i—from something besides general cultural or societal forces. Only after the revolution had taken hold in Iran were the human wave attacks possible. The fact that this fervor then died down as the war went on also casts doubt on broad cultural explanations of Iranian performance.

Nonetheless, the human wave attacks—and their consequences for Iran's war effort—reinforce the idea that unit cohesion by itself is not synonymous with battlefield effectiveness. The former is a necessary but insufficient condition of the latter. Iran's seemingly limitless supply of martyrs helped it avoid losing the war for a number of years but never translated into a decisive battlefield edge, because these forces were still so utterly lacking in tactical proficiency and the ability to conduct complex operations. Moreover, the reason that Iran lacked these latter two

[229]

capacities stemmed directly from the military organizational practices its leaders had adopted in response to the threats they faced.

The Role of Material Capabilities and Third Party Support

One also might point to the balance of material capabilities and third party support to explain the battlefield performance of the two sides. Iraq had a substantial superiority in both the quality and quantity of arms throughout the war. Not only did revolutionary Iran alienate most of the nations that could have sold it weapons, but many countries, especially in the Gulf, actively sought to support Iraq. After 1982, even the United States shared intelligence with the Iraqis, although it refrained from direct weapons sales.[209] Given these advantages, perhaps the eventual Iraqi victory, Pyrrhic though it was, is not so surprising, irrespective of any changes in military organizational practices.

Still, it is important not to overstate the impact of such advantages. First, Iraq had an indisputable weaponry advantage for essentially six years before it demonstrated significant improvements in effectiveness (see table 5.9 comparing the two sides' arsenals of main battle tanks, for example). The gap widened as the war went on, but it is hard to understand why a 6:1 advantage (as seen in 1986) would suddenly confer battlefield benefits that a 5:1 advantage (as seen in 1984) had not already provided.

Second, although Iraq received extensive foreign military assistance, most of it arrived from 1981 to 1983.[210] Despite the enormous capital advantage this assistance should have afforded Iraq, there was little to no change in Iraqi battlefield performance until much later in the war. In fact, during the period when the Iraqi military began to improve, Iranian defense spending actually was higher than Iraq's (see table 5.10).

Similarly, Iraq had been receiving U.S. tactical intelligence for years before it seemed to perform better militarily.[211] Until shifts in Iraqi military organizational practices allowed for better use of these resources, they did not make a substantial difference. Saddam flatly distrusted the United States, and as late as February 1986, internal U.S. government correspondence suggested that the Iraqis were "unable or unwilling" to act on the information provided to them.[212] Even many years later, U.S. officials were skeptical about whether Iraq ever really used or needed the intelligence it received.[213] The U.S. secretary of state at the time privately characterized the intelligence sharing as "limited," though useful.[214]

In sum, the role of third parties should not be overestimated as a factor in Iraq's eventually improved battlefield effectiveness. Once the nature of Iraqi military organizational practices shifted, it certainly was able to

Table 5.9. Comparing arsenals: Main battle tanks

	1980	1984	1986
Iraq	2,750	4,820	6,150
Iran	1,735	1,000	1,000

Sources: All data are from Iran and Iraq estimates in "The Middle East and North Africa," *Military Balance*, vols. 80, 84, 86 (1980, 1984, 1986), 42, 61–62, and 96–97, respectively.

Table 5.10. Comparing capital: Defense spending (in billions of dollars)

	1980	1984	1986
Iraq	2.67	10.296	12.866
Iran	4.2	17.370	14.091

Sources: All data are from Iran and Iraq estimates in "Middle East and North Africa," *Military Balance*, vols. 80, 84, 86, 42, 61–62, and 96–97, respectively.
Note: The table does not include foreign military assistance to Iraq.

take advantage of these resources, but prior to 1986, Iraqi performance looked very similar to how it had looked in 1980.[215]

The evidence from the battles of the Iran-Iraq War shows that countries' ability to generate fighting power from their resources depends in large part on the military organizational practices that they adopt, which stem from the nature of threats facing a given regime.

First, in the Iranian case, Iranian regular forces that had been subject to some conventional war practices with respect to training during the time of the Shah did demonstrate tactical proficiency and a minimal ability to conduct some complex operations in the early years of the war. Although the contrast should not be overdrawn, there was a clear difference between the regular forces' effectiveness and that of Iranian revolutionary forces, which had been subject only to coup prevention practices. This difference speaks again to the importance of variation in such practices.

Unfortunately for Iran, its leaders mistakenly credited the country's early victories to the revolutionary rather than the regular forces, accelerating the imposition of coup prevention practices in the regular forces. Exogenous events such as the disastrous 1981 crash that killed key military leaders also played a role in erasing any legacy of effectiveness lingering from the time of the Shah. As a result, the regular and revolutionary forces increasingly converged toward poor effectiveness as the war went on, at least in terms of tactical proficiency and the ability to conduct complex operations.

Iraqi units also displayed poor effectiveness in the early years of the war. Their battlefield performance reflected little tactical proficiency and an inability to conduct complex operations. From 1982 to 1986, the war's stalemate reflected the mutual ineffectiveness of the two sides, both subject to coup prevention practices. After 1986, however, Saddam shifted practices in the Republican Guard and select army divisions, and there was substantial improvement in the battlefield effectiveness of those units. They proved to be tactically proficient and capable of at least some complex operations. Notably, they were more effective than they or regular army or Popular Army units had been earlier in the war and were also more effective than their Iranian counterparts.

In general, then, the timing, nature, and direction of the observed variation in effectiveness were linked to shifts in military organizational practices, which in turn were tied to the threat environments facing the two regimes. Indeed, the behavior of both Iran and Iraq should induce significant caution about explanations of effectiveness focused solely on weapons (the Iraqi advantage) or numbers (the Iranian advantage). Neither of these advantages was enough to generate good battlefield performance in the absence of the crucial organizational traits emphasized here: merit-based promotion structures, rigorous training, unified and decentralized command structures, and information sharing. These variables had to be in place for the material factors to exert their force. Ultimately, it is impossible to explain why the war lasted as long as it did, imposed the costs that it did, and or ended when it did absent an understanding of the full range of threats facing the two regimes and the military organizational practices that these threats engendered.

Conclusion

Threats, Military Organizational Practices, and the Battlefields of the Future

Battlefield effectiveness is about more than victory or defeat. It requires militaries to generate tactically proficient fighting units capable of complex modern operations. Whether a given military can perform these key tasks depends on the organizational practices it adopts with respect to promotion patterns, training regimens, command arrangements, and information management. These practices are the critical missing link between broad material and political variables and the generation of battlefield effectiveness. By elucidating the military structures and behaviors most conducive and detrimental to effectiveness, this book identifies the key causal mechanisms that explain variation in military performance, both across and within states.

The case studies in this book make clear that these military organizational practices do not float freely. Rather, they spring from the threat environments that regimes face. Weakly institutionalized regimes with conflictual civil-military histories are much more likely to prioritize protection against coup threats, leading to the adoption of military organizational practices poorly suited to the demands of conventional warfighting. By contrast, robustly institutionalized regimes with harmonious or at least nonconflictual relationships between political leaders and military officers are much less likely to be concerned about coups. This security leaves them the option of adopting conventionally oriented military organizational practices that maximize battlefield effectiveness. Where such regimes face threatening external adversaries or have foreign policy goals that require territorial revision, they are particularly likely to gravitate toward such policies, even when their national resources may be limited.

[233]

This concluding chapter reviews the empirical evidence that supports the main claims; draws out the implications for scholarship; discusses possible extensions of the work that would require further research; and presents several real-world applications of the findings.

SUMMARY OF THE EMPIRICAL FINDINGS

Relying on documentary evidence, the book presented two controlled, paired comparisons of states at war: North and South Vietnam (1963–1975), and Iran and Iraq (1980–1988). These two cases offered strong controls for alternative explanations of effectiveness and therefore a relatively clean opportunity to test the book's argument. The wars examined were "fair" fights—that is, instances in which states were similar or evenly matched along the major dimensions often said to matter for military effectiveness. These included wealth, population, democracy, external threats, culture, and the degree of political intervention in the military. This approach sought to avoid examining cases whose value of the dependent variable, battlefield effectiveness, was overdetermined. In each of the four cases, different threats gave rise to different military organizational practices, both within and across the armies examined, which in turn resulted in differing abilities to generate tactical and operational fighting power on the battlefield. Though puzzling from the perspective of existing explanations of effectiveness, the pattern was generally what we would expect if the book's argument is correct.

Chapter 2 began by comparing the threat environments in North and South Vietnam, and the military organizational practices that these different environments engendered. South Vietnam was characterized first by personalist and then military dictatorship. Deeply concerned about the possibility of both coups and state failure, and deliberately insulated from external conventional military threats due to U.S. aid, South Vietnam's leaders imposed coup protection practices in most of their army units. In a notable exception, however, the 1st Division—stationed farthest from Saigon and closest to North Vietnam—was allowed to adopt conventional war practices. Meanwhile, North Vietnamese leaders, facing virtually no internal threats due to the robust development of a single-party state, and possessing national goals that actively required revision of the country's borders and conquest of foreign territory, adopted conventional war practices.

Chapter 3 explored the dramatic consequences of these divergent practices by examining five of the Vietnam War's major battles or campaigns. The evidence shows that North and South Vietnam consistently fought differently. Despite the fact that the two countries were both

Table C.1. The case studies

State	Variation in practices, if any	Battlefield impact
South Vietnam	From coup prevention practices to conventional war practices in 1st Division	1st Division much more effective than other units from South Vietnamese army and just as effective as comparable North Vietnamese units
North Vietnam	Consistent conventional war practices	Consistent effectiveness
Iraq	From coup prevention practices to conventional war practices in Republican Guard and select army divisions	Dramatic improvement in effectiveness of Republican Guard and select army divisions compared to their earlier performance and to that of other Iraqi units and of Iranian units
Iran	From coup prevention practices in revolutionary forces only to coup prevention practices in both revolutionary and regular forces	Regular forces initially more effective than revolutionary forces, followed by uniformly poor effectiveness across all units

nondemocratic and had almost identical levels of economic development, the same size populations, and common cultural underpinnings, North Vietnam's organizational practices maximized combat power, while South Vietnam's squandered it. The major exception, again, was the South Vietnamese 1st Division, which had less potential to threaten the regime with a coup. After adopting organizational practices geared much more closely to conventional war, the 1st Division generated combat power nearly indistinguishable from that of comparable North Vietnamese units. Though not enough to overcome the deficits in the rest of the South Vietnamese army, the 1st Division's performance provides fine-grained evidence of the posited connections among threats, practices, and effectiveness, showing that the book's framework helps us understand both broad patterns at the state level as well as unit-level exceptions to those patterns.

Chapters 4 and 5 conducted a similar comparison of Iran and Iraq during their war. The evidence showed that Saddam Hussein had a quite rational fear of coups, much as one would expect in a personalist dictatorship, and that he entered the Iran-Iraq War with exactly the practices needed to maintain himself in power against this threat. As the war went on, however, the detrimental battlefield effects of these practices increasingly became apparent, especially by 1986 when a particularly devastating series of operational setbacks not only threatened defeat in the war but also risked a coup by senior officers. Saddam at that point ordered his Republican Guard and select regular army units to adopt conventional war practices. Although confined to only a few divisions, this shift produced rapid improvements in Iraqi battlefield effectiveness, again consistent with what one would expect in a personalist dictatorship where decisions can be made quickly by a single individual rather than by bureaucratic institutions. The result was a highly successful series of Iraqi counteroffensives in 1987 and 1988 that ended the war. These victories occurred despite the fact that Iran remained larger, wealthier, and more populous than Iraq, and the Iraqi military remained infused with Arab culture and high levels of political intervention in the military, which other theories of effectiveness would expect to stymie combat performance.

This Iraqi triumph was possible only because it faced in Iran an adversary who gave it the luxury of time to adapt. Iran's leaders arguably faced the most complicated threat environment of the four states examined here. The revolutionary regime simultaneously faced threats of coup, secession, civil war, and external conventional war, each of which also threatened some variety of counterrevolution. Consistent with the book's framework, Iranian leaders prioritized coup protection even though they needed the military to be a functional institution to deal with all the threats they faced besides coups. In particular, Khomeini imposed harsh coup protection measures on the legacy military inherited from the Shah, which had the greatest motive and capability to unseat the new regime. It is interesting to note, though, that the revolutionary regime was not able to erase overnight the vestiges of the somewhat better military organizational practices that had evolved under the Shah. These intramilitary differences were evident in the early stages of the Iran-Iraq War, as the Shah's legacy units were clearly more tactically proficient and capable of complex operations than the newer units established by the revolutionary regime.

Unfortunately for Iran, its leaders never successfully integrated the prerevolutionary and revolutionary armed forces, and in fact mistakenly credited the revolutionary forces rather than the legacy units with early battlefield successes. As a result, Iran's leaders only deepened their imposition of coup protection practices as the war went on, decimating whatever effectiveness lingered from the Shah's era. They instead relied on soldiers who were ideologically motivated to be cohesive but who lacked any ability to convert that cohesion into tactical proficiency or complex operations. Once the Iraqis finally adopted conventional war practices in their Republican Guard and select regular army units, Iranian forces became highly vulnerable to Iraqi combined arms assaults.

Put simply, both Iran and Iraq performed poorly when their militaries were uniformly subject to coup protection practices: in the Iranian case, after about 1982, and in the Iraqi case, before about 1986. By contrast, in the period before these practices exerted their full effects on the regular military in Iran and in the period after these practices were lifted on the Republican Guard and select army units in Iraq, military performance by those forces was noticeably better compared both to the opponent's military and to other units drawn from the same state. The contrast was subtle in the Iranian case and dramatic in the Iraqi case but in both instances directly attributable to differing military organizational practices that stemmed from threat environments in which coups rather than other states were the major concern. These distinctions—similar to those seen in the Vietnam comparisons—suggest the importance of threats and military organizational practices in explaining variations in battlefield effectiveness both across and within states.

IMPLICATIONS: THE CONTRIBUTION TO SCHOLARSHIP

This book began with a puzzle: If the basic activities that produce success on the modern battlefield are more or less known, then why don't all states do those things? The framework here suggests that even where it may be in a *state's* best interest to perform those key tasks, the *regime* ruling a given state may eschew the benefits of conventional military effectiveness because of the coup risk that such expertise poses. In particular, personalist and military dictatorships are likely to be very sensitive to this risk, as are any states that have a history of conflict-ridden civil-military relations. The book's empirical chapters showed that Saddam's Iraq, Diem's and Thieu's South Vietnam, and Khomeini's Iran all evinced this tendency.

Conversely, some authoritarian regimes, particularly single-party states, are well-institutionalized in ways that safely channel opposition to the government and mute internal threats, resulting in largely harmonious civil-military relations. The absence of coup fears in these regimes does not guarantee the adoption of military organizational practices geared toward conventional war, but it makes such adoption possible—especially in cases where the regime has foreign policy goals that require territorial revision. The experience of the North Vietnamese regime illustrated these dynamics at work, explaining why North Vietnam was able to generate so much more fighting power from its

[237]

resources than was its southern counterpart. As this contrast suggests, political institutions and civil-military history offer important *ex ante* clues as to the nature of military organizational practices that a given state is likely to adopt. When combined with other indicators of the internal and external threat environments facing a particular regime, the result is a strong predictor of the military power the state is likely to generate.

All this suggests that traditional ways of thinking about power in international relations merit some reconsideration. Power is often treated as synonymous with material assets, and no doubt having a booming economy, large population, and top-of-the-line weapons position a state to perform well militarily, other things being equal. But in fact other things rarely are equal. Material assets have to be converted into military organizational strength, because it is military organizations that compete on the battlefield, not national economies, birthrates, or storehouses of weapons. Furthermore, military organizational strength is a double-edged sword for some regimes, which is why they may generate less conventional military power than we might expect based solely on calculations of their material resources. In fact, this was exactly the scenario illustrated by the Iraqi military from 1980 to 1986: Iraq enjoyed significant and ever-increasing material advantages over Iran, but the nature of internal threats to the Iraqi regime led to military organizational practices that hindered the conversion of that latent material power into actual fighting capability.

For those already convinced of the power of nonmaterial variables, the book's framework improves our understanding of what exactly these factors are and when their causal power is turned on and off. The framework does this in part by drawing on insights from the study of comparative politics, which traditionally has paid great attention to the nature of internal threats across different types of regimes exhibiting varied civil-military histories. In much international relations research, by contrast, the notion of "regime type" has essentially become synonymous with a black-and-white distinction between dictatorship and democracy. Indeed, this distinction has driven one of the most prominent and provocative findings in the existing literature on military effectiveness: that democracy confers a major battlefield advantage by producing better strategic assessment of which wars to enter and by inculcating soldiers with liberal political values that motivate them to fight better.

Beginning with Huntington's *Political Order in Changing Societies*, however, scholars of comparative politics have emphasized that there exist important variations within—and not just between—democratic and nondemocratic regimes. Political institutions can be strong or weak in both, with important implications for such regimes' behavior. A more recent wave of scholarship in international relations has drawn on these insights to explain states' conflict behavior, especially conflict initiation. Jessica Weeks, in particular, has theorized that different types of authoritarian institutions produce varying levels of accountability for leaders, resulting in differing propensities for conflict initiation across authoritarian regimes. As she notes, when we move beyond "the usual dichotomy between democracy and authoritarianism," it becomes clear that many autocracies are just as selective as democracies in their choices about conflict initiation.[1]

This book both joins that promising approach and pushes it in some new directions. Most notably, my analysis explores states' intrawar behavior rather than conflict initiation—what happens after wars start, rather than why they start. It is important to know what causes states to initiate conflict, of course, but how they actually fight once engaged on the battlefield also has critical independent implications for war outcomes, war duration, and the costs that war imposes on both winners and losers. These variables all shape the impact of war on the international system as a whole, and the book's framework provides a useful tool for gauging that impact by assessing the likely combat effectiveness of war participants.

The focus on intrawar behavior also is important because arguments about democratic wartime advantages have rested on claims not only about democratic selection into winnable wars but also about the superior battlefield fighting capabilities of democratic regimes once wars have started. By focusing on variation among authoritarian regimes' fighting power, the book enables us to probe the logic of democratic superiority in a way that arguments focused on initiation have not. The centrality of threats and military organizational practices in the cases examined suggests that liberal political values may have little to do with conventional military effectiveness. Rather, liberal regimes may simply be more likely to face threat environments that allow the development of conventionally useful military organizational practices. Where authoritarian regimes face similar threat environments, they too can develop conventionally useful military organizational practices. Hence the book's argument not only helps explain puzzling instances of autocratic effectiveness but encourages a reconsideration of the sources of apparent democratic military prowess as well.

The book's focus on threats as the central variable also differs from previous work on authoritarian conflict behavior. Institutions are important here not because of their effects on accountability but because of what they tell us about the domestic threat environment. Past civil-military relations are important for the same reason. By focusing on threats, the book's framework avoids the determinism that sometimes

[239]

results from an emphasis on institutions alone. After all, organizational behavior and war are both dynamic, and threats can shift even where institutions do not. So although institutions provide an important initial clue as to a regime's likely choice of military organizational practices, the book's framework enables us to situate these institutions in a larger context that allows for change over time and/or across different military units within the same state. Such adaptation and innovation is puzzling from the perspective of existing theories yet absolutely vital to explaining how real wars unfold.

Furthermore, institutions often can tell us when and how we should expect to see such variation occur. For example, we should expect faster military organizational adaptation in personalist regimes—once the leader is convinced it's necessary— because institutions are essentially nonexistent. The experience of Saddam's Iraq from 1986 to 1988 confirms this intuition. By contrast, the factional nature of the military regime in South Vietnam was a barrier to adjustments in military organizational practices, even when many individual officers recognized that existing policies were deeply problematic. This pattern suggests that institutions offer useful clues not only to the likely initial nature of military organizational practices but also to the processes by which such practices may change.

Finally, the research presented here contributes to the study of civil-military relations, a subject at the nexus of comparative politics and international relations. Existing scholarship has pointed to the detrimental impact of coup-proofing techniques on conventional military effectiveness, but these promising studies have focused almost entirely on Arab autocracies, leaving it unclear whether coup concerns underlie a broader pattern of military organizational behavior that extends beyond the Middle East. The book's case studies demonstrate that coup-proofing is indeed a far-reaching phenomenon with roots in the threat environments that different regimes face. It can happen in postcolonial Southeast Asia and revolutionary Iran just as easily as in the Arab world.

That said, autocracy and coup-proofing are not synonymous. The variation seen in the Iraqi and South Vietnamese cases demonstrates that nothing about being an autocracy guarantees permanent or categorical adherence to coup prevention practices. In fact, some nondemocratic regimes do not engage in this behavior at all, enabling them to generate surprisingly high levels of military power from their material resources, despite their lack of liberal political values. This was the case in North Vietnam.

In addition, the book's framework provides a general, deductively grounded explanation of the actual mechanisms by which coup-proofing wreaks havoc on conventional military effectiveness: by altering a core set of military organizational practices. Using this same logic, the framework shows that excellent battlefield performance requires more than simply the absence of coup-proofing. Rather, militaries must adopt a distinct, affirmative set of policies with respect to core areas of military activity in order to convert resources into fighting power. States such as North Vietnam, which lack significant internal coup threats and have foreign policy goals that require territorial revision, are likely to gravitate toward such policies. But even states with conflictual civil-military relations, such as Saddam's Iraq, can adopt different practices when the external threat environment generates enough pressure and the adversary provides the space and time needed for adaptation. Iraq enjoyed this luxury; South Vietnam did not.

EXTENSIONS: AREAS FOR FURTHER RESEARCH

Like all research, the argument and evidence in this book have their limits. Several aspects of this work might profitably be extended to new areas, however. First, the book argues that a regime's foreign policy goals are critical in propelling the adoption of conventional war practices, but it takes these goals largely as givens rather than examining their sources. Additional research could explore the causes and consequences of these goals more explicitly, examining whether they, too, are systematically related in any way to a given state's political institutions or other observable traits. Understanding these connections, if they exist, would further improve our ability to predict *ex ante* which regimes are most likely to adopt which types of military organizational practices.

Second, the book set aside unit cohesion as an aspect of battlefield effectiveness, focusing instead on militaries' tactical proficiency and ability to conduct complex operations. This choice stemmed not from the assumption that unit cohesion does not matter but from the belief that alone it is inadequate to explain the observed variation in battlefield effectiveness. In fact, the case studies bear out this view, as the two most cohesive militaries examined—communist North Vietnam and revolutionary Iran—diverged dramatically in their battlefield performance. Their differing trajectories reinforce the idea that having highly motivated soldiers with a strong willingness to fight is a necessary but far from sufficient condition for generating fighting power.

That said, unit cohesion does underlie battlefield performance, and as the experience of the South Vietnamese 1st Division in 1975 attests, units can collapse from loss of morale even when they have the tactical skills and weapons needed to continue resisting. Further research could explore the drivers of this vital component of effectiveness, particularly

[241]

given that its sources may be ideological or psychological, and therefore quite different from the causes of effectiveness emphasized in this book's framework. Again, the North Vietnamese and Iranian cases offer at least tentative support for the notion that cohesion has ideational roots in the larger society from which a military is drawn, and other recent research confirms this intuition.[2]

Third, scholars could use the book's framework to examine other non-democracies, particularly through the exploration of primary source documents in original languages, as well as interviews. This book has focused on developing key concepts and trying to show their range across a breadth of settings, but there are limitations to this approach. Deeper research on individual cases would enable us to subject the book's argument to more rigorous tests and amend it if necessary.

Such efforts also might enable better understanding of how regimes themselves perceive their threat environments. The book's framework has focused on objective, observable indicators of internal and external threats, more or less assuming that regimes accurately perceive these in-dicators and act accordingly. I justified this approach at the outset by ar-guing that in many instances regimes do behave as if they pay attention to these indicators, and so by making this assumption we can better pre-dict the military organizational practices such regimes will adopt than we could if we assume that adoption is random. The empirical evidence from the cases bore out this approach, as the threat environments gener-ally did correlate with the practices that the different regimes adopted.

Yet threat perceptions are highly contingent and often biased or dis-torted in various ways. Regimes may not adopt the practices that the framework predicts that they should, or they may adopt such practices belatedly or haphazardly. Further research could explore the conditions under which regimes will or will not respond to the incentives posed by the threat environment, and why. It would be particularly useful if future scholarship could identify any systematic conditions under which par-ticular types of bias or distortion are likely, enabling us to see when the book's framework is most likely to apply.

In addition, future research could focus more directly on instances in which the primary internal danger to a given regime is something be-sides coups: revolution, social unrest, secession, or civil war, for example. Which military organizational practices are ideal for combating these dangers, and to what extent do they trade off with preparation for con-ventional interstate war? This book focused on coups in part because the trade-off is so stark, but other types of internal threats may be less damaging to the development of military skill. For example, the prac-tices needed to fight effectively in a conventional civil war might not di-verge dramatically from those identified here as being necessary in

[242]

conventional interstate wars. Or, regimes that do not face significant coup risks might be able to build entirely distinct and highly robust coercive institutions to deal with internal security threats, while still maintaining a regular military to fight conventional wars. In general, we would expect organizational choices to reflect the threat environment, consistent with the argument made here, but the battlefield consequences might look different.

Beyond this research, more empirical work is needed on the role of threats and military organizational practices in explaining the battlefield effectiveness of democracies. The analytical strategy here deliberately excluded such regimes for reasons of both methodology and substance. Methodologically, the case studies sought to hold constant the variable most often credited in existing research with explaining poor military performance: autocracy. Focusing only on nondemocracies made it easier to isolate the causal impact of other variables often treated as synonymous with autocracy, such as politicization of the military, and to explore puzzling variations within nondemocratic regimes. Substantively, autocracies also have received less scholarly attention despite the fact that such states are likely to be central to future conflicts, which provided a second set of reasons to narrow the book's empirical scope to these regimes.

Nevertheless, the book's broader argument should point the way toward explaining variation in battlefield effectiveness among democratic regimes as well. Although we might expect that democracies will on average have stronger institutions, face lower risk of coups, and therefore be more likely to adopt military organizational practices geared toward conventional warfare, this tendency will not be universal. Some democracies do look like Sweden and the United States, but many also look like Pakistan, Afghanistan, Egypt, Russia, and Iraq—they hold elections but are weakly institutionalized and have conflictual civil-military relations that expose them to many of the same trade-offs as their nondemocratic counterparts when it comes to the design of coercive institutions. Even some better institutionalized democracies, such as India and Turkey, have histories of significant civil-military tension that might create pressures for the adoption of coup prevention practices. The framework here suggests the general utility of exploring these possible differences and using them as a source of leverage to explain variation in conflict behavior beyond nondemocracies.

Finally, the book has focused on states as the primary actors, but further research could explore the application of its central premises to nonstate actors. Much like states, nonstate actors generate fighting power through the building, maintenance, and adaptation of fighting organizations.[3] Also like states, nonstate violent actors vary in their internal cohesion and the extent to which the leaders of a given group face challenges from their own members.

One would expect nonstate actors that manage to stamp out these internal threats to be better positioned to focus on organizational tasks that bolster the generation of externally directed combat power, much as is the case for their state counterparts. For example, the fighting power of nonstate groups such as Hezbollah, the Tamil Tigers, and the Provisional Irish Republican Army clearly owes much to the high levels of organizational cohesion each achieved by minimizing internal dissent early.[4] By contrast, groups plagued by enduring fissures and leadership struggles have to devote more organizational resources to self-policing, leaving less bandwidth for combating their adversaries. For example, this dynamic partly explains why the armed opposition in Syria has been unable to overthrow the Assad regime even though the opposition often has controlled more territory and ostensibly represents a much larger segment of the country's majority Sunni population. Insurgents have to prepare to fight the regime but also have to battle one another and even potential splinter movements in their own ranks.[5] By the same token, regime forces in that country must protect Asad from both coups and civil war, which partly explains why his forces, too, have fared poorly in many battles despite enormous material advantages. Neither side has been able to optimize its military organizational practices for dealing solely with the threat posed by the opponent.

Dealing with these types of internal threats often trades off with battlefield effectiveness, for states and nonstates alike. Many of the same organizational practices that I have argued produce success for state militaries seem likely to apply to armed groups. Promotion on merit, rigorous training, decentralized yet unified command structures, and information sharing all seem vital for the fighting power of such organizations. For example, supposedly formidable Shi'i militias in Iraq initially foundered in trying to retake territory lost to the Islamic State of Iraq and Syria largely because of the militias' highly politicized promotion processes and lack of serious training.[6] Although the nature of the battlefield tasks that nonstate actors might seek to perform are likely to be distinct from those of conventional warfare, many of the relevant organizational traits seem likely to be similar.

Applications: The Framework's Relevance to Foreign Policy

The framework and empirical evidence in this book speak to several real-world policy issues. Chief among these are the net assessment of potential adversaries, along with efforts to estimate and build the fighting capabilities of potential allies. This final section discusses each of these in turn.

The book's emphasis on the distinction between victory and effectiveness paves the way for more fine-grained net assessments of potential adversaries than are often possible in academic studies that focus solely on war outcomes. War outcomes surely matter, but the manner in which those outcomes are achieved is of vital concern to policymakers. The question preceding U.S. conventional military operations is rarely, Will this operation ultimately result in victory for the United States? Given the United States' overwhelming material power, its tendency to fight wars of choice, and the benefits it usually enjoys from working with allies, it can almost always eke out something resembling conventional military victory against weaker states. The real question is, What costs can potential opponents impose on the United States during the fight, even if the United States still gets the eventual conventional outcome it seeks?

The findings here shed light on this question, illuminating a vital set of factors to be analyzed in assessing potential adversaries. When facing opponents that have managed to build relatively strong institutions and mute internal threats, especially coup concerns, the United States can expect military conflict to last longer, cost more, and impose greater casualties. Slobodan Milošević's regime presented one such case. Despite Serbia's relative weakness compared to NATO, its military adopted practices that enabled it to hold out against coalition airpower for more than nine weeks, rather than the mere days NATO expected. Although the 1999 war is viewed as a defeat for Serbia, the country's ability to generate conventional fighting power arguably secured for it several significant concessions compared to the deal it would have achieved from the Rambouillet Agreement.[7] As this case shows, even weak states can fight well when their internal conditions are right, with significant consequences for U.S. military operations and foreign policy.

By contrast, when the United States faces adversaries worried about coup threats, it can expect an opponent likely to suffer rapid military collapse. For example, Muammar Qaddafi's coup fears led to precisely the sort of damaging military organizational practices predicted by the book's framework and resulted in the rapid collapse of his regime under conventional military pressure from the United States.[8] Indeed, sometimes such regimes can collapse too rapidly, setting the stage for a security vacuum in the aftermath of military defeat. The instability of post-Qaddafi Libya illustrates this concern. So, too, does post-Saddam Iraq.[9] Had the United States understood in 2003 how brittle the Iraqi military actually was, it might have prepared for the post-conflict environment differently, or it might have decided that military operations

[245]

were unnecessary for achieving its goals. In all such situations, a clear understanding of the internal and external threat environments facing an opponent is essential to solid calculations about whether to go to war, how to fight, and how to prepare for the aftermath.

The experiences of the two countries examined in this book that also fought wars against the United States—North Vietnam and Iraq—reinforces this logic. The contrast in the performance of these two relatively weak, authoritarian regimes against a materially superior, democratic adversary is quite striking, yet it is highly consistent with what we would expect based on the book's framework.[10] The conventional war practices employed by the North Vietnamese enabled them to impose significant costs on the United States in terms of time, resources, and casualties. Ultimately, the United States had to settle for a draw at best. By contrast, when the Iraqis fought the United States in 1991 and 2003, Saddam had reverted to coup prevention practices, which helps explain why the coalitions managed to achieve such rapid, low-cost conventional military victories, despite the large size of the Iraqi army and, in 1991 at least, the excellent quality of many of its weapons.[11]

The book's framework also is relevant for assessing the fighting capabilities of great powers. For example, modern-day China is an authoritarian regime, but one with a well-developed single party that seems to have all but eliminated any serious danger of military-backed coups.[12] Indeed, the country has virtually none of the indicators of coup risk identified in the book's framework. Although the regime still faces myriad other internal threats, including secession, rebellion, and mass protests, the book's framework would expect China to have little reason to adopt the coup prevention practices so damaging to conventional military effectiveness.

Furthermore, it is not controversial to note that China harbors foreign policy goals that require territorial revision, notably with respect to Taiwan. This external imperative, combined with the lack of internal dangers posed by the Chinese military—especially the air and naval forces that are the subject of most concern in the region—suggests that China's military should be a prime candidate for the adoption of conventional war practices. The United States and China are not destined to experience conflict, of course, but the book's framework suggests that the United States should not underestimate China's ability to generate a conventionally effective fighting organization, were such conflict to occur. China is not a democracy, but it is a different breed of autocracy from that the United States has faced in targeting personalist regimes such as Qaddafi's Libya.

Beyond assessing potential adversaries, the book also improves the tools we have for estimating and building the fighting power of coalition partners and allies. U.S. defense strategy increasingly calls for "building partner capacity," that is, for bolstering the fighting effectiveness of other armies, particularly the armies of nondemocratic or nascent democratic states.[13] For example, the U.S. exit strategies for both Iraq and Afghanistan relied heavily on the building of indigenous army and police forces that could operate independently of the United States. Broader U.S. strategies in East Asia and the Middle East also depend on building or sustaining the militaries of allies such as South Korea, Japan, Saudi Arabia, Israel, and Egypt. This also has been a significant component of the U.S. approach to counterterrorism in places such as Yemen.

The factors here present an important set of indicators that U.S. policymakers should seek to examine and to influence in such countries. It is worth noting, for example, that two other countries examined in this book—South Vietnam and Iran—both received enormous infusions of U.S. weapons and military assistance just prior to or during the wars examined here. Saddam Hussein's regime also received some indirect support and the provision of tactical intelligence. But the adoption of military organizational practices stemming from the nature and severity of internal threats in all three regimes greatly eroded the potential battlefield value of these U.S. contributions. Only in the Iraqi case, after the shift in Saddam's military organizational practices late in the war, was the recipient of U.S. assistance actually able to generate fighting power, and in South Vietnam U.S. assistance arguably became counterproductive, shielding the regime from the very threats that would have been most likely to prompt much-needed adaptation. In general, the sheer scale of U.S. assistance to South Vietnam, as well as to Iran under the Shah, underscores how important it is to look beyond purely material factors in estimating the likely return on U.S. security assistance. If any regimes should have been able to fight effectively due to U.S. provision of aid, surely South Vietnam in the 1960s and Iran in the early 1980s would have qualified. Yet their performances were generally poor, largely because aid did little to address the core threats facing recipient regimes.

These realities have important implications for efforts to implement security assistance to foreign militaries. Such efforts often focus on rapidly building foreign militaries to a particular size, with the metric of success defined as the number of men in uniform who have completed some modicum of basic training. As this book has tried to make clear, however, all training is not created equal, and rigorous, realistic training at both the small- and large-unit levels is only one of several organizational practices vital to military effectiveness. Training must be paired with merit-based promotion systems, appropriate command arrangements, and systems that encourage necessary information sharing. Only then are consistent tactical proficiency and competence in complex operations likely.

[247]

Without attention to these organizational "guts," and to the threat conditions shaping them, foreign militaries may look effective on paper but are likely to collapse on the battlefield, even when they have the benefit of good hardware or technical intelligence. The rapid 2014 collapse of the U.S.-built Iraqi army in the face of attacks by the Islamic State painfully illustrated this point.[14] The United States poured years of efforts and billions of dollars into forming and equipping the post-Saddam Iraqi army, but Prime Minister Nouri al-Maliki almost immediately began implementing coup prevention practices when the United States withdrew in late 2011, and the army's combat capability rapidly declined from whatever minimal baseline it had reached as a result.[15]

These same dynamics bode poorly for the fighting capabilities of other U.S. allies as well. In Afghanistan, for example, it is not clear that the regime trusts its own military enough to allow merit-based promotions, rigorous training, and a clear chain of command.[16] Certainly, the country's weak institutions and civil-military history do not inspire much confidence.[17] That said, the regime's primary armed threat is insurgency, not conventional war, so adherence to some coup prevention practices might not be as devastating to Afghan effectiveness as it was to the armies examined here—after all, the Afghans need to be effective at a somewhat different set of tasks than the South Vietnamese or Iraqis did. Still, the record of the Afghan National Army to date strongly suggests that the country's military organizational practices are unlikely to generate as much fighting power as one would predict based purely on the infusion of resources the security forces have received.

Similarly, the United States has sold tens of billions of dollars in weapons to the Gulf states, especially Saudi Arabia and the United Arab Emirates, but coup fears continue to plague both regimes.[18] These concerns raise serious questions as to whether either regime is likely to implement the conventional war practices that would maximize the fighting power afforded by such weapons. The United States would want to factor in this constraint in estimating how much it could depend on these allies' effectiveness during a regional military crisis. That said, the fact that most U.S. weapons sales have gone to these regimes' naval and especially air forces—rather than their ground forces—may be a partial saving grace. Compared to the armies examined in this study, air and naval forces have less inherent ability to mount a coup. As a result, even weakly institutionalized regimes with substantial coup worries might be willing to allow greater adoption of conventional war practices in these units, as compared to ground units.[19]

U.S. allies are likely to fight better—and make better use of foreign security assistance—when their regimes have managed to mute coup threats. For example, the book's framework would predict that despite

Singapore's small size and population, the country is likely to generate substantial combat power from its arms purchases.[20] The country is not a democracy, but it is a well-institutionalized, consolidated authoritarian regime that faces essentially no internal dissent. Civilian control of the military is well established, and the regime is focused primarily on external dangers, particularly from Malaysia and China.[21] Given this threat environment, it is not surprising that Singapore's military has adopted organizational practices well suited to conventional war. For example, Singapore's promotion system is merit-based, and training is rigorous and realistic.[22]

In general, those designing programs for foreign military assistance must consider carefully the full range of threats facing recipient regimes. Often U.S. assistance aims to improve a foreign military's proficiency in dealing with a single threat, one that the United States shares. But most regimes face a multiplicity of dangers, especially internal ones, and the book's framework shows how powerful coup threats can be in shaping military organizational practices, irrespective of outside aid. Force generation plans that ignore these aspects of the recipient regime's threat calculus will meet with little success. In such cases, efforts to strengthen political institutions and reduce civil-military conflict may do more than weapons sales and training programs to align the regime's threat calculus with that of its outside patron.

More broadly, the case studies encourage humility about the perverse effects that even well-designed security assistance can induce.[23] The problem of moral hazard already has been mentioned: that by doing more, the United States creates incentives for its partners to do less, which in the long run may make them even more vulnerable when U.S. assistance inevitably tapers off. In other words, U.S. presence can shield regimes from the very threats that would otherwise stimulate needed adaptation in military organizational practices. This dilemma may be inescapable in some cases, which should induce caution in policymakers considering intervention in the first place.

An additional problem is that U.S. ties to foreign military units actually can heighten coup fears in partner regimes. In South Vietnam, for example, the United States' tacit support for the 1963 coup was well known, leading subsequent regimes to harbor deep suspicions about any units or individuals that had close relationships with the Americans. U.S. trainers found Saigon's repeated failures to promote officers they deemed effective puzzling, but such intransigence was only logical from the perspective of coup protection: ties to the Americans may have been a sign of conventional military proficiency but also were viewed as a dangerous marker of conspiracy by political leaders who had seen the Americans back previous military plots. The United States' failure to appreciate this dimension of the South Vietnamese regime's threat calculus no doubt hindered the effort to create a conventionally effective partner military.

Analysts and policymakers must move beyond bean counting in efforts to assess and influence the fighting effectiveness of both enemy and friendly forces. Combat power depends not only on men and materiel but also on organizational structure and behavior, which are functions of the broader threat environment into which a given coercive apparatus is born and in which it subsequently evolves. Only by understanding these origins, the processes of organizational adaptation, and the implications for core military activities can scholars accurately account for the wide-ranging and often puzzling fates of military organizations on the battlefield—and it is knowledge of these same factors that can endow political leaders with the ability to shape and re-shape such organizations in the real world.

Notes

INTRODUCTION

1. Stephen Biddle, *Military Power: Explaining Victory and Defeat in Modern Battle* (Princeton: Princeton University Press, 2004).

2. James Quinlivan, "Coup-Proofing: Its Practice and Consequences in the Middle East," *International Security* 24, no. 2 (1999), 131–165; Risa Brooks, *Political-Military Relations and the Stability of Arab Regimes* (New York: Oxford University Press, 1998); and Stephen Biddle and Robert Zirkle, "Technology, Civil-Military Relations, and Warfare in the Developing World," *Journal of Strategic Studies* 19, no. 2 (1996), 171–212.

3. Zeev Maoz and Bruce Russett, "Normative and Structural Causes of the Democratic Peace, 1946–1986," *American Political Science Review* 87, no. 3 (1993), 624–638; and Bruce Bueno de Mesquita, James D. Morrow, Randolph Siverson, and Alastair Smith, "An Institutional Explanation of the Democratic Peace," *American Political Science Review* 93, no. 4 (1999), 791–807.

4. Robert Gates, "Helping Others Defend Themselves," *Foreign Affairs* 89, no. 3 (May/June 2010), 2–6.

5. Allan R. Millett and Williamson Murray, "The Effectiveness of Military Organizations," in *Military Effectiveness*, vol. 1, *The First World War*, ed. Allan R. Millett and Williamson Murray (Boston: Allen & Unwin, 1988), 6–7, 12, and 19.

6. Martin van Creveld, *Fighting Power: German and U.S. Army Performance, 1939–1945* (Westport, CT: Greenwood Press, 1982), 3.

7. *Military Effectiveness*, vol. 1, 3.

8. Biddle, *Military Power*.

9. For critical reviews of Biddle, see the June 2005 special issue of the *Journal of Strategic Studies*. Like Biddle, I focus on mid-to-high intensity conventional land warfare, but the basic logic of the argument should extend to air and naval conflict and irregular warfare. See also Ryan Grauer and Michael Horowitz, "What Determines Military Victory? Testing the Modern System," *Security Studies* 21 (2012), 83–112.

10. Andrew Krepinevich, *The Army and Vietnam* (Baltimore: Johns Hopkins University Press, 1986); and John Nagl, *Learning to Eat Soup with a Knife: Counterinsurgency Lessons from Malaya and Vietnam* (Chicago: University of Chicago Press, 2005).

11. Nora Kinzer Stewart, *Mates and Muchachos: Unit Cohesion in the Falklands/Malvinas War* (New York: Brassey's, 1991).

12. Daniel Kon, *Los Chicos de la Guerra* (Sevenoaks, UK: New English Library, 1983), 28.

13. See note 10; Austin Long, *Refighting the First War: Military Culture and Counterinsurgency Doctrine in the United States and United Kingdom* (Ithaca, NY: Cornell University Press, forthcoming); and Robert Cassidy, *Russia in Afghanistan and Chechnya: Military Strategic Culture and the Paradoxes of Asymmetric Conflict* (Fort Carlisle, PA: Strategic Studies Institute, 2003).

14. This is not to claim that such transitions are easy, successful, or guarantors of overall military effectiveness, as the U.S. experience in Iraq shows. See Long, *Refighting the First War*; Brian Burton and John Nagl, "Learning as We Go: The U.S. Army Adapts to Counterinsurgency in Iraq, July 2004–December 2006," *Small Wars and Insurgencies* 19, no. 3 (September 2008), 303–327; Colin Kahl, "COIN of the Realm: Is There a Future for Counterinsurgency?" *Foreign Affairs* 86, no. 6 (November/December 2007), 169–176; and Joshua Rovner, "The Heroes of COIN," *Orbis* (Spring 2012), 215–232.

1. A Framework for Explaining Battlefield Effectiveness

1. On North Vietnam, see chapter 2 in this book. On the Israelis, see Chaim Herzog, *The Arab-Israeli Wars: War and Peace in the Middle East* (New York: Random House, 1982); and Martin van Creveld, *The Sword and the Olive: A Critical History of the Israeli Defense Force* (New York: Public Affairs, 2002). On the United States, the literature is voluminous. Two starting points are Van Creveld, *Fighting Power*; and Stephen Peter Rosen, *Winning the Next War: Innovation and the Modern Military* (Ithaca, NY: Cornell University Press, 1991).

2. Charles Tilly, "Reflections on the History of European State-Making," in *The Formation of National States in Western Europe*, ed. Charles Tilly (Princeton: Princeton University Press, 1975), 42. On non-European neighborhoods, see Jeffrey Herbst, "War and the State in Africa," *International Security* 14, no. 4 (Spring 1990), 117–139; Cameron G. Thies, "War, Rivalry, and State Building in Latin America," *American Journal of Political Science* 49, no. 3 (July 2005), 451–465; and Miguel Centeno, "Blood and Debt: War and Taxation in Nineteenth-Century Latin America," *American Journal of Sociology* 102, no. 6 (May 1995), 1565–1605.

3. Successful coups almost always involve military participation or at least acquiescence. In fact, regimes' anticipation of this danger may explain why we observe relatively few instances of professional, conventionally effective militaries launching coups. Pakistan is an important exception. In general, the fact that regimes choose their military organizational practices strategically, knowing the threats they face, means that coups launched by militaries employing conventional war practices should be rare.

4. Quinlivan, "Coup-Proofing"; Brooks, *Political-Military Relations*; and Biddle and Zirkle, "Technology, Civil-Military Relations."

5. Indeed, as the rest of this section shows, the actual mechanisms in my argument differ from those identified in past studies. For example, Quinlivan emphasizes "the fostering of expertness in the regular military" (151) as a coup-proofing technique. In his view, "improving the technical skills of regular military officers increases not only their ability to deal with foreign regular armies, but also their sense of the

military risks involved in a coup attempt. Understanding these risks in turn renders them less likely to attempt a coup and more susceptible to detection should they try" (152–153). By contrast, I argue that regimes fearful of coups *limit* training because they fear the development of military skill, and I find no evidence that they are interested in "fostering expertness." Similarly, Quinlivan argues that coup-fearing regimes will prize political loyalty and family/sectarian/ethnic ties in the formation of military units and selection of key officers. I agree that these traits are important but emphasize that the distinctive feature of such regimes is that they select against competence in the promotion process. Many good armies, including the PAVN and the Wehrmacht, required political loyalty for officers to get ahead—but these regimes did not punish competence, which is the phenomenon we see in armies such as the ARVN, where leaders actually weeded out officers who performed well in battle. In general, Quinlivan and I share the intuition that states focused on coup prevention are less likely to perform well in interstate wars, but we do not have the same explanation as to why. Quinlivan, "Coup-Proofing."

6. On the Soviets, see David Glantz, *Stumbling Colossus: The Red Army on the Eve of World War* (Lawrence: University Press of Kansas, 1998); and Donald Cameron Watt, "The High Command: Who Plotted against Whom? Stalin's Purge of the Soviet High Command Revisited," *Journal of Soviet Military Studies* 3, no. 1 (1990), 46–65; and Earl F. Ziemke, "The Soviet Armed Forces in the Interwar Period," in *Military Effectiveness*, vol. 2, 1–38. On Argentina, see Stewart, *Mates*, and Kon, *Los Chicos*.

7. Terrence Lee, "Military Cohesion and Regime Maintenance: Explaining the Role of the Military in 1989 China and 1998 Indonesia," *Armed Forces and Society* 32, no. 1 (October 2005), 80–104; Terrence Lee, "The Armed Forces and Transitions from Authoritarian Rule: Explaining the Role of the Military in 1986 Philippines and 1998 Indonesia," *Comparative Political Studies* 42, no. 5 (May 2009), 640–669; and Sheena Chestnut Greitens, *Dictators and Their Secret Police: Coercive Institutions and State Violence under Authoritarianism,* book manuscript, 2014.

8. Theoretically, states could try to forge a third path by creating a separate coercive organization to monitor or counterbalance the military and then allowing the regular military to adopt conventional war practices. Empirically, however, few leaders facing intense coup threats feel comfortable with this arrangement as their sole protection against military overthrow. After all, even a good internal security organization is unlikely to have the ability to beat a robust professional military in a contest for domestic power. Fearful regimes often do build nonmilitary internal security apparatuses, but rarely does this step relieve them of the fundamental trade-off between conventional military effectiveness and domestic protection from coups.

9. On the concept of offense and defense dominance, see Robert Jervis, "Cooperation under the Security Dilemma," *World Politics* 30, no. 2 (January 1978), 167–214.

10. Dan Reiter and Allan Stam, *Democracies at War* (Princeton: Princeton University Press, 2002). For criticism, see Risa Brooks, "Making Military Might: Why Do States Fail and Succeed?" *International Security* 28, no. 2 (Fall 2003), 149–191; Michael Desch, *Power and Military Effectiveness: The Fallacy of Democratic Triumphalism* (Baltimore: Johns Hopkins University Press); and Alexander Downes, "How Smart and Tough Are Democracies? Reassessing Theories of Democratic Victory in War," *International Security* 33, no. 4 (Spring 2009), 9–51. See also Dan Reiter, Allan Stam, and Alexander Downes, "Correspondence: Another Skirmish in the Battle over Democracies and War," *International Security* 34, no. 2 (Fall 2009), 194–204.

11. Samuel Huntington, *Political Order in Changing Societies* (New Haven: Yale University Press, 1968), 1.

12. Watt, "The High Command."

13. Barbara Geddes, "What Do We Know about Democratization after 20 Years?" *American Political Science Review* 2 (1999), 121–122.

14. Geddes, "What Do We Know," 130.

15. This approach echoes that used in Dan Slater, *Ordering Power: Contentious Politics and Authoritarian Leviathans in Southeast Asia* (New York: Cambridge University Press, 2010), 12–13.

16. John B. Londregan and Keith T. Poole, "Poverty, the Coup Trap, and the Seizure of Executive Power," *World Politics* 42, no. 2 (January 1990), 152; and Aaron Belkin and Evan Schofer, "Toward a Structural Understanding of Coup Risk," *Journal of Conflict Resolution* 47, no. 5 (October 2003), 611.

17. Geddes, "What Do We Know," 121.

18. Huntington, *Political Order*, 91.

19. Geddes, "What Do We Know," 115–144; Jennifer Gandhi and Adam Przeworksi, "Authoritarian Institutions and the Survival of Autocrats," *Comparative Political Studies* 40, no. 11 (November 2007), 1279–1301; Beatriz Magaloni, "Credible Power-Sharing and the Longevity of Authoritarian Rule," *Comparative Political Studies* 41, nos. 4–5 (April 2008), 715–741; Jason Brownlee, *Authoritarianism in an Age of Democratization* (New York: Cambridge University Press, 2007); Jennifer Gandhi, *Political Institutions under Dictatorship* (New York: Cambridge University Press, 2008); and Carles Boix and Milan W. Svolik, "The Foundations of Limited Authoritarian Government: Institutions, Commitment, and Power-Sharing in Dictatorships," *Journal of Politics* 75, no. 2 (April 2013), 300–316.

20. James Mahoney, "Path Dependence in Historical Sociology," *Theory and Society* 29, no. 4 (August 2000), 507–548; Paul Pierson, *Politics in Time: History, Institutions, and Social Analysis* (Princeton: Princeton University Press, 2004); Kathleen Thelen, "Historical Institutionalism in Comparative Politics," *Annual Review of Political Science* 2 (1999), 369–404; and Stephen D. Krasner, "Sovereignty: an Institutional Perspective," in *The Elusive State: International and Comparative Perspectives*, ed. James A. Caporaso (Newbury Park, CA: Sage, 1989).

21. Barry R. Posen, *The Sources of Military Doctrine: France, Britain, and Germany Between the World Wars* (Ithaca, NY: Cornell University Press, 1984); Rosen, *Winning the Next War*; and Deborah Avant, *Political Institutions and Military Change: Lessons from Peripheral Wars* (Ithaca, NY: Cornell University Press, 1994).

22. The Soviet Union is best characterized as a personalist regime until Stalin's death in 1953, after which Soviet decision-making authority became much more vested in the party as an institution rather than in the hands of any single leader.

23. Roman Kolkowicz, *The Soviet Military and the Communist Party* (Boulder, CO: Westview Press, 1985), chap. 3; Glantz, *Stumbling Colossus*; Earl F. Ziemke, "The Soviet Armed Forces in the Interwar Period," in *Military Effectiveness*, vol. 2, 1–38; Gabriel Gorodetsky, *Grand Delusion: Stalin and the German Invasion of Russia* (New Haven: Yale University Press, 1999), 121; Roger Reese, *Red Commanders: A Social History of the Soviet Army Officer Corps, 1918–1991* (Lawrence: University of Kansas Press, 2005), 159–160.

24. On Egypt, see Risa Brooks, "An Autocracy at War: Explaining Egypt's Military Effectiveness, 1967 and 1973," *Security Studies* 15, no. 3 (2006), 396–430. On China, see Roderick MacFarquhar and Michael Schoenhals, *Mao's Last Revolution* (Cambridge: Harvard University Press, 2006); Andrew Scobell, "Military Coups in the People's Republic of China: Failure, Fabrication, or Fancy?" *Journal of Northeast Asian*

Studies 14, no. 1 (1995), 25–46; and Ellis Joffe, "The Military as a Political Actor in China," in *Soldiers, Peasants, and Bureaucrats: Civil-Military Relations in Communist and Modernizing Societies*, ed. Roman Kolkowicz and Andrzej Korbonski (Boston: Allen & Unwin, 1982), 139–158.

25. Biddle, *Military Power*; and Biddle, "Explaining Military Outcomes," in *Creating Military Power: The Sources of Military Effectiveness*, ed. Elizabeth Stanley and Risa Brooks (Stanford: Stanford University Press, 2007), 207–227.

26. Biddle, *Military Power*; and Biddle, "Explaining Military Outcomes," 207–227.

27. On China, see Roy Appleman, *Disaster in Korea: The Chinese Confront MacArthur* (College Station: Texas A&M University Press, 1989); Edwin Hoyt, *The Day the Chinese Attacked: Korea, 1950* (New York: McGraw-Hill, 1990); and Allen Whiting, *China Crosses the Yalu: The Decision to Enter the Korean War* (Stanford: Stanford University Press, 1968). On Serbia, see Ivo Daalder and Michael O'Hanlon, *Winning Ugly: NATO's War to Save Kosovo* (Washington, DC: Brookings Institution Press, 2000); and Barry R. Posen, "The War for Kosovo: Serbia's Political-Military Strategy," *International Security* 24, no. 4 (Spring 2000), 39–84.

28. Herzog, *Arab-Israeli Wars*.

29. Andrew Scobell, *China's Use of Military Force: Beyond the Great Wall and the Long March* (New York: Cambridge University Press, 2003).

30. Biddle, *Military Power*, chap. 8.

31. Posen, *Sources*; Michael Desch, *Civilian Control of the Military: The Changing Security Environment* (Baltimore: Johns Hopkins University Press, 1998); and Kenneth Waltz, *Theory of International Politics* (New York: McGraw-Hill, 1979). A similar though not explicitly realist argument appears in Rosen, *Winning the Next War*.

32. Otto Hintze, "Military Organization and the Organization of the State," in *The Historical Essays of Otto Hintze*, ed. Felix Gilbert (New York: Oxford University Press, 1975); Charles Tilly, *Coercion, Capital, and European States, AD 990–1992* (Cambridge, MA: Blackwell, 1992); Charles Tilly, "Reflections on the History of European State-Making," in *The Formation of National States in Western Europe*, ed. Charles Tilly (Princeton: Princeton University Press, 1975); and Thomas Ertman, *Birth of the Leviathan: Building States and Regimes in Early Modern Europe* (New York: Cambridge University Press, 1997).

33. Michael Gordon and Bernard Trainor, *The Generals' War: the Inside Story of the Conflict in the Gulf* (New York: Little, Brown, 1995), chap. 19.

34. Steven R. David, *Choosing Sides: Alignment and Realignment in the Third World* (Baltimore: Johns Hopkins University Press, 1991); and Steven R. David, "Explaining Third World Alignment," *World Politics* 43, no. 2 (January 1991), 233–256. These works draw on the idea that states balance against threat rather than just power. Stephen Walt, *The Origins of Alliances* (Ithaca, NY: Cornell University Press, 1987).

35. Bruce Bueno de Mesquita et al., *The Logic of Political Survival* (Cambridge: MIT Press, 2005).

36. Slater, *Ordering Power*, 5. See also Paul Staniland, "States, Insurgents, and Wartime Political Orders," *Perspectives on Politics* 10, no. 2 (June 2012), 243–264.

37. *The Art of War*, trans. Samuel B. Griffith (New York: Oxford University Press, 1971), 83. For important context regarding Sun Tzu's claims, see Andrew Meyer and Andrew R. Wilson, "Inventing the General: A Re-appraisal of the *Sunzi binfga*," in

War, Virtual War and Society: The Challenge to Communities (New York: Rodopi, 2008), 151–168.

38. Samuel Huntington, *The Soldier and the State* (Cambridge: Harvard University Press, 1957). For a critical view, see Peter Feaver, *Armed Servants: Agency, Oversight, and Civil-Military Relations* (Cambridge: Harvard University Press, 2003).

39. Carl von Clausewitz, *On War*, ed. and trans. Michael Howard and Peter Paret (Princeton: Princeton University Press, 1984), 605. On the notion that the contrast between Sun Tzu and Clausewitz is overdrawn, see Michael Handel, *Masters of War: Classical Strategic Thought* (Portland, OR: Frank Cass, 1996).

40. Posen, *Sources*; and Eliot Cohen, *Supreme Command: Soldiers, Statesmen, and Leadership in Wartime* (New York: Free Press, 2002).

41. On Saddam, see chapter 4 in this book. See also Williamson Murray and Kevin Woods, "Saddam and the Iran-Iraq War: Rule from the Top," paper presented at the London School of Economics, September 24, 2010, available upon request; Kevin M. Woods et al., *Iraqi Perspectives Project: A View of Operation Iraqi Freedom from Saddam's Senior Leadership* (Norfolk, VA: U.S. Joint Forces Command, 2006). On Hitler, see Albert Seaton, *The German Army, 1933–1945* (New York: St. Martin's Press); MacGregor Knox, *Common Destiny: Dictatorship, Foreign Policy, and War in Fascist Italy and Nazi Germany* (Cambridge: Cambridge University Press, 2000), chap. 5; Joachim Fest, *Plotting Hitler's Death: The Story of the German Resistance* (New York: Henry Holt, 1996); Manfred Messerschmidt, "German Military Effectiveness between 1919 and 1939," in Murray and Millett, *Military Effectiveness*, vol. 2, 218–255; Jurgen E. Forster, "The Dynamics of Volkegemeinschaft: The Effectiveness of the German Military Establishment in the Second World War," in Murray and Millett, *Military Effectiveness*, vol. 3, 180–220; and Williamson Murray, "Net Assessment in Nazi Germany in the 1930s," in *Calculations: Net Assessment and the Coming of World War II*, ed. Williamson Murray and Allan R. Millett (New York: Free Press, 1992), 85.

42. Given the Prussian martial tradition, Hitler had unusual, perhaps unique, advantages. For the most part, he did not have to choose between competence and political loyalty in his officer corps—there was an ample supply of men who possessed both, significantly reducing the coup risk that Hitler faced from building an externally effective army. It is notable, however, that even within this context, the Wehrmacht, as the successor to the conventionally oriented imperial army, generally fought more effectively than the SS, where adherence to Nazi ideology mattered much more for advancement. Despite this, Hitler "commented that he often bitterly regretted not having purged his officer corps the way Stalin did." Fest, *Plotting Hitler's Death*, 332. See also sources in note 41.

43. Though concerned about coups, Hitler knew that his foreign policy aims required a conventionally effective military. He continued the long-established German dedication to rigorous, realistic military training, as well as the tradition of devolving significant tactical and operational authority to commanders (although this approach changed starting in 1942–1943 when Hitler assumed personal command of field armies in Russia, with predictably disastrous results). Hitler did purposely divide his military and limit information sharing at the highest levels in order to increase his own control of the armed forces, so he could not be said to have adopted all conventional war practices. See sources in notes 41 and 42.

44. Stephen Cohen, *The Pakistan Army* (Karachi: Oxford University Press, 1998); and Paul Staniland, "Explaining Civil-Military Relations in Complex Political Environ-

ments: India and Pakistan in Comparative Perspective," *Security Studies* 17, no. 2 (2008), 322–362.

45. Quinlivan, "Coup-Proofing"; Brooks, *Political-Military Relations*; and Biddle and Zirkle, "Technology, Civil-Military Relations."

46. Reiter and Stam, *Democracies at War*. See also David Lake, "Powerful Pacifists: Democratic States and War," *American Political Science Review* 86, no. 1 (1992), 24–37; Bruce Bueno de Mesquita and Randolph Siverson, "War and the Survival of Political Leaders: A Comparative Study of Regime Types and Political Accountability," *American Political Science Association* 89, no. 4 (December 1995), 841–855; Ulrich Pilster and Tobias Bohmelt, "Do Democracies Engage in Less Coup-Proofing? On the Relationship between Regime Type and Civil-Military Relations," *Foreign Policy Analysis* 8, no. 4 (2012), 1–17; and Ulrich Pilster and Tobias Bohmelt, "Coup-Proofing and Military Effectiveness in Interstate Wars, 1967–99," *Conflict Management and Peace Science* 28 (2011), 331–350.

47. Jessica L. P. Weeks, "Strongmen and Straw Men: Authoritarian Regimes and the Initiation of International Conflict," *American Political Science Review* 106, no. 2 (May 2012), 326–347; Jessica L. Weeks, "Autocratic Audience Costs: Regime Type and Signaling Resolve," *International Organization* 62 (Winter 2008), pp. 35–64; Jessica L. P. Weeks, *Dictators at War and Peace* (Ithaca, NY: Cornell University Press, 2014); Mark Peceny and Caroline C. Beer, "Peaceful Parties and Puzzling Personalists," *American Political Science Review* 97, no. 2 (May 2003), 339–342; Mark Peceny, Caroline C. Beer, and Shannon Sanchez-Terry, "Dictatorial Peace?" *American Political Science Review* 96, no. 1 (March 2002), 15–26; and Brian Lai and Dan Slater, "Institutions of the Offensive: Domestic Sources of Dispute Initiation in Authoritarian Regimes, 1950–1992," *American Journal of Political Science* 50, no. 1 (January 2006), 113–136.

48. Geddes, "What Do We Know," 121.

49. Statistical tests show that countries with higher Polity scores are less likely to experience coups. Jonathan Powell, "Regime Vulnerability and the Diversionary Threat of Force," *Journal of Conflict Resolution* 58 (December 2012), 169–196.

50. Helen Graham, *The Spanish Republic at War, 1936–1939* (New York: Cambridge University Press, 2002); and Gerald Howson, *Arms for Spain: The Untold Story of the Spanish Civil War* (London: J. Murray, 1998).

51. Srinath Raghavan, "Civil-Military Relations in India: The China Crisis and After," *Journal of Strategic Studies* 32, no. 1 (February 2009), 149–175; Stephen P. Cohen, *The Indian Army: Its Contribution to the Development of a Nation* (New York: Oxford University Press, 1990), esp. 175–176; and V. Longer, *Red Coats to Olive Green: A History of the Indian Army, 1600–1974* (Bombay: Allied Publishers, 1974), 277–398.

52. See, for example, Michael Beckley, "Economic Development and Military Effectiveness," *Journal of Strategic Studies* 33, no. 1 (2010), 43–79.

53. For a discussion of these issues, see Daryl Press, "Lessons from Ground Combat in the Gulf," *International Security* 22, no. 2 (Fall 1997), 137–146; Stephen Biddle, "Victory Misunderstood: What the Gulf War Tells Us about the Future of Conflict," *International Security* 21, no. 2 (Fall 1996), 139–179; Stephen Biddle, "The Gulf War Debate Redux," *International Security* 22, no. 2 (Fall 1997), 163–174; and Thomas G. Mahnken and Barry D. Watts, "What the Gulf War Can (and Cannot) tell Us about the Future of Warfare," *International Security* 22, no. 2 (Fall 1997), 151–162.

54. Korea Institute of Military History, *The Korean War*, vol. 1, ed. Allan Millett (Lincoln: University of Nebraska Press, 2000–2001).

55. Trevor Dupuy, David Bongard, and Richard Anderson, *Hitler's Last Gamble: The Battle of the Bulge, December 1944–January 1945* (New York: HarperCollins, 1994); and Charles MacDonald, *A Time for Trumpets: The Untold Story of the Battle of the Bulge* (New York: Morrow, 1985).

56. Dan Slater and Daniel Ziblatt, "The Enduring Indispensability of the Controlled Comparison," *Comparative Political Studies*, January 2013, available at http://cps.sagepub.com/content/early/2013/01/15/0010414012472469, 12.

57. I choose 1917 because it is the year in which the modern system of force employment first emerged. Biddle, *Military Power*.

58. On folk Bayesianism, see Timothy K. McKeown, "Case Studies and the Limits of the Quantitative World View," in *Rethinking Social Inquiry: Diverse Tools, Shared Standards*, ed. Henry Brady and David Collier (New York: Rowman & Littlefield, 2004), 158–167; and Slater and Ziblatt, "The Enduring," 13.

59. McKeown, "Case Studies," 158–167.

60. On the role of Arab culture, see Ken Pollack, "The Influence of Arab Culture on Arab Military Effectiveness," Ph.D. dissertation, Massachusetts Institute of Technology, 1996.

61. Alexander George and Andrew Bennett, *Case Studies and Theory Development in the Social Sciences* (Cambridge: MIT Press, 2004), chaps. 8, 9, and 10.

62. George and Bennett, *Case Studies*, 152.

63. Slater and Ziblatt, "The Enduring," 13.

2. Threats and Military Organizational Practices in North and South Vietnam

1. A note about terminology: the two primary actors of interest are described as North and South Vietnam. However, many native southerners supported and even helped lead the communist regime based in Hanoi, while as many as a million northerners came to live in the South after partition. As a result, the terms "North" and "South," and references to "Northern" and "Southern" forces, should not be taken as literal geographic references, but as shorthand for the governments in the two capitals and the military apparatuses they directed. Robert K. Brigham, "Why the South Won the American War in Vietnam," in *Why the North Won the Vietnam War*, ed. Marc Jason Gilbert (New York: Palgrave, 2002), 97–99, 107, 113.

2. This section draws heavily on Fredrik Logevall, *Embers of War: The Fall of an Empire and the Making of America's Vietnam* (New York: Random House, 2013); and Anthony James Joes, *The War for South Vietnam* (New York: Praeger, 1990).

3. French control was always tightest in Cochin China. Later anticolonial movements were stronger in Tonkin and Annam. Logevall, *Embers of War*, 17.

4. Joes, *The War*, 9.

5. Lien-Hang T. Nguyen, *Hanoi's War: An International History of the War for Peace in Vietnam* (Chapel Hill: University of North Carolina Press, 2012), 22.

6. Joes, *The War*, chap. 2.

7. Stein Tonnesson, *Vietnam 1946: How the War Began* (Los Angeles: University of California Press, 2010).

8. Arthur J. Dommen, *The Indochinese Experience of the French and the Americans: Nationalism and Communism in Cambodia, Laos, and Vietnam* (Bloomington: Indiana University Press, 2001), 196, 469. At this time the MAAG was limited to 685 military personnel.

9. Dommen, *The Indochinese Experience*, 195.

10. These events are chronicled in much greater detail in Dommen, *The Indochinese Experience*, chap. 4.

11. Joes, *The War*, chap. 3. On Diem, see Seth Jacobs, *Cold War Mandarin: Ngo Dinh Diem and the Origins of America's War in Vietnam, 1950–1963* (New York: Rowman and Littlefield, 2006).

12. Dommen, *The Indochinese Experience*, chap. 5.

13. Logevall, *Embers of War*, 655; and Dommen, *The Indochinese Experience*, 343–348.

14. Joes, *The War*, chaps. 4–5.

15. George Herring, *America's Longest War: The United States and Vietnam, 1950–1975* (New York: McGraw-Hill, 2002), 81; and Tuong Vu, *Paths to Development in Asia: South Korea, Vietnam, China, and Indonesia* (New York: Cambridge University Press, 2010), 124.

16. William J. Duiker, "Victory by Other Means: The Foreign Policy of the Democratic Republic of Vietnam," in Gilbert, *Why the North*, 58–59; and Brigham, "Why the South," in ibid., 98–99, 102.

17. Dommen, *The Indochinese Experience*, 423–424.

18. Duiker, "Victory by Other Means," 50.

19. Logevall, *Embers of War*, 691; and William J. Duiker, "Foreword: The History of the People's Army," in The Military History Institute of Vietnam, *Victory in Vietnam: The Official History of the People's Army of Vietnam, 1954–1975*, trans. Merle L. Pribbenow (Lawrence: University of Kansas Press, 2002), ix–xvi.

20. Duiker, "Victory by Other Means," 60.

21. Dommen, *The Indochinese Experience*, 475.

22. Dommen, *The Indochinese Experience*, 501. This program was not the first of its kind. Joes, *The War*, chaps. 5–6; and Ronald Spector, *Advice and Support: The Early Years, 1941–1960* (Honolulu: University Press of the Pacific, 2005), 332–333.

23. James Lawton Collins, Jr., *The Development and Training of the South Vietnamese Army, 1950–1972* (Washington, DC: Department of the Army, 1975), 123.

24. Nguyen Cao Ky, *How We Lost the Vietnam War* (New York: Cooper Square Press, 2002), 48; and Jeffrey D. Clarke, *Advice and Support: The Final Years, 1965–1973* (Washington, DC: U.S. Army Center of Military History, 1988), 81.

25. This uneasy arrangement was ratified by a flawed but accepted election in 1967. Joes, *The War*, chap. 7.

26. Clarke, *Advice and Support*, 23.

27. For a detailed analysis of the escalation decisions, see Fredrik Logevall, *Choosing War: The Lost Chance for Peace and the Escalation of the War in Vietnam* (Los Angeles: University of California Press, 1999).

28. Clarke, *Advice and Support*, 13, 109, 213.

29. James H. Willbanks, *Abandoning Vietnam: How America Left and South Vietnam Lost Its War* (Lawrence: University of Kansas Press, 2004), 29–31.

30. Willbanks, *Abandoning Vietnam*, 202.

31. George Veith, *Black April: The Fall of South Vietnam, 1973–75* (New York: Encounter Books, 2012).

32. Ky, *How We Lost*; and Clarke, *Advice and Support*. The combined populations of the two states was believed to be somewhere above 30 million people. South Vietnam's estimated population was 16 million by 1970.

33. Joes, *The War*, 3.

34. The end of chapter 3 of this book discusses this point in detail. Nguyen Duy Hinh and Tran Dinh Tho, *The South Vietnamese Society* (Washington, DC: U.S. Army Center of Military History, 1980), 3–5, 9; Logevall, *Embers of War*, 17, 78, 110.

35. The South was still more than 80 percent ethnic Vietnamese. The remainder of the population included a tiny proportion of Indians, Pakistanis, Malays, and Arabs, along with the larger minority groups: the Chams, Cambodians, Chinese, and Montagnards. Hinh and Tho, *South Vietnamese Society*, 96. On religious differences, see Hinh and Tho, *South Vietnamese Society*, 142.

36. Ngo Quang Truong, *Territorial Forces* (Washington, DC: Center of Military History, 1981), 16.

37. Collins, *Development and Training*, 10.

38. Calculations made based on figures in Spector, *Advice and Support*, chap. 15; Collins, *Development and Training*, 10; Andrew Wiest, *Vietnam's Forgotten Army: Heroism and Betrayal in the ARVN* (New York: New York University Press, 2008), 34; and Thomas R. Cantwell, "The Army of South Vietnam: A Military and Political History, 1955–75," Ph.D. dissertation, University of New South Wales, 1989, 153–155.

39. Jessica Chapman, *Cauldron of Resistance: Ngo Dinh Diem, the United States, and 1950s Southern Vietnam* (Ithaca, NY: Cornell University Press, 2013), 74–77.

40. General Cao Van Vien, *Leadership*, Indochina Monograph (Washington, DC: U.S. Army Center of Military History, 1981), 22.

41. Hinh and Tho, *South Vietnamese Society*, 30.

42. Spector, *Advice and Support*, 225.

43. Hinh and Tho, *South Vietnamese Society*, 30.

44. Cantwell, "The Army of South Vietnam," 60–61; and Ky, *How We Lost*, 28–29.

45. Cao Van Vien, *Leadership*, 42.

46. For background on the Cao Dai and Hoa Hao, see Jeanne S. Mintz, Herbert M. Silverberg, and James E. Trinnaman, *A Short Guide to Psychological Operations in the Republic of Vietnam* (Washington, DC: Special Operations Research Office, July 7, 1965), unclassified assessment available at the Center of Military History, Fort McNair, Washington, DC, 27–34.

47. Cao Van Vien, *Leadership*, 42–49; Hinh and Tho, *The South Vietnamese Society*, 32. Unfortunately, "the Cao Dai and Hoa Hao adherents and members of the Binh Xuyen were the most dedicated anti-Communists of South Vietnam" (Hinh and Tho, *South Vietnamese Society*, 27).

48. Chapman, *Cauldron of Resistance*; and Brigham, "Why the South," in Gilbert, *Why the North*, 100–101.

49. Vien, *Leadership*, 55.

50. Allan E. Goodman, *An Institutional Profile of the South Vietnamese Office Corps*, RM-6189-APRA (Santa Monica, CA: RAND, June 1970), 3, available through Defense Technical Information Center.

51. Quoted in Spector, *Advice and Support*, 301.

52. Quoted in Clarke, *Advice and Support*, 47.

53. Collins, *Development and Training*, 75. Naturally, one must take U.S. assessments blaming the South Vietnamese with a grain of salt. The U.S. military exhibited plenty of its own deficits in the war and had obvious incentives to downplay them afterward.

54. Hinh and Tho, *South Vietnamese Society*, 129.

55. Goodman, *Institutional Profile*, vi.

56. Stephen T. Hosmer, Konrad Kellen, and Brian M. Jenkins, *The Fall of South Vietnam: Statements by Vietnamese Military and Civilian Leaders*, R-2208-OSD (HIST) (Santa Monica, CA: RAND, December 1978), 31.

57. Tran Van Don, quoted in Hosmer et al., *The Fall of South Vietnam*, 45.

58. "RVNAF Leadership," October 1969, in *A Systems Analysis View of the Vietnam War: 1965–1972*, vol. 6: *Republic of Vietnam Armed Forces*, 165, in the unclassified collection of the Southeast Asia Analysis Report, available at the Center of Military History, Fort McNair, Washington, DC.

59. Goodman, *Institutional Profile*, 26–81. The same statistic appears in "RVNAF Leadership," June 1968, in *A Systems Analysis View of the Vietnam War*, vol. 6, 149.

60. "RVNAF Leadership," June 1968, 151.

61. "The Situation in South Vietnam," January 1969, in *A Systems Analysis View of the Vietnam War*, vol. 1: *The Situation in Southeast Asia*, 33, in the unclassified collection of the Southeast Asia Analysis Report, available at the Center of Military History, Fort McNair, Washington, DC.

62. "RVNAF Leadership," March 1970, section from *Systems Analysis View*, vol. 6, 178.

63. Clarke, *Advice and Support*, 219–220.

64. Clarke, *Advice and Support*, 245. In 1969, the commanders of the 5th and 18th divisions were removed, although their replacements were of questionable ability. Also unfortunate: the original commanders of these divisions were reassigned to training commands. "RVNAF Leadership," February 1970, section from *Systems Analysis View*, vol. 6, 7.

65. Clarke, *Advice and Support*, 514; see also chaps. 14 and 20.

66. Veith, *Black April*, pp. 5, 52.

67. Ibid., 26, 18.

68. Collins, *Training and Development*, chap. 5.

69. Ibid., 123.

70. Clarke, *Advice and Support*, 378.

71. Quoted in Hosmer et al., *The Fall of South Vietnam*, 58.

72. Clarke, *Advice and Support*, p. 161.

73. Ibid.

74. "RVNAF Leadership," October 1969, p. 3.

75. Collins, *Training and Development*, chap. 5.

76. Cantwell, "The Army of South Vietnam," 177–178.

77. Quoted in Hosmer et al., *The Fall of South Vietnam*, 58.

78. Collins, *Training and Development*, 126.

79. Vien, *Leadership*, 157.

80. Hosmer et al., *The Fall of South Vietnam*.

81. Quoted in Clarke, *Advice and Support*, 259.

82. Truong, *Territorial Forces*, 16.

83. Cantwell, "The Army of South Vietnam," 41, 125

84. Collins, *Training and Development*, 17.

85. Cantwell, "The Army of South Vietnam," 42.

86. Vien, *Leadership*, 39.

87. Collins, *Training and Development*, 10–11, 90.

88. Neil Sheehan, *A Bright Shining Lie: John Paul Vann and America in Vietnam* (New York: Random House, 1988), 122–123.

89. Goodman, *Institutional Profile*, 14.

90. Collins, *Training and Development*, 75.

91. David M. Toczek, *The Battle of Ap Bac: They Did Everything But Learn from It* (Westport, CT: Greenwood Press, 2001), 41.

92. Collins, *Training and Development*, 32.

93. Cantwell, "The Army of South Vietnam," 102.

94. United States Army Command and General Staff College, Staff Study on Army Aspects of Military Assistance, quoted in Spector, *Advice and Support*, 279.

95. Spector, *Advice and Support*, 347, 279–280.

96. Ibid., 316.

97. Ibid., 279, 342–344.

98. For background on the Can Lao, as well as on the other major political party in South Vietnam, the Viet Nam Quoc Dan Dang (VNQDD), or Vietnamese Nationalist Party, see Mintz et al., *A Short Guide*, 39.

99. Clarke, *Advice and Support*, 31.

100. Cantwell, "The Army of South Vietnam," 166.

101. Hosmer et al., *The Fall of South Vietnam*, 23.

102. Wiest, *Vietnam's Forgotten Army*, 48.

103. Ibid., 62, 53, 50.

104. Ibid., 63.

105. Cantwell, "The Army of South Vietnam," 310; and Wiest, *Vietnam's Forgotten Army*, 63, 70.

106. Wiest, *Vietnam's Forgotten Army*, 69–70, 99.

107. Quoted in Wiest, *Vietnam's Forgotten Army*, 63.

108. Wiest, *Vietnam's Forgotten Army*, 147–148, 181.

109. Vu, *Paths to Development*, 135.

110. The Military History Institute of Vietnam, *Victory in Vietnam: The Official History of the People's Army of Vietnam, 1954–1975*, trans. Merle L. Pribbenow (Lawrence: University of Kansas Press, 2002), 29, 10–11; and William Turley, "The Vietnamese Army," in *Communist Armies in Politics*, ed. Jonathan R. Adelman (Boulder, CO: Westview Press, 1982), 71.

111. Regular military forces included the People's Army, by far the largest component, as well as a People's Navy and People's Air Force, which lacked independent service status. Among the Paramilitary Forces were the People's Regional Force at the provincial level, the People's Self-Defense Force in the cities, the People's Militia in rural district areas, the Armed Youth Assault Force, and additional reserves. Douglas Pike, *PAVN: People's Army of Vietnam* (Novato, CA: Presidio Press, 1986), 90–92.

112. Military History Institute, *Victory in Vietnam*, 32, 211, 431. Pike reports that the PAVN had grown to twenty-five divisions by 1975. Pike, *PAVN*, 103.

113. Merle Pribbenow, "North Vietnam's Master Plan," *Vietnam* 12, no. 2 (August 1999), 30–31; Brigham, "Why the South," in Gilbert, *Why the North*, 107–108, 110–111; and Veith, *Black April*, 5–6.

114. William Duiker, *The Communist Road to Power in Vietnam* (Boulder, CO: Westview Press, 1981), pp. 212–13.

115. Nguyen, *Hanoi's War*, 71; and Duiker, *Communist Road*, 302–303.

116. Wherever possible, I specify whether the forces in question are PLAF or PAVN, generally using the term PLAF prior to 1965 and PAVN afterward. Almost any ARVN opponent force, whether from the PLAF or PAVN, Main Force or otherwise, was at times referred to by the contraction "Viet Cong," short for Viet Cong-san, meaning Vietnamese communist. I avoid this derogatory and ambiguous term. But because it is more accurate than referring simply to "the North Vietnamese," I do use the term "communist" to describe PLAF forces, although I recognize that not all NLF members participating in the PLAF would have identified themselves as such. Veith, *Black April*, 5–6; Turley, "The Vietnamese Army," 81; Herring, *America's Longest War*, 82; and Brigham, "Why the South," in Gilbert, *Why the North*, 115n44.

117. Logevall, *Embers of War*, 151, 154.

118. Nguyen, *Hanoi's War*, chaps. 1 and 2, esp. 21, 49.

119. Ibid., 54–55, 63–70, 81–83, 88, 91–92, 102–103, 155–157, 197–198, 262–263.

120. Ibid., 34–35.

121. Turley, "The Vietnamese Army," in *Communist Armies*, 63.

122. William S. Turley, "Civil-Military Relations in North Vietnam," *Asian Survey* 9, no. 12 (December 1969), 880; and Turley, "The Vietnamese Army," in *Communist Armies*, 68.

123. For a representative example, see Tu Van Vien, "Political Achievements within the Armed Forces to Be Perpetuated," translated from *Hoc Tap*, no. 12 (December 1964), 39, available through the Vietnam Archive, Texas Tech University, document number 2321310012.

124. General Nguyen Chi Thanh, quoted in Khan, "Notebook II," 4.

125. *People's War, People's Army* (Hanoi: Foreign Languages Publishing House, 1961), 129.

126. "Prospects for North and South Vietnam," National Intelligence Estimate Number 63-59, May 26, 1959, available through foia.cia.gov, 9.

127. For example, "Prospects for North and South Vietnam," National Intelligence Estimate Number 14.3/53-61, August 15, 1961, available through foia.cia.gov, 8.

128. Pike, *PAVN*, 157.

129. Military History Institute, *Victory in Vietnam*, 35.

130. Lieutenant General Song Hao, "Party Leadership Is the Cause of the Growth and Victories of Our Army," Document No. 72, Vietnam Documents and Research Notes, January 1970, 24, available through the Vietnam Archive, Texas Tech University, document number 4080319006.

131. Hao, "Party Leadership," 32.

132. Quoted in Lanning and Cragg, *Inside the VC and the NVA: The Real Story of North Vietnam's Armed Forces* (College Station: Texas A&M University Press, 2008), 91.

133. Pike, *PAVN*, 21. These debates are discussed in more detail in Nguyen, *Hanoi's War*, 28.

134. Khan, "Notebook II," 9.

135. Pike, *PAVN*, 167.

136. Military History Institute, *Victory in Vietnam*, 99.

137. Giap, *People's War*, 59, 138.

138. Military History Institute, *Victory in Vietnam*, 39.

139. This policy was not without its detractors. The debate over whether to emphasize political indoctrination or modern tactics in training was vociferous in the mid-1950s, with General Giap seeking to focus on the latter and Truong Chinh, secretary general of the Party until 1956, believing the former was more important. Giap won this argument. Turley, "Civil-Military Relations," 882.

140. Turley, "The Vietnamese Army," in *Communist Armies*, 72.

141. Military History Institute, *Victory in Vietnam*, 14.

142. Lanning and Cragg, *Inside the VC*, 41.

143. Melvin Gurtov, *The War in the Delta: Views from Three Viet Cong Battalions* (Santa Monica, CA: RAND, 1967), 18.

144. This conclusion could reflect some selection bias, in that the least politically indoctrinated soldiers might have been the most likely to end up speaking with Gurtov. Nevertheless, his conclusions are consistent with evidence from PAVN leaders' own discussion of their training curriculum, cited above. Gurtov, *War in the Delta*, 21.

145. Lanning and Cragg, *Inside the VC*, 42, 54, 55.

146. Ibid., 181.

147. Quoted in William Darryl Henderson, *Cohesion, the Human Element in Combat: Leadership and Societal Influence in the Armies of the Soviet Union, United States, and North Vietnam* (Washington, DC: National Defense University Press, 1985), 29.

148. Military History Institute, *Victory in Vietnam*, 39–42, 104, 106, 39, 105.

149. Pike, *PAVN*, 147.

150. Ibid., 167.

151. Khan, "Notebook II," 9.

152. Ibid., 15.

153. Pike, *PAVN*, 167.

154. Khan, "Notebook II," 10–11.

155. Pike, *PAVN*, 164.

156. Military History Institute, *Victory in Vietnam*, 103.

157. Pike, *PAVN*, 153–155; and Lanning and Cragg, *Inside the VC*, 85–86.

158. For example, "Report on Political and Ideological Situation," in "Self-Criticism: Report from a North Vietnamese Division," document no. 19, Vietnam Documents and Research Notes, November 19, 1967, 5–6, Vietnam Center and Archive, Texas Tech University, item no. 2120908016; and Military History Institute, *Victory in Vietnam*, 113.

159. Duiker, *Communist Road*, 250; Duiker, "Victory by Other Means," in Gilbert, *Why the North*, 66; Brigham, "Why the South," in *Why the North*, 110–111; and Nguyen, *Hanoi's War*, 28–29.

160. Duiker, *Communist Road*, 254–255.

161. Military History Institute, *Victory in Vietnam*, 173, 25.

162. Duiker, *Communist Road*, 230.

3. Battlefield Effectiveness in North and South Vietnam

1. Lt. Gen. Ngo Quang Truong, *RVNAF and U.S. Operational Cooperation and Coordination* (Washington, DC: U.S. Army Center of Military History, 1980), 165.

2. Neither does this chapter explore instances in which North Vietnam fought against U.S.-only forces, as in the air defense of North Vietnam—though the scholarship about North Vietnam's effectiveness in such battles is consistent with the findings here. Merle L. Pribbenow, "The -Ology War: Technology and Ideology in the Vietnamese Defense of Hanoi, 1967," *Journal of Military History* 67, no. 1 (January 2003), 175–200.

3. Debates on these and other offensives are discussed in great detail in Nguyen, *Hanoi's War*.

4. I report whatever casualty figures are available for this and the other battles, noting ranges where sources disagree. The information is not standardized, because some battle accounts report soldiers killed, others killed and wounded, and others just "losses." I do not rely on these numbers as a measure of effectiveness, not least because they may be biased, but they do provide additional information in the context of a larger battle.

5. Lt. Col. John Vann, *After Action Report on Dinh Tuong*, January 9, 1963, Historian's Files and Working Papers, Center of Military History, Washington, DC, 4; Toczek, *The Battle of Ap Bac*, 71; General Donn A. Starry, *Armoured Combat in Vietnam* (Dorset, UK: Blandford Press, 1981), 25.

6. Vann, *After Action Report*, 4.

7. Toczek, *Battle of Ap Bac*.

8. Sheehan, *Bright Shining Lie*, 205.

9. Working paper from the *Stennis Report*, February 14, 1963, Historian's Notes and Working Papers, Center of Military History, Washington, DC, 1.

10. Sheehan, *Bright Shining Lie*, 205.

11. Toczek, *Battle of Ap Bac*, 75–76.

12. Toczek, *Battle of Ap Bac*, 73; and Dave Richard Palmer, *Summons of the Trumpet: U.S.-Vietnam in Perspective* (San Rafael, CA: Presidio, 1978).

13. Cantwell, "Army of South Vietnam," 69–70; and Sheehan, *Bright Shining Lie*, 121.

14. Toczek, *Battle of Ap Bac*, 73.

15. Sheehan, *Bright Shining Lie*, 231; and Toczek, *Battle of Ap Bac*, 73.

16. Sheehan, *Bright Shining Lie*, 206. Similar figures are reported in Vien, *Leadership*, 55.

17. Sheehan, *Bright Shining Lie*, 207.

18. Toczek, *Battle of Ap Bac*, 85.

19. Ibid., 70.

20. Sheehan, *Bright Shining Lie*, 209–210; Starry, *Armoured Combat*, 25; and Toczek, *Battle of Ap Bac*, 70.

21. Toczek, *Battle of Ap Bac*, 78.

22. Col. James M. Winterbottom, "Translation of VC Document on Ap Bac Battle 2 Jan 63," April 20, 1963, Historian's Files and Working Papers, the Center of Military History, Washington, DC, 10.

23. Sheehan, *Bright Shining Lie*, 215.

24. 1st Lt. Arthur L. Bloch, "Field Advisor Narrative Analysis: Task Force A, 2 January 1963," January 6, 1963, Historian's Files and Working Papers, Center of Military History, Washington, DC, 1. These events are also described in Palmer, *Summons*, 34.

25. Maj. Jack A. Macslarrow, "Field Advisor Analysis, Dan Thang 1," 2–4 January, 1963, Historian's Files and Working Papers, Center of Military History, Washington, DC, 5.

26. Bloch, "Field Advisor Narrative," 2.

27. Macslarrow, "Field Advisor Analysis," 2. See also Letter from Maj. Jack A. Macslarrow to Major Tho, January 3, 1963, Historian's Files and Working Papers, Center of Military History, Washington, DC, 1–2, and 5.

28. Macslarrow, "Field Advisor Analysis," 4.

29. Macslarrow, "Field Advisor Analysis," 2. See also Letter Macslarrow to Tho, 1–2; and Major William J. Hart, "Field Advisor Narrative Analysis, Task Force B: 2 January 1963," January 7, 1963, Historian's Files and Working Papers, Center of Military History, Washington, DC, 1.

30. Macslarrow, "Field Advisor Analysis," 2. See also Letter Macslarrow to Tho, 1–2.

31. Toczek, *Battle of Ap Bac*, 80.

32. Sheehan, *Bright Shining Lie*, 220.

33. Toczek, *Battle of Ap Bac*, 81.

34. Sheehan, *Bright Shining Lie*, 238.

35. Captain James B. Scanlon, "Field Advisor Narrative Analysis," January 7, 1963, Historian's Files and Working Papers, Center of Military History, Washington, DC, 1–2.

36. Toczek, *Battle of Ap Bac*, 90–91.

37. Ibid, 92.

38. Toczek, *Battle of Ap Bac*, 86, 91.

39. Sheehan, *Bright Shining Lie*, 256.

40. Starry, *Armoured Combat*, 27.

41. Scanlon, "Field Advisor Narrative," 2.

42. Sheehan, *Bright Shining Lie*, 254.

43. U.S. adviser quoted in Toczek, *Battle of Ap Bac*, 94.

44. Sheehan, *Bright Shining Lie*, 253.

45. Ibid., 255.

46. Ibid., 257.

47. Toczek, *Battle of Ap Bac*, 94.

48. Ibid., 95–96.

49. Sheehan, *Bright Shining Lie*, 262.

50. Winterbottom, "Translation of VC Document," 21–23.

51. Mays, "Field Advisor Narrative," 3.

52. Cantwell, "The Army of South Vietnam," 125

53. Vann, *After Action Report*, 17.

54. Ted Surong, "The Lesson of Ap Bac," *Conflict* 9 (1989), 334.

55. Vann, *After Action Report*, 3, 8; and Sheehan, *Bright Shining Lie*, 233.

56. Starry, *Armoured Combat*, 27.

57. Vann, *After Action Report*, 17; Palmer, *Summons*, 36–37; Cantwell, "The Army of South Vietnam," 69–70; and Sheehan, *Bright Shining Lie*, 121.

58. Quoted in David Halberstam, "Vietnam Defeat Shocks U.S. Aides," *New York Times*, January 6, 1963, 2.

59. Mark Moyar, *Triumph Forsaken: the Vietnam War, 1954–1965* (New York: Cambridge University Press, 2006), 195–196. Moyar gives these factors significant weight in his account.

60. David Halberstam, "Harkins Praises Vietnam Troops," *New York Times*, January 10, 1963, 3.

61. Vann, *After Action Report*, 19.

62. Toczek, *Battle of Ap Bac*, 127.

63. Winterbottom, "Translation of VC Document," 36.

64. Lieutenant Colonel Andrew O'Meara, "Recollections of Ap Bac," undated, historians' files on South Vietnam, Center of Military History, Washington, DC, B-2 and B-3.

65. Winterbottom, "Translation of VC Document," 36.

66. O'Meara, "Recollections of Ap Bac," B-2 and B-3.

67. Winterbottom, "Translation of VC Document," 42–44.

68. Toczek, *Battle of Ap Bac*, 124.

69. Winterbottom, "Translation of VC Document," 29.

70. Ibid.

71. "The Use of U.S. Helicopters in Support of Vietnamese Operations on 2 Janu-

ary 1963," memo to Major General Fred C. Weyand, subject: Information Regarding U.S. Military Operations in Vietnam for Chair, House Armed Services Committee, January 30, 1963, available in the Historian's Files and Working Papers, Center of Military History, Washington, DC, 5.

72. These estimates appear in W.B. Rosson, "Foreword," in Toczek, *Battle of Ap Bac*, xv. One South Vietnamese general claimed the ARVN casualties were much higher, around 400 men. See also Vien, *Leadership*, 55.

73. James H. Willbanks, *The Tet Offensive: A Concise History* (New York: Columbia University Press, 2007), xvi.

74. For background, see Dommen, *Indochinese Experience*, 661–664, 668–669.

75. Willbanks, *Tet Offensive*, 81, 40–41. Unfortunately, information on many of these engagements is sparse.

76. Ibid., 31–39.

77. Ibid., 44–49.

78. George Smith, *The Siege at Hue* (Boulder, CO: Lynne Rienner, 1999), 8.

79. Willbanks, *Tet Offensive*, 46; and Smith, *Siege*, 13–14.

80. Smith, *Siege*, 23.

81. Willbanks, *Tet Offensive*, 39, 45.

82. Ibid., 49.

83. Col. Hoang Ngoc Lung, *The General Offensives of 1968–69* (Washington, DC: U.S. Army Center of Military History, 1981), 78; and Smith, *Siege*, 125.

84. Smith, *Siege*, 20.

85. Willbanks, *Tet Offensive*, 31.

86. Smith, *Siege*, 23.

87. Ibid, 24.

88. Ibid., 25–26.

89. Ibid., 27.

90. Ibid., 25–26, 27, 28.

91. Ibid., 64.

92. Lung, General Offensives, 80.

93. Wiest, *Vietnam's Forgotten Army*, 110.

94. Smith, *Siege*, 121, 91, 128.

95. Ibid., 120–126.

96. Ibid., 135, 125–127, 131; and Wiest, *Vietnam's Forgotten Army*, 112.

97. Smith, *Siege*, 141–143.

98. Ibid., 145.

99. Wiest, Vietnam's Forgotten Army, 113.

100. Ibid.

101. Smith, *Siege*, 167.

102. Willbanks, *Tet Offensive*, 54.

103. Wiest, Vietnam's Forgotten Army, 112.

104. Ibid., 114–115.

105. Smith, *Siege*, 146, 161.

106. Willbanks, *Tet Offensive*, 54.

107. Smith, *Siege*, 163.

108. Willbanks, *Tet Offensive*, 54.

109. Lung, General Offensives, 84.

110. Keith Nolan, *Battle for Hue: Tet, 1968* (Novato, CA: Presidio Press, 1983), 172.

111. Smith, *Siege*, 141.

112. Ibid., 168.

113. Lung, *General Offensives*, 84. This view is echoed in Smith, *Siege*, 165.

114. Nolan, *Battle*, 76, 87–88.

115. Smith, *Siege*, 167.

116. Willbanks, *Tet Offensive*, 31.

117. Ibid., 45; and Military History Institute, *Victory in Vietnam*, 219.

118. Military History Institute, *Victory in Vietnam*, 218.

119. Wiest, Vietnam's Forgotten Army, 110.

120. Smith, *Siege*, 55.

121. *LAMSON 719 After Action Report*, Department of the Army, Headquarters, XXIV Corps, May 14, 1971, 99, available in the Historian's Working Files and Papers at the Center of Military History, Fort McNair, Washington, DC. Restrictions on U.S. action stemmed from the Cooper-Church Amendment passed after the invasion of Cambodia. U.S. airpower and firepower from support bases inside South Vietnam did play a role in the battle, though even these were circumscribed due to poor weather. James H. Willbanks, *Abandoning Vietnam: How America Left and South Vietnam Lost Its War* (Lawrence: University of Kansas Press, 2004), 98, 102; and Maj. Gen. Nguyen Duy Hinh, *Lam Son 719*, Indochina Monograph (Washington, DC: U.S. Army Center of Military History, 1977), 64.

122. Keith William Nolan, *Into Laos: the Story of Dewey Canyon II/Lam Son 719; Vietnam 1971* (Novato, CA: Presidio Press, 1986), 14.

123. Hinh, *Lam Son 719*, 26–28.

124. Ibid., 127.

125. Nolan, *Into Laos*, 105, 104.

126. Wiest, Vietnam's Forgotten Army, 209.

127. Nolan, *Into Laos*, 105.

128. Ibid., 103–104.

129. On Cambodia, see John M. Shaw, *The Cambodian Campaign: The 1970 Offensive and America's War in Vietnam* (Lawrence: University of Kansas Press, 2005); and Tran Dinh Tho, *The Cambodian Incursion* (Washington, DC: U.S. Army Center of Military History, 1978).

130. Military History Institute, *Victory in Vietnam*, 272–274.

131. Hinh, *Lam Son 719*, 131.

132. Military History Institute, *Victory in Vietnam*, 274.

133. Hinh, *Lam Son 719*, 74.

134. Willbanks, *Abandoning Vietnam*, 105.

135. Hinh, *Lam Son 719*, 76, 86.

136. Ibid., 84, 145.

137. On Thieu's concerns, see "Cables from LTG Sutherland to GEN Abrams COMUS-MACV," February 12, 1971, 11:44 am and 12:20 pm; February 27, 1971, 6:45 am; February 28, 2:10 pm; and March 5, 1971, 11:55 am; all available in the Historian's Working Files and Papers at the Center of Military History, Fort McNair, Washington, DC.

138. Hinh, *Lam Son 719*, 89.

139. "Cables from LTG Sutherland to GEN Abrams COMUSMACV," March 2, 1971, 2:20 pm, available in the Historian's Working Files and Papers at the Center of Military History, Fort McNair, Washington, DC; and Hinh, *Lam Son 719*, 89.

140. Hinh, *Lam Son 719*, 90.

141. Ibid., 96.

142. Willbanks, *Abandoning Vietnam*, 108–109.

143. Hinh, *Lam Son 719*, 98.

144. "Cable from LTG Sutherland to GEN Abrams COMUSMACV," March 10, 1971, 9:40 am, available in the Historian's Working Files and Papers at the Center of Military History, Fort McNair, Washington, DC.

145. Hinh, *Lam Son 719*, 98.

146. Ibid., 113, 127.

147. Military History Institute, *Victory in Vietnam*, 277; Hinh, *Lam Son 719*, 153; and Willbanks, *Abandoning Vietnam*, 112.

148. Hinh, *Lam Son 719*, 108, 118, 163.

149. Ibid., 154; and "Cable from LTG Sutherland to GEN Abrams COMUSMACV," March 24, 1971, 2:46 pm, available in the Historian's Working Files and Papers at the Center of Military History, Fort McNair, Washington, DC.

150. Hinh, *Lam Son 719*, 127–132.

151. Ibid., 144.

152. Nolan, *Into Laos*, 129.

153. Hinh, *Lam Son 719*, 153, 162.

154. "Cable from LTG Sutherland to GEN Abrams COMUSMACV," March 4, 1971, 9:52 am, available in the Historian's Working Files and Papers at the Center of Military History, Fort McNair, Washington, DC.

155. Ibid.

156. Hinh, *Lam Son 719*, 88, 169.

157. Starry, *Armoured Combat*, 197; and Hinh, *Lam Son 719*, 155.

158. Hinh, *Lam Son 719*, 119.

159. Nolan, *Into Laos*, 259.

160. Hinh, *Lam Son 719*, 153; and "Cables from LTG Sutherland to GEN Abrams COMUSMACV," March 11, 1971, 11:45 am, and March 18, 1971, 2:25 pm, available in the Historian's Working Files and Papers at the Center of Military History, Fort McNair, Washington, DC.

161. Hinh, *Lam Son 719*, 161.

162. Willbanks, *Abandoning Vietnam*, 106–107.

163. Collins, 37.

164. "Cable from LTG Sutherland to GEN Abrams COMUSMACV," March 11, 1971, 11:45 am, and March 23, 1971, 11:55 am, available in the Historian's Working Files and Papers at the Center of Military History, Fort McNair, Washington, DC.

165. Willbanks, *Abandoning Vietnam*, 112.

166. Nolan, *Into Laos*, 119.

167. Ibid., 155.

168. Willbanks, *Abandoning Vietnam*, 106 and 112.

169. Hinh, *Lam Son 719*, 158.

170. "Cable from LTG Sutherland to GEN Abrams COMUSMACV," March 18, 1971, 2:25 pm, available in the Historian's Working Files and Papers at the Center of Military History, Fort McNair, Washington, DC.

171. Nolan, *Into Laos*, 105

172. Terry L. Florence, *Final Combat Operation After Action Feeder Report, Lam Son 719*, memo to Headquarters, U.S. Army Advisory Group, 1st Infantry Division (ARVN), April 25, 1971, 5, available in the Historian's Working Files and Papers at the Center of Military History, Fort McNair, Washington, DC.

173. Wiest, Vietnam's Forgotten Army, 209.

174. Willbanks, *Abandoning Vietnam*, 108.

175. *Appendix 6 (Enemy Tactics) to Annex C (Intelligence) to Combat After Action Report: Lam Son 719*, Headquarters, U.S. Army Vietnam, April 1, 1971, 2, available in the Historian's Working Files and Papers at the Center of Military History, Fort McNair, Washington, DC.

176. *Appendix 6 (Enemy Tactics)*, 1–2.

177. Hinh, *Lam Son 719*, 143.

178. *Appendix 6 (Enemy Tactics)*, 1.

179. Military History Institute, *Victory in Vietnam*, 277–278.

180. *Appendix 6 (Enemy Tactics)*, 1.

181. Hinh, *Lam Son 719*, 145.

182. *Appendix 6 (Enemy Tactics)*, 1.

183. "Cable from LTG Sutherland to GEN Abrams COMUSMACV," March 4, 1971, 7:40 am, available in the Historian's Working Files and Papers at the Center of Military History, Fort McNair, Washington, DC.

184. At the end of 1971, the United States had 158,120 soldiers in South Vietnam, but by the end of 1972, only 24,000 remained. Dale Andradé, *America's Last Vietnam Battle: Halting Hanoi's 1972 Easter Offensive* (Lawrence: University Press of Kansas, 2001), 7.

185. Lt. Gen. Ngo Quang Truong, *The Easter Offensive of 1972* (Washington, DC: U.S. Army Center of Military History, 1980), esp. 172; Capt. David K. Mann, *The NVA 1972 Invasion of Military Region I: Fall of Quang Tri and Defense of Hue*, Project CHECO Report, January 22, 1973, available in the Historian's Working Files and Papers at the Center of Military History, Fort McNair, Washington, DC; Stephen Randolph,

Powerful and Brutal Weapons: Nixon, Kissinger, and the Easter Offensive (Cambridge: Harvard University Press, 2007); and Caitlin Talmadge, "Explaining Military Effectiveness: Political Intervention and Battlefield Performance," Ph.D. dissertation, Massachusetts Institute of Technology, 2011, 142–160.

186. Military History Institute, *Victory in Vietnam*, 289.

187. Truong, *Easter Offensive*, 1.

188. Andradé, *America's Last Vietnam Battle*, 34.

189. Truong, *Easter Offensive*, 16.

190. Ibid., 24–25; and Military History Institute, *Victory in Vietnam*, 290–291.

191. Truong, *Easter Offensive*, 25.

192. Military History Institute, *Victory in Vietnam*, 291.

193. Truong, *Easter Offensive*, 29. This account is also echoed in Military History Institute, *Victory in Vietnam*, 291.

194. Truong, *Easter Offensive*, 25, 31.

195. Mann, *NVA 1972 Invasion*, chap. 3.

196. Truong, *Easter Offensive*, 31 and 75.

197. Andradé, *America's Last Vietnam Battle*, 102–103.

198. Truong, *Easter Offensive*, 38–39.

199. Andradé, America's Last Vietnam Battle, 2.

200. Truong, *Easter Offensive*, 33.

201. Andradé, *America's Last Vietnam Battle*, 64.

202. Truong, *Easter Offensive*, 38.

203. Andradé, *America's Last Vietnam Battle*, 105.

204. Truong, *Easter Offensive*, 33.

205. Ibid., 39–40.

206. Ibid., 41.

207. Military History Institute, *Victory in Vietnam*, 292.

208. Truong, *Easter Offensive*, 44. A nearly identical account of these events appears in Mann, *The NVA 1972 Invasion*.

209. Andradé, *America's Last Vietnam Battle*, 143.

210. Truong, *Easter Offensive*, 45.

211. Military History Institute, *Victory in Vietnam*, 292.

212. Truong, *Easter Offensive*, 45, 62.

213. Andradé, *America's Last Vietnam Battle*, 151.

214. Ibid., 152–153.

215. Truong, *Easter Offensive*, 48.

216. Col. G.H. Turley, *The Easter Offensive: Vietnam, 1972* (Novato, VA: Presidio, 1985), epilogue.

217. Truong, *Easter Offensive*, 53.

218. Ibid., 54, 60.

219. Ibid., 75–77, 53.

220. Military History Institute, *Victory in Vietnam*, 303.

221. Truong, *Easter Offensive*, 59, 60, 62.

222. Ibid., 65, 66.

223. Ibid., 67; see also Military History Institute, *Victory in Vietnam*, 304–305.

224. Truong, *Easter Offensive*, 67.

225. Ibid., 69-70.

226. Military History Institute, *Victory in Vietnam*, 304.

227. Andradé, *America's Last Vietnam Battle*, 487–488.

228. Truong, *Easter Offensive*, 172.

229. Veith, *Black April*.

230. Frank Snepp, *Decent Interval: An Insider's Account of Saigon's Indecent End Told by the CIA's Chief Strategy Analyst in Vietnam* (New York: Random House, 1977), 56.

231. Hosmer et al., *The Fall of South Vietnam*, 66–76.

232. Snepp, *Decent Interval*, 122, 131.

233. Ibid., 159–161.

234. Military History Institute, *Victory in Vietnam*, 356.

235. Turley, *The Easter Offensive*, epilogue.

236. Veith, *Black April*, 268.

237. Hosmer et al., *The Fall of South Vietnam*, 102.

238. Ibid., 70, 112; and Snepp, *Decent Interval*, 55.

239. Snepp, *Decent Interval*, 193.

240. Hosmer et al., *The Fall of South Vietnam*, 82.

241. Military History Institute, *Victory in Vietnam*, 362.

242. Snepp, *Decent Interval*, 140.

243. Military History Institute, *Victory in Vietnam*, 336, 351.

244. Veith, *Black April*, 46, 69.

245. Military History Institute, *Victory in Vietnam*, 352.

246. Hosmer et al., *The Fall of South Vietnam*, 80–82.

247. Snepp, *Decent Interval*, 174.

248. Hosmer et al., *The Fall of South Vietnam*, 84.

249. Ibid., 85, 90–91.

250. Nguyen Ba Can, quoted in Hosmer et al., *The Fall of South Vietnam*, 89.

251. Hosmer et al., *The Fall of South Vietnam*, 93, 94.

252. Preceding quotations all from Hosmer et al., *The Fall of South Vietnam*, 95-96.

253. Military History Institute, *Victory in Vietnam*, 381.

254. Hosmer et al., *The Fall of South Vietnam*, 98.

255. Ibid., 99, 101.

256. Veith, *Black April*, 276.

257. Hosmer et al., *The Fall of South Vietnam*, 87.

258. Veith, *Black April*, 280.

259. Hosmer et al., *The Fall of South Vietnam*, 120; and Snepp, *Decent Interval*, 239–242.

260. Hosmer et al., *The Fall of South Vietnam*, 104.

261. Ibid., p. 89.

262. Ibid., 107.

263. Lam Quang Thi, *The Twenty-Five Year Century: A South Vietnamese General Remembers the Indochina War to the Fall of Saigon* (Denton: University of North Texas Press, 2001), chap. 14.

264. Hosmer et al., *The Fall of South Vietnam*, 108.

265. Ibid.

266. Military History Institute, *Victory in Vietnam*, 383.

267. Veith, *Black April*, 316; and Hosmer et al., *The Fall of South Vietnam*, 109.

268. Hosmer et al., *The Fall of South Vietnam*, 109–110.

269. Ibid., 110.

270. Ibid.

271. Ibid., 111.

272. Military History Institute, *Victory in Vietnam*, 391.

273. Hosmer et al., *The Fall of South Vietnam*, 111.

274. Ibid., 114.

275. Ibid., 116.

276. George J. Veith and Merle L. Pribbenow II, " 'Fighting Is an Art': the Army of the Republic of Vietnam's Defense of Xuan Loc, 9–21 April 1975," *Journal of Military History* 68 (January 2004), 163–213; and Veith, *Black April*, chap. 17.

277. Hosmer et al., *The Fall of South Vietnam*, 117-118.

278. Ibid., 118, 410, 123–125.

279. Ibid., 112. The same conclusion is reached in Smith, *The Siege*, 175.

280. Hosmer et al., *The Fall of South Vietnam*, 96.

281. Ibid., 96.

282. Ibid., 79.

283. Ibid., 65.

284. Military History Institute, *Victory in Vietnam*, 372.

285. Ibid., 372, 371.

286. Ibid., 393, 395.

287. Cantwell, "The Army of South Vietnam."

288. William Duiker, *Sacred War: Nationalism and Revolution in a Divided Vietnam* (New York: McGraw-Hill, 1995), esp. chap. 7; and Thomas Ahern, *Vietnam Declassified: The CIA and Counterinsurgency* (Lexington: The University Press of Kentucky, 2010), esp. conclusion.

289. Douglas Pike, *Viet Cong: The Organization and Techniques of the National Liberation Front of South Vietnam* (Cambridge: MIT Press, 1966), 377.

290. Joes, *The War*, 92; and Collins, *Training and Development* 60 and 94–95. Conversely, in 1969, 47,000 communist personnel defected to South Vietnam, as did 32,000 the following year. Hinh, *Lam Son 719*, 5. Desertions in South Vietnam also

dropped substantially in response to basic efforts to improve soldiers' quality of life, such as ensuring regular mail delivery, better food, clothing, and medical care, occasional entertainment, and better care for dependents. This reduction suggests that most desertions did not have a political motivation. Vien, *Leadership*, 70.

291. Lanning and Cragg, *Inside the VC*, chap. 3.

292. Joes, *The War*, 132–133, 154.

293. For examples, see Frances Fitzgerald, *Fire in the Lake: The Vietnamese and the Americans in Vietnam* (Boston: Little, Brown, 2002); Melvin Gurtov and Konrad Kellen, *Vietnam: Lessons and Mislessons* (RAND, June 1969); Konrad Kellen, *A Profile of the PAVN Soldier in South Vietnam* (Santa Monica, CA: RAND, June 1966); and Ahern, *Vietnam Declassified*, esp. conclusion.

294. This general logic draws on John Lynn, *The Bayonets of the Republic: Motivation and Tactics in the Army of Revolutionary France, 1791–94* (Chicago: University of Illinois Press, 1984).

295. Logevall, *Embers of War*, 17, 78, 110.

296. Logevall, *Embers of War*, 18, 77, 151; and Marc Jason Gilbert, "Introduction," in *Why the North*, 14.

297. Brigham, "Why the South," in Gilbert, *Why the North*, 99.

298. Duiker, "Victory by Other Means," in Gilbert, *Why the North*, 53.

299. Vu, *Paths to Development*, chap. 5; and Nguyen, *Hanoi's War*, esp. chaps. 1 and 2.

300. The term comes from Philip Selznick, *The Organizational Weapon: A Study of Bolshevik Strategy and Tactics* (New York: McGraw-Hill, 1952).

301. Logevall, *Embers of War*, xviii.

302. Brigham, "Why the South," in Gilbert, *Why the North*, 100–101.

303. Duiker, *Sacred War*, chap. 3.

304. For further discussion, see Talmadge, "Explaining Military Effectiveness," 172–180.

305. Veith, *Black April*, 264–266.

4. Threats and Military Organizational Practices in Iraq and Iran

1. Gary Sick, "Trial by Error: Reflections on the Iran-Iraq War," *Middle East Journal* 43, no. 2 (Spring 1989), 230.

2. Ibid., 240.

3. Following convention, I use "Saddam" as shorthand for "Saddam Hussein," instead of "Hussein." For the transliteration of Arabic words, I generally follow Gregory Gause, *The International Relations of the Persian Gulf* (New York: Cambridge University Press, 2010). I do not change alternative transliterations used in quoted sources.

4. Sick, "Trial by Error, 230.

5. "The Implications of the Iran-Iraq Agreement," paper produced by the Central Intelligence Agency, State Department, and Defense Intelligence Agency, May 1, 1975, available at www.gwu.edu/~nsarchiv/NSAEBB/NSAEBB167/01.pdf.

6. Sick, "Trial by Error," 231–232.

7. Ibid., 233.

8. Said K. Aburish, "How Saddam Hussein Came to Power," in *The Saddam Hussein Reader*, ed. Turi Munthe (New York: Thunder's Mouth Press, 2002), 48; and Adeed Dawisha, *Iraq: A Political History from Independence to Occupation* (Princeton: Princeton University Press, 2009), 214.

9. Efraim Karsh and Inari Rautsi, *Saddam Hussein: A Political Biography* (New York: Free Press, 1991), 138.

10. Anthony Cordesman and Abraham Wagner, *The Lessons of Modern War, vol. 2: The Iran-Iraq War* (Boulder, CO: Westview, 1990), 25–26.

11. Dilip Hiro, *The Longest War: The Iran-Iraq Military Conflict* (New York: Routledge, 1991), 28–9, 35.

12. "More Arrests Expected from Hussein Execution Video," CNN.com, January 3, 2007, available at http://www.cnn.com/2007/WORLD/meast/01/03/saddam.execution/index.html.

13. Sick, "Trial by Error," 232.

14. Shahram Chubin and Charles Tripp, *Iran and Iraq at War* (London: I.B. Tauris, 1988), chap. 1.

15. Hiro, *Longest War*, 36.

16. Kenneth Pollack, *Arabs at War: Military Effectiveness, 1948–1991* (Lincoln: University of Nebraska Press, 2002), 183.

17. Stephen Walt, *Revolution and War* (Ithaca, NY: Cornell University Press, 1996), 238–243 and 259–268; and Cordesman and Wagner, *Lessons*, 24.

18. Cordesman and Wagner, *Lessons*, 73.

19. I borrow this periodization from Gause, *International Relations of the Persian Gulf*, 57–58.

20. For background on the Tanker War and War of the Cities, see Hiro, *Longest War*, chap. 6.

21. Remark by an Iraqi general, quoted in Kevin M. Woods, Williamson Murray, and Thomas Holaday, *Saddam's War: An Iraqi Military Perspective of the Iran-Iraq War* (Washington, DC: National Defense University, 2009), 39.

22. The terms had been established in UN Resolution 598, passed in 1987. Sick, "Trial by Error," 242.

23. Steven R. Ward, *Immortal: A Military History of Iran and Its Armed Forces* (Washington, DC: Georgetown University Press, 2009), 297.

24. Clodfelter, *Warfare and Armed Conflicts* (Jefferson, NC: McFarland, 2001), 629.

25. Hiro, *Longest War*, 1, 250.

26. Sick, "Trial by Error," 233–236.

27. Chubin and Tripp, *Iran and Iraq*, 207.

28. "Discussion Paper for SIG on Policy Options for Dealing with Iran-Iraq War," mid-1982, origin unknown, available at the National Security Archive, the George Washington University, Washington, DC.

29. Vietnam was an ideal supplier because many of Iran's weapons were U.S.-made, and Hanoi had captured significant quantities of U.S. spare parts when it conquered

South Vietnam. Hiro, *Longest War*, 72. Britain reportedly provided large quantities of spare parts for Iran's Chieftain tanks, including engines. Cordesman and Wagner, *Lessons*, 120–121.

30. "Discussion Paper for SIG."

31. Hiro, *Longest War*, chap. 5; and Bryan R. Gibson, *Covert Relationship: American Foreign Policy, Intelligence, and the Iran-Iraq War, 1980–1988* (Denver, CO: Praeger, 2010), 71–72.

32. Cordesman and Wagner, *Lessons*, 13, 41, and 54.

33. Ibid., 54, based on CIA data.

34. Pollack, "The Influence of Arab Culture."

35. Cordesman and Wagner, *Lessons*, 25, 413.

36. Karsh and Rautsi, *Saddam Hussein*, 88.

37. Pollack, *Arabs at War*, 182; and "Iraq's Role in the Middle East," National Intelligence Estimate, Director of Central Intelligence, June 21, 1979, D-1, available at www.gwu.edu/~nsarchiv/NSAEBB/NSAEBB167/02.pdf.

38. Pollack, *Arabs at War*, 207.

39. Ibrahim Al-Marashi and Sammy Salama, *Iraq's Armed Forces: An Analytical History* (New York: Routledge, 2008), 3; Charles Tripp, *A History of Iraq* (New York: Cambridge University Press, 2007), chap. 2; and Joseph Sassoon, *Saddam Hussein's Ba'th Party: Inside an Authoritarian Regime* (New York: Cambridge University Press, 2012), chap. 5.

40. Pollack, *Arabs at War*, 149.

41. Karsh and Rautsi, *Saddam Hussein*, 7.

42. Tripp, *History of Iraq*, chaps. 4–5; Karsh and Rautsi, *Saddam Hussein*, 24.

43. FBI Interview with Saddam Hussein, session 2, conducted by George Piro, Baghdad Operations Center, February 8, 2004, 6, available at http://www.gwu.edu/~nsarchiv/NSAEBB/NSAEBB279/index.htm.

44. FBI Interview with Saddam Hussein, session 5, conducted by George Piro, Baghdad Operations Center, February 8, 2004, 7, available at http://www.gwu.edu/~nsarchiv/NSAEBB/NSAEBB279/index.htm.

45. Karsh and Rautsi, *Saddam Hussein*, chap. 2.

46. Tripp, *History of Iraq*, chap. 5; and FBI Interview, session 5, 3–5.

47. Karsh and Rautsi, *Saddam Hussein*, 47.

48. Tripp, *History of Iraq*, 188; and Karsh and Rautsi, *Saddam Hussein*, 40–41.

49. Al-Marashi and Salama, *Iraq's Armed Forces*, 113.

50. Dawisha, *Iraq*, 212.

51. Karsh and Rautsi, *Saddam Hussein*, 189.

52. Chubin and Tripp, *Iran and Iraq*, 294. For more background on the Popular Army, see Sassoon, *Saddam Hussein's Ba'th Party*, 146–147.

53. Different sources provide slightly different estimates of the number of Republican Guard brigades by the end of the war. Pollack counts twenty-eight, while Al Marashi and Salama count twenty-five. *Arabs at War*, 218–219; and *Iraq's Armed Forces*, 168. Many accounts of the Iraqi order of battle actually obscure this growth by counting divisions only, and they often list Iraq as having only one Republican

Guard division throughout the war. Although this may have been true as a matter of nomenclature, it is important to remember that Iraqi divisions often had many more than the typical three brigades under their command.

54. Karsh and Rautsi, *Saddam Hussein*, 15, 35.

55. For detailed analysis of the role of the Ba'th party in Iraqi politics, see Sassoon, *Saddam Hussein's Ba'th Party*.

56. Karsh and Rautsi, *Saddam Hussein*, 41, 88; and Dawisha, *Iraq*, 211.

57. "Iraq's Role in the Middle East," 7; and Marion Farouk-Sluglett and Peter Sluglett, *Iraq Since 1958: From Revolution to Dictatorship* (New York: I.B. Tauris, 2001), 206.

58. Karsh and Rautsi, *Saddam Hussein*, chaps. 4–5.

59. Al-Marashi and Salama, *Iraq's Armed Forces*, 127.

60. The background to these events can be seen in "Correspondence between the Baghdad and the General Security Directorates Requesting Confirmation of Miscellaneous Information on an Attempted Coup," CRRC Number SH-GMID-D-000-190, June 19, 1979, 1.

61. Aburish, "How Saddam Hussein Came to Power," 51–54.

62. Dawisha, *Iraq*, 214.

63. Quoted in Samir al-Khalil, *Republic of Fear: The Politics of Modern Iraq* (Berkeley: University of California Press, 1989), 20.

64. Aburish, "How Saddam Hussein Came to Power," 52.

65. Karsh and Rautsi, *Saddam Hussein*, 2.

66. "A Meeting, Dated 1 May 1991, between Saddam Hussein and the General Command of the Army Regarding the Enlargement of the Army, and Assessment of Performance/Problems in Recent Conflict," CRRC Number SH-SHTP-A-000-849, May 1, 1991, 1–2.

67. Cordesman and Wagner, *Lessons*, 28, 60.

68. "Iraq's Role in the Middle East," 7.

69. Dawisha, *Iraq*, 222.

70. Hiro, *Longest War*, 51, 68, and 197.

71. Amazia Baram, "The Ruling Political Elite in Bathi Iraq, 1968–1986: The Changing Features of a Collective Profile," *International Journal of Middle East Studies* 21, no. 4 (November 1989), 447–493.

72. Quoted in Murray and Woods, *The Iran-Iraq War*, 287.

73. Intelligence Assessment, CIA Directorate of Intelligence, "Is Iraq Losing the War?" April 1986, 9, available at the National Security Archive, the George Washington University, Washington, DC. See also Cordesman and Wagner, *Lessons*, 228; Hiro, *Longest War*, 171–172; and Al-Marashi and Salama, *Iraq's Armed Forces*, 164

74. *The Negative Impact of the War on the Iraqi Domestic Situation*, report of the Hungarian Embassy in Baghdad to Hungarian Foreign Minister Peter Varkony, April 24, 1986, available at the National Security Archive, the George Washington University, Washington, DC.

75. Charles Tripp, "The Iran-Iraq War and Iraqi Politics," in *The Iran-Iraq War: Impact and Implications*, ed. Efraim Karsh (New York: St. Martin's Press, 1989), 232–233; and Stephen C. Pelletiere and Douglas V. Johnson, *Lessons Learned: The Iran-Iraq War*,

vol. 1 (Carlisle, PA: Strategic Studies Institute of the U.S. Army War College, 1990), published as "Fleet Marine Force Reference Publication 3-202," 37, 259–260.

76. Quoted in Woods et al., *Saddam's War*, 4 and 25.

77. Ibid., 4.

78. "Text Versions of Cassettes Recorded of 1980 Meetings Held among Saddam Hussein and Iraqi Officials Regarding Tactics and Plotting against the Iraqi Enemy," CRRC Number SH-SHTP-D-000-624, December 28–29, 1980, 112, 119; and "Written Transcripts of Audio Tapes of Meetings between Saddam Hussein and Senior Military Commanders Discussing Nominations to Ba'ath Party Leadership and Iran-Iraq War Battles," CRRC Number SH-SHTP-D-000-864, September 1982, 123–128.

79. "Written Transcripts," CRRC Number SH-SHTP-D-000-864, 130–132.

80. "Text Versions," CRRC Number SH-SHTP-D-000-624, 107–110.

81. Cordesman and Wagner, *Lessons*, 43–44, 59, 110.

82. Lieutenant General Ra'ad Majid Rashid al-Hamdani, quoted in Kevin M. Woods et al., *Saddam's Generals: Perspectives of the Iran-Iraq War* (Alexandria, VA: Institute for Defense Analyses, 2011), 37. This is confirmed by other interviews discussed in the same volume, 122–123.

83. Cordesman and Wagner, *Lessons*, 149; and "Prospects for Iraq," Special National Intelligence Estimate 36.2-83, Director of Central Intelligence, 1983, 15, available at https://www.gwu.edu/~nsarchiv/NSAEBB/NSAEBB167/04.pdf.

84. Karsh and Rautsi, *Saddam Hussein*, 191–192.

85. Pollack, *Arabs at War*, 208; and Hiro, *Longest War*, 89.

86. Hamdani, quoted in Woods et al., *Saddam's Generals*, 30–31, 73.

87. Hamdani, quoted in Woods et al., *Saddam's War*, 59.

88. Woods et al., *Saddam's War*, 14, 77.

89. "A Meeting on 18 October 1984 between Saddam Hussein and Unknown Officials in which They Discuss Military Operations and a Large Secret Project," CRRC Number SH-SHTP-A-000-735, October 1984, 9–10.

90. General al-Khazraji had proven himself a competent commander in numerous battles by this point in the war. Woods et al., *Saddam's Generals*, 40–44.

91. Woods et al., *Saddam's War*, 83.

92. Al-Marashi and Salama, *Iraq's Armed Forces*, 166.

93. Saddam's reflections on the process are discussed in "A Meeting," CRRC Number SH-SHTP-A-000-849, 4–5. Further details in Pollack, *Arabs at War*, 219–220.

94. Pollack, *Arabs at War*, 219–220; and Woods et al *Saddam's Generals*, 77.

95. Tripp, "The Iran-Iraq War," in *Iran-Iraq War*, 233.

96. Karsh and Rautsi, *Saddam Hussein*, 185.

97. Woods et al., *Saddam's War*, 97.

98. Kevin Woods et al., "Saddam's Delusions: The View from the Inside," *Foreign Affairs* 85, no. 3 (May/June 2006), 2; and Kevin Woods et al., *Iraqi Perspectives Project: A View of Operation Iraqi Freedom from Saddam's Senior Leadership* (U.S. Joint Forces Command and the Institute for Defense Analyses, 2006), esp. chap. 3.

99. Cordesman and Wagner, *Lessons*, 69; and Williamson Murray and Kevin Woods,

The Iran-Iraq War: A Military and Strategic History (United Kingdom: Cambridge University Press, 2014), 65–66.

100. Marashi and Salama, *Iraq's Armed Forces*, 154–155.

101. Cordesman and Wagner, *Lessons*, 426.

102. Pollack, *Arabs at War*, 219.

103. Cordesman and Wagner, *Lessons*, 44.

104. "Audio Recorded Meeting," CRRC Number SH-SHTP-A-000-627, 20–21.

105. "Meetings between Saddam Hussein and Various Iraqi Officials," CRRC Number SH-MISC-D-000-695, October 12–13, 1980, 700–701.

106. "Audio Recorded Meeting," CRRC Number SH-SHTP-A-000-627, 21–22.

107. "Saddam Hussein Discusses Neighboring Countries and Their Regimes," CRRC Number SH-SHTP-A-000-626, exact date unknown, sometime after 1980 and before 1985, 10.

108. Woods et al., *Saddam's Generals*, 111, 133–140; and "Audio Recorded Meeting," CRRC Number SH SHTP-A-000-627, 33–34.

109. Woods et al., *Saddam's Generals*, 134.

110. "Defense in Strong Points, by Staff Brigadier General Abd-al-Zuhrah Shikarah al-Maliki," in "Military Journal, vol. 61, no. 3, July 1984 (U)," CRRC Number SH-MODX-D-000-853, July 1984, 56.

111. This military journal is listed in the CRRC only as "Iraqi Military Journal," without a specific title. "Security and Safety of the Unit in Peace and War, by Staff Major General Faruq Umar al-Hariri," in "Military Journal," CRRC Number SH-MODX-D-000-853, 12.

112. Intelligence Appraisal, Defense Intelligence Agency, "Iran-Iraq: The Second Year of War," December 8, 1982, 2, available at the National Security Archive, the George Washington University, Washington, DC. See also Cordesman and Wagner, *Lessons*, 353.

113. "Audio Recorded Meeting," CRRC Number SH-SHTP-A-000-627, 32.

114. Woods et al., *Saddam's Generals*, 136.

115. "Transcript of a Conversation between Saddam Hussein and High Ranking Officers during the Iraq-Iran War," CRRC Number SH-SHTP-D-000-607, February 25, 1985–July 31, 1986, 6.

116. "Meeting between Saddam and the Military Corps Commanders," CRRC Number SH-SHTP-A-000-634, March 28, 1987, 12.

117. "Meeting between Saddam," CRRC Number SH-SHTP-A-000-634, 15.

118. Woods et al., *Saddam's War*, 70; and Pollack, *Arabs at War*, 219.

119. Quoted in Woods et al., *Saddam's Generals*, 140–141.

120. Woods et al., *Saddam's War*, 14.

121. Ward, *Immortal*, 291; and Pollack, *Arabs at War*, 220–221.

122. Woods et al., *Saddam's War*, 60, 78.

123. Woods et al., *Saddam's Generals*, 77–78; Pollack, *Arabs at War*, 220; and Murray and Woods, *The Iran-Iraq War*, 291.

124. Cordesman and Wagner, *Lessons*, 355–356.

125. Woods et al., "Saddam's Delusions"; and Woods et al., *Iraqi Perspectives Project*, especially chap. 3.

126. Cordesman and Wagner, *Lessons*, 420.

127. Sassoon, *Saddam Hussein's Ba'th Party*, 138.

128. Hiro, *Longest War*, 109; and Woods et al., *Saddam's Generals*, 32.

129. A taste of these sort of orders appears in "Meeting between Saddam," CRRC Number SH-SHTP-A-000-634, 10.

130. Cordesman and Wagner, *Lessons*, 80.

131. Iraqi general quoted in Woods et al., *Saddam's Generals*, 44–45.

132. Al-Marashi and Salama, *Iraq's Armed Forces*, 126, 145, 156.

133. "Audio Recorded Meeting," CRRC Number SH-SHTP-A-000-627, 25.

134. "Defense in Strong Points, by Staff Brigadier General Abd-al-Zuhrah Shikarah al-Maliki," in "Military Journal," CRRC Number SH-MODX-D-000-853, 60.

135. "Audio Recorded Meeting," CRRC Number SH-SHTP-A-000-627, 9–10, 45.

136. Cordesman and Wagner, *Lessons*, 133.

137. Tripp, "The Iran-Iraq War," in *Iran-Iraq War*, 69.

138. Ward, *Immortal*, 276.

139. Cordesman and Wagner, *Lessons*, 356.

140. Pelletiere and Johnson, *Lessons Learned*, vii; Chubin and Tripp, *Iran and Iraq*, 119; and Al-Marashi and Salama, *Iraq's Armed Forces*, 153, 166.

141. Al-Marashi and Salama, *Iraq's Armed Forces*, 166–167.

142. Woods et al., "Saddam's Delusions"; and Woods et al., *Iraqi Perspectives Project*, esp. chap. 3.

143. Al-Marashi and Salama, *Iraq's Armed Forces*, 147.

144. Pelletiere and Johnson, *Lessons Learned*, 30.

145. "A Meeting between Saddam Hussein and High-Ranking Officers Discussing Battles in the Iran-Iraq War," CRRC Number SH-SHTP-D-000-612, late 1980s, 7.

146. "GMID Daily Intelligence Reports sent by the Military Attaché in Iran Concerning the Loss of Iran and Iraq Forces, during the War in 1981," CRRC Number SH-GMID-D-000-883, March 5, 1981–April 28, 1981, 9.

147. "GMID Daily Intelligence," CRRC Number SH-GMID-D-000-883, 18.

148. "Accuracy in the Transmission of Information, by Staff Brigadier General Ihsan Qasim Bakr," in "Military Journal," CRRC Number SH-MODX-D-000-853, 31.

149. Woods et al., *Saddam's War*, 38.

150. Al-Marashi and Salama, *Iraq's Armed Forces*, 147; and Woods et al. *Saddam's Generals*, 73.

151. Cordesman and Wagner, *Lessons*, 80.

152. Al-Marashi and Salama, *Iraq's Armed Forces*, 147.

153. Pelletiere and Johnson, *Lessons Learned*, 30.

154. Al-Marashi and Salama, *Iraq's Armed Forces*, 153; and Chubin and Tripp, *Iran and Iraq*, 117.

155. "Presidential Direction during War in 1984," CRRC Number SH-AFGC-D-000-686, February–December 1984, 41.

156. Al-Marashi and Salama, *Iraq's Armed Forces*, 166.

157. Cordesman and Wagner, *Lessons*, 356. See also Al-Marashi and Salama, *Iraq's Armed Forces*, 164–166.

158. Woods et al., "Saddam's Delusions"; and Woods et al., *Iraqi Perspectives Project*, esp. chap. 3.

159. All data from "The Middle East and North Africa," *Military Balance* (1980), 42; and "The Middle East and North Africa," *Military Balance* (1986), 96–97.

160. Chubin and Tripp, *Iran and Iraq*, 37.

161. Ward, *Immortal*, 134.

162. Ward, *Immortal*, 139, 149–150; and Sepehr Zabih, *The Iranian Military in Revolution and War* (New York: Routledge, 1988), 3.

163. Ward, *Immortal*, chapter 6.

164. Ibid., 186–187.

165. Ward, *Immortal*, 188–191.

166. Ibid., 180, 202; and Nikola Schahgaldian, with the assistance of Gina Barkhordarian, *The Iranian Military under the Islamic Republic* (Santa Monica, CA: RAND Corporation, 1987), 13.

167. Mark Roberts, *Khomeini's Incorporation of the Iranian Military*, McNair Paper 48 (Washington, DC: National Defense University, January 1996), 6.

168. Schahgaldian, *Iranian Military*, 13.

169. Ward, *Immortal*, 202, 203.

170. "The Evolution of the U.S.-Iranian Relationship," U.S. Department of State report, January 29, 1980, 37–38, 42, 50, and 54, available through the Digital National Security Archive, item number IR03556.

171. Ward, *Immortal*, chap. 8.

172. Ibid., 216–224.

173. Afshon Ostovar, "Guardians of the Islamic Revolution: Ideology, Politics, and the Development of Military Power (1979–2009)," Ph.D. diss., University of Michigan, 2009, 50; and Ward, *Immortal*, 222.

174. David Menashri, *Iran: A Decade of War and Revolution* (New York: Holmes and Meier, 1990), 10.

175. Ostovar, "Guardians," 72.

176. Ward, *Immortal*, 211; and Cordesman and Wagner, *Lessons*, 28.

177. Ward, *Immortal*, 226.

178. Cordesman and Wagner, *Lessons*, 26; and Ward, *Immortal*, 233–234.

179. Ostovar, "Guardians," 75.

180. Ibid.; and Reza Kahlili, *A Time to Betray* (New York: Simon & Schuster, 2010), 52–53.

181. Ward, *Immortal*, 228; and Menashri, *Iran*, 217.

182. Hiro, *Longest War*, 52; and Menashri, *Iran*, 219.

183. Ward, *Immortal*, 101, 225.

184. Schahgaldian, *Iranian Military*, 28.

185. Ward, *Immortal*, 226–227, 238.

186. Cordesman and Wagner, *Lessons*, 192.

187. Menashri, *Iran*, 11; and Gause, *International Relations*, 73.

188. Cordesman and Wagner, *Lessons*, 117.

189. Menashri, *Iran*, 11.

190. "Implications for U.S. Interests and Policy of Iranian Invasion of Southern Iraq," U.S. Department of State discussion paper, July 14, 1982, available at the National Security Archive, the George Washington University, Washington, DC.

191. Intelligence Appraisal, "Iran-Iraq," 1.

192. Menashri, *Iran*, 239, 281–282.

193. Letter, Islamic Republic of Iran, Abolhassan Bani Sadr to Kurt Waldheim, October 1, 1980, available at the National Security Archive, the George Washington University, Washington, DC.

194. Cordesman and Wagner, *Lessons*, 28–29, 122; and Zabih, *Iranian Military*, 130, 152–153.

195. Ward, *Immortal*, 209.

196. Ibid., 202–209; and Schahgaldian, *Iranian Military*, vi, 14.

197. Schahgaldian, *Iranian Military*, 21, 22.

198. Ward, *Immortal*, 229. For more background on the purges, see Zabih, *Iranian Military*, chap. 5.

199. Ward, *Immortal*, 228–229; Schahgaldian, *Iranian Military*, vi, 34, 44, 49.

200. Ward, *Immortal*, 255.

201. Schahgaldian, *Iranian Military*, 25, 44; and Zabih, *Iranian Military*, 16–17.

202. Ward, *Immortal*, 206–207.

203. Cordesman and Wagner, *Lessons*, 60.

204. Ward, *Immortal*, 206.

205. Cordesman and Wagner, *Lessons*, 42.

206. Ward, *Immortal*, 245.

207. Schahgaldian, *Iranian Military*, 43.

208. "Intelligence Report about Iran, Issued by the General Military Intelligence Directorate (GMID) in 1980," CRRC Number SH-GMID-D-000-842, January–June 1980, 54–59.

209. Ward, *Immortal*, 228, 230, 245; Zabih, *Iranian Military*, 143–146.

210. Zabih, *Iranian Military*, 15.

211. Ward, *Immortal*, 246; and Cordesman and Wagner, *Lessons*, 55.

212. "General Military Intelligence Directorate Correspondence about the Iranian Military Sites and Plans during the Iraq-Iran War," CRRC Number SH-GMID-D-000-266, April 1–14, 1987, 13.

213. Ward, *Immortal*, 94.

214. Cordesman and Wagner, *Lessons*, 55–6.

215. Schahgaldian, *Iranian Military*, 75.

216. Chubin and Tripp, *Iran and Iraq*, 44.

217. Roberts, *Khomeini's Incorporation*, 7.

218. Ward, *Immortal*, 202–209.

219. Zabih, *Iranian Military* 5.

220. Ward, *Immortal*, 218.

221. Roberts, *Khomeini's Incorporation*, 4.

222. Woods et al., *Saddam's War*, 7–8; and Ostovar, "Guardians," chap. 3.

223. Schahgaldian, *Iranian Military*, vii.

224. Ward, *Immortal*, 227.

225. Cordesman and Wagner, *Lessons*, 420; and Schahgaldian, *Iranian Military*, 30.

226. Cordesman and Wagner, *Lessons*, 67.

227. Schahgaldian, *Iranian Military*, 48.

228. "Intelligence Report," CRRC Number SH-GMID-D-000-842, 53.

229. Ward, *Immortal*, 226.

230. Cordesman and Wagner, *Lessons*, 420.

231. "Intelligence Report," CRRC Number SH-GMID-D-000-842, 42–43.

232. Cordesman and Wagner, *Lessons*, 324, 420.

233. Ibid., 431.

234. Schahgaldian, *Iranian Military*, vii, 31; Cordesman and Wagner, *Lessons*, 169; Zabih, *Iranian Military*, 213; and Ward, *Immortal*, 255.

235. Ward, *Immortal*, 209; and Zabih, *Iranian Military*, 8.

236. Roberts, *Khomeini's Incorporation*, 6.

237. Schahgaldian, *Iranian Military*, 14.

238. Roberts, *Khomeini's Incorporation*, 6.

239. Schahgaldian, *Iranian Military*, vii.

240. Ward, *Immortal*, 102.

241. Schahgaldian, *Iranian Military*, 32.

242. Ward, *Immortal*, 230.

243. Cordesman and Wagner, *Lessons*, 59.

244. Schahgaldian, *Iranian Military*, 28.

245. Roberts, *Khomeini's Incorporation*, 41.

246. Schahgaldian, *Iranian Military*, 34.

5. Battlefield Effectiveness in Iraq and Iran

1. These battles occurred in the central and southern sectors of the border, where there was little Kurdish participation in the fighting. Kurdish forces were relatively autonomous from the national governments of both states and subject to their own distinct organizational practices.

2. Hiro, *Longest War*; Edgar O'Ballance, *The Gulf War* (Washington, DC: Brassey, 1988); Sick, "Trial by Error," 230–245; and Cordesman and Wagner, *Lessons*.

3. Chaim Hertzog, "A Military-Strategic Overview," in *The Iran-Iraq War: Impact and Implications*, ed. Efraim Karsh (New York: St. Martin's Press, 1989), 255.

4. Iraqi and Iranian military performance in these other campaigns is generally consistent with the patterns observed in ground warfare. Shahram Chubin, "Iran and the War: From Stalemate to Ceasefire," in *The Gulf War: Regional and International Dimensions*, eds. Hanns W. Maull and Otto Pick (New York: St. Martin's Press, 1989), 12; and Cordesman and Wagner, *Lessons*, 380.

5. Pollack, *Arabs*, 228.

6. Cordesman and Wagner, *Lessons*, 86–87.

7. Ward, *Immortal*, 248.

8. Ibid.; and Cordesman and Wagner, *Lessons*, 88–89.

9. Ward, *Immortal*, 249–251; and Cordesman and Wagner, *Lessons*, 85.

10. Cordesman and Wagner, *Lessons*, 93.

11. Al-Marashi and Salama, *Iraq's Armed Forces*, 157.

12. Ward, *Immortal*, 251.

13. Woods et al., *Saddam's War*, 47.

14. Ward, *Immortal*, 251–252; and Cordesman and Wagner, *Lessons*, 93

15. Cordesman and Wagner, *Lessons*, 95.

16. Pollack, *Arabs at War*, 190.

17. Cordesman and Wagner, *Lessons*, 95–96.

18. Pollack, *Arabs at War*, 193.

19. Ward, *Immortal*, 253.

20. Pollack, *Arabs at War*, 193.

21. Cordesman and Wagner, *Lessons*, 78, 81, 97; and Pollack, *Arabs at War*, 192.

22. Cordesman and Wagner, *Lessons*, 90, 97.

23. Pollack, *Arabs at War*, 187–9.

24. Ibid., 184, 186. See also Murray and Woods, *The Iran-Iraq War*, chap. 4, esp. 114.

25. Cordesman and Wagner, *Lessons*, 78.

26. Pollack, *Arabs at War*, 187–189.

27. Alert Memorandum, Director of Central Intelligence, for the National Security Council, "Iran-Iraq," September 17, 1980, 3, available at the National Security Archive, the George Washington University, Washington, DC.

28. Cordesman and Wagner, *Lessons*, 111.

29. Pollack, *Arabs at War*, 193.

30. Ward, *Immortal*, 248.

31. Ibid., 256.

32. Hiro, *Longest War*, 59.

33. Ward, *Immortal*, 253.

34. Cordesman and Wagner, *Lessons*, 112–4.

35. Ward, *Immortal*, 254.

36. Murray and Woods, *The Iran-Iraq War*, 144.

37. Cordesman, *Lessons*, 115.

38. An example of this public castigation appears in "Speech, Ali Khamenei, Friday Prayer Sermon, June 19, 1981," available at the National Security Archive, the George Washington University, Washington, DC. See also Murray and Woods, *The Iran-Iraq War*, 149.

39. Cordesman and Wagner, *Lessons*, 123–124.

40. Pollack, *Arabs at War*, 195.

41. Cordesman and Wagner, *Lessons*, 123–124.

42. Hiro, *Longest War*, 53.

43. Cordesman and Wagner, *Lessons*, 124–125.

44. Ibid., 125.

45. Pelletiere and Johnson, *Lessons Learned*, 10.

46. Ward, *Immortal*, 256.

47. Ibid., 257; and Hiro, *Longest War*, 55–56.

48. Pollack, *Arabs at War*, 198.

49. Ward, *Immortal*, 257.

50. Pollack, *Arabs at War*, 198–199.

51. Ward, *Immortal*, 257–258.

52. Cordesman and Wagner, *Lessons*, 131.

53. Ward, *Immortal*, 257–258; and Cordesman and Wagner, *Lessons*, 130–131.

54. Pollack, *Arabs at War*, 198–199.

55. Ibid.; Cordesman and Wagner, *Lessons*, 139; and Murray and Woods, *The Iran-Iraq War*, 179.

56. Ward, *Immortal*, 258; and Cordesman and Wagner, *Lessons*, 133.

57. "Implications of Iran's Victory Over Iraq," Special National Intelligence Estimate 34/36.2-82, Director of Central Intelligence, 1982, vii, available at https://www.gwu.edu/~nsarchiv/NSAEBB/NSAEBB167/03.pdf.

58. Cordesman and Wagner, *Lessons*, 140, 142; and Intelligence Appraisal, Defense Intelligence Agency, "Iran-Iraq: the Second Year of War," December 8, 1982, 2, available at the National Security Archive, the George Washington University, Washington, DC.

59. Cordesman and Wagner, *Lessons*, 142.

60. "Saddam Hussein Discusses Neighboring Countries and their Regimes," CRRC Number SH-SHTP-A-000-626, date unknown, sometime after 1980 and before 1985, 20–21.

61. Pollack, *Arabs at War*, 200.

62. "Discussion Paper for SIG."

63. Cordesman and Wagner, *Lessons*, 130–131, 140.

64. Pollack, *Arabs at War*, 199.

65. Cordesman and Wagner, *Lessons*, 131.

66. Pollack, *Arabs at War*, 199–200; and Cordesman and Wagner, *Lessons*, 115.

67. Cordesman and Wagner, *Lessons*, 124–125.

68. Pollack, *Arabs at War*, 200.

69. Ward, *Immortal*, 259.

70. Cordesman and Wagner, *Lessons*, 149; and Memorandum, White House, William Clark to President Reagan, "An Iranian Invasion of Iraq: Considerations for US Policy," July 1982, 1, available at the National Security Archive, the George Washington University, Washington, DC.

71. Cordesman and Wagner, *Lessons*, 149.

72. Hiro, *Longest War*, 88.

73. Cordesman and Wagner, *Lessons*, 149–150.

74. Pollack, *Arabs at War*, 204.

75. Ibid., 205.

76. Cordesman and Wagner, *Lessons*, 150–151.

77. Pollack, *Arabs at War*, 205.

78. Cordesman and Wagner, *Lessons*, 151.

79. Pollack, *Arabs at War*, 205.

80. These included the Iranian Wal Fajr (By the Dawn) offensives, beginning with battles just north of the Hawizeh Marshes in early 1983. The summer saw an offensive in the central part of the front, near Mehran, and in July and October Iran conducted offensives in Kurdistan in the north. Ward, *Immortal*, 261–263; and Cordesman and Wagner, *Lessons*, 155, 161, 168, 178–179.

81. Pollack, *Arabs at War*, 210.

82. Cordesman and Wagner, *Lessons*, 185.

83. Ward, *Immortal*, 261.

84. Cordesman and Wagner, *Lessons*, 168.

85. Pollack, *Arabs at War*, 206.

86. Cordesman and Wagner, *Lessons*, 155.

87. Pollack, *Arabs at War*, 211.

88. Cordesman and Wagner, *Lessons*, 177.

89. Ibid., 179–183, 200–203; and Ward, *Immortal*, 264–266.

90. Pollack, *Arabs at War*, 211.

91. Woods et al., *Saddam's War*, 76.

92. Al-Marashi and Salama, *Iraq's Armed Forces*, 160.

93. Cordesman and Wagner, *Lessons*, 204.

94. Iraq regained some of this territory in January 1986. Cordesman and Wagner, *Lessons*, 217–218.

95. Hiro, *Longest War*, 88, 105.

96. Ward, *Immortal*, 259.

97. Ibid.

98. Cordesman and Wagner, *Lessons*, 152.

99. Ibid., 147.

100. Ibid., 152.

101. Intelligence Appraisal, "Iran-Iraq," 5.

102. Cordesman and Wagner, *Lessons*, 219.

103. Ibid., 218.

104. Woods et al., *Saddam's War*, 74.

105. Hiro, *Longest War*, 168.

106. Cordesman and Wagner, *Lessons*, 218.

107. Ward, *Immortal*, 273.

108. Woods et al, *Saddam's War*, 74.

109. Cordesman and Wagner, *Lessons*, 219–220; and Ward, *Immortal*, 275.

110. Ward, *Immortal*, 275.

111. Ibid., 274–275.

112. Cordesman and Wagner, *Lessons*, 220.

113. Woods et al., *Saddam's War*, 74.

114. Al-Marashi and Salama, *Iraq's Armed Forces*, 160–161.

115. Cordesman and Wagner, *Lessons*, 220–221; and Pollack, *Arabs at War*, 217.

116. Ward, *Immortal*, 275–276.

117. Cordesman and Wagner, *Lessons*, 222.

118. Pollack, *Arabs at War*, 217–218.

119. Cordesman and Wagner, *Lessons*, 222–223.

120. Ward, *Immortal*, 275–276.

121. Hiro, *Longest War*, 169.

122. Ward, *Immortal*, 275–276; Cordesman and Wagner, *Lessons*, 224.

123. Hiro, *Longest War*, 169.

124. Cordesman and Wagner, *Lessons*, 226.

125. Ibid., 225–226.

126. Murray and Woods, *The Iran-Iraq War*, 288–289.

127. Cordesman and Wagner, *Lessons*, 245; and Sick, "Trial by Error," 239.

128. *The Negative Impact of the War on the Iraqi Domestic Situation.*

129. Intelligence Assessment, CIA Directorate of Intelligence, "Is Iraq Losing the War?" April 1986, 9, available at the National Security Archive, the George Washington University, Washington, DC.

130. Cordesman and Wagner, *Lessons*, 228.

131. Hiro, *Longest War*, 171–172.

132. Al-Marashi and Salama, *Iraq's Armed Forces*, 164.

133. Cordesman and Wagner, *Lessons*, 228.

134. Al-Marashi and Salama, *Iraq's Armed Forces*, 164.

135. Tripp, "The Iran-Iraq War," 232–233.

136. Cordesman and Wagner, *Lessons*, 222.

137. Ward, *Immortal*, 275–276.

138. Cordesman and Wagner, *Lessons*, 223.

139. Woods et al., *Saddam's War*, 74; and Ward, *Immortal*, 275.

140. Hiro, *Longest War*, 167–168.

141. Pelletiere and Johnson, *Lessons Learned*, 52; and Zabih, *Iranian Military*, 196.

142. Zabih, *Iranian Military*, 198.

143. Cordesman and Wagner, *Lessons*, 249.

144. Hiro, *Longest War*, 180–181.

145. Cordesman and Wagner, *Lessons*, 249.

146. Ibid., 247; and Ward, *Immortal*, 277.

147. Cordesman and Wagner, *Lessons*, 246–247.

148. Ibid., 248.

149. Ward, *Immortal*, 278,

150. Cordesman and Wagner, *Lessons*, 250; Pollack, *Arabs at War*, 223.

151. Pollack, *Arabs at War*, 223; and Cordesman and Wagner, *Lessons*, 251–252.

152. Pollack, *Arabs at War*, 223.

153. Cordesman and Wagner, *Lessons*, 252–253.

154. Hiro, *Longest War*, 183; and Pollack, *Arabs at War*, 224.

155. Cordesman and Wagner, *Lessons*, 257, 259–260.

156. Cordesman and Wagner, *Lessons*, 261–262.

157. Pollack, *Arabs at War*, 223.

158. Woods et al., *Saddam's War*, 15.

159. Cordesman and Wagner, *Lessons*, 261–262, 357.

160. Pollack, *Arabs at War*, 223.

161. Cordesman and Wagner, *Lessons*, 261–262.

162. Hiro, *Longest War*, 181.

163. Ward, *Immortal*, 278–279.

164. Ibid., 292.

165. Woods et al., *Saddam's War*, 15; and Cordesman and Wagner, *Lessons*, 231–232, 260–261, 324.

166. Hiro, *Longest War*, 203; and Cordesman and Wagner, *Lessons*, 373.

167. Cordesman and Wagner, *Lessons*, 373.

168. Woods et al., *Saddam's War*, 15.

169. Ward, *Immortal*, 292–293.

170. Pollack, *Arabs at War*, 225.

171. Ibid.; and Cordesman and Wagner, *Lessons*, 374.

172. Cordesman and Wagner, *Lessons*, 374.

173. Pollack, *Arabs at War*, 225; and Al-Marashi and Salama, *Iraq's Armed Forces*, 170.

174. Cordesman and Wagner, *Lessons*, 374.

175. Ward, *Immortal*, 292–293.

176. Murray and Woods, "Saddam and the Iran-Iraq War," 21, available upon request.

177. Cordesman and Wagner, *Lessons*, 375.

178. Cable, CIA Directorate of Intelligence, "Middle East Brief [Excised] for April 20, 1988," April 20, 1988, available at the National Security Archive, the George Washington University, Washington, DC.

179. Al-Marashi and Salama, *Iraq's Armed Forces*, 171.

180. See, for example, Pelletiere and Johnson, *Lessons Learned*.

181. Cordesman and Wagner, *Lessons*, 353.

182. Pollack, *Arabs at War*, 229, 231.

183. Cordesman and Wagner, *Lessons*, 353.

184. Woods et al., *Saddam's War*, 15.

185. Pollack, *Arabs at War*, 225–227.

186. Cordesman and Wagner, *Lessons*, 381–382.

187. Pollack, *Arabs at War*, 225–227.

188. Cordesman and Wagner, *Lessons*, 381–382.

189. Pollack, *Arabs at War*, 225–227.

190. Cordesman and Wagner, *Lessons*, 382–383.

191. Ibid., 383.

192. Pollack, *Arabs at War*, 227.

193. Ward, *Immortal*, 293.

194. Woods et al., *Saddam's War*, 88; Pollack, *Arabs at War*, 227–8; and Cordesman and Wagner, 389.

195. Pollack, *Arabs at War*, 227–228.

196. Ward, *Immortal*, 293–294; and Cordesman and Wagner, *Lessons*, 389.

197. Pollack, *Arabs at War*, 227–228.

198. Ibid., 228.

199. Cordesman and Wagner, *Lessons*, 395–398.

200. Ibid., 76, 382, 388.

201. Pelletiere and Johnson, *Lessons Learned*, 48.

202. Pollack, *Arabs at War*, 230–231.

203. Pelletiere and Johnson, *Lessons Learned*, 2.

204. Cordesman and Wagner, *Lessons*, 396.

205. See, for example, Schahgaldian, *Iranian Military*, vi–vii; and O'Ballance, *Gulf War*, 211.

206. Hiro, *Longest War*, 52, 106.

207. Chubin, "Iran and the War," in Maull and Pick, *Gulf War*, 6.

208. Sepehr Zabih, *The Iranian Military in Revolution and War* (New York: Routledge, 1988), 17 and 11.

209. The United States did sell weapons to Iran in the arms-for-hostages deal known as the Iran–Contra scandal. Hiro, *Longest War*, chap. 5. On the tilt in U.S. policy

toward supporting Iraq after 1982, see Nicholas A. Veliotes and Jonathan T. Howe to Lawrence S. Eagleburger, "Iran-Iraq War: Analysis of Possible U.S. Shift from Position of Strict Neutrality," Information Memorandum, U.S. Department of State, October 7, 1983; Geoffrey Kemp, "Near-Term Options in the Iran-Iraq War," Memorandum for the Record, National Security Council, March 26, 1984; "Briefing Material for Ambassador Wisner: Iran-Iraq," Cable, State Department to American Embassy Cairo, August 28, 1986; Dennis Ross to John M. Poindexter, "Expanding Intelligence to [sic] Provided to the Iraqis," PROFS Message, White House, October 3, 1986; Ronald C. St. Martin to Robert C. McFarlane, "U.S. Targeting Support re Iran-Iraq War," October 16, 1986, Memorandum, National Security Council. All documents available at the National Security Archive, the George Washington University, Washington, DC.

210. Iraq received an estimated $25–35 billion in foreign military assistance in this period. "The Middle East and North Africa," *Military Balance* 84 (1984), 62.

211. Pollack, *Arabs at War*, 211.

212. Murray and Woods, *The Iran-Iraq War*, 280–284; and Bob Pearson forwarding message from Ken DeGraffenreid to Donald Fortier and John M. Poindexter, "Intelligence Exchange with Iraq," PROFS Message, White House, February 24, 1986, available at the National Security Archive, the George Washington University, Washington, DC.

213. "Towards an International History of the Iran-Iraq War, 1980–1988: A Critical Oral History Workshop," Woodrow Wilson International Center for Scholars, July 19, 2004, 20.

214. "U.S. Intelligence for Iraq," Background paper, December 15, 1986, 1, available through the Digital National Security Archive, item number IG00383.

215. For additional discussion, see Caitlin Talmadge, "The Puzzle of Personalist Performance: Iraqi Battlefield Effectiveness in the Iran-Iraq War," *Security Studies* 22 (2013), 215–219.

CONCLUSION

1. Weeks, "Strongmen," 343; Weeks, *Dictators at War and Peace*.

2. Jasen J. Castillo, *Endurance and War: The National Sources of Military Cohesion* (Stanford: Stanford University Press, 2014).

3. Paul Staniland, *Networks of Rebellion: Explaining Insurgent Cohesion and Collapse* (Ithaca, NY: Cornell University Press, 2014); and Peter Krause, "The Political Effectiveness of Non-State Violence: a Two-State Framework to Transform a Deceptive Debate," *Security Studies* 22, no 2 (2013), 259–294.

4. Staniland, *Networks of Rebellion*.

5. Kenneth Pollack, "Breaking the Stalemate: The Military Dynamics of the Syrian Civil War and Options," Middle East memo no. 30, Brookings Institution, August 2013.

6. Mitchell Prothero, "Weeks of Combat in Iraq Show Shiite Militias Have Few Offensive Capabilities," McClatchy News, July 16, 2014.

7. On expectations about the war and Serbia's likely performance, see Daalder and O'Hanlon, *Winning Ugly*; Elaine Sciolino and Ethan Bronner, "How a President,

Distracted by Scandal, Entered Balkan War," *New York Times*, April 18, 1999, 1. On Serbian effectiveness, see Benjamin S. Lambeth, *Kosovo and the Continuing SEAD Challenge*, RAND report RP-1018, 2002, Santa Monica, CA; Darrel Whitcomb, "The Night They Saved Vega 31," *Air Force Magazine* 89, no. 2 (December 2006), 70–74; and Andrew Stigler, "A Clear Victory for Air Power: NATO's Empty Threat to Invade Kosovo," *International Security* 27, no. 3 (Winter 2002–2003), 129–130. On Serbia's gains in the postwar settlement compared to Rambouillet, see Posen, "War for Kosovo," 79.

8. Florence Gaub, "The Libyan Armed Forces between Coup-Proofing and Repression," *Journal of Strategic Studies* 26, no. 2 (2013), 221–244.

9. Woods et al., "Iraqi Perspectives Project."

10. A useful comparison of the two countries' air defense efforts against the United States appears in Biddle and Zirkle, "Technology, Civil-Military Relations," 171–212.

11. Talmadge, The Puzzle of Personalist Performance.

12. Michael Kiselycznyk and Phillip C. Saunders, "Civil-Military Relations in China: Assessing the PLA's Role in Elite Politics," *China Strategic Perspectives no. 2*, Institute for National Strategic Studies (Washington, DC: National Defense University, August 2010).

13. Gates, "Helping Others," 2–6.

14. Austin Long, Keren Fraiman, and Caitlin Talmadge, "Why the Iraqi Army Collapsed," *Monkey Cage* blog post, *Washington Post*, June 13, 2014.

15. Yasir Abbas and Dan Trombly, "Inside the Collapse of the Iraqi Army's 2nd Division," War on the Rocks blog post, July 1, 2014.

16. Antonio Giustozzi with Peter Quentin, "The Afghan National Army: Sustainability Challenges beyond Financial Aspects," Royal United Services Institute issue paper, February 2014.

17. Steve Coll, "Dodging a Coup in Kabul, for Now," *New Yorker*, July 17, 2014.

18. "U.S. Seeks $10.8 Billion Weapons Sale to U.A.E., Saudis," Bloomberg, October 15, 2013; "UAE Islamists Convicted for Plotting Government Coup," BBC News Middle East, July 2, 2013.

19. The apparently successful strikes by the United Arab Emirates on Libya in August 2014 lend credence to this prediction. "Arab Nations Strike in Libya, Surprising U.S.," *New York Times*, August 25, 2014.

20. "Singapore: Small State, Big Weapons Buyer," Al Jazeera, March 28, 2014, available online.

21. Chan Heng Chee, "Singapore," in *Military-Civilian Relations in South-East Asia* (Oxford: Oxford University Press, 1985), 136–156; and Tim Huxley, *Defending the Lion City: The Armed Forces of Singapore* (New South Wales: Allen & Unwin, 2000).

22. Derek Da Cunha, "Sociological Aspects of the Singapore Armed Force," *Armed Forces and Society* 25, no. 3 (Spring 1999), 459–475; Chee, "Singapore," 145–154.

23. For more on these dilemmas, see Walter Ladwig, *The Trouble with Allies in Counterinsurgency: U.S. Indirect Intervention in the Philippines, Vietnam, and El Salvador* (Cambridge University Press, forthcoming).

Index